VGM's Careers Encyclopedia

Fifth Edition

The Editors of VGM Career Books

VGM Career Books

Chicago   New York   San Francisco   Lisbon   London   Madrid   Mexico City
Milan   New Delhi   San Juan   Seoul   Singapore   Sydney   Toronto

Library of Congress Cataloging-in-Publication Data

VGM's careers encyclopedia / the editors of VGM Career Books.—5th ed.
        p.   cm.
    ISBN 0-658-01653-9
        1. Vocational guidance—United States.   2. Occupations—United States.   I. VGM Career
Books (Firm).

HF5382.5.U5 C337   2001
331.7'02'03—dc21   2001033252

VGM Career Books
A Division of The *McGraw·Hill* Companies

1 2 3 4 5 6 7 8 9 0   LBM/LBM   0 9 8 7 6 5 4 3 2 1

ISBN 0-658-01653-9

This book was set in Goudy
Printed and bound by Lake Book Manufacturing

Cover design by Amy Yu Ng
Cover illustration copyright © The Stock Illustration Source

McGraw-Hill books are available at special quantity discounts to use as premiums and sales
promotions, or for use in corporate training programs. For more information, please write to the
Director of Special Sales, Professional Publishing, McGraw-Hill, Two Penn Plaza, New York, NY
10121-2298. Or contact your local bookstore.

This book is printed on acid-free paper.

■ Contents ■

▪ Foreword ▪

VGM Career Books is pleased to bring you this fifth edition of *VGM's Careers Encyclopedia*. Thoroughly revised and updated, this comprehensive and timely publication offers a wealth of career information in one source that will be extremely useful to students, parents, and guidance counselors.

Since the publication of the first edition, there have been many changes in America's job market. The nation's economy continues to shift away from manufacturing toward an economy based on services and technology. The number and types of jobs available have changed considerably, as have the salaries commanded in each career. We have incorporated all this new information into the fifth edition, blending the updated material into the A-to-Z descriptions of almost 200 careers.

We hope that *VGM's Careers Encyclopedia* serves you well and provides you with the career information you seek. If it helps you or someone you know to pursue an enjoyable and rewarding career, the book has served its purpose.

The Editors
VGM Career Books

VGM's Careers Encyclopedia

ACCOUNTANT

The job

Accountants prepare and analyze the financial reports that furnish up-to-date information for businesses, government agencies, and other organizations. The data that accountants provide influence just about every choice in business and government because the financial condition of an organization is an ever-present ingredient in any decision. Competent accountants are essential to the success of small businesses and large corporations alike.

The four major accounting fields are public, management, government, and internal auditing. *Public accountants* may work for the government, a corporation, a nonprofit group, or individual small business clients. Their work varies from preparing individual tax returns to advising large corporations about employee compensation and benefits packages. Public accountants often specialize in a particular phase of accounting such as auditing or taxes. Many also function as management consultants, advising clients on accounting systems and equipment.

Certified public accountants (CPAs) hold a certificate issued by the state board of accountancy. To obtain certification in most states, candidates must be college graduates who have passed the CPA examination prepared by the American Institute of Certified Public Accountants. Most states require a four-year degree, but nearly a third of all states now require course work beyond the four-year degree.

Management accountants are employed by a single company to handle the company's financial records. Some management accountants function as *internal auditors*, an increasingly important specialization. Auditing entails reviewing financial records and reports to judge their reliability. The internal auditor's evaluation of the company's financial systems and management control procedures enables the company to function efficiently and economically. Computer systems allow internal auditors to provide management with timely, accurate data on which to base business decisions.

In some companies, a management accountant may function as a credit manager, handling the company's accounts receivable and making decisions on extending credit to customers. (See the separate job description for **credit manager**.)

Government accountants maintain and examine the financial records of government agencies and audit the records of businesses and individuals whose financial activities are subject to government regulations. These accountants are employed by federal, state, and local government agencies.

Beginners in accounting usually start as ledger accountants or junior internal auditors, or as trainees for technical accounting positions. Junior public accountants usually assist with auditing work for several clients.

Related jobs are appraiser, loan officer, and internal revenue agent.

Places of employment and working conditions

All business, industrial, and government organizations use the services of accountants. Accountants work for the corner deli operator as well as for AT&T, for the smallest municipal government as well as for the government of the United States. They work throughout the country, with the heaviest concentrations of job opportunities in large urban areas such as Chicago, Los Angeles, New York City, and Washington, D.C., where many public accounting firms and central offices of large businesses are located.

Accountants have desk jobs and usually work no more than 40 hours a week. Those employed by accounting firms carry heavy workloads during tax season, roughly from early December to May. Accountants employed by national firms may travel extensively to conduct audits and perform other services for their clients or employers.

Qualifications, education, and training

If you want to be an accountant, you need an aptitude for mathematics. In addition, you must be neat, accurate, articulate, honest, able to work with little supervision, and able to handle responsibility.

Training in accounting is available at business schools and correspondence schools as well as at colleges and universities. However, most large public accounting and business firms, and the federal government, require beginning accountants and internal auditors to have at least a bachelor's degree in accounting or in a closely related field. In addition, at least 32 states now require 150 semester hours of course work as a prerequisite for taking the CPA exam. Many employers prefer a master's degree. Most companies also require some, if not extensive, familiarity with computer technology. The federal government requires four years of college with at least 24 semester hours of accounting, or an equivalent combination of college and work experience.

Work experience is important and can help an applicant get a job after graduation. Therefore, many colleges provide students with an opportunity to gain experience while still in school, through internship programs.

Accountants who wish to advance professionally must continue studying accounting throughout their careers. Many employers and professional associations offer seminars and courses. More and more accountants are studying computer operation and programming in addition to accounting subjects.

In the field of internal auditing, the designation certified internal auditor (CIA) is awarded by the Institute of Internal Auditors to those who have two years' experience and complete a four-part examination. Candidates for this designation must also have a bachelor's degree from an accredited college or university.

Nearly all states require CPAs and licensed public accountants to complete continuing education courses for license renewal.

Potential and advancement

There are more than 1,080,000 accountants and auditors in the United States. Job opportunities for accountants likely will increase at an average pace through 2008. CPAs should have a wider range of job opportunities than other accountants. A master's degree is an asset for those competing for jobs with prestigious firms. Mastery of computer technology or specialization in a field such as international business also is advantageous.

Accountants may advance to such jobs as chief plant accountant, chief cost accountant, budget director, or manager of internal auditing. Some achieve corporate-level positions such as controller, treasurer, financial vice president, or president.

Public accountants can advance from beginner through intermediate-level positions in one or two years and to senior positions in another few years, as they gain experience and handle more complex accounts. In large accounting firms, they often become supervisors, managers, or partners. Some transfer to executive positions in private firms or open their own public accounting offices. Entry-level accountants employed by the federal government are usually promoted within two years.

Income

The median salary for accountants and auditors is $37,860. Overall, salaries range from about $23,800 to more than $76,000. Owners and partners of firms may earn more.

According to Robert Half International, accountants and auditors average $26,000 to $36,250 during their first year of employment; from year one to year three, they earn $29,250 to $41,250. Senior accountants and auditors average $34,750 to $51,000, managers earn between $41,750 and $68,500, and directors of accounting and auditing average between $56,250 and $91,000 per year.

In the federal government, junior accountants and auditors begin at about $20,600 a year; those with superior academic records can begin as high as $25,500. A beginner with a master's degree or two years of professional experience starts at about $31,200 a year.

Additional sources of information

American Institute of Certified Public Accountants
Harborside Financial Center
201 Plaza III
Jersey City, NJ 07311-3881
www.aicpa.org

American Society of Women Accountants
1595 Spring Hill Road, Suite 330
Vienna, VA 22182
www.aswa.org

Institute of Internal Auditors
249 Maitland Avenue
Altamonte Springs, FL 32701-4201
www.theiia.org

Institute of Management Accountants
10 Paragon Drive
Montvale, NJ 07645
www.imanet.org

National Society of Public Accountants and the Accreditation
    Council for Accountancy and Taxation
1010 North Fairfax Street
Alexandria, VA 22314-1574
www.acatcredentials.org

ACTOR

The job

Probably the most famous people in today's society are the leading actors who perform in motion pictures and stage plays and on television and radio. Through these mediums, actors entertain their audiences—using words, gestures, and facial expressions to bring characters to life.

Few actors achieve great fame and popularity and become stars. More become fairly well known and play important supporting roles. Most, however, struggle to find employment and accept small acting roles to gain experience and earn a reputation in the field; these actors often face periods of unemployment and are forced to supplement their incomes by working at other jobs—for example, as waiters or salespeople.

Actors usually begin their careers in short roles, or bit parts. As they gain experience, they may move on to supporting roles, and then a few move on to the principal parts.

Some actors work as extras, who rarely have any lines. They appear as people walking by or in crowd scenes.

Places of employment and working conditions

Most actors working in motion pictures are employed in Hollywood and New York City. Film studios are also located in Florida, Texas, and other parts of the United States. Television actors find the most opportunities at the headquarters for the major networks—New York City and Los Angeles. Stage actors work in New York City and other large cities.

Acting can be a stressful career. Acting jobs are usually temporary, and many actors find themselves unemployed frequently. Those who have the talent, persistence, and stamina to land acting jobs must often travel and work long hours, including evenings. The work itself is at times tedious, involving memorization of lines and repetitious rehearsals. Motion picture actors sometimes film on location in places with uncomfortable climates.

Qualifications, education, and training

Aspiring actors should get involved in as much amateur theater as possible, such as high school and college plays and local theater groups.

While some people enter the acting field and achieve success without formal training and experience, such preparation is usually necessary. Formal training is available at dramatic arts schools in New York City and Los Angeles and at many colleges and universities throughout the United States that have bachelor's- and master's-degree programs in drama and theater arts. Having formal training in singing and dancing may provide opportunities for employment.

Actors need not only talent but also confidence, persistence, the ability to portray a convincing character, and, often, an attractive physical appearance.

Potential and advancement

Employment opportunities for actors are expected to increase faster than the average for all careers through 2008. New jobs will be created as the number of theatrical and motion picture productions increases and as audiences continue to support live theater productions. Nevertheless, there will be significant competition for jobs—with many people auditioning for available parts. Federal funding for the arts also will influence the total number of jobs.

Actors typically develop the creative skills and experience they need by taking advantage of amateur acting opportunities. They then move on to local and regional theater, which may help them find opportunities in New York City, Hollywood, and Los Angeles. Modeling experience is sometimes helpful.

Income

Several unions represent workers and negotiate salaries in the different branches of the acting field. The Actors' Equity Association represents stage actors; actors in motion pictures, television, commercials, and films are represented by the Screen Actors Guild and the Screen Extras Guild; and actors in television and radio are represented by the American Federation of Television and Radio Artists.

Actors in Broadway productions earn a minimum weekly salary of $1,135. Those working in off-Broadway productions earn a minimum of $450 to $650 a week, depending on the size of the theater. Actors working in traveling shows are paid an additional $100 per day for living expenses.

Motion picture and television actors earn a minimum of $576 a day. Television actors often earn residuals for reruns.

Those few actors who achieve stardom receive salaries many times the size of the minimum.

Additional sources of information

Actors' Equity Association
165 West 46th Street, 15th Floor
New York, NY 10036
www.actorsequity.org

Theatre Communications Group
355 Lexington Avenue
New York, NY 10017
www.tcg.org

ACTUARY

The job

Actuaries are, for the most part, mathematicians. They assemble and analyze statistics on probabilities of death, illness, injury, disability, unemployment, retirement, and property losses to design insurance and pension plans and determine the premium structure for the policies.

For example, actuaries employed by a company selling auto insurance gather and analyze statistics on auto accidents. The actuaries then base the premiums for the company's policies on the accident statistics for different groups of policyholders. They consider age, miles driven annually, and geographic location, among other variables.

The insurance company is assuming a risk, so the premium rates developed by company actuaries must enable the company to pay all claims and expenses and must be adequate to provide the company with a reasonable profit for taking on that risk. To function effectively, actuaries must keep up-to-date on general economic and social trends and on any legislative developments that could affect insurance practices.

Actuaries provide information to executives in the company's investments, group underwriting, and pension planning departments; they prepare material for policyholders and government requirements; and they may be called on to testify before public agencies on proposed legislation on insurance practices.

Actuaries employed by the federal government usually work on a specific insurance or pension program such as Social Security. Those in state government positions regulate insurance companies, supervise state pension programs, and serve in the unemployment insurance and workers' compensation programs.

Consulting actuaries set up pension and welfare plans for private companies, unions, and government agencies. Some consulting actuaries evaluate pension plans and certify their solvency in compliance with federal law.

Life insurance companies employ the most actuaries; others work for property and liability companies. Large companies may employ as many as 100 actuaries, while many smaller companies use the services of consulting firms or rating bureaus. Other actuaries work for private organizations that administer independent pension or welfare plans or for federal and state agencies.

Beginning actuaries often rotate among various jobs within a company's actuarial operation to become familiar with its different phases. In the process, they gain a broad knowledge of insurance and related fields.

Other related jobs include mathematician, statistician, accountant, and claim representative.

Places of employment and working conditions

Many actuaries work in Boston, Chicago, Hartford, New York City, and Philadelphia in insurance company headquarters.

Actuaries have desk jobs and usually work at least 40 hours a week. Occasional overtime and travel may be necessary, especially for consulting actuaries.

Qualifications, education, and training

A strong background in mathematics is necessary for anyone interested in a career as an actuary.

About 55 colleges and universities offer a degree in actuarial science. However, a bachelor's degree with a major in mathematics, statistics, or business administration is also a good educational background for an actuary. Courses in insurance law, economics, accounting, and computer science are valuable.

Some companies will also accept an applicant who has a degree in engineering, economics, or business administration if courses in calculus, probability, and statistics have been included.

Of equal importance to a strong mathematics background are the examination programs offered to prospective actuaries by the Society of Actuaries and the Casualty Actuarial Society. Examinations are given twice a year, and extensive home study is required to pass the more advanced ones. Completion of one or more of these examinations while still in school helps students to evaluate their potential as actuaries; those who pass one or more examinations usually have better employment opportunities and receive higher starting salaries. Actuaries are encouraged to complete an entire series of examinations as soon as possible in their careers to achieve full professional status. This usually takes from 5 to 10 years.

Consulting pension actuaries who service private pension plans and certify the plans' solvency to the federal government must be enrolled and licensed by the Joint Board for the Enrollment of Actuaries, which stipulates the experience, education, and examination requirements.

Potential and advancement

About 16,000 persons are employed as actuaries in the United States. Competition for jobs is expected to increase as the field experiences slow growth through 2008. Mergers and downsizing in the insurance industry will reduce job opportunities overall but create some growth for consultants. Evaluation of natural and environmental disasters may stimulate demand for property and casualty actuaries. Growth is also expected in managed health plans.

Advancement within the field depends on job performance, experience, and the number of actuarial examinations completed successfully. Actuaries can be promoted to assistant, associate, and chief actuary within their companies. Also, because they have a broad knowledge of insurance and its related fields, actuaries are often selected for administrative positions in other departments such as underwriting, accounting, or data processing. Many actuaries advance to top executive positions, where they help determine company policy.

Income

Most college graduates just beginning their careers earn about $37,300 a year, slightly less if they have not passed any actuarial examinations. Earnings increase with experience and advancement in the examination program, with many companies giving merit increases for each examination successfully completed.

Actuaries have a median annual income of $65,560. Starting salaries for those with a bachelor's degree average about $37,300. The top 10 percent of actuaries earn more than $123,810.

Additional sources of information

American Society of Pension Actuaries
4350 North Fairfax Drive, Suite 820
Arlington, VA 22203
www.aspa.org

Casualty Actuarial Society
1100 North Glebe Road, Suite 600
Arlington, VA 22201
www.casact.org

National Association of Insurance Women (International)
P.O. Box 4410
Tulsa, OK 74159
www.naiw.org

Society of Actuaries
475 North Martingale Road, Suite 800
Schaumburg, IL 60173-2226
www.soa.org

ADVERTISING ACCOUNT EXECUTIVE

The job

Each client of an advertising agency is assigned to an account executive, who is responsible for every aspect of the client's advertising campaign. The account executive must know the client's product and marketing plans and the agency's resources for successfully carrying out the client's objectives. Together they plan the advertising campaign and create its components.

The account executive studies a client's company, paying particular attention to its sales, its public image, and its advertising requirements and budget. In developing an advertising campaign to suit the client's needs, the account executive calls on all the resources of the agency artists and designers, copywriters, media buyers, production staff, and market researchers.

The account executive then has the job of selling the client on the planned advertising campaign. Account executives may spend considerable time changing and reworking the plan before the client grants approval. As the advertising campaign progresses, the account executive keeps track of sales figures and may further alter the campaign to achieve the results the client wants.

The job can be glamorous—account executives get to wine and dine clients and sometimes go on location to oversee the production of commercials or other material—but it also carries with it a heavy responsibility. The account executive must ensure that artists, copywriters, and production people meet schedules and must act as liaison between the agency and the client, keeping costs within the client's budget.

In some large agencies, account executives report to an *account supervisor*, but in most agencies they are supervised by top management or owners. In small agencies, the owners of the firm often function as account executives and may even do some of the creative work, such as copywriting.

Places of employment and working conditions

Advertising agencies exist in many cities, but the heaviest concentrations are in New York City, Los Angeles, and Chicago. "Madison Avenue" is the familiar term for the many large and prestigious agencies in New York City. Other rapidly growing advertising centers are Atlanta, Houston, Dallas, and Detroit.

Pressures are extreme, and working hours can be long and unpredictable. Many positions involve substantial travel. Advertising is a competitive field, and there is little job security. The loss of a major account can mean the firing or laying off of everyone who worked on the account, including the account executive.

Qualifications, education, and training

Job experience in sales, advertising, or market research is valuable, but you also need at least a bachelor's degree to become an advertising account executive. A major in advertising, marketing, business administration, or liberal arts is preferred, and some large agencies prefer a master's degree in business administration. Account executives need to be computer literate and should have an understanding of database applications.

Training programs for account executives are offered by some agencies. Completion of an internship program during school is highly recommended.

Potential and advancement

The employment outlook for advertising is good, and job opportunities should continue to grow through 2008. The advertising field is strongly affected by general business conditions, however, because most firms adjust their advertising budgets according to their sales, which are influenced by economic conditions. Entry-level jobs and trainee positions usually have an overabundance of applicants, but experienced account executives with a proven track record will continue to be in demand.

Skilled and experienced account executives can advance to the highest positions in an agency. In a large agency, they can become account supervisors of one or more accounts, advance to the executive suite, become partners in the firm, or open their own agencies. Some leave their agency jobs to become advertising managers for former clients.

Income

Trainees start at about $31,900, depending on education and the size of the agency. Account executives earn an average annual salary of $57,300.

Additional sources of information

American Advertising Federation
Education Services Department
1101 Vermont Avenue NW, Suite 500
Washington, DC 20005
www.aaf.org

American Association of Advertising Agencies
405 Lexington Avenue
New York, NY 10174-1801
www.aaa.org

International Advertising Association
521 Fifth Avenue, Suite 1807
New York, NY 10175
www.iaaglobal.org

ADVERTISING MANAGER

The job

In many companies, the considerable amount of advertising done to place the company's product or service before the public requires the time and talents of a full-time advertising manager. Working in close cooperation with the marketing department, or as part of the marketing department, the advertising manager develops advertising appropriate to the consumers the company wants to attract.

In some companies, the advertising manager is the only one on the staff, creating the art and written copy and placing it in newspapers or magazines, on radio or television, and on the Internet as well. Other advertising managers supervise a staff that may include artists, copywriters, production and research teams, and media buyers. The department may turn out display ads, point-of-sale and direct-mail advertising, a company product catalog, and trade show displays. In such advertising departments, the advertising manager administers a large budget, coordinates the activities of the department to meet deadlines and schedules, places the company's advertising in the appropriate media, and handles the day-to-day administration of the department.

In a company that uses the services of an advertising agency for all or part of its advertising, the advertising manager represents the company in its dealings with the agency. Depending on the extent of the manager's authority, he or she might select the advertising agency, supervise the management of the account by the agency, supply market research information, apportion the advertising budget, and approve the final advertising campaign. In some companies, top management has the final approval of the advertising campaign and budget.

Whether the advertising manager works with an advertising agency or supervises an in-house advertising department, and regardless of the size of the company or its advertising budget, he or she must produce visible results in the form of increased sales of the company's product or service.

Places of employment and working conditions

Advertising managers work in all areas of the country, with the most job opportunities in large metropolitan areas.

Advertising managers work under considerable pressure. They generally work long hours and are required to successfully coordinate the ideas, personalities, and talents of a variety of people—from top management to the creative staff of the advertising department. Some positions require extensive travel.

Qualifications, education, and training

Success in advertising depends on imagination, creativity, a knowledge of what motivates consumers, and the ability to function as part of a team. An advertising manager must also have supervisory ability, budgeting experience, and a solid grounding in all areas of advertising.

The first step is a college degree. The most useful degrees are liberal arts, business administration, and marketing.

After graduation, beginners in this field usually start in one of the specialty areas of advertising such as art, copywriting, research, production, or media buying in either an advertising department or an advertising agency to gain as much experience as possible. Experience in several specialties provides the best training for a prospective advertising manager.

Potential and advancement

As with all top-management positions, there is competition for the top spot in an advertising department. The job outlook is good because the number of company advertising departments is expected to grow overall, although the rate of growth will vary in each industry. The best jobs will go to those with education, experience, and proven abilities.

Advertising managers are already in top positions. They advance by moving to larger companies or to advertising agencies where they will have greater responsibilities and more challenging work. Some open their own agencies.

Income

Salaries vary with location, sales volume, and size of company, ranging from an average of $57,300 to a high of $145,000 and above. In general, salaries for advertising managers are higher in consumer product firms than in industrial firms.

Many advertising managers also receive bonuses or company stock for effective advertising campaigns and participate in profit-sharing plans.

Additional sources of information

American Advertising Federation
Education Services Department
1101 Vermont Avenue NW, Suite 500
Washington, DC 20005
www.aaf.org

Association of National Advertisers
708 Third Avenue
New York, NY 10017-4270
www.ana.net

International Advertising Association
521 Fifth Avenue, Suite 1807
New York, NY 10175
www.iaaglobal.org

ADVERTISING SALESPERSON

The job

The money necessary to finance the activities of radio and television stations and most of the publication costs of newspapers and magazines comes from the sale of time or space to clients who wish to advertise a product or service.

Advertising salespeople sell directly to clients or to advertising agencies that represent the clients. Technically, the sales worker is selling broadcasting time segments on the station's programming or space in a publication based on content and the amount and type of audience that each attracts.

Advertising salespeople for newspapers work locally and as national sales representatives. There are three principal categories of newspaper advertising: general, retail, and classified. General, also known as national, advertising is the advertising of products and services marketed nationally or regionally through local retail outlets. This type of newspaper advertising is usually handled by independent national sales representatives who deal with national advertisers and their advertising agencies. They usually represent a number of local newspapers.

Retail advertising is local advertising. Salespeople handling this type of newspaper advertising may also provide some of the copywriting and layout required or provide advice on ad content and design. Classified advertising is sold by outside salespersons, who call on auto dealers, real estate brokers, and other regular advertisers, and by inside salespeople, who handle walk-in or telephone classified advertising. *Retail* and *classified advertising salespeople* keep close track of clients and often provide pickup service for advertising copy, execute changes in ads, and suggest advertising approaches.

On small newspapers, advertising may be sold by all members of the staff, or the paper may employ a part-time advertising salesperson.

Even more advertising dollars are spent on magazine advertising. Magazines use national sales representatives more than newspapers do because most magazines have a wider, often national, distribution. Local and regional magazines employ more local salespeople.

Radio stations employ *radio advertising salespeople* to sell airtime to local businesses and use national sales representatives on a commission basis to sell local time to national and regional advertisers. The radio advertising salesperson sells radio time in the form of entire programs, portions of programs, or spot announcements. He or she must know not only the type of audience that listens to a particular station but also the time of day during which a specific segment of the audience is most likely to be listening. Radio advertising salespeople must be well versed in the latest market-research analysis of their local marketing areas and must be prepared to advise a client on the best advertising approach for the money.

At small radio stations, everyone may sell advertising, or the station manager may handle all advertising. Larger stations employ several salespeople, and stations in major marketing areas may have sizable sales staffs.

The largest advertising medium by far is television. The typical television station in a major city employs six to eight *television advertising salespeople* to call on local businesses. A large percentage of television advertising time is also sold by national sales representatives who have branch offices in major cities. These "sales reps" sell most television advertising and act as the go-betweens for local stations and the national advertisers.

Network salespeople work for the national television and radio networks and sell network time to national advertisers. They handle accounts worth hundreds of thousands of dollars.

Places of employment and working conditions

Advertising sales jobs can be found in all communities, with the most opportunities in large metropolitan areas. National sales representatives are concentrated in cities such as Chicago, Los Angeles, and New York City.

Advertising sales is a combination of office duties, telephone calls, and legwork. The salespeople work long hours. It is often necessary to spend significant time on a particular account, including the preparation of sales presentations and cost estimates.

Qualifications, education, and training

The personal qualities of a good salesperson include aggressiveness, enthusiasm, perseverance, and the ability to get along with people.

Experience in selling advertising is especially helpful, but sales experience of any kind is valuable.

Although a college degree is not required by all employers, large metropolitan newspapers, mass-circulation and trade magazines, major radio and television stations, networks, and national sales representative firms require a bachelor's degree in marketing or journalism. Some require a major in advertising.

Potential and advancement

The future for magazine, newspaper, radio, and television advertising is promising. Media sales will continue to grow and provide many opportunities. The Internet has opened up a new advertising avenue and new opportunities for salespeople.

Beginners will find the best opportunities with small local newspapers and magazines and small radio and television stations, where they can gain valuable experience. There will continue to be opportunities for part-time work with small newspapers and small or local radio and television stations.

Newspaper advertising salespeople can advance to positions such as general advertising manager, retail advertising manager, classified advertising manager, or advertising director.

Radio advertising salespeople can advance to sales manager positions that involve developing sales plans as well as policies and programming.

In television, advertising salespeople can advance to regional, national, and general sales manager positions. The top-level positions in television station management are often filled by former general sales managers.

Income

Advertising salespeople work on a commission basis, and the amount of their earnings is governed by their ability and ambition. Some employers provide a base salary plus a commission. The median salary for advertising salespeople is about $34,910. Radio salespeople tend to earn less, while sales managers at large magazines earn considerably more.

Earnings of television national sales representatives are better than sales earnings in just about any other industry. Earnings of experienced national salespeople often approach six figures. People in these positions also take part in company stock or profit-sharing plans.

Additional sources of information

National Association of Broadcasters
1771 N Street NW
Washington, DC 20036
www.nab.org

Radio Advertising Bureau
261 Madison Avenue
New York, NY 10016
www.rab.com

Television Bureau of Advertising
3 East 54th Street
New York, NY 10022
www.tvb.org

ADVERTISING WORKER

The job

For the thousands of people working in advertising, job satisfaction may come from having their work appear in print or on television or radio.

The work of a group of people with special talents goes into every advertising campaign, and the end result, when the campaign is successful, can make a meaningful difference in the sales figures of a product or service.

Artists, *designers*, and *layout artists* create the visual aspects of magazine and newspaper ads, television commercials, and product packaging. They select photographs, draw illustrations, and decide on the colors and style of type to be used. They also prepare samples of artwork for account executives who are planning advertising campaigns with clients and prospective clients.

Copywriters provide the words. A copywriter usually works closely with the account executive to produce just what the client wants to say about his or her product or service. The work of the copywriter is an integral part of almost all advertising but is especially important in radio, where words are the only vehicle for delivering the advertiser's message.

Production managers arrange for the filming, recording, or printing of the completed advertisement. They must be able to produce the finished product on time and within the budget allocated by the client. They normally deal with models, actors, and photographers.

Media buyers are specialists who are well informed on costs and audiences of the various media. They work with account executives to decide on how to reach the largest and most appropriate consumer audience for a client's product or service. Working within the client's budget, they buy advertising time on radio or television and advertising space in newspapers and magazines. In some agencies, the functions are separated into *time buyers* and *space buyers*.

Employers include advertising agencies and the advertising departments of commercial and industrial firms, retail stores, and newspapers and magazines. Printing companies, package design firms, sign companies, and mail-order catalogs also employ persons with advertising skills.

Beginners in advertising usually start as assistants in research, production, or media buying. Those with writing ability usually start as *junior copywriters*.

Related jobs are advertising account executive, advertising manager, advertising salesperson, and marketing researcher.

Places of employment and working conditions

About half of all advertising workers are employed in the New York City and Chicago areas, but opportunities exist in most cities.

All advertising workers function under great pressure. The usual 35- to 40-hour workweek often includes overtime because of deadlines, the demands of clients, and production schedules.

Although advertising agencies are considered glamorous places to work, there may be little job security. If an agency loses a big account, all the people who worked on the account, including the account executive, may lose their jobs.

Qualifications, education, and training

Creativity and a knowledge of what motivates consumers are the keys to success in advertising.

Successful advertising workers also have imagination, a flair for language, and the ability to sell ideas. They must get along well with people, be able to function as part of a team, enjoy challenge and variety, and thrive on excitement and competition.

High school courses in art and writing are valuable, as is experience in selling advertising for a school newspaper or a summer job at a radio station or newspaper office. Any education or professional experience in marketing, art, writing, journalism, or business and marketing research is valuable.

There are no specific educational requirements in the advertising field, but most employers prefer college graduates; they will accept a degree in almost any field. Some have a preference for a liberal arts background with majors in art, literature, and social sciences; others want applicants with degrees in marketing, business, or journalism.

When seeking a position in advertising, certain job applicants are expected to provide samples of their work. A beginning artist should supply a portfolio of drawings; a writer should supply samples of published material. Experienced advertising workers should include samples of the ads they have produced for previous employers.

Potential and advancement

This is a popular field with stiff competition for entry-level jobs and for jobs with the best companies. Employment opportunities should increase steadily, but because the amount of money spent on advertising is strongly affected by general business conditions, they may be better in some years than in others.

Opportunities for advancement usually exist within each specialty area. An artist or designer can become an art director; a copywriter can be promoted to copy chief. Advancement to management is possible from any of the specialties, and experienced advertising workers sometimes open their own advertising agencies.

Income

Salaries vary by field and according to experience. For artists, the median salary in advertising agencies is $34,800. Newspapers offer average annual salaries of $24,100, commercial printers pay $24,700 on average, and magazine layout artists average $33,000.

Writers earn averages of $38,100 in advertising agencies, $35,900 working for periodicals, $28,500 with newspapers, and $26,300 in radio and television broadcasting.

Additional source of information

American Advertising Federation
Education Services Department
1101 Vermont Avenue NW, Suite 500
Washington, DC 20005
www.aaf.org

AEROSPACE ENGINEER

The job

Aerospace engineers are responsible for developing extraordinary machines, from airplanes that weigh more than half a million pounds to spacecraft that travel in excess of 17,000 miles an hour. They design, develop, and test aircraft, spacecraft, and missiles and supervise the manufacturing of these products. Aerospace engineers who work with aircraft are considered *aeronautical engineers*, and those working specifically with spacecraft are considered *astronautical engineers*.

Aerospace engineers develop new technologies for use in aviation, defense systems, and space exploration, often specializing in areas such as structural design, guidance, navigation and control, instrumentation and communication, or production methods. They also may specialize in a particular type of aerospace product, such as commercial transports, military fighter jets, helicopters, spacecraft, or missiles and rockets. Aerospace engineers may be experts in aerodynamics, thermodynamics, celestial mechanics, propulsion, acoustics, or guidance and contol systems.

Places of employment and working conditions

California, Washington, Texas, and Florida—states with large aerospace manufacturers—employ the most aerospace engineers. Almost one-half of those jobs are in the aircraft and parts, guided missile, and space vehicle manufacturing industries. Federal government agencies, primarily the Department of Defense and the National Aeronautics and Space Administration, provide about one out of seven jobs. Business services, engineering and architectural services, research and testing services, and electrical and electronics manufacturing firms account for most of the remaining jobs.

Qualifications, education, and training

The ability to think analytically, a capacity for details, and the ability to work as part of a team are necessary. Good communication skills are also important.

Mathematics and the sciences must be emphasized in high school.

A bachelor's degree in engineering is the minimum requirement in this field. In a typical curriculum, the first two years are spent in the study of basic sciences such as physics and chemistry, mathematics, introductory engineering, and some liberal arts courses. The remaining years are usually devoted to specialized engineering courses.

Engineering programs can last from four to six years. Those that require five or six years to complete may award a master's degree or may provide a cooperative plan of study plus practical work experience with a nearby industry.

Because of rapid changes in technology, many aerospace engineers continue their education throughout their careers. A graduate degree is necessary for most teaching and research positions and for many management jobs. Some persons obtain graduate degrees in business administration.

All states require licensing of engineers whose work may affect life, health, or property or who offer their services to the public. Those who are licensed are called registered engineers. Requirements for licensing include graduation from an accredited engineering school, four years of experience, and passing an examination.

Potential and advancement

There are about 53,000 aerospace engineers in the country. Employment in this field is expected to grow more slowly than the average for all occupations through 2008. A large proportion of aerospace engineering jobs are defense related, so employment opportunities with the federal government will be limited unless there is an increase in defense and space exploration spending. Faster growth for this field is expected in the civilian sector as airliners are replaced with quieter and more fuel-efficient aircraft and demands increase for spacecraft, helicopters, and business aircraft. However, increasing foreign competition and small orders from airlines will limit growth in the private sector as well.

Income

Starting salaries for engineering graduates with a bachelor's degree average about $40,700 a year in private industry. Starting offers for those with a master's degree average $54,200 a year and for those with a Ph.D., $64,400.

The average yearly salary for aerospace engineers employed by the federal government is about $70,000; engineers working with aircraft and parts average $72,200 yearly; and those working with missiles, space vehicles, and parts average $58,200.

Additional sources of information

Accreditation Board for Engineering and Technology
111 Market Place, Suite 1050
Baltimore, MD 21202-4012
www.abet.org

American Institute of Aeronautics and Astronautics
AIAA Student Programs
The Aerospace Center
1801 Alexander Bell Drive, Suite 500
Reston, VA 20191

Junior Engineering Technical Society
1420 King Street, Suite 405
Alexandria, VA 22314-2794
www.jets.org

National Society of Professional Engineers
1420 King Street
Alexandria, VA 22314-2794
www.nspe.org

Society of Women Engineers
120 Wall Street, 11th Floor
New York, NY 10005
www.swe.org

AIR-CONDITIONING, REFRIGERATION, AND HEATING TECHNICIAN

The job

These skilled workers install, maintain, and repair a large variety of complicated equipment and machinery. They usually specialize in one area of the field but often work in several. About one out of seven is self-employed.

Air-conditioning and *refrigeration technicians* install and repair equipment that ranges in size from small (a window air conditioner) to massive (a central air-conditioning system for a large building or the refrigeration system for a frozen food processor). Following blueprints and design specifications, they put the components of a system into place—connecting ductwork, refrigerant lines, piping, and electrical power. They are busiest in the spring and summer months.

Furnace installers, or *heating equipment technicians*, install oil, gas, and electrical heating units. They install fuel supply lines, air ducts, pumps, and other components and connect electrical wiring and controls. Most furnace installers, as well as air-conditioning and refrigeration technicians, are employed by cooling and heating equipment dealers and contractors.

Oil burner mechanics keep oil-fueled heating systems in good operating condition. They are busiest in the fall and winter months. Most are employed by fuel oil dealers.

Gas burner mechanics have duties similar to those of oil burner mechanics. In addition, they repair stoves, clothes dryers, and hot water heaters that use gas as their fuel. Their busiest seasons are also fall and winter, and most are employed by gas utility companies.

Related jobs are appliance repairer, electrician, plumber, and pipe fitter.

Places of employment and working conditions

Air-conditioning and refrigeration mechanics and furnace installers work in all parts of the country. Oil burner mechanics are concentrated in areas that use oil as a major heating fuel, which means that more than half work in Illinois, Massachusetts, Michigan, New Jersey, New York, and Pennsylvania. About half of all gas burner mechanics work in California, Illinois, Michigan, Ohio, and Texas, where gas is a major heating fuel.

Most air-conditioning, refrigeration, and heating mechanics work a 40-hour week, with overtime and irregular hours during peak seasons. Employers try to provide a full workweek year-round, usually by servicing both air-conditioning and heating equipment or by providing inspection and repair services during off-season months. Reduced hours or layoffs may occur during slow periods, however.

When installing new equipment, mechanics often work at great heights; much of their work is also done in awkward or cramped positions. They are subject to hazards such as electrical shock, burns, and muscle strain from lifting heavy equipment.

Qualifications, education, and training

Good physical condition is an absolute necessity in this field because agility and strength are often required for installation and repair work. Mechanical aptitude is also important.

High school and college courses in mechanical drawing or blueprint reading, mathematics, physics, computer applications, and microelectronics are helpful.

Although many air-conditioning, refrigeration, and heating technicians still acquire their skills through on-the-job training, employers increasingly prefer to hire those trained by a technical school or formal apprenticeship program. Trade schools, community colleges, and the armed forces offer six-month to two-year programs. Three- to four-year apprenticeship programs, which combine class-room instruction with on-the-job training, are sponsored by various industry associations.

Those who purchase or work with refrigerants must also pass an exam approved by the Environmental Protection Agency to be certified to purchase and handle refrigerants.

Potential and advancement

There are about 286,000 technicians in this field. Employment is expected to increase at an average rate through 2008. Jobs will be created by economic growth; as new residential, commercial, and industrial structures are built, mechanics will be needed to install and repair climate control systems. Mechanics will also be in demand to replace climate control systems in existing buildings with more modern energy-saving systems. The overall outlook for opportunities in this field is good, but job availability is closely related to trends in the construction industry.

Income

Hourly earnings for technicians range from $8.78 to $22.29, with average earnings at about $14.02.

Apprentices usually begin at about 50 percent of the wage rate paid to experienced mechanics. Their earnings increase as they gain experience and improve their skills.

Additional sources of information

Associated Builders and Contractors
1300 North 17th Street
Rosslyn, VA 22209

National Association of Home Builders
Home Builders Institute
1201 15th Street NW
Washington, DC 20005

National Association of Plumbing-Heating-Cooling
  Contractors
180 South Washington Street
P.O. Box 6808
Falls Church, VA 22046

AIRPLANE MECHANIC

The job

Airplane mechanics perform scheduled maintenance, make repairs, and complete inspections required by the Federal Aviation Administration (FAA).

Many airplane mechanics specialize in either repair work or scheduled maintenance. They specialize further and are licensed as *power plant mechanics*, who work on the engine; *airframe mechanics*, who work on the wings, landing gear, and structural parts of the plane; or *aircraft inspectors*. Some mechanics specialize in one type of plane or in one section of a plane, such as the electrical system.

In the course of their work, airplane mechanics take engines apart; replace worn parts; use x-ray and magnetic inspection equipment; repair sheet-metal surfaces; check for rust, distortion, or cracks in wings and fuselages; check electrical connections; repair and replace gauges; and then test all work after completion.

About two-thirds of all airplane mechanics work for airlines; one in eight works for the federal government as a civilian mechanic at a military air base. The remainder are employed in general aviation, including those who work for airports, in small repair shops, and for companies that own and operate their own planes.

Mechanics employed by most major airlines belong to either the International Association of Machinists and Aerospace Workers or the Transport Workers Union of America. Some belong to the International Brotherhood of Teamsters.

Places of employment and working conditions

Airplane mechanics in general aviation work in every part of the country, as do civilians employed by the federal government at military bases. Most airline mechanics work near large cities at airports where the airlines have installations.

Mechanics usually work in hangars or other indoor areas; when repairs must be made quickly, however, they may work outdoors. Work areas are often noisy, and mechanics do a lot of standing, bending, stooping, and climbing.

Qualifications, education, and training

Physical strength, ability, good eyesight and eye-hand coordination, and mechanical aptitude are necessary.

High school courses in mathematics, physics, chemistry, and mechanical drawing are good preparation for this field. Automotive repair or other mechanical work is helpful, as is a background in electronics.

A few airplane mechanics learn through on-the-job training, but most acquire their skills in 24- to 30-month training programs at FAA-approved trade schools, including people with experience in the armed forces. Employers view people who have both trade school training and military experience as the most desirable job applicants.

Most mechanics who work on civilian aircraft are certificated by the FAA. Applicants for all certificates must pass written and oral tests, give a practical demonstration of their ability to do the work authorized by the particular certificate, and fulfill the experience requirements.

At least 18 months of work experience is required for an airframe, power plant, or repairer's certificate, and 30 months is required for a combination airframe/power plant certificate. To obtain an inspector's authorization, a mechanic must first hold a combination certificate for at least three years. Uncertified mechanics must work under the supervision of certified mechanics.

Mechanics must have current job experience to maintain their certification. Those who have not worked at least 1,000 hours in the last two years must take a refresher course.

Potential and advancement

There are about 133,000 airplane mechanics. On the whole, this job field is expected to grow steadily. In general aviation, job opportunities should be good. Many openings occur as experienced mechanics retire and fewer people enter the military. Competition is keen for airline jobs because the pay scale is high. Federal job opportunities will fluctuate with changes in defense spending.

Income

Airline mechanics earn hourly rates of $11.92 to $24.40. Median hourly earnings are $18.30. Workers usually receive the added benefit of reduced airfares for themselves and their family.

Additional sources of information

Aviation Maintenance Foundation International
P.O. Box 2826
Redmond, WA 98073

Professional Aviation Maintenance Association
636 I Street NW, Suite 300
Washington, DC 20001

AIRPLANE PILOT

The job

Pilots work in facilities from tiny county airfields to the huge international complexes located near large cities. In addition to working as airline pilots, they work as crop dusters, power line inspectors, aerial photographers, charter pilots, or flight instructors. Many work for federal, state, and local governments, and a rapidly growing number work for businesses that own and operate their own company aircraft.

Except on the smallest aircraft, two pilots are usually needed. The more experienced pilot (called *captain* by the airlines) is in command and supervises all other crew members on board. A *copilot* assists in communicating with air traffic controllers and monitoring instruments in addition to assisting with flying the plane. Most larger airliners carry a third pilot in the cockpit, a *flight engineer*, who aids the pilots by monitoring and operating instruments, making minor in-flight repairs, and monitoring other traffic.

Before takeoff, the pilot plans the flight carefully, using information on weather en route and at the destination. Once decisions are made regarding route, altitude, and speed, the pilot files the flight plan and notifies air traffic control so that the flight can be coordinated with other air traffic. Pilots also check the plane thoroughly before each flight—testing engines, controls, and instruments.

Takeoff and landing are the most difficult parts of a flight and require close cooperation between pilot and copilot. Once in the air, the flight is relatively easy unless the weather is bad. Pilots steer the plane along the planned route, maintain radio contact with air traffic control stations along the route, and keep close watch on instruments and fuel gauges. In bad weather, pilots can request information on changes in route or altitude from air traffic controllers as they search for better flying conditions. If visibility is poor, pilots must depend on instruments to fly safely over mountains or other obstacles and to land completely "blind" at their destination.

When a flight is over, pilots must file a complete record of the flight with the airline or other employer and with the Federal Aviation Administration (FAA).

Most airline pilots are members of the Airline Pilots Association; one major airline's pilots are members of the Allied Pilots Association.

Places of employment and working conditions

Most pilots work out of the larger airports located in major population centers such as Los Angeles, San Francisco, New York City, Dallas–Fort Worth, Chicago, Miami, and Atlanta.

The mental stress of flying can be tiring, especially for a pilot who is responsible for the safety of passengers and a crew.

By law, airline pilots cannot fly more than 100 hours a month or more than 1,000 hours a year; they actually fly an average of 75 hours a month and work an additional 75 hours a month performing nonflying duties. Because most flights involve layovers away from their assigned base, pilots spend much of their free time away from home. While pilots are on layover, airlines provide hotel accommodations and living expense allowances. Pilots with little seniority get the less-desirable night and early-morning flights.

Pilots employed by other than major airlines often work odd hours and have irregular schedules, perhaps flying 30 hours one month and 90 hours the next. About 20 percent of pilots work more than 40 hours per week. Other nonflying duties add to the work schedule in many instances. Airline pilots have the advantage of large support staffs that handle almost all nonflying duties, but business pilots often make minor plane repairs, schedule and supervise aircraft maintenance, oversee refueling, and load passengers and baggage for proper balance and safety.

Qualifications, education, and training

The FAA regulates the licensing of pilots at all levels of competence and experience. There are about 600 FAA-certified civilian flying schools, including some colleges and universities that offer degree credit for pilot training.

Flying can be learned in either military or civilian flying schools, but service in the armed forces provides an additional opportunity to gain substantial experience with jet aircraft. Airlines and many businesses prefer to hire applicants with this experience.

All pilots who are paid to transport passengers or cargo must have a commercial pilot's license. The license is issued by the FAA, and to qualify, pilots must be at least 18 years old and have at least 250 hours of flight experience. In addition, they must pass a strict physical examination and have 20/20 vision with or without glasses, good hearing, and no physical handicaps that would prevent quick reactions. Applicants for a commercial license must also pass a written examination covering principles of safe flight, navigation, and FAA regulations, and demonstrate their flying ability to FAA examiners.

Pilots who want to fly in all types of weather must be licensed by the FAA for instrument flying. To qualify for this license, pilots must have 105 hours of flight experience, including 40 hours flying by instruments. They also must pass a written examination and demonstrate their ability to fly by instruments.

There are additional FAA requirements for airline pilots. They must pass written and flight examinations. Airlines sometimes prefer to hire pilots who already have a flight engineer license, although they may provide this training to applicants with a commercial license. Captains must also have an airline transport pilot's license. Applicants for this license must be at least 23 years old and have a minimum of 1,500 hours of flying experience, including night and instrument flying.

All licenses are valid so long as a pilot can pass the physical examinations and periodic tests of flying skills required by government regulations.

To be considered for airline jobs, pilots must be high school graduates. Most airlines also require at least two years of college and prefer to hire college graduates. Airlines give all applicants psychological and aptitude tests to assess their ability to make the quick decisions and accurate judgments that are part of an airline pilot's duties. All new airline pilots receive several weeks of intensive training, including classroom instruction and simulator experience, before assignment to a flight, usually as flight engineer.

Companies other than airlines usually do not require as much experience or formal education, but a commercial license is necessary. Most companies prefer to hire pilots who have experience in the type of plane they will be flying for the company and will generally start them as copilots.

Potential and advancement

There are about 94,000 civilian pilots in the country; 84 percent work for major airlines. Pilots are expected to face keen competition for jobs through 2008. Many commercial and military pilots have lost or left their jobs following recent restructuring of the airline industry and federal budget cuts. Few new jobs will be created, as the industry expects slow growth. Increased passenger and cargo traffic will create demand for more pilots and flight instructors. However, this trend will be offset by the use of larger planes and computerized flight management systems, which eliminate the need for flight engineers on newer planes.

Advancement for pilots is generally limited to other flying jobs. As they gain experience and accumulate flying time, they may become flying instructors, fly charter planes, or work for small air transportation firms such as air taxi companies. Some pilots advance to jobs with large companies where they can progress from copilot to pilot and occasionally to chief pilot in charge of aircraft scheduling, maintenance, and flight procedures.

For airline pilots, advancement depends on seniority as established by union contract provisions. It takes one to five years for a flight engineer to advance to copilot, and 5 to 15 years to advance from copilot to captain. Choice of the more desirable routes also depends on seniority.

A few specially trained pilots become evaluators, or "check pilots," who test pilots and copilots at least twice a year by flying with them and evaluating their proficiency.

Income

Airline pilots' salaries are among the highest in the nation. The average salary for pilots and flight engineers is $91,750. Per diem can add as much as $500 per month to this salary.

Additional sources of information

For information about job opportunities in companies other than airlines, consult the classified sections of aviation trade magazines or apply to companies that operate aircraft at local airports.

For information on requirements for airline pilots, contact:

Airline Pilots Association
1625 Massachusetts Avenue NW
Washington, DC 20036

Air Transport Association of America
1301 Pennsylvania Avenue NW, Suite 1110
Washington, DC 20006

AIRPORT MANAGER

The job

Whether it is a small local airport or an elaborate complex handling international flights, there has to be an airport manager in charge. An airport manager is responsible for the efficient day-to-day operation of the airport, including provisions for aircraft maintenance and fuel, maintenance and safety of runways and other facilities, budget and personnel, negotiation of leases with airport tenants such as airlines and terminal concessionaires, enforcement of airport and government regulations, record keeping, and public relations.

An airport manager must be familiar with state and federal regulations pertaining to airports and must strive to maintain good relations with local communities. An important part of the job is making local businesses and industries aware of the services available at the airport. In an airport operated by a local government agency, the airport manager may be responsible for reporting to a variety of boards or committees.

At a small installation, the owner-operator may handle all duties, while at a large airport the manager, or director, is assisted by a number of specialists, each of whom is responsible for specific areas of airport operation.

An *assistant airport director* assists the director or manager with administrative responsibilities and may be in charge of public relations, maintenance, personnel, or tenant relations. An *engineer* handles maintenance of runways, terminal buildings, hangars, and grounds. The engineer oversees new construction, handles real estate and zoning matters, and administers Federal Aid to Airports programs.

An important position at all but the smallest airports is that of *fixed based operator* (FBO). At owner-operated airports, the manager may fulfill this function personally, but at other airports it is handled by a retail firm employing from one or two people to several hundred. The FBO provides (sells) general aviation products and/or services at an airport. This can include aircraft repair services, flight training, aircraft sales, fuel and spare parts, air taxi service, and charter flights.

Places of employment and working conditions

Airport managers are employed throughout the United States in airports of all sizes. The most job opportunities are in California, Florida, Illinois, Indiana, Michigan, Missouri, New York, Ohio, Pennsylvania, and Texas.

In a small airport, the manager usually works long hours, many of them outdoors. At large facilities, the manager usually works regular hours, in an office, but is on call for emergency situations. Managers do some traveling in the course of their work as they negotiate with airport tenants, such as airlines, or when they appear before state and federal regulatory agencies. Community activities and meetings usually require some evening hours.

Qualifications, education, and training

Leadership qualities, tact, initiative, good judgment, and the ability to get along with people are important qualities. Managers of airports with airline service usually need a college degree in airport management, business or public administration, or aeronautical or civil engineering. Colleges and universities that offer these degrees sometimes offer flight training as well.

At smaller airports, experience as a fixed base operator or superintendent of maintenance plus a pilot's license is often sufficient for the position of airport manager.

Potential and advancement

This is a relatively small field. Some growth is expected as existing airports are enlarged and new ones are built to handle increased passenger travel, air cargo tonnage, and general aviation activity.

Advancement usually takes the form of moving to a larger airport with more complex responsibilities. Some airport managers move up to state or federal positions in regulatory agencies.

Income

At a major international airport, salaries are usually in excess of $65,000. Smaller airports may offer salaries approximately half that size.

Additional source of information

Office of General Aviation
Federal Aviation Administration
Washington, DC 20591

AIR TRAFFIC CONTROLLER

The job

The safe and efficient operation of the nation's airways and airports is the responsibility of air traffic controllers. They coordinate all flight activities to prevent accidents. Some regulate airport traffic; others regulate planes in flight between airports.

Airport traffic controllers monitor all planes in and around an airport. Planes that are not visible from the control tower are monitored on a radar screen. When the airport is busy, controllers fit the planes into a holding pattern with other planes waiting to land. The controller must keep track of all planes in the holding pattern while guiding them in for landings and instructing other planes for takeoffs.

After a plane departs the airport, the airport traffic controller notifies the appropriate *en-route controller*. There are 21 en-route control centers in the

United States where en-route controllers work in teams of two or three. Each team is assigned a specific amount of airspace along one of the designated routes generally flown by all airplanes.

Before taking off, each pilot files a flight plan that is sent to the appropriate control center. When a plane enters a team's airspace, one member of the team communicates with the pilot by radio and monitors the flight path on radar. This controller provides information on weather, nearby planes, and other hazards and can approve and monitor such things as altitude changes. The Federal Aviation Administration (FAA) is currently automating air traffic control so that computers will assist controllers with the demands of increased air traffic.

All civilian air traffic controllers work for the FAA, most of them at major airports and air traffic control centers located near large cities. Military and naval air installations use their own personnel as air traffic controllers, and many civilian controllers acquire their skills during military service.

Places of employment and working conditions

Air traffic controllers work at civilian and military installations throughout the country, but most work at main airports and air traffic control centers near large cities.

Because control towers and centers operate around the clock, seven days a week, controllers work night and weekend shifts on a rotating basis. They work under stress because they usually have several planes under their control at one time. They must make quick decisions that affect the safety of many people.

Qualifications, education, and training

Potential controllers need a decisive personality because they must make quick decisions, and they should be articulate because instruction to pilots must be given quickly and clearly. A quick and retentive memory is a must, as is the ability to work under pressure and to function calmly in an emergency.

Air traffic controller trainees are selected through the federal civil service system. Applicants must be under 31 years of age for airport tower and en-route center positions. Those over 31 may work at flight service stations. They must pass a physical exam and a written exam that measures their ability to learn and their aptitude for the work. In addition, applicants must have three years of general work experience or four years of college, or a combination of both. Applicants with experience as military controllers, pilots, or navigators can improve their test ratings by scoring well on the occupational knowledge portion of the examination. Passing a drug screen is also a requirement for applicants.

Trainees receive seven months of intensive training at the FAA Academy. They learn the fundamentals of the airway system, federal aviation regulations, aircraft performance characteristics, and the use of controller equipment. The training also includes operation of the new automated air traffic control system currently being installed at airports nationwide.

After training, it usually takes several years of progressively more responsible work experience to become a fully qualified controller.

A yearly physical examination is required of all controllers, and they must pass a job performance examination twice a year. Drug screening is also a condition of continued employment.

Potential and advancement

There are about 30,000 air traffic controllers nationwide.

Competition for jobs will be stiff through 2008; the number of applicants is expected to exceed the number of openings. Employment in this field is expected to show little or no change in this period. The need for air traffic controllers during the coming decade will be reduced because of the introduction of a new air traffic control system that will involve the use of a computer radar network; this network will perform many of the tasks now performed by air traffic controllers.

Controllers can advance by transferring to different locations and larger airports. In installations with a number of air traffic controllers, experienced controllers can advance to supervisory positions. Some advance to management jobs in air traffic control or to administrative jobs in the FAA.

Income

The average annual salary for controllers is about $64,880 for civilians and $48,300 for those employed by the federal government. Air traffic controllers receive overtime pay or equal time off for any hours worked over 40 hours per week.

Depending on length of service, controllers receive 13 to 26 days of paid vacation and 13 days of paid sick leave each year; they also receive life insurance, health benefits, and a retirement program. Because of the stress of this occupation, the retirement program is more liberal than for other federal employees.

Additional source of information

A pamphlet on air traffic controllers is available from any U.S. Office of Personnel Management Job Information Center. To find the telephone number of your local Job Information Center, look in your telephone book under U.S. Government, Office of Personnel Management.

APPLIANCE REPAIRER

The job

Appliance repairers service the many laborsaving appliances in use in just about every home today. These include stoves and ovens, washing machines and dryers, dishwashers, refrigerators and freezers, and small appliances. Appliance repairers usually specialize in one or two of these items.

Large appliances are usually serviced in the customer's home, while small appliances or parts from large appliances may be taken back to a repair shop by the appliance repairer.

Most appliance repairers work in independent appliance stores and repair shops. Others work for service centers operated by appliance manufacturers, department stores, and utility companies. Every community also has its share of appliance repairers who conduct their own small businesses.

In addition to servicing appliances, the repairer sometimes gives instruction in the correct use and care of an appliance; prepares estimates of repair costs; keeps records of service, parts, and working time on each job; and may collect payment for completed work.

Related jobs are air-conditioning, refrigeration, and heating technician; television and radio service technician; and business machine service technician.

Places of employment and working conditions

Appliance repairers work in just about every community, with the highest concentrations in highly populated areas.

Those who work in repair shops usually work in quiet, well-lighted areas. Repairers who work on the customers' premises must sometimes work in cramped or dusty areas and often spend several hours a day in travel. Repairers are subject to electrical hazards and muscle strain from moving large appliances.

Independent appliance repairers must supply their own tools, equipment, trucks, and parts inventory.

Qualifications, education, and training

Anyone interested in pursuing this field should have mechanical aptitude and manual dexterity. The ability to work independently is important, and a pleasant personality is an asset when dealing with customers.

High school shop classes in electricity and electronics are helpful, as are mechanical drawing and mechanics.

Some appliance repairers acquire their skills in other jobs and then transfer into appliance repair. Although formal training in appliance repair is available from some vocational and technical schools and community colleges, additional on-the-job training is also necessary to become fully qualified.

In companies that repair major appliances, trainees start as helpers and accompany experienced repairers as they make house calls. Those who work in repair shops learn basic skills by repairing and rebuilding increasingly more complicated appliances or parts. Trainees receive supplementary training by attending one- and two-week courses conducted by appliance manufacturers. Some large companies, such as department store chains, have formal training programs that include shop classes and home-study courses.

Experienced appliance repairers attend manufacturers' training courses periodically to keep up with the changes in the field.

The Environmental Protection Agency requires a certification examination for repairers who handle refrigerants. Some states also demand licensing or registration. Written, and sometimes practical, testing is required. Certification by examination is also offered through the National Appliance Service Technicians Certification Program and the Professional Service Association.

Potential and advancement

There are about 51,000 appliance repairers. Most work in retail trade establishments such as department stores, household appliance stores, and dealerships that sell or service appliances and power tools. Other employers are gas and electric utility companies, wholesalers, and electrical repair shops. More than 15 percent of workers in this field are self-employed.

The employment of appliance repairers is expected to increase more slowly than the average for all occupations through 2008. Although the number of appliances used is expected to increase with the number of households, advanced technology will reduce the need for repairs.

Appliance repairers who work in large shops or for service centers may be promoted to supervisor or service manager. A few may advance to management positions such as regional service manager or parts manager for appliance manufacturers.

Income

Earnings of appliance repairers vary according to skill level, geographic location, and the type of equipment serviced. Salaries range from abut $15,730 to $42,090, with the average salary being $26,010. Trainees earn less, and more experienced repairers earn more. In general, repairers earning the highest salaries are those who work for large firms or who service gas appliances.

Additional sources of information

Local appliance repair shops, appliance dealers, chain stores, and utility companies can provide information about job opportunities. Local technical and vocational schools can provide information on courses available.

Other information about training programs or work opportunities is available from:

Appliance Service News
P.O. Box 809
St. Charles, IL 60174

ARCHITECT

The job

An architect designs buildings and other structures—anything from a private home to a large office building or an entire city's redevelopment.

The architect must oversee all phases of the project from initial idea to completed structure. He or she must solve complex technical problems while retaining artistic design and must be able to function in a highly competitive atmosphere.

After discussing ideas, needs, and concepts with the client, the architect prepares preliminary drawings and then detailed plans for the project, including the plumbing, electrical, and heating systems. He or she must specify materials that comply with local building regulations and must stay within the client's budget.

All through this process, the architect may have to make changes at the request of the client. Once plans are ready and approved, the architect may help the client select a contractor and will continue to check the work while it is in progress to ensure that all design specifications are being carried out. The architect's responsibility does not end until the structure is completed and has passed all required inspections.

Architects can work in salaried positions for architectural firms or can go into private practice. Those who decide to open their own businesses usually begin their careers with a few years in salaried positions to accumulate experience.

Most architects are employed by architectural firms, building contractors, and community planning and redevelopment authorities. A few work for government agencies such as the Department of Defense, the Department of Housing and Urban Development, and the General Services Administration.

Related fields are building contractor, urban planner, and landscape architect.

Places of employment and working conditions

Architects are employed throughout the country, in towns and cities of all sizes. A large proportion of all architectural work, however, is concentrated in Boston, Chicago, Los Angeles, New York City, Philadelphia, San Francisco, and Washington, D.C.

Architects generally work in comfortable offices and spend much of their time advising clients, developing reports and drawings, and working with other architects and engineers. They sometimes must put in overtime to meet deadlines. Once building is under way, they spend much time outdoors inspecting the progress of construction.

Qualifications, education, and training

Architecture requires a wide variety of technical, artistic, and social skills. Anyone planning a career in this field should be able to work independently, have a capacity for solving technical problems, and be artistic. Good business skills are also helpful.

High school students interested in architecture should take courses in mathematics, physics, and art. Summer jobs with architects or building contractors can provide useful experience.

Computer skills are important for architects because the use of computer-aided design and drafting techniques is standard.

Several types of degrees are granted in architecture. Most architecture degrees are from five-year bachelor of architecture programs intended for students continuing their education after high school. Another type of bachelor of architecture program requires three to four years and is for students with a prior degree in another discipline. There are also two master of architecture programs; these require two years for students with undergraduate degrees in architecture or a related area and three to four years for students with a degree in another discipline. Courses typically include architectural history and theory, design, graphics, engineering, urban planning, English, mathematics, chemistry, sociology, economics, and a foreign language.

Although many architects work without a license, all states require that a licensed architect take final legal responsibility for a completed project. To qualify for the licensing examination, the applicant must have a bachelor's degree plus experience in an architect's office and must pass all sections of the Architect Registration Examination. Many states require than an architect's degree be from a school accredited by the National Achitectural Accrediting Board.

Potential and advancement

There are approximately 99,000 architects in the country, most of them in large cities. Prospects for employment in architecture are expected to be average through 2008, with the number of job openings depending on the number of degrees being granted and cycles in the building market. Competition is expected to be keen for jobs with the most prestigious firms. Most openings will occur in architectural firms, but some jobs will also be available in government agencies and in colleges and universities.

New graduates usually begin as assistants in architectural firms. Their tasks include helping in the preparation of architectural documents or drawings, researching building codes and materials, and writing specifications. Experienced architects may be promoted to supervisory or management positions in large firms. Some may become partners in firms, while others set up their own firms.

Income

Salaries for experienced architects average about $47,710 a year. Partners and principals in architectural firms earn $132,500 on average; in large practices, they may earn more.

Architects in private practice usually undergo a period of high expenses and low income. Once a practice is established, partners earn much more than their salaried employees, but income will fluctuate with the cyclical changes in the construction industry.

Additional sources of information

American Institute of Architects
1735 New York Avenue NW
Washington, DC 20006
www.aiaonline.com

Society of American Registered Architects
1245 South Highland Avenue
Lombard, IL 60148

ATHLETE, PROFESSIONAL

The job

One of the most difficult aspects of the move from amateur or college sports to the world of professional sports for many players is the change in attitude from sports as a game to sports as big business. The drive to get to the top and the constant pressure to stay there can prove disillusioning to some players.

Athletes who reach the professional ranks usually developed their interest in sports at an early age. By the time they reach high school, they have usually already decided on a particular sport as their favorite or the one they are best at playing.

Professional teams recruit most of their players from among the top-notch college players. A few are hired from industrial and business leagues, the military, and minor and semipro teams. On rare occasions, an exceptional player is hired right out of high school.

In the past, women as professional athletes have appeared mostly in golf and figure skating. However, today, women also play professional tennis and basketball and are securing a limited number of positions as professional jockeys. Although there are some regional women's softball and hockey leagues, they have never gained a money-making professional status.

Places of employment and working conditions

Many professional athletes face the possibility of being traded or dropped, and older players are constantly pressured by talented newcomers. Injuries are always a danger, and, for the most part, an athlete's playing years are limited to the early 20s through the mid-30s. Only golfers regularly play longer.

Travel is a constant necessity during the playing season, with little time off for personal life and family. Rigorous training schedules, the need to be in top physical form, and the strict training rules and curfews of some coaches are a hardship for some players.

Qualifications, education, and training

Competitiveness, top playing skills, physical stamina, strength, good eyesight and hearing, self-discipline, and the ability to work as part of a team are necessary for a professional athlete. Quick reflexes, concentration, timing, and speed are also necessary in most sports.

High school athletic training is fundamental. Good coaching at this level develops basic skills and physical condition and introduces the player to the regimen of exercise, dieting, practice, and training that will be necessary throughout a professional career. Good coaching in high school also increases the player's chances for a college scholarship.

Although a college education is not required to play professionally, college does offer some unique advantages. College-level coaching refines and upgrades the skills developed in high school. There is also greater emphasis on technique and application of skills. Moreover, college games usually reach a wider audience, including scouts from professional teams.

The biggest advantage of a college education, however, is the opportunity to prepare for an alternative lifetime career. Not every talented player reaches the professional ranks, and even those who do have a limited playing career. Not everyone gets to be a coach or a celebrity who earns a lifetime living as a result of sports fame.

Potential and advancement

A very few make it to the top professional leagues. Even those who do can play for only a limited time. Athletes who have college training can move into fields such as radio, television, and journalism after they retire. Others open restaurants or sporting goods stores or work for community recreation departments.

Other opportunities exist in local amateur, semipro, and industrial leagues. Former college players may fill openings for coaching positions in small colleges and secondary schools, some of which require teaching certification.

Professional athletes may also move into coaching and management positions after their professional playing careers end.

Income

Highly publicized three- and five-year contracts of several million dollars or more, earned by a few superstars, are few and far between. Nevertheless, many athletes are well paid. Salaries range from about $20,000 to well over $1 million a year.

Salaries in individual sports, as opposed to team sports, vary a great deal. These athletes earn their income by participating in tournaments and meets. Usually only the top players in sports such as golfing, boxing, and horse racing earn high salaries.

Many professional athletes earn additional income through endorsements and personal appearances. Many also have businesses that they operate during off-season months.

Additional sources of information

National Association of Professional Baseball Leagues
P.O. Box A
St. Petersburg, FL 33731

National Basketball Association
645 Fifth Avenue
New York, NY 10022

National Football League
410 Park Avenue
New York, NY 10022

ATHLETIC COACH

The job

A coach must be a leader who can draw out the talent of each individual player and, at the same time, mold players into an effective team. A good coach uses sports as a means of developing the personal qualities as well as the professional abilities of the athletes under his or her charge.

Most athletic coaches are employed in secondary schools, where they serve as regular members of the faculty. They usually teach physical education classes and some classroom subjects and may coach several sports.

Athletic coaches are also employed by colleges, professional teams, and, in a few instances, elementary schools. Colleges, professional teams, and secondary schools employ one or more assistant coaches as well as head coaches.

A coach is usually an experienced player in the sport that he or she coaches. A coach must be able to teach the finer points of the sport, direct the performance of the team members, judge abilities and personalities, plan game strategies, draw up playing schedules, and, in some instances, function as a substitute player. In addition, a coach should be able to administer first aid in emergency situations.

Recent laws that require equality for women in school sports programs have resulted in a substantial increase in athletic programs and scholarships for female athletes. Because high school sports for girls have grown especially fast in recent years, the need for qualified women coaches should remain steady.

Places of employment and working conditions

Athletic coaches work throughout the country, with the most job opportunities in metropolitan areas large enough to support a number of secondary schools.

Working conditions depend on the employer. In some communities, a coach will have modern equipment and a liberal budget. In other areas, a coach will have a tight budget and poor facilities. During the sports season, life can be hectic, but in balance, coaches have off-season months free.

Qualifications, education, and training

Coaches need physical stamina and good health and, of course, must possess athletic ability. They should like to work with young people and be honest and fair.

High school courses should include English, public speaking, and biology. Volunteer work or a part-time job at a summer camp or community center can provide valuable experience.

In college, a physical education major plus experience in competitive sports at the varsity level is considered the minimum requirement. A graduate of a private college who has varsity experience will find it easier to get a job than a physical education major from a big university who lacks varsity experience.

Most states require high school coaches to be certified teachers, and some require them to be certified coaches. Coaches can maximize their job opportunities by being certified in at least one additional area besides coaching. Budget restrictions in some schools require that the athletic coach be qualified to fill a teaching position as well.

Potential and advancement

Approximately 52,000 athletic coaches are employed in the United States. The demand for qualified coaches should increase in the next decade because of population growth and the expansion of athletic opportunities for girls and women.

Coaches usually advance by moving to larger schools or colleges as they build a reputation for turning out winning teams. In large schools, a coach can be promoted to athletic director or move into educational administration as a school principal or superintendent. As they reach the end of their peak physical years, some coaches prefer to move into related fields such as sportswriting, physical rehabilitation, or sporting goods sales. Some become managers or owners of health clubs or summer camps.

Income

High school and college coaches earn salaries ranging from about $11.00 to $13.70 an hour. Many coaches earn extra salaries for their coaching responsibility, depending on the sport and the amount of time involved. Top colleges pay their coaches $63,500 a year or more. Top professional coaches earn substantially more.

Additional sources of information

American Alliance for Health, Physical Education, Recreation,
    and Dance
1900 Association Drive
Reston, VA 20191
www.aahperd.com

National High School Athletic Coaches Association
2265 Lee Road, 3321 B
Winter Park, FL 32789-5020

AUTOMOTIVE MECHANIC

The job

One of the disadvantages of automobile ownership is that cars require maintenance and, sometimes, repairs to keep them operating. Automotive mechanics
are workers who have the skills to provide repair and service to cars and light
trucks, such as vans and pickups.

For a car that's not performing properly, the mechanics' first task is to diagnose the vehicle's problem. They discuss the symptoms with the owner or with
the worker who wrote the service report. Then they may test-drive the vehicle or
use equipment such as spark plug testers or compression gauges to troubleshoot.

Once mechanics have determined the source of the problem, they make
repairs or adjustments that are necessary. They sometimes have to replace damaged parts.

Automotive mechanics also provide regular maintenance service. This
includes inspecting, lubricating, and adjusting the engine and replacing parts that
are damaged.

In large automotive repair shops, mechanics often specialize in certain types
of repairs, such as automatic transmissions, air conditioning, alignment, brakes,
or radiators.

Places of employment and working conditions

Automotive mechanics work for automotive dealers, independent auto repair
shops, and gasoline service stations. Other employers are automotive centers at
department, automotive, and home supply stores; taxicab and auto leasing companies; and federal, state, and local governments.

Automotive mechanics usually work indoors, and some repair shops are dusty
and noisy. Mechanics often have to work with dirty, greasy parts in awkward positions. They are sometimes subject to minor injuries.

Mechanics usually work 40 hours a week, but self-employed mechanics often
work more.

Qualifications, education, and training

While some automotive mechanics learn their skills on the job, the increasing complexity and sophistication of automotive technology are making it necessary for mechanics to complete a formal training program after graduating from high school. Knowledge of electronics and computer science also is increasingly important.

Training programs are offered in high schools, community colleges, and public and private vocational and technical schools. Trade and technical school programs usually last six months to a year, while community college programs are spread out over two years. The course combines hands-on practice and classroom instruction.

Some automobile manufacturers and their participating dealers also offer training programs. They sponsor associate-degree programs at community colleges throughout the country. Because these programs combine classroom instruction with actual work experience, they may take up to four years to complete. However, they provide students with money, a guaranteed job—and, sometimes, financial aid.

Beginners usually start as trainee mechanics, helpers, lubrication workers, or service station attendants and develop and learn skills by working with experienced mechanics. It usually takes one to two years to become a journey service mechanic, except for those who graduate from the better mechanic training programs; they often achieve this level after a few months. To become knowledgeable and experienced with all types of repairs takes another one or two years. Difficult specialties may take an additional one or two years of training and experience.

Automotive mechanics continue to receive training throughout their careers. They are sometimes sent by their employers to factory training centers to learn to repair new models or receive special instruction. Many also seek voluntary certification through the National Institute for Automotive Service Excellence, a credential that is widely recognized in the field. Certification is available in eight specializations; master mechanics specialize in all eight.

Potential and advancement

There are currently about 790,000 automotive mechanics. Employment opportunities should be good for graduates of formal training programs. Workers without formal training will face competition for entry-level jobs.

Experienced mechanics may advance to supervisory or managerial positions. Other mechanics advance by opening their own shops.

Income

Mechanics earn an average hourly wage of $13.16. Top mechanics earn more than $21.25 per hour. Many automotive dealers and repair shops offer a commission tied to the labor cost of each job. Under this system, weekly earnings vary with the amount of work completed.

Master technicians earn the most, from $70,000 to $100,000 per year.

Additional sources of information

Automotive Service Association
1901 Airport Freeway
Bedford, TX 76021-5732
www.asashop.org

Automotive Service Industry Association
25 Northwest Point
Elk Grove Village, IL 60007-1035

National Automotive Technicians Education Foundation
13505 Dulles Technology Drive
Herndon, VA 20171-3415
www.natef.org

BANK OFFICER

The job

Bank officers are responsible for carrying out the policy set by the board of directors of the bank and for overseeing the day-to-day operations of departments. A thorough knowledge of business and economics is necessary, along with expertise in the specialized banking area for which the officer is responsible.

Bank officers and their responsibilities include: *loan officer*, who evaluates the credit and collateral of individuals and businesses applying for loans; *trust officer*, who administers estates and trusts, manages property, invests funds for customers, and provides financial counseling; *operations officer*, who plans and coordinates procedures and systems; *branch manager*, who is responsible for all functions of a branch office; *international officer*, who handles financial dealings abroad or for foreign customers; and *cashier*, who is responsible for all other customer transactions. Other officers handle auditing, personnel administration, public relations, and operations. In small banks there may be only a few officers, each of whom heads several functions or departments.

A related job is credit manager.

Places of employment and working conditions

Bank officers are employed in cities of all sizes throughout the United States.

Bank officers are usually involved in the civic and business affairs of their communities and are often called on to serve as directors of local companies and community organizations. This can entail evenings spent away from home attending meetings and functions related to these positions.

Qualifications, education, and training

The ability to inspire confidence in others is a necessary characteristic of a successful bank officer. Officers should also display tact and good judgment with customers and employees. The ability to work independently and analyze information is also important.

High school students interested in banking should study math and take any available courses in economics.

Potential bank officers usually start their careers at a bank by entering the company's management training program after graduation from college. A few outstanding clerks and tellers work their way up the ladder to positions with more responsibility and are also accepted into these training programs, but the usual requirement is a college degree.

The ideal preparation for a banking officer is generally a bachelor's degree in social science along with a master of business administration degree. A business administration degree with a major in finance or a bachelor's degree with courses in accounting, economics, commercial law, political science, and statistics is also a good college background.

Continuing education courses are helpful for those seeking promotion. The American Institute of Banking and other associations sponsor specialized training for banking professionals.

Potential and advancement

Expanding bank services and the increased use of computers will require trained personnel at all levels of banking. Substantial competition for job openings is expected, however, as the number of qualified candidates outpaces demand. The banking industry is still experiencing mergers and acquisitions, reducing the need for bank officers, especially in middle management.

It usually takes many years of experience to advance to senior management positions. Experience in several banking departments and continuing education in management-sponsored courses can aid in acquiring promotion.

Income

Income varies, with banks in large cities paying more than those in small towns. Bank officers usually earn about $45,800 a year.

Additional sources of information

American Bankers Association
1120 Connecticut Avenue NW
Washington, DC 20036
www.aba.com

Financial Women International
200 North Glebe Road, Suite 820
Arlington, VA 22203-3728
www.fwi.org

BANK TELLER

The job

Bank tellers are the most visible employees of a bank and should project an efficient, pleasant, and dependable image, both of themselves and of the employer. Tellers cash checks, process deposits and withdrawals, sell savings bonds and traveler's checks, keep records, and process paperwork. In the course of their day, tellers must be thorough and accurate in checking identification, verifying the dollar amounts of checks and cash, and counting out money to customers. At the end of the day, all transactions must balance.

Opportunities for part-time teller work exist in larger banks where extra tellers are used during peak banking hours and on peak banking days.

Places of employment and working conditions

Bank tellers work in all areas of the country, in communities of all sizes.

In small banks, tellers usually perform a variety of duties, while those in larger ones typically work in one specialty area. Boredom can be a problem, and some bank tellers object to the close supervision that is part of their working atmosphere.

Tellers stand during much of the workday; anyone who does not like to be confined to a small space might find the teller cages of some banks unpleasant.

Some evening and weekend hours are required in most positions.

Qualifications, education, and training

Personal qualities of honesty and integrity are necessary for a job as a teller. An aptitude for working with numbers, attention to detail, and the ability to be part of a closely supervised team are essential. Tellers should have a pleasant personality and like to work with people.

A high school diploma is adequate preparation for entry-level jobs if the applicant has had courses in typing, bookkeeping, computer science, and business arithmetic.

Tellers receive anywhere from a few days to three weeks or more of training and spend some time observing an experienced teller before working on their own.

Bank training courses generally are available to all bank employees throughout their working years. Employees who avail themselves of these courses can continue gaining new skills. The successful completion of specific banking courses may lead to promotion.

Potential and advancement

There are about 560,000 bank tellers. Though the burgeoning use of automated tellers and direct deposit means fewer tellers will be needed through 2008, there should still be good opportunities for qualified applicants. Part-time tellers are in demand for busy periods, and the banking industry traditionally has high turnover.

Income

The banking industry also has traditionally paid lower salaries than many other industries, and this trend has not changed in recent years.

The principal factors determining salaries are range of responsibilities, experience, length of service, and the location and size of the institution. The median annual salary for full-time bank tellers is $17,200, with the lowest 10 percent earning about $12,970 and the top 10 percent earning more than $23,000.

Additional sources of information

American Bankers Association
1120 Connecticut Avenue NW
Washington, DC 20036
www.aba.com

American League of Financial Institutions
900 19th Street NW, Suite 400
Washington, DC 20006

BIOCHEMIST

The job

Biochemists study the chemical composition and behavior of living things and the effects of food, drugs, hormones, and other chemicals on various organisms. Their work is essential to a better understanding of health, growth, reproduction, and heredity in human beings and to progress in the fields of medicine, nutrition, and agriculture.

Most biochemists are involved in basic research; those engaged in applied research use the results of basic research to solve practical problems. For example, basic research into how an organism forms a hormone has been used to synthesize and produce hormones on a mass scale.

Laboratory research can involve weighing, filtering, distilling, and culturing specimens or the operation of electron microscopes and centrifuges. Biochemists sometimes design new laboratory apparatuses or develop new techniques to carry out specific research projects.

About half of all biochemists are employed in colleges and universities, where they combine their research work with teaching positions. Other job opportunity fields for biochemists are the drug, insecticide, and cosmetic industries and non-profit research foundations and government agencies in the areas of health and agriculture.

Places of employment and working conditions

Biochemists are employed in all regions of the country, mainly in areas where chemical, food, and drug industries and colleges and universities are located.

Laboratory work can involve the handling of dangerous or unpleasant substances. Biochemists involved in research projects may work irregular or extended hours during certain phases of a project.

Qualifications, education, and training

Keen powers of observation, a curious mind, patience and perseverance, mechanical aptitude, and good communication skills are among the abilities necessary for the biochemist. Anyone planning a career in this field should be able to work either independently or as part of a team.

An advanced degree is the minimum requirement, even for many beginning jobs in this field. The prospective biochemist should begin with an undergraduate degree in chemistry, biology, or biochemistry, which will also involve courses in mathematics and physics. Some research assistant or testing and inspection positions require only a bachelor's degree. For most positions, however, a master's degree is mandatory.

A Ph.D. degree is almost mandatory for anyone who hopes to do significant biochemical research or advance to management and administrative levels. This degree requires extensive original research and the writing of a thesis. Those who work directly with human patients, in drug or gene therapy, need an M.D.

Potential and advancement

Job prospects in the next 10 years are expected to be good, as a result of efforts to cure major diseases, concern for the safety of food and drug products, and public awareness of environmental and pollution problems. Biochemists will also be needed in the drug manufacturing industry, in hospitals and health centers, in colleges and universities, and in federal regulatory agencies.

Beginners in biochemistry jobs usually start as technicians or assistants, doing testing and analysis. They may advance, through increased experience and education, to positions that involve planning and supervising research. Positions in administration and management can be achieved by those with experience and advanced degrees, but many biochemists prefer to remain in the laboratory— doing biochemical research.

Despite generally good prospects in the field, competition for basic research positions is expected to increase as the federal government awards fewer research grants.

Income

Salaries for experienced biochemists in industry average $27,930 to $86,020 a year. Those with a Ph.D. earn the most.

Biochemists employed by colleges and universities receive salaries comparable to those of other faculty members, with average salaries much lower than in industry.

Additional source of information

American Society for Biochemistry and Molecular Biology
9650 Rockville Pike
Bethesda, MD 20814

BIOMEDICAL ENGINEER

The job

Biomedical engineers apply engineering principles to medical and health-related problems.

Most engineers in this field are involved in research. They work with life scientists, chemists, and members of the medical profession to design and develop medical devices such as artificial hearts, pacemakers, dialysis machines, and lasers for surgery. Others work for private industry in the development, design, and sale of medical instruments and devices.

Biomedical engineers with computer expertise adapt computers to medical needs and design and build systems to modernize laboratory and clinical procedures. Some work for the National Aeronautics and Space Administration developing life support and medical monitoring systems for astronauts.

Places of employment and working conditions

Some phases of this work involving certain illnesses or medical conditions may be unpleasant.

Qualifications, education, and training

The ability to think analytically, a capacity for details, and the ability to work as part of a team are necessary. Good communication skills are also important.

Mathematics and the sciences must be emphasized in high school.

A bachelor's degree in engineering is the minimum requirement in this field. In a typical curriculum, the first two years are spent in the study of basic sciences such as physics and chemistry, mathematics, introductory engineering, and some liberal arts courses. The remaining years are usually devoted to specialized engineering courses. For this field, that means a sound background in mechanical, electrical, industrial, or chemical engineering along with additional specialized biomedical training.

Engineering programs can last from four to six years. Those that require five or six years to complete may award a master's degree or may provide a cooperative plan of study plus practical work experience with a nearby industry.

All states require licensing of engineers whose work may affect life, health, or property or who offer their services to the public. Those who are licensed, about one-third of all engineers, are called registered engineers. Requirements for licensing include graduation from an accredited engineering school, four years of experience, and passing an examination.

Additional sources of information

Accreditation Board for Engineering and Technology
111 Market Place, Suite 1050
Baltimore, MD 21202-4012
www.abet.org

Alliance for Engineering in Medicine and Biology
1101 Connecticut Avenue NW, Suite 700
Washington, DC 20036

Biomedical Engineering Society
8401 Corporate Drive, Suite 110
Landover, MD 20785-2224
http://mecca.org/BME/BMES/society/index.htm

Junior Engineering Technical Society
1420 King Street, Suite 405
Alexandria, VA 22314-2794
www.jets.org

National Society of Professional Engineers
1420 King Street
Alexandria, VA 22314-2794
www.nspe.org

Society of Women Engineers
120 Wall Street, 11th Floor
New York, NY 10005
www.swe.org

BROADCAST TECHNICIAN

The job

The operation and maintenance of the electronic equipment used to record and transmit radio and television programs is the responsibility of broadcast technicians, also called broadcast engineers.

In small stations, broadcast technicians perform a variety of duties. In large stations and in networks, technicians are more specialized. They may perform any or all of the following functions.

Transmitter technicians monitor and log (keep records of) outgoing signals and are responsible for transmitter operation. *Maintenance technicians* set up, maintain, and repair the broadcasting equipment. *Audio control technicians* regulate sound; *video control technicians* regulate the quality of television pictures; and *lighting technicians* direct the lighting. *Recording technicians* operate and maintain sound recording equipment, while *video recording technicians* operate and maintain videotape recording equipment. When programs originate outside of a radio or television station, *field technicians* set up and operate the broadcasting equipment.

Radio stations usually employ only a few broadcast technicians, 3 to 10, depending on the size and broadcasting schedule of the station. Television broadcasting is more complex, and television stations usually employ between 10 and 30 technicians in addition to supervisory personnel.

Related jobs are drafter, engineering and science technician, and surveyor.

Places of employment and working conditions

Broadcast technicians are employed throughout the United States, especially in large metropolitan areas. The highest-paid and most specialized jobs are in Los Angeles, New York City, Chicago, and Washington, D.C., where most network programs originate.

In large stations, broadcast technicians work a 40-hour week. In smaller stations, the workweek is usually longer. In stations that broadcast 24 hours a day, seven days a week, some weekend, evening, and holiday work is necessary. Network technicians covering an important event often have to work continuously and under concerted pressure until the event is over.

Qualifications, education, and training

Manual dexterity, good eyesight and hearing, reliability, and the ability to work as part of a team are requisites for anyone interested in this field.

High school should include algebra, trigonometry, physics, and electrical shop. Electronics courses can also provide valuable background.

Many technical schools and colleges offer special courses for broadcast technicians.

Anyone who operates a transmitter in a television station must have a restricted radiotelephone operator permit, according to federal law. No examination is required to obtain one. While some states require anyone working with a microwave to have a general radiotelephone operator license, this is not a Federal Communications Commission requirement.

A college degree in engineering is becoming necessary for many supervisory and executive positions in broadcasting.

Potential and advancement

Candidates should expect strong competition for broadcast technician jobs in major metropolitan areas, where the number of broadcast technicians typically exceeds the number of openings. There is better potential for entry-level positions in small cities and towns.

Employment of broadcast technicians is expected to grow slowly through 2008. Any job openings that occur will likely be to replace technicians who retire or transfer to other occupations. The increasing use of automated equipment will eliminate the need for broadcast technicians in some areas.

One potential area of growth is in nonbroadcast organizations that use video for employee communications, training, and marketing and promotion.

Income

In general, television stations pay higher salaries than radio stations. Commercial broadcasting pays more than educational broadcasting. Stations in large cities pay more than stations in smaller cities and towns.

Average annual earnings for technicians are $25,270. The top 10 percent earn more than $67,020.

Additional sources of information

Corporation for Public Broadcasting
901 E Street NW
Washington, DC 20004-2037

Federal Communications Commission
Consumer Assistance Office
1270 Fairfield Road
Gettysburg, PA 17325-7245

National Association of Broadcasters
Broadcast Education Association
1771 N Street NW
Washington, DC 20036
www.nab.org

BUILDING CONTRACTOR

The job

A building contractor, or *builder*, is responsible for the actual erection of a structure. The contractor is hired at an agreed-upon fee to handle all phases of building. Working within the client's budget, the contractor orders all materials, schedules work, and hires all necessary labor. The contractor usually assigns specific parts of the construction to subcontractors such as electricians and plumbers.

Places of employment and working conditions

Building contractors work in all areas of the country, in communities of all sizes and in urban areas.

The building contractor has all the headaches—bad weather that delays construction, materials that don't arrive on time, security concerns at the building site, subcontractors that don't complete their work on schedule and hold up subsequent construction steps, labor unrest, cost overruns. A few of these problems on a single job can put small contractors out of business.

For further information

Building contractors usually start out in one of the building trades. See the job descriptions for **carpenter; electrician; air-conditioning, refrigeration, and heating technician;** and **plumber and pipe fitter** for specific information on training, potential, and income.

BUILDING OR PROPERTY MANAGER

The job

A building or property manager is responsible for overseeing the day-to-day happenings of a site with multiple tenants such as office buildings, apartment houses, or shopping centers.

A building or property manager is a combination administrator, rental agent, accountant, public relations expert, purchasing agent, and maintenance person. The manager may simply have an office on the premises or may live there in an apartment supplied by the owners of the building.

In a single building with only a handful of tenants, the manager performs all duties with the help of a small clerical and maintenance staff. In large units, the manager supervises a sizable staff that carries out the details of maintenance, security, leases and rent collection, accounting, and other matters.

One of the most important duties of a building manager is soliciting and retaining tenants. That involves showing available units to prospective occupants, arranging leases, and providing renovations to suit commercial tenants. Each of these activities is of prime importance to the profitable operation of the building. The reputation of the building manager and staff for competence and service may influence a prospective tenant's decision to move into a building.

Most building managers are employed by either real estate and development firms, banks or trust companies, or insurance companies that own investment property. Government agencies also employ building managers in subsidized public housing projects. Some building managers are self-employed.

A beginner in this field usually works under the supervision of an experienced manager. To gain experience, the beginner might be given responsibility for a small building or be hired as a resident supervisor or maintenance manager.

A related job is real estate agent/broker.

Places of employment and working conditions

Building and property managers work in offices, but they often spend blocks of time away from their desks, visiting the properties that they manage. They also confer with various members of the maintenance staff and tenants.

Building managers must recognize that tenants can sometimes be demanding, troublesome, and unreasonable, and the building manager is on call at all times for emergencies and problems.

Qualifications, education, and training

Reliability, good judgment, tact, and diplomacy are all necessary. A building manager must also have initiative and a well-honed sales ability.

High school preparation should include business courses and the development of communication skills.

A college education is becoming more and more important in this field. A background in accounting, law, finance, management, government, or economics is helpful; a business degree with a major in real estate is ideal. Junior and community colleges offer two-year programs leading to an associate degree, which is also acceptable to many employers.

Various professional and trade organizations associated with the real estate field offer short-term formal training programs. A number of organizations also offer certification programs; certification is granted to candidates who complete training programs, meet job experience standards, and pass written examinations.

Potential and advancement

There are about 315,000 building and property managers in the United States. Large metropolitan regions, retirement and resort communities, and industrial areas provide numerous job opportunities. Growth in the demand for office buildings, retail establishments, and apartments and houses should create average demand for building and property managers through 2008. Those who hold bachelor's degrees in business administration and related fields should have the best opportunities.

Income

Earnings vary greatly with geographic area, size of building, and level of responsibility.

Managers can earn from $14,570 to $74,500 or more a year.

Additional sources of information

American Industrial Real Estate Association
Sheraton Grande Office Center
345 South Figueroa, Suite M-1
Los Angeles, CA 90071

Building Owners and Managers Institute
1521 Ritchie Highway
Arnold, MD 21012
www.bomi-edu.org

Institute of Real Estate Management
430 North Michigan Avenue
Chicago, IL 60611
www.irem.org

BUSINESS MACHINE SERVICE TECHNICIAN

The job

Maintenance and repair of business and office machines is the work of business machine service technicians. Most of these technicians work for business machine manufacturers and dealers or repair shops; a few work for large organizations that have enough machines to employ an in-house, full-time technician.

Business machine service technicians work on typewriters, computers, fax machines, calculators and adding machines, and copiers and duplicating equipment. A few repair and service dictating machines; the remainder service cash registers, and postage and mailing equipment.

Technicians usually specialize in one type of business machine, such as computers or copiers. Those who work for a manufacturer or dealer generally service only the brand produced or sold by the employer.

Related jobs are appliance repairer, computer service technician, communications equipment mechanic, and television and radio service technician.

Places of employment and working conditions

Business machine service technicians work in communities of all sizes throughout the country. Even small communities tend to have at least one repair shop or self-employed technician.

Technicians may work in a repair shop or service center, or they may repair equipment on-site at hospitals, factories, or offices.

Servicing business machines is cleaner work than most other mechanical jobs, and business machine service technicians usually wear business clothes. There are no slow periods, since business machines must be serviced regardless of slack economic conditions.

Some technicians do shift work that includes weekends and holidays because they service machines at computer centers, hospitals, and other locations that are open 24 hours a day.

Qualifications, education, and training

Mechanical ability, manual dexterity, good eyesight and color vision, good hearing, and the ability to work without supervision are required. Technicians interact directly with the customer, so they must also be pleasant and tactful.

High school classes in electrical shop, mechanical drawing, mathematics, physics, and computer science are helpful.

There are no specific educational requirements for this field, but many employers prefer some technical training in electricity or electronics. Courses are available at trade and technical schools and at junior and community colleges. Training received in the armed forces is also valuable.

Trainees who are hired by a manufacturer or dealer attend a training program sponsored by the manufacturer. Such programs last from several weeks to several months and are followed by one to three years of on-the-job training. Training offered by independent repair shops is less formal but basically the same.

All business machine service technicians keep up with technological changes by attending frequent training seminars sponsored by manufacturers when new machines are developed. Many companies also provide tuition assistance for technicians who take additional work-related courses in colleges or technical schools.

Additional sources of information

Local offices of firms that sell and service business machines can provide information on job opportunities and training.

CARPENTER

The job

Carpenters are the largest group of building trade workers in the United States and are employed in almost every type of construction activity. Carpentry is divided into rough and finish work, and a skilled carpenter is able to do both.

Rough work comprises erecting the wood framework in buildings, including subfloors, partitions, and floor joists; installing the heavy timbers used in the building of docks and railroad trestles; erecting scaffolds and temporary buildings at construction sites; and making the chutes for pouring concrete and the forms to enclose the concrete while it hardens. Rough work must be completed before finish work can begin.

Installing molding, wood paneling, cabinets, windows and doors, and hardware, as well as building stairs and laying floors, is finish work. In some construction jobs, finish work may also include installing wallboard and floor coverings such as linoleum or asphalt tile.

In small communities and rural areas, carpenters often install glass and insulation and do the painting; in large metropolitan areas, carpenters tend to specialize in just one phase of carpentry.

Carpenters work from blueprints or from instructions given by supervisors and must use materials and building techniques that conform to local building codes. They use hand tools such as hammers, saws, chisels, and planes (which carpenters usually provide for themselves), as well as portable power saws, drills, and rivet guns (which are usually supplied by the builder or contractor).

Places of employment and working conditions

Carpenters work throughout the country in communities of all sizes and in rural areas.

Most carpenters work for contractors and builders who construct new buildings or renovate and remodel older structures; many are self-employed or combine wage employment with a part-time business of their own. Some are employed by government agencies, manufacturing firms, and other large organizations.

A large proportion of carpenters belong to the United Brotherhood of Carpenters and Joiners of America.

A carpenter's work is always active and sometimes strenuous, depending on whether it is rough or finish work. Prolonged standing, climbing, and squatting are necessary, and there is danger of injury from falls, sharp or rough materials, and the use of sharp tools and power equipment.

Qualifications, education, and training

Manual dexterity is an extremely important qualification, as is the ability to solve mathematical problems quickly and accurately. Anyone interested in carpentry as a career should also be in good physical condition, have a good sense of balance, and be unafraid of working on high structures.

Although a large number of workers in this field have acquired their skills by working as carpenters' helpers or for contractors who provide some training, the best training is obtained in a formal apprenticeship program. Carpenters with such training are in greater demand, command better pay, and have more opportunities for advancement.

Apprenticeship applicants generally must be at least 17 years old and meet local requirements. Courses in carpentry shop, mechanical drawing, and general mathematics are helpful. Applicants are usually given an aptitude test to assess their suitability for carpentry work, so students interested in carpentry should make sure they acquire the best technical skills possible during high school.

An apprenticeship consists of three to four years of on-the-job training supplemented by related classroom instruction. The classroom instruction includes drafting, blueprint reading, mathematics for layout work, and the use of woodworking machines to familiarize the apprentice with the materials, tools, and principles of carpentry.

Most apprenticeship programs are sponsored and supervised by a joint committee of local contractors, builders, and representatives of the local chapter of the carpenters' union. The committee determines the number of carpenters the local job market can support and establishes the minimum standards of education, training, and experience. If specialization by local contractors is extensive, the committee sometimes rotates apprentices among several employers to provide training in all areas of carpentry.

Potential and advancement

There are about 1.1 million carpenters in the United States. Job opportunities should be plentiful through 2008 due to replacement needs. However, the construction industry is sensitive to the national economy, and the field is expected to show below-average growth as compared with other occupations.

Carpenters have greater opportunity for advancement to general supervisory positions than other construction workers because they are involved in the entire construction process. For this same reason, carpenters often become building contractors.

Income

For carpenters who are not self-employed, median hourly earnings are $13.82. Those in the middle of the salary range earn between $11.88 and $20.50 per hour. Those at the top of the salary range earn more than $23.57 per hour, while those at the bottom earn less than $8.74.

Carpenters' earnings may be affected at times by bad weather that causes them to lose work time or reduces the number of available jobs.

Additional sources of information

Associated Builders and Contractors
1300 North 17th Street
Rosslyn, VA 22209

Associated General Contractors of America
1957 E Street NW
Washington, DC 20006

National Association of Women in Construction
327 South Adams Street
Fort Worth, TX 76104

United Brotherhood of Carpenters and Joiners of America
101 Construction Avenue NW
Washington, DC 20001

CARTOONIST

The job

Cartoonists are specialized artists who use small drawings to illustrate ideas, concepts, text, customers' products, or humorous situations. Many cartoonists are freelancers and may work for multiple clients. Often, their work is syndicated and appears in several publications. A cartoonist may specialize in one of a number of areas.

A *political* or *editorial cartoonist* uses his or her skills to focus attention on political issues and personalities of the day, local issues, or other community activities and personalities. Political cartoons are not always humorous—many are sad, and some are almost brutal. The political cartoonists, the fewest in number of all cartoonists, usually have both artistic talent and a broad background in history, politics, literature, and human behavior.

Sports cartoonists use their talents to depict sports figures and situations. They usually work for newspapers and must have an eye for physical action and a knowledge of the fine points of various sports.

Commercial or *advertising cartoonists* work in the field of advertising. This is a rapidly growing field and one that offers many opportunities to beginners. Most cities have at least one art studio that supplies drawings for local businesses and industries to use in their ads; larger cities have several such studios. Experienced commercial cartoonists are also employed by advertising agencies, advertising departments of large industries and businesses, educational publishers, and many federal and state agencies.

Comic strip cartoonists combine writing and drawing techniques to produce a small story in cartoon form. In longer, continuous comic strips or comic books, in which a more complex story line is used, the cartoonist often works in conjunction with a writer.

Magazine cartoonists usually work on a freelance basis by submitting humorous cartoons to magazines. Some specialize in a particular topic such as industrial safety or sales and submit their work to trade magazines.

Caricaturists are basically talented portrait artists who exaggerate and distort to portray the qualities of a personality in terms of physical characteristics. Caricature is subtler and usually less kind than political cartooning.

Motion picture cartoonists draw by hand or use computers to create a series of pictures, or frames, each one differing only slightly from the preceding one. When the images are reproduced on film and projected, the cartoon characters appear to move. More than any other cartoonists, motion picture cartoonists work as part of a team. Some cartoonists draw and paint-in the background; others make rough sketches of the main points of the story. *Animators* fill in these sequences by preparing the detailed drawings of every movement.

One of the newest fields is that of television cartoonist. These cartoonists usually have a solid background in several phases of cartooning—especially advertising and animation—and a working knowledge of television production techniques and requirements.

Places of employment and working conditions

Job opportunities are everywhere, especially for a beginner. Boston, Chicago, Los Angeles, and New York City provide many jobs in the newspaper and publishing fields, while most motion picture cartoonists, animators, and television cartoonists work in Los Angeles or New York City.

Most cartoonists work regular schedules of 35 to 40 hours a week. Comic strip and editorial cartoonists must meet deadlines. Freelance cartoonists set their own hours.

Qualifications, education, and training

Artistic talent and a sense of humor are the prime requisites. Creativity, imagination, an understanding of human nature, manual dexterity, good color vision, and perseverance are also necessary.

Sometimes talent alone is enough, but a solid foundation provided by formal art training is the best preparation. This training can begin in high school. An aspiring cartoonist should take any available art courses and should follow an academic program as preparation for college or art school. Any opportunity to draw for school or local publications or to make posters for community events can provide valuable experience.

Most art schools provide a few courses in cartooning plus comprehensive training in commercial art; a few offer special programs in cartooning. These are Chouinard Art Institute (Los Angeles), Corcoran School of Art (Washington, D.C.), Chicago Academy of Fine Arts (Chicago), and Cartoonists and Illustrators School (New York City). Some accredited home-study courses provide art training, but students should check these out thoroughly before deciding to enroll.

Walt Disney Studios offers a limited number of apprenticeships to artists who have completed two or three years of formal art training. Some large art studios also have apprenticeship programs.

The accumulation of a portfolio should start as early as possible. Samples of the cartoonist's work are always the best way to impress an employer or a school with the quality of his or her product and imagination.

Potential and advancement

This is a growing field with many job opportunities for those with talent and training. Competition is keen, but beginners with persistence will find opportunities, especially for freelance work or in small art studios. The biggest money is in syndication, but this is the toughest field to break into.

Income

Salaries for cartoonists vary widely and depend on the location and type of work. Earnings range from $17,910 to $64,580 or more a year. Syndicated artists working on commission earn much more. Freelance cartoonists can earn from $50 to $1,200 or more for a single cartoon, depending on their talent and reputation.

Additional sources of information

Association of American Editorial Cartoonists
242 West 18th Street
Ohio University
Columbus, OH 43210

Cartoonists Guild
11 West 20th Street
New York, NY 10003

National Cartoonists Society
9 Ebony Court
Brooklyn, NY 11229

CERAMIC ENGINEER

The job

Ceramic engineers work not only with ceramics (as in pottery) but also with all other nonmetallic, inorganic materials that require high temperatures in their processing. Thus, these engineers work on such diverse products as glassware, heat-resistant metals, electronic components, and nuclear reactors. They also design and supervise construction of plants and equipment used in the manufacture of these products.

Ceramic engineers normally specialize in one or more ceramic products—whiteware (porcelain and china or high-voltage electrical insulators), structural material such as brick tile, electronic ceramics, or glass or fuel elements for atomic energy, to name a few. Most are employed in the stone, clay, and glass industries. Others work in industries that use ceramic products, including the iron and steel, electrical equipment, aerospace, and chemical industries.

Places of employment and working conditions

Ceramic engineers are employed in all areas of the country. Their work locations vary from laboratories to factory production areas, depending on the product and the industry.

Qualifications, education, and training

The ability to think analytically, a capacity for details, and the ability to work as part of a team are necessary. Good communication skills are also important for the ceramic engineer.

Mathematics and the sciences must be emphasized in high school.

A bachelor's degree in engineering is the minimum requirement in this field. In a typical curriculum, the first two years are spent in the study of basic sciences such as physics and chemistry, mathematics, introductory engineering, and some liberal arts courses. The remaining years are usually devoted to specialized engineering courses.

Engineering programs can last from four to six years. Those that require five or six years to complete may award a master's degree or may provide a cooperative plan of study plus practical work experience with a nearby industry.

Because of rapid changes in technology, many ceramic engineers continue their education throughout their careers. A graduate degree is necessary for most teaching and research positions and for many management jobs. Some persons obtain graduate degrees in business administration.

Engineering graduates usually work under the supervision of an experienced engineer or in a company training program until they become acquainted with the requirements of a particular company.

All states require licensing of engineers whose work may affect life, health, or property or who offer their services to the public. Those who are licensed are called registered engineers. Requirements for licensing include graduation from an accredited engineering school, four years of experience, and passing an examination.

Potential and advancement

Job growth in this field is expected to be slower than average through 2008. Some new opportunities are expected in research and testing, health, engineering, and architectural services.

Income

The starting salary in private industry averages $43,400 a year for beginning ceramic engineers. Experienced ceramic engineers earn annual salaries of about $57,970, and those who are the most highly qualified earn $89,600 and more.

Additional sources of information

Accreditation Board for Engineering and Technology
111 Market Place, Suite 1050
Baltimore, MD 21202-4012
www.abet.org

American Ceramic Society
735 Ceramic Place
P.O. Box 6136
Westerville, OH 43086-6136

Junior Engineering Technical Society
1420 King Street, Suite 405
Alexandria, VA 22314-2794
www.jets.org

National Society of Professional Engineers
1420 King Street
Alexandria, VA 22314-2794
www.nspe.org

Society of Women Engineers
120 Wall Street, 11th Floor
New York, NY 10005
www.swe.org

CHEF

The job

The preparation of food for public consumption in restaurants, schools, hospitals, hotels, and numerous other establishments is the work of chefs and cooks.

Cooks vary from the short-order cook in a small restaurant serving only a few easily prepared dishes to a highly trained specialist in a large institution or expensive restaurant. These large facilities employ several cooks and assistant cooks who specialize in one type of food, such as pastry or sauces.

In a kitchen that employs numerous cooks, a head cook—or *chef*—coordinates the activities of the entire staff and may personally prepare certain foods. The chef is also responsible for planning menus and ordering food supplies.

Places of employment and working conditions

Cooks and chefs are employed throughout the country in communities of all sizes.

Many kitchens are spacious and pleasant, with air-conditioning and the latest appliances. In older buildings or in small restaurants, conditions are not always as pleasant. All cooks and chefs must stand most of the time, lift heavy pots and kettles, and work near hot ovens and stoves. They are also subject to burns and cuts from sharp implements.

Working evenings, holidays, and weekends is typical for restaurant employees. Those who work in institutional settings may have more regular hours.

Qualifications, education, and training

Cleanliness, a keen sense of taste and smell, and physical stamina are important qualities for cooks and chefs. They must also work well as part of a team.

High school or vocational school courses in business arithmetic and food preparation are helpful; part-time or summer work in a fast-food restaurant also can be valuable.

Although many cooks acquire their skills through on-the-job training, larger institutions and the better hotels and restaurants prefer more formal training.

Some professional associations and trade unions offer apprenticeship programs in cooperation with local employers and junior colleges, and a few large hotels and restaurants have their own training programs. Colleges and universities offer courses in commercial food preparation as part of the hotel management curriculum. Courses and training programs vary in length from a few months to several years. Students study basic food preparation, care of kitchen equipment, food storage, menu planning, and food purchasing.

Most states require cooks and chefs to have health certificates indicating that they are free from contagious diseases.

Potential and advancement

Employment opportunities for cooks and chefs are expected to be plentiful through 2008. Small restaurants, school cafeterias, and other places serving simple fare offer the best opportunities for beginners.

Employment in restaurants is expected to grow rapidly. Food and beverage sales and employment in eating and drinking establishments are associated with the general growth of the economy. Increased business activity results in more workers' lunches and more entertainment of clients. Population growth, rising family and personal incomes, and additional leisure time will allow more people to dine out more often. Also, because more women have joined the workforce, families eat out more often for convenience.

Employment of institutional chefs and fast-food cooks will not grow as rapidly. However, there will be many opportunities in institutions associated with elderly people as the population ages.

Advancement in this field usually takes the form of moving to larger food-service facilities or restaurants. Some chefs gradually advance to supervisory or management positions in hotels, clubs, or the more elegant restaurants. Others open their own restaurants or catering businesses.

Income

Restaurant cooks earn about $7.81 an hour, fast-food and short-order cooks earn about $6.12, and bread and pastry makers earn $8.17 on average.

Chefs earn more, with those in the very best restaurants earning much more. Executive chefs earn salaries of about $45,520. Many are paid bonuses in addition to their base salaries.

Additional sources of information

American Culinary Federation
Educational Institute
P.O. Box 3466
St. Augustine, FL 32085

National Restaurant Association
1200 17th Street NW
Washington, DC 20036-3097

CHEMICAL ENGINEER

The job

The duties of chemical engineers entail a working knowledge of chemistry, physics, and mechanical and electrical engineering.

Chemical engineers design chemical plants, manufacturing equipment, and production methods; they develop processes for such activities as removing chemical contaminants from waste materials.

This is one of the most complex and diverse areas of engineering. Chemical engineers often specialize in a particular operation such as oxidation or polymerization. Others specialize in plastics or rubber or in a field such as pollution control.

Most chemical engineers work in manufacturing firms, primarily in chemicals, petroleum, and related industries. A smaller number work in the nuclear energy field.

Places of employment and working conditions

Chemical engineers work in many different parts of the country. They may be subject to hazards that occur when working with dangerous chemicals.

Qualifications, education, and training

The ability to think analytically, a capacity for details, and the ability to work as part of a team are necessary. Good communication skills are also important for anyone who holds chemical engineering as a career goal.

Mathematics and the sciences must be emphasized as much as possible in high school.

A bachelor's degree in engineering is the minimum requirement in this field. In a typical curriculum, the first two years are spent in the study of basic sciences such as physics and chemistry, mathematics, introductory engineering, and some liberal arts courses. The remaining years are usually devoted to specialized engineering courses.

Engineering programs can last from four to six years. Those requiring five or six years to complete may award a master's degree or may provide a plan of study plus work experience in a relevant industry.

Because of rapid changes in technology, many engineers continue their education throughout their careers. A graduate degree is necessary for most teaching and research positions and for many management jobs. Some chemical engineers obtain graduate degrees in business administration.

Graduates usually work under the supervision of an experienced chemical engineer or in a company training program until they become acquainted with the requirements of a particular company.

All states require licensing of engineers whose work may affect life, health, or property or who offer their services to the public. Those who are licensed are called registered engineers. Requirements for licensing include graduation from an accredited engineering school, four years of experience, and passing an examination.

Potential and advancement

There are more than 48,000 chemical engineers in the United States. The field is expected to experience average growth through 2008. It's likely that competition for jobs will be marked because the number of gradutes will exceed job openings. The best opportunities are expected in the fields of pharmaceuticals, specialty chemicals, and plastics.

Income

Starting salaries for chemical engineers with a bachelor's degree average about $46,900 a year in private industry. Starting offers for those with a master's degree average $52,100 a year and for those with a Ph.D., $67,300. Senior engineers working in private industry with management responsibilities earn $92,240 or more.

Additional sources of information

Accreditation Board for Engineering and Technology
111 Market Place, Suite 1050
Baltimore, MD 21202-4012
www.abet.org

American Institute of Chemical Engineers
Three Park Avenue
New York, NY 10016-5901
www.aiche.org

Junior Engineering Technical Society
1420 King Street, Suite 405
Alexandria, VA 22314-2794
www.jets.org

National Society of Professional Engineers
1420 King Street
Alexandria, VA 22314-2794
www.nspe.org

Society of Women Engineers
120 Wall Street, 11th Floor
New York, NY 10005
www.swe.org

CHEMIST

The job

Chemists search for and put to use new knowledge about chemicals, which make up everything in the environment, whether naturally occurring or of human design. Chemists also develop processes that save energy and reduce pollution. Research on the chemistry of living things spurs advances in medicine, agriculture, food processing, and other important fields.

Chemists often specialize in one of the subfields of chemistry. *Analytical chemists* study the structure, composition, and nature of substances. *Organic chemists* study all elements made from carbon compounds, which include vast areas of modern industry. The development of plastics and many other synthetics is a result of the work of organic chemists. *Inorganic chemists* study compounds other than carbon and are involved in the development of such materials as solid-state electronic components. *Physical chemists* study energy transformation and are engaged in finding new and better energy sources.

Related jobs are chemical engineer, agricultural scientist, and biological scientist.

Places of employment and working conditions

Nearly half of all chemists are employed in manufacturing firms—mostly in the chemical manufacturing industry. Chemists also work for state and local governments and for federal agencies. Others work for research, development, and testing services. In addition, thousands of persons hold chemistry faculty positions in high schools, colleges, and universities.

Although chemists work in all parts of the country, the largest concentrations are in highly industrial areas.

Chemists usually work regular hours in modern facilities, including laboratories, classrooms, and offices. In certain industries, hazards are present in the handling of explosive or otherwise dangerous materials, but safety regulations in these industries are correspondingly strict.

Qualifications, education, and training

Anyone who plans a career as a chemist should enjoy performing experiments and building things and should have a genuine liking for math and science. A wide range of abilities is necessary, including perseverance, concentration on detail, good eye-hand coordination, and the ability to work independently.

High school students who are looking forward to a career in chemistry should take as many math and science courses as possible and should develop good laboratory skills. Foreign language and computer science courses can also prove valuable. Most employers prefer to hire those who understand computerized laboratory equipment and can apply computer skills to modeling and simulation tasks.

Many colleges and universities offer a bachelor's degree in chemistry. Courses include analytical, organic and inorganic, and physical chemistry, as well as mathematics and physics. This is the minimum educational requirement for most jobs; however, many research jobs require a Ph.D.

A master's degree in chemistry, usually requiring extensive, independent research, is offered by several hundred colleges and universities. Independent research is required for master's and Ph.D. degrees.

Potential and advancement

About 96,000 people are presently employed as chemists across the nation. The field is expected to grow at an average rate through 2008, with the best employment opportunities for analytical, environmental, and synthetic organic chemists. Drug research, environmental issues, and advances in biotechnology will create the greatest demand.

In all areas, advanced degrees will continue to be the key to administrative and managerial positions. College professors, chemists doing basic research, and those employed in the top administrative positions in both industry and teaching will need a Ph.D. degree to achieve these levels.

Income

Salaries for chemists vary according to experience, education, and place of employment. Entry-level starting salaries in private industry average $29,500 for people with a bachelor's degree, $38,500 with a master's degree, and $59,300 with a Ph.D.

Median salaries for all chemists with comparable degrees are $50,100, $61,000, and $76,000, respectively.

Chemists working for the federal government earn an average salary of $62,800.

Additional source of information

American Chemical Society
Department of Career Services
1155 16th Street NW
Washington, DC 20036
www.acs.org

CHILD CARE WORKER

The job

Child care workers look after children whose parents work outside their homes or cannot be with them for some reason. Job duties depend on the age of the children. Infants must be fed, diapered, calmed, and played with. Preschool children must also be given this basic care plus activities that will stimulate them physically, emotionally, and socially.

Child care workers begin their workdays by greeting children at the door and helping them get settled. They plan activities that will provide both physical and mental exercise such as outdoor and indoor games, drawing and coloring, singing, and reading.

In addition, child care workers are responsible for the children's physical welfare. They provide healthy meals and snacks and make sure that the children have appropriate rest time.

Workers may be employed by a day care center, or they may be self-employed and provide care in their own homes.

Places of employment and working conditions

Places of employment include the child care workers' homes, churches, schools, day care centers within workplaces, and independent day care centers.

Child care workers have an active and hectic day. They often have to put in long hours to accommodate parents' schedules. The job can be physically tiring, requiring a lot of time standing, walking, bending, stooping, and lifting. Sometimes children can be difficult to manage, and child care workers must provide firm discipline.

Qualifications, education, and training

People choosing this field naturally must enjoy working with children. They also need to be patient and have high energy.

The level of training of child care workers varies widely and depends on the specific location and setting. Each state has its own licensing requirements, and these range from a high school diploma to a college degree in child development or early childhood education. Some states require continuing education.

One valuable credential for child care workers is the child development associate (CDA) designation, which is awarded by the Council for Early Childhood Professional Recognition. To get a CDA, candidates may complete a one-year training program or pass a direct assessment of skills, offered to experienced child care workers.

Potential and advancement

There are more than a million child care workers in America, many of whom work part-time. Opportunities are expected to be good through 2008 due to increased demand and high turnover.

Child care workers may advance as they gain experience and training. In large child care centers, they may become supervisors or administrators. Some child care workers advance by starting their own businesses.

Income

Median annual earnings for full-time child care workers are $17,310. Teachers working in the public schools earn more; the average is in excess of $23,300.

Additional source of information

Council for Early Childhood Professional Recognition
2460 16th Street NW
Washington, DC 20009
www.cdacouncil.org

CHIROPRACTOR

The job

Chiropractors treat patients by manual manipulations (called adjustments) of parts of the body, especially the spinal column. This system of treatment is based on the theory that pressure on nerves that pass from the spinal cord to different parts of the body interferes with nerve impulses and their functioning, causing disorders in parts of the body. By means of certain manipulations of the vertebrae, the chiropractor seeks to relieve the pressure of specific nerves and thus remove the cause of a particular ailment.

Most chiropractors also employ x-rays to aid in locating the source of an ailment. They use supplementary treatment with water, light, or heat therapy and may prescribe diet, exercise, and rest. Drugs and surgery are not used in this system of treatment.

Newly licensed chiropractors often start their careers by working in salaried positions—as assistants to established practitioners or in chiropractic clinics.

A practice can be conducted on a part-time basis, making this a good field for people with family responsibilities.

Places of employment and working conditions

Chiropractors often locate in small communities or near chiropractic colleges.

Most chiropractors are in private practice, which allows them to schedule their own working hours. Evening and weekend hours are sometimes necessary to accommodate patients.

Qualifications, education, and training

Manual dexterity rather than strength is necessary for a chiropractor. A keen sense of observation, good interpersonal skills, and a sympathetic manner with sick people are also important.

High school courses in science are important. Two to four years of college is required before entrance into chiropractic school; college programs must include chemistry, biology, and physics courses.

There are 16 chiropractic colleges that are accredited by the Council on Chiropractic Education. The four-year course of study emphasizes courses in manipulation and spinal adjustment, but most schools also offer a broad curriculum that includes basic and clinical sciences.

The first two years of study include classroom and laboratory work in anatomy, physiology, and biochemistry. The last two years are devoted to practical experience in college clinics. The degree of D.C. (doctor of chiropractic) is awarded upon completion.

All chiropractors must be licensed to practice. In addition to a state board examination and a national board test, licensing requirements usually include two years of college and the successful completion of an accredited four-year chiropractic course. A four-year college degree is required in some states, and this may eventually become the standard. Some states also require a basic science examination. Most states also mandate a specified number of hours of continuing education each year.

Specialty certifications are available through certain chiropractic associations.

Potential and advancement

Currently there are about 46,000 practicing chiropractors in the country. This number will increase as a result of greater public acceptance of the profession. Expanded interest in alternative medicine is also expected to create greater demand for chiropractors.

Income

As in any type of independent practice, earnings are relatively low in the beginning and gradually increase. Experienced chiropractors generally earn between $63,930 and $110,820 a year, with some earning considerably more.

Additional sources of information

American Chiropractic Association
1701 Clarendon Boulevard
Arlington, VA 22209
www.amerchiro.org

Council on Chiropractic Education
7975 North Hayden Road, Suite A-210
Scottsdale, AZ 85258

CITY MANAGER

The job

A city manager, usually appointed by the elected officials of a community, administers and coordinates the day-to-day activities of the community. The city manager oversees such functions as tax collection and disbursement, law enforcement, public works, budget preparation, studies of current problems, and planning for future needs. In a small city, the manager handles all functions; in a larger city, the manager usually has a number of assistants, each of whom manages a department.

City managers and their assistants supervise city employees, coordinate city programs, greet visitors, answer correspondence, prepare reports, represent the city at public hearings and meetings, analyze work procedures, and prepare budgets.

Most city managers work for small cities (populations of less than 25,000) that have a council-manager type of government. The council, which is elected, hires the manager, who is then responsible for running the city as well as for hiring a staff. In cities with a mayor-council type of government, the mayor hires the city manager as his or her top administrative assistant. A few managers work for counties and for metropolitan and regional planning bodies.

Most city managers begin as management assistants in one of the city departments such as finance, public works, or planning. Experience in several departments is valuable and can provide a well-rounded background.

There are few women in this field, but this is a new and growing profession, with room for people who have training in a variety of disciplines that relate to the functions and problems of urban life.

Places of employment and working conditions

City managers are employed in cities of all sizes, but job opportunities are greatest in the eastern states.

Working conditions for a city manager are usually those of an office position with considerable public contact. More than 40 hours a week is usually required, and emergency situations and public meetings frequently involve evening and weekend work.

Qualifications, education, and training

Persons planning a career in city management must be dedicated to public service and willing to work as part of a team. They should have self-confidence, be able to analyze problems and suggest solutions, and function well under stress. Tact and the ability to communicate effectively are also important.

A graduate degree is required even for most entry-level positions in this field. An undergraduate degree in a field such as engineering, recreation, social work, or political science should be followed by a master's degree in public or municipal administration or business administration.

Many colleges and universities that offer advanced degrees in this field include an internship of six months to a year, in which the candidate must work in a city manager's office to gain experience.

Potential and advancement

Little to no growth is expected in this field through 2008. A few jobs will be created as smaller towns expand enough to hire a city manager for the first time. Also, some nonpaid positions may be converted to paid positions.

Generally, one begins as an assistant to a city manager or department head, with promotions leading to greater responsibility. A city manager will probably work in several types and sizes of cities in his or her career, which will further broaden the person's experience and promotion potential.

Income

Salaries for city managers depend on education, experience, job responsibility, and the size of the employing city. The average salary for a city manager ranges from about $70,500 to $101,800.

Benefits usually include travel expenses, and a car is often provided for official business.

Additional source of information

International City/County Management Association
777 North Capitol Street NE, Suite 500
Washington, DC 20002
www.icma.org

CIVIL ENGINEER

The job

Civil engineering is the oldest branch of the engineering profession. Civil engineers design and supervise construction of buildings, roads, harbors, airports, dams, tunnels and bridges, and water supply and sewage systems.

Specialties include structural, hydraulic, environmental (sanitary), transportation, geotechnical, and soil mechanics. Many civil engineers are in supervisory or administrative positions. They may supervise a construction site or administer a large municipal project such as highway or airport construction.

Most civil engineers work for construction companies or for federal, state, and local government agencies. Others work for public utilities, railroads, architectural firms, and engineering consulting firms.

Places of employment and working conditions

Civil engineers work in all parts of the country, usually in or near major industrial and commercial centers. Some work for American firms in foreign countries.

Much of civil engineers' time is spent outdoors. They sometimes operate in remote areas and may have to move from place to place as they work on different projects.

Qualifications, education, and training

The ability to think analytically, a capacity for details, and the ability to work as part of a team are necessary. Good communication skills are also important.

Mathematics and the sciences must be emphasized in high school.

A bachelor's degree in engineering is the usual minimum requirement in this field. In a typical curriculum, the first two years are spent in the study of basic sciences such as physics and chemistry, mathematics, introductory engineering, and some liberal arts courses. The remaining years are usually devoted to specialized engineering courses.

Engineering programs can last from four to six years. Those requiring five or six years to complete may award a master's degree or may provide a cooperative plan of study plus practical work experience in a nearby industry.

Because of rapid changes in technology, many engineers continue their education throughout their careers. A graduate degree is necessary for most teaching and research positions and for many management jobs. Some persons obtain graduate degrees in business administration.

Engineering graduates usually work under the supervision of an experienced engineer or in a company training program until they become acquainted with the requirements of a particular company or industry.

All states require licensing of engineers whose work may affect life, health, or property or who offer their services to the public. Those who are licensed are called registered engineers. Requirements for licensing include graduation from an accredited engineering school, four years of experience, and passing a written examination.

Potential and advancement

There are about 195,000 civil engineers in the country. Job opportunities in this field likely will be plentiful through 2008 because population growth will create an increasing demand for housing, transportation, power generating plants, and other energy sources. Opportunities will vary by region and depend somewhat on the health of the general economy and the rate of new construction.

Income

Starting salaries for civil engineers with a bachelor's degree average about $36,100 a year in private industry. Starting offers for those with a master's degree average $42,300 a year and for those with a Ph.D., $58,600. Senior engineers working in private industry with management responsibilities earn salaries in excess of $90,000.

Additional sources of information

Accreditation Board for Engineering and Technology
111 Market Place, Suite 1050
Baltimore, MD 21202-4012
www.abet.org

American Society of Civil Engineers
1801 Alexander Bell Drive
Reston, VA 20191-4400
www.asce.org

Junior Engineering Technical Society
1420 King Street, Suite 405
Alexandria, VA 22314-2794
www.jets.org

National Society of Professional Engineers
1420 King Street
Alexandria, VA 22314-2794
www.nspe.org

Society of Women Engineers
120 Wall Street, 11th Floor
New York, NY 10005
www.swe.org

CLAIM REPRESENTATIVE

The job

Claim representatives, including claim adjusters and claim examiners, investigate claims for insurance companies, negotiate settlements with policyholders, and authorize payment of claims.

Claim adjusters work for property-liability (casualty) insurance companies and usually specialize in specific types of claims such as fire, marine, or automobile. They determine whether the company is liable (that is, whether the customer's claim is a valid one covered by the customer's policy) and recommend the amount of settlement. In the course of investigating a claim, adjusters consider physical evidence, testimony of witnesses, and any applicable reports. They strive to protect the company from false or inflated claims and at the same time settle valid claims quickly and fairly. In some companies, adjusters submit their findings to *claim examiners*, who review the reports and authorize payment as appropriate.

In states with no-fault auto insurance, adjusters do not have to establish responsibility for a covered loss but must decide the amount. Many auto insurance companies employ special inside adjusters who settle smaller claims by mail, by telephone, or at special drive-in centers where claims are settled immediately.

Most claim adjusters work for insurance companies, but some work for independent firms that contract their services to insurance companies. These firms vary in size from local companies employing two or three adjusters to large national organizations with hundreds of adjustment specialists.

A few adjusters represent insured parties rather than insurance companies. These public adjusters are retained by banks, financial organizations, and other businesses to negotiate settlements with insurers.

In life insurance companies, claim examiners are the equivalent of claim adjusters. In the course of settling a claim, an examiner might correspond with policyholders or their families, consult medical specialists, calculate benefit payments, and review claim applications for completeness. Questionable claims or those exceeding a specified amount would be even more thoroughly investigated by the examiner.

Claim examiners also maintain records of settled claims and prepare reports for company data processing departments. More experienced examiners serve on company committees, survey claim settlement procedures, and work to improve the efficiency of claim-handling departments.

Related jobs are actuary, insurance agent and broker, and underwriter.

Places of employment and working conditions

Claim adjusters work in all sections of the United States, in cities and towns of all sizes. Claim examiners, on the other hand, work in home offices of insurance companies, most of which are located in and around Boston, Chicago, Dallas, New York City, Philadelphia, and San Francisco.

Adjusters set their own schedules, doing whatever is necessary to dispose of a claim promptly and fairly. Most firms provide 24-hour claim service, so adjusters are on call all the time and may work some weekends and evenings. They may be called to the site of an accident, a fire, or a burglary or the scene of a riot or hurricane. They must be physically fit because they spend much of the day traveling, climbing stairs, and actively investigating claims. Much of their time is spent outdoors—this is not a desk job.

Claim examiners, by contrast, do have desk jobs. Their usual workweek is 40 hours, but they may work longer hours during peak loads or when preparing quarterly and annual reports. They may travel occasionally in the course of their investigations and are sometimes called on to testify in court regarding contested claims.

Qualifications, education, and training

Claim representatives should be able to communicate tactfully and effectively, have a good memory, and enjoy working with details. Knowledge of computers is important because they are used extensively for record keeping. Claim examiners must also be familiar with medical and legal terms, understand insurance laws and regulations, and have mathematical skills.

Insurance companies prefer to hire college graduates for positions as claim representatives but will sometimes hire high school graduates with specialized experience; for example, automobile repair experience is desirable for automobile claims adjuster positions. Because of the complexity of insurance regulations and claim procedures, however, claim representatives without a college degree may advance more slowly than those with a two- or four-year degree.

Many large insurance companies provide on-the-job training combined with home-study courses for newly hired claim adjusters and claim examiners. Throughout their careers, claim representatives continue to take a variety of courses and programs designed to certify them in specific areas of the profession.

Licensing of adjusters is required in some states. Requirements vary, but an applicant usually must be 20 or 21 years of age and a resident of the state, complete an approved training course in insurance or loss adjusting, provide character references, pass a written examination, and file a surety bond (a bond guaranteeing performance of a contract or obligation).

Potential and advancement

While all indications point to a steady need for claim representatives, persons trying to enter the field will have an advantage if they can demonstrate certain specialized skills. The growing trend toward drive-in claim centers and claim handling by telephone will probably reduce the demand for automobile adjusters but increase the demand for inside adjusters. Those who specialize in workers' compensation, product liability, and other types of complex business insurance will be in particular demand.

Claim representatives are promoted as they gain experience and complete courses and training programs. Those who demonstrate exceptional ability or administrative skills may become department supervisors or may advance to management jobs. Some qualified adjusters, however, prefer to broaden their knowledge by transferring to other departments such as underwriting or sales.

Income

Salaries for claim adjusters and investigators average about $38,290. Adjusters are often provided with a company car or reimbursed for using their own cars for business purposes.

Additional sources of information

Alliance of American Insurers
1501 Woodfield Road, Suite 400 W
Schaumburg, IL 60173-4980

American Council of Life Insurance
1001 Pennsylvania Avenue NW
Washington, DC 20004-2599

Insurance Information Institute
110 William Street
New York, NY 10038
www.iii.org

National Association of Independent Insurers
Public Relations Department
2600 River Road
Des Plaines, IL 60018

National Association of Public Adjusters
300 Water Street
Baltimore, MD 21202

COMMUNICATIONS EQUIPMENT MECHANIC

The job

The installation, maintenance, and repair of communications equipment are the responsibility of communications equipment mechanics. This equipment includes telephone, telegraph, wireless, fax, and cable equipment as well as radio, television, and radar broadcasting equipment. (The job of **broadcast technician**, another type of equipment operator, is covered separately.)

Communications equipment mechanics are employed by communications companies, manufacturers of communication equipment, airlines, police and fire departments, government agencies, and radio and television studios.

Communications equipment mechanics have various duties and specialties.

Central office equipment installers handle the installation of switchboards, dialing systems, and other equipment in the central office of a telephone company. *Station installers* and *repair persons* install and service telephone equipment in homes, offices, businesses, and telephone booths and maintain outside facilities. *PBX installers* and *repair persons* work on private switchboard equipment. *Line persons* and *cable splicers* install and maintain aerial and underground wires and cables.

Radio and telephone technical operators set up and adjust overseas radio-telephone communication equipment. They contact foreign terminals and make mutually agreed-upon adjustments in transmitting power, frequency, and speech levels.

In radio and television studios, a *construction technician* installs broadcasting equipment, assembles and wires units of technical equipment, and assists in testing the equipment.

Radar technicians install and service radar equipment.

Related jobs are broadcast technician, television and radio service technician, business machine service technician, and computer service technician.

Places of employment and working conditions

Positions for communications technicians are available throughout the United States and in many locations overseas.

Because most communications systems operate 24 hours a day, seven days a week, most communications equipment mechanics work shifts, weekends, and holidays. They are also usually required to be on 24-hour call to take care of equipment-failure emergencies.

Mechanics usually work in comfortable surroundings, but, depending on the job, they may have to stand for long periods, climb, reach, stoop, and lift light objects. They must be careful to avoid electrical shocks. Workers who wear headsets may suffer hearing loss from acoustic shock, a high-pitched, shrill noise produced by some headsets.

Qualifications, education, and training

Mechanical aptitude, manual dexterity, normal eyesight and hearing, physical stamina, and the ability to work as part of a team are necessary.

High school should include courses in mathematics, physics, and electronics. Hobbies that involve electronics and communication equipment are also helpful.

Large companies have reduced the size of their training programs and consequently are seeking employees with work experience who already have the skills necessary for doing the job. These workers often come from smaller companies or the armed forces.

Companies' second preference is to hire people who have an associate degree or postsecondary vocational school training in telecommunication technology, electronics, computer maintenance, or related subjects.

If there are no available applicants with these credentials, some companies will promote from within and provide training. The trend, however, is to reduce company costs by phasing out internal training programs.

Many telephone companies are replacing traditional classroom training programs with modular training programs, in which employees work at a chosen pace using entry tests, videotapes, movies, computer terminals, and programmed workbooks. Larger companies may send mechanics to outside training sessions to study repair procedures or new equipment.

Potential and advancement

There are about 125,000 communications equipment mechanics nationwide. Job opportunities are expected to grow at an average rate through 2008. Increased demand for installers is expected as companies upgrade their telecommunications systems. Maintenance work, however, is expected to decline because of self-monitoring, self-diagnosing equipment.

Income

Earnings for communications equipment mechanics vary greatly with the size and location of the employer. Central office installers and technicians, PBX installers, and repairers represented by the Communications Workers of America and the International Brotherhood of Electrical Workers earn between $283 and $996 a week. The average hourly rate is $21.00.

Most communications equipment mechanics are members of the Communications Workers of America or the International Brotherhood of Electrical Workers. For these workers, wage rates, increases, and the time needed to advance in the job are determined by union contracts. Union contracts also require extra pay for work beyond the normal eight hours a day or five days a week and for all work on Sundays and holidays. Contracts also provide for additional pay for night work; paid vacations; paid sick leave; group life, medical, and dental insurance; and several other employee benefits.

Additional sources of information

Local telephone companies and radio and television stations can provide further information on job requirements and salaries.

Also, more information on career opportunities in the telephone industry is available from:

United States Telephone Association
1401 H Street NW, Suite 600
Washington, DC 20005-2136

COMPUTER PROGRAMMER

The job

Computer programmers write detailed instructions, called programs, that list the orderly steps a computer must follow to perform a function. Once programming is completed, the programmer runs a sample of the data to make sure the program is correct and will produce the desired information. If there are any errors, the program must be changed and rechecked until it produces the correct results. This is called debugging. The final step is the preparation of an instruction sheet for the computer operator who will run the program.

A simple program can be written and debugged in a few days. Those that use many data files or complex mathematical formulas may require a year or more of work. On such large projects, several programmers work together under the supervision of an experienced programmer.

Programmers usually work from problem descriptions prepared by *systems analysts* who have examined a given situation and determined the next steps necessary to achieve the desired outcome. In organizations that do not employ systems analysts, employees called *programmer-analysts* handle both functions. An *applications programmer* then writes detailed instructions for programming the data. Applications programmers usually specialize in business or scientific work.

A *systems programmer* is a specialist who maintains the general instructions (software) that control the operation of the entire computer system.

Beginners in this field spend several months working under supervision before they begin to handle all aspects of the job.

Most programmers are employed by manufacturing firms, banks, insurance companies, data processing services, utilities, and government agencies. Systems programmers usually work in research organizations, computer manufacturing firms, and large computer companies.

Places of employment and working conditions

Programmers are employed in all areas of the country.

Most programmers work a 40-hour week, but their hours are not always 9:00 to 5:00. They may occasionally work on weekends or other odd hours to have access to the computer when it is not needed for scheduled work.

Qualifications, education, and training

Patience, persistence, and accuracy are necessary characteristics for a programmer. Ingenuity, imagination, and the ability to think logically are also important.

High school experience should include as many mathematics courses as possible.

There are no standard training requirements for programmers, but the field is becoming more competitive, and three out of five programmers now have a B.A. or higher degree. Some, especially those who work for scientific organizations, have a graduate degree in computer science, mathematics, engineering, or physical sciences.

Computer programming courses are offered by vocational and technical schools, colleges and universities, and junior colleges. Home-study courses are also available, and a few high schools offer some training in programming.

Because of rapidly changing technologies, programmers take periodic training courses offered by employers, software vendors, and computer manufacturers. Like physicians, they must keep constantly abreast of the latest developments in their field. These courses also aid in advancement and promotion.

Some programmers also receive certification from product vendors or software firms. Such certification may be an advantage in seeking jobs.

Potential and advancement

There are about 648,000 computer programmers in the country. Employment opportunities should grow at a faster than average rate, as compared with other occupations, through 2008. Both systems and applications programmers should find many job opportunities because data processing services are expected to expand more than any other area of the economy.

There are many opportunities for advancement in this field. In large organizations, programmers may be promoted to lead programmers with supervisory responsibilities. Both applications programmers and systems programmers can be promoted to systems analyst positions.

Income

Programmers earn an average of $47,550 a year. Those in the middle of the salary range earn between $36,020 and $70,610 annually; those at the top of the salary range earn more than $88,730, and those at the bottom earn less than $27,670.

Programmers who work in the West and Northeast generally earn more than those who work in the South and Midwest.

Additional sources of information

Association for Computing Machinery
1515 Broadway
New York, NY 10036
www.acm.org

Data Processing Management Association
505 Busse Highway
Park Ridge, IL 60068

COMPUTER SERVICE TECHNICIAN

The job

Computer systems perform a wide variety of tasks in business and industry. Keeping the systems in working order is the responsibility of computer service technicians.

Computer service technicians not only do repair work but also provide regular scheduled maintenance checks to prevent emergency breakdowns of equipment. Some computer technicians install new equipment, while others design and develop maintenance and repair schedules and manuals. Some technicians specialize in a particular computer model or system or in a certain type of repair.

Most computer service technicians are employed by the manufacturers of computer equipment or by firms that contract to provide maintenance service to a manufacturer's customers. A few are employed directly by organizations that have large computer installations.

Related jobs are appliance repairer, business machine service technician, communications equipment mechanic, and television and radio service technician.

Places of employment and working conditions

Computer service technicians work throughout the country. Most are in large cities, where computer equipment is concentrated.

The normal workweek is 40 hours, but large amounts of overtime are standard. Many service technicians work rotating shifts or are on call 24 hours a day because many businesses run their computers around the clock.

Qualifications, education, and training

Mechanical aptitude, manual dexterity, good eyesight and color vision, normal hearing, patience, and the ability to work without supervision are necessary. Because technicians work directly with customers, they must get along well with people.

A high school student interested in this field should take courses in mathematics, physics, and electrical shop. Hobbies that involve electronics, such as ham radio operation or building stereo equipment, are helpful.

Employers usually prefer to hire trainees with one or two years of technical training in electronics or electrical engineering. Technical and vocational schools, junior colleges, and the armed forces provide this training.

Trainees usually receive instruction from the employer for three to six months and then complete six months to two years of on-the-job training. Because of constant technological changes in the field, all technicians normally take periodic training courses as new equipment is developed.

Experienced technicians may take advanced courses for specialization in particular systems or repairs. Some technicians study computer programming and systems analysis to broaden their knowledge of computer operation.

Additional sources of information

Manufacturers of computers can provide information on job opportunities and training programs.

CONTROLLER

The job

The briefest and broadest definition of a controller (or comptroller) is the key financial executive who controls, analyzes, and interprets the financial results and records of a company or an organization.

The *treasurer*, on the other hand, is responsible for the receipt, custody, and properly organized disbursement of an organization's or a company's funds.

Some organizations also have a *vice president of finance* who has overall financial responsibility and reports to the chief executive officer—president or chairman of the board—of the company.

A company may have one or all of these financial officers or may combine all three into one executive-level position with any of the mentioned titles. This job description is confined to the usual duties of a controller in an organization that has a separate treasurer position.

The controller is responsible for the design of a company's accounting system(s), preparation of budgets and financial forecasts, internal auditing of company operations and records, control of company funds kept by the treasurer, establishment and administration of tax policies and procedures, and preparation of reports to government agencies. Because an organization's financial operations involve the accumulation, interpretation, and storage of vast amounts of detailed information, a controller is often also in charge of the company's computerized data processing operation.

Places of employment and working conditions

Controllers are employed throughout the country. They work for government agencies, businesses, industry, nonprofit organizations, hospitals, and other institutions of all sizes.

As with many top-level jobs, controllers often work long hours under great pressure. Peak workloads occur when tax reports and stockholders' reports are prepared.

Qualifications, education, and training

A controller needs more than facility with mathematics and the ability to do accurate work. At this level of responsibility, sound judgment, planning proficiency, administrative and management skills, ability to motivate people, communication skills, and computer literacy must be combined with expertise in cost accounting, budgeting, taxes, and other specialized areas.

A college background in finance, accounting, economics, mathematics, or business administration is usually the basic education for this profession. The majority of people who reach this level have a master's degree in business administration or a CPA (certified public accountant) certificate (see page 2 for information on CPA requirements).

Continuing education is essential. Professional certifications, sponsored by associations in the field, are also desired.

Potential and advancement

The career paths to the post of controller are varied. Cost analysis and accounting, budgeting, tax auditing, financial analysis, planning and programming, credit collections, systems and procedures, and data processing are training grounds for executive-level financial positions.

Once the top management level has been reached, the usual method of advancement for a controller is to transfer to a larger organization where the responsibilities are greater and more complex. Some advance by moving from a top financial position in a large organization to the chief executive post in a smaller company.

Income

Salaries for controllers depend in large part on the size of the organization and its location and are generally higher in larger institutions and cities. Controllers' annual salaries average $109,700. Many controllers receive bonuses, which vary according to the size of the firm and other factors.

Additional source of information

Financial Executives Institute
10 Madison Avenue
P.O. Box 1938
Morristown, NJ 07962-1938
www.fei.org

CORRECTIONS OFFICER

The job

Corrections officers, more commonly known as prison guards, supervise the daily activities of prisoners. They guard prisoners both inside and outside the prison. They explain prison rules to inmates and listen to their complaints and needs.

Inside the prison, corrections officers escort inmates to their daily activities, such as meals, classes, work, and chapel. If a prisoner is sick, the corrections officer sees that he or she gets to the hospital. Corrections officers oversee recreational activities and make sure that all bars, gates, doors, and windows are secure so that prisoners cannot escape. They must count the prisoners at certain times during the day and report any who are missing. In addition, corrections officers must intervene to quell fights, disturbances, or escape attempts. They must also make sure prisoners do not have any forbidden articles.

Some corrections officers oversee prisoners outside the boundaries of the prison. They escort prisoners to and from jobs and on court-ordered trips, and they return escapees and parole violators.

Places of employment and working conditions

Most corrections officers work in state and county correctional institutions. Some work in federal prisons.

Corrections officers usually work a 40-hour week. Prisons must be guarded around the clock, so some guards work nights, evenings, and weekends.

Corrections officers may be put in dangerous situations at times. They must be able to remain calm and make sound decisions quickly.

Qualifications, education, and training

Corrections officers must be U.S. citizens and, in most states, at least 18 to 21 years old. They must have no felony convictions.

A high school education is necessary for most jobs. Postsecondary education in a relevant field, such as criminal justice or police science, is beneficial, especially for promotion.

Most states test applicants on their ability to read and follow directions. Other states administer a civil service examination. Some states require a psychological examination, and all require a physical exam. Some candidates for federal jobs and for some state jobs are screened for drug abuse and must pass a background check.

All beginning officers must undergo a training program lasting from one to six months. Trainees learn modern correctional methods, personal defense, physical restraint of prisoners, and the use of guns. Federal corrections officers are formally trained at the Federal Bureau of Prisons residential training center in Georgia.

Potential and advancement

The job outlook for corrections officers is favorable through 2008. The inmate population is rising, in part because of mandatory sentencing laws. Opportunities will result from the expansion of existing prisons and the construction of new ones. Turnover will also create opportunities.

As they gain additional training, experience, and education, corrections officers advance in rank and salary. The route is from corrections officer to sergeant to lieutenant to corrections captain to deputy keeper. Titles for ranks may vary from institution to institution.

Income

Pay scales vary by rank, branch of government that is the employer, and geographic location. Corrections officers working for the federal government earn an average of $36,500. In the public sector, the average is $32,600.

Additional sources of information

American Correctional Association
8025 Laurel Lakes Court
Laurel, MD 20707-5075

National Council on Crime and Delinquency
685 Market Street, No. 620
San Francisco, CA 94105

COSMETOLOGIST

The job

An attractive personal appearance is important to many people. Cosmetologists, also called hairstylists or beauticians, help people look good and feel better about themselves.

Cosmetologists cut, shampoo, and style hair. In addition, they advise clients on suitable hairstyles and teach them how to care for their hair. Sometimes cosmetologists straighten or permanent wave a client's hair. They are also trained to either lighten or darken hair color. Other job duties include giving manicures and scalp and facial treatments; providing makeup analysis for women; and cleaning and styling wigs and hairpieces.

Cosmetologists also make appointments and maintain records of their clients' hair care preferences. They must keep their work areas clean and sell hair products and other supplies.

In addition, some cosmetologists own their businesses and have managerial responsibilities.

Places of employment and working conditions

Cosmetologists work in all cities and towns, but opportunities are greatest in the most populated cities and states. Cosmetologists who set fashion trends usually work in New York City or Los Angeles.

Most full-time cosmetologists work 40 hours a week, sometimes during evenings and weekends. They spend a great deal of time on their feet.

Qualifications, education, and training

Cosmetologists should be creative. They must enjoy interacting closely with people and have skill in working with their hands.

All states require cosmetologists to be licensed. In most states, a candidate must graduate from a state-licensed cosmetology school, pass a physical exam, and be at least 16 years old. Some states require graduation from high school, while others require only an eighth-grade education.

Cosmetology training is offered in public and private vocational schools. Daytime courses usually last 10 months to a year; night courses take longer. Programs include classroom study, demonstrations, and hands-on experience. Some cosmetologists train by working as apprentices for one to three years.

Students take the state licensing exam after graduating from a cosmetology program. In addition to a written exam, some states have an oral test and/or a practical test of cosmetology skills.

Potential and advancement

There are about 723,000 cosmetologists in the country, and the field should grow at an average rate through 2008. Population gains, higher incomes, the large number of working women, and expansion of the beauty salon industry will result in many job opportunities.

Cosmetologists advance as they gain experience and their client rosters grow. Some are promoted into management positions or open their own salons. Some teach in cosmetology schools. Others advance by becoming sales representatives for cosmetology firms. Cosmetologists can also become examiners for state cosmetology boards.

Income

Cosmetologists earn an average of about $12,270 to $20,540 per year, excluding tips. The top 10 percent earn more than $27,270.

Additional sources of information

American Association of Cosmetology Schools
901 North Washington Street, Suite 206
Alexandria, VA 22314-1535

National Cosmetology Association
401 North Michigan Avenue, 22nd Floor
Chicago, IL 60611
www.nca.now.com

CREDIT INVESTIGATOR

The job

The work of a credit investigator varies by employer and size of the organization.

In a local department store that extends credit in the form of a charge account or for the purchase of a home appliance, the credit investigator is usually a clerical employee who calls an applicant's employer to verify employment and earnings and contacts the local credit bureau to ascertain the applicant's credit ranking.

In a bank or savings and loan association, the credit department is more comprehensive and is usually called a loan department. Credit investigators in this setting do more in-depth analysis of a credit applicant's finances and require more information than a retail store credit department because the amounts of bank loans are usually much larger. In the case of business loans, significant sums of money may be involved. The credit investigation often includes acquisition and analysis of a firm's records, such as financial statements, inventory figures, details of operation, and similar information.

Manufacturers, wholesalers, and distributors who extend credit to their customers also employ credit investigators. Because the sums of money involved are often substantial, the credit investigation is a thorough one and often as detailed as a bank's investigation.

Additional information relative to this occupational field is contained in the job description for **credit manager**.

CREDIT MANAGER

The job

When either a business or an individual requests credit, the financial background of the requestor is investigated by the lender. Final acceptance or rejection of an application for credit is the responsibility of a credit manager.

In extending credit to a business (commercial credit), the credit manager or an assistant analyzes financial reports submitted by the applicant, reviews the firm's credit record, and consults with banks or other institutions that service the firm's accounts.

In extending credit to individuals (consumer credit), credit managers must rely on personal interviews, credit bureau reports, and the applicant's bank to provide relevant information.

In large companies, credit managers analyze the information gathered by application clerks or *credit investigators* and data provided in financial reports. In small companies, credit managers do much of the information gathering themselves and may also be involved in collecting delinquent accounts. In some large organizations, executive-level credit managers formulate company credit policies and establish credit department procedures.

Some credit managers are employed in wholesale and retail trade; others work for manufacturing firms and financial institutions.

Beginners in this field usually gain experience as management trainees. They learn to deal with credit bureaus, banks, and other businesses and receive a thorough grounding in the company's credit procedures and policies.

Related jobs are accountant, bank officer, and economist.

Places of employment and working conditions

Credit managers work in all areas of the country, in communities of all sizes. Most job opportunities are in urban areas supporting many financial and business firms.

This is an office job and usually consists of a 35- to 40-hour week. In some businesses, seasonal peak workloads may require overtime.

Qualifications, education, and training

The ability to analyze and draw conclusions, a pleasant personality, and communication skills are necessary for this career.

High school courses in business, bookkeeping, computer science, and public speaking are helpful. Summer or part-time jobs in business offices or credit agencies provide valuable experience.

Even though some employers will promote high school graduates to the position of credit manager if they have substantial experience in credit collection or processing of credit information, a college degree is becoming increasingly important, even for entry-level jobs. A bachelor's degree in business administration, economics, accounting, or liberal arts with a business or accounting major is the preferred educational background.

Some professional organizations in the credit and finance field offer formal training programs that include home-study courses, college courses, or other special instruction. These programs aid beginners who are developing their skills and help experienced credit managers keep abreast of new developments.

Potential and advancement

Average growth is expected in this field through 2008. The health of the general economy and the number of real estate, retail sales, and other transactions requiring credit will influence the demand for workers. Job openings will also result from workers leaving this field or the workforce.

Advancement is limited in small and medium-size companies, but in large companies, credit managers can advance to top executive positions.

Income

Credit investigators earn average annual salaries of about $45,500. Credit managers earn median annual salaries of $56,600.

Additional source of information

International Credit Association
Education Department
Box 27357
St. Louis, MO 63141-1757

CRIMINOLOGIST

The job

The broad field of criminology encompasses all men and women who work in law enforcement, criminal courts, prisons and other correctional institutions, and counseling and rehabilitation programs for offenders. Many jobs in these categories are outlined elsewhere in this book. This job description focuses on the term *criminologist* as it applies to those who are involved in the scientific investigation of crime through analysis of evidence.

The scientific gathering, investigation, and evaluation of evidence is known as criminalistics, and professionals in this field are called *forensic scientists*. These technical experts, including specially trained police officers and detectives, carefully search victims, vehicles, and scenes of crimes. They take photographs, make sketches, lift fingerprints, make casts of footprints and tire tracks, and gather samples of any other relevant materials.

Once the evidence has been gathered, scientists and technicians trained in various natural sciences analyze it along with reports from medical examiners and pathologists. Other specialists interview victims to prepare composite pictures or psychological profiles of the criminal. Those who specialize in firearms and ballistics conduct tests that identify weapons used in specific crimes.

Forensic specialists also include handwriting experts, fingerprint and voice-print specialists, polygraphy (lie detector) examiners, and odontologists (teeth and bite-mark specialists).

Almost all the members of this field work for federal, state, or local law enforcement and investigative agencies. Municipal and state police departments have investigative responsibilities that include the processing of evidence. Some employ civilian scientists and technicians, but many utilize specially trained police officers in police crime laboratories.

The federal government employs forensic scientists in several agencies, including the Federal Bureau of Investigation and the Secret Service.

Related jobs are chemist, medical laboratory technologist, biochemist, and police officer.

Places of employment and working conditions

Forensic scientists may be on call at all hours and may be required to work outdoors or in unpleasant conditions when gathering evidence.

Qualifications, education, and training

Curiosity, aptitude for detail, patience, and good eyesight and color vision are necessary traits.

High school curricula should include mathematics and science courses.

Optimal college training depends on the specialty field selected. A degree in chemistry, biology, electronics, or whatever related field is appropriate should be obtained. Course work in forensic science is offered by some colleges as well as by some law enforcement training programs and police departments.

Potential and advancement

There are relatively few positions for criminologists. The number of available positions in the future will depend on the amount of public funding for crime prevention.

Income

Beginning criminologists earn about $28,200 a year. Those who are experienced earn from about $35,540 to $62,520.

Additional sources of information

American Society of Criminology
1314 Kinnear Road, Suite 212
Columbus, OH 43212

Federal Bureau of Investigation
U.S. Department of Justice
Washington, DC 20535
www.fbi.gov

DANCER

The job

Professional dancers perform classical ballet, modern dance, and other forms of dance; work in opera, musical comedy, movies, and television; and teach dancing. Some specially trained dance teachers also use dance therapy to promote mental health.

Dancers who perform lead a demanding life with little job security. Shows can close unexpectedly, and movie and television assignments are of short duration. Unemployment rates are significant, and even highly qualified dancers find it difficult to obtain year-round work. Dancers who are part of an established dance company or who are in a long-running hit show have the most stable performing lives. Many dancers take part-time jobs to support themselves between dancing assignments, and those who are qualified to teach often combine teaching and performing.

Dancers who teach full-time have the most stable working lives. Those who teach at colleges and universities have the same schedule as other faculty members. Others teach in private studios, professional dance schools, and dance companies. Those who work for dance companies also travel with the group when it goes on tour.

Professionals who create dance routines or new ballets are called *choreographers*. They usually have experience as performers and can continue their careers as choreographers long after the conclusion of their active performing years. *Dance directors* train dancers in new routines or productions.

Dancers who perform usually are members of one of the unions affiliated with the Associated Actors and Artists of America.

Places of employment and working conditions

New York City is *the* place for performing dancers. Other cities that provide substantial numbers of job opportunities are Atlanta, Boston, Philadelphia, Cleveland, Dallas, Miami, Cincinnati, Chicago, Milwaukee, Pittsburgh, Houston, Salt Lake City, Seattle, and Washington, D.C.

Just about every town and city has at least one dance school that employs teachers. Job openings for dance teachers also exist in colleges and universities and in secondary schools, dance companies, and private studios.

A dancer's life is one of rigorous practice and self-discipline, with strict dieting a constant factor. Performances are scheduled on evenings and weekends, and lessons and practice take up daytime hours, leaving little time for personal life. Heavy travel schedules and the unstable nature of show business can drain a performer's physical and emotional strength. The physical demands of this career mean that a dancer's active performing career is usually over by his or her late 30s.

Qualifications, education, and training

Good health and physical stamina are essential for a dancer. Body build and height should be average, with good feet and normal arches. Agility, grace, creativity, and a feeling for music are also necessary. In addition, dancers should be able to take direction and function as part of a group.

Selection of a good professional dance school is important. Serious training for a dancer begins before the age of 12. In ballet, training must begin even earlier, at about age 5 to 7. Most dancers are ready for professional auditions by age 17 or 18, but training never ends. Ten to 12 lessons a week and many hours of practice make up the life of a dancer, even when he or she is performing with a dance company or in a show.

Because of the strenuous training schedule, a dancer's general education may suffer. Some dancers solve this problem by taking correspondence courses. In addition to dance, professional dance schools usually teach music, literature, and history to aid students in dramatic interpretation of dance.

An alternative to professional school training is a college or university degree in dance. About 250 schools confer degrees in dance. Bachelor's and master's degrees are typically offered in the departments of physical education, music, theater, or fine arts. A college degree is usually necessary for teaching at the college or university level but is not required for teaching in a professional school or dance studio, where performing experience is preferred. College-trained dancers who wait to begin a performing career until graduation from college may find themselves at a disadvantage when competing with beginners of 17 or 18.

Potential and advancement

There are about 29,000 dancers across the nation performing on stage, screen, and television, and many others are involved in teaching. This is a field in which qualified applicants always exceed the number of job openings. Expanded employment opportunities exist in teaching dance.

Income

Basic agreements between unions and producers specify minimum wages, working hours, and other employment conditions, but individual contracts signed by each dancer with a producer may be more favorable than the basic union agreement.

The annual salary for dancers averages between $21,430 and $25,000. Dancers on tour receive an additional allowance for room and board.

The normal workweek for a dancer under a union contract is 30 hours (6 hours per day maximum) of rehearsals and performances. Extra compensation is paid for any additional hours worked.

Dancers who teach earn salaries that vary with location, prestige of the school or dance company, and reputation of the teacher. At colleges and universities, dance teachers earn the same salaries as other faculty members.

Additional sources of information

American Dance Guild
31 West 21st Street, Third Floor
New York, NY 10010

National Dance Association
1900 Association Drive
Reston, VA 20191

DENTAL ASSISTANT

The job

Dental assistants work with dentists and oral hygienists as they examine and treat patients. They are usually employed in private dental offices and often combine office duties, such as making appointments, maintaining patient records, and billing, with chair-side assisting.

Dental assistants prepare instruments and materials for treatment procedures, process dental x-ray films, sterilize instruments, prepare plaster casts of teeth from impressions taken by the dentists, and sometimes provide oral health instructions to patients. In some states, they are permitted to apply medications to teeth and gums, remove excess filling materials from surfaces of teeth, and fit rubber isolation dams on individual teeth before treatment by the dentist.

Dental assistants are also employed in dental schools, hospital dental departments, state and local public health departments, and private clinics. The federal government employs them in the Public Health Service, the Veterans Administration, and the armed forces.

Most dental assistants are women. Opportunities for part-time work are numerous, making this an attractive career choice for people with family responsibilities.

A related job is dental hygienist.

Places of employment and working conditions

Dental assistants are employed in communities of all sizes, with the most job opportunities in large metropolitan areas.

A 40-hour workweek is usual for full-time dental assistants, but this includes some evening and Saturday hours in most dental offices.

Qualifications, education, and training

Neatness and the ability to help people relax are important personal qualities.

High school courses in biology, chemistry, health, computer science, and office practices are helpful.

Most dental assistants acquire their skills on the job. Office skills often provide entry into a dental office, where a beginner handles appointments, acts as receptionist, and performs routine clerical and record-keeping chores. Dental assisting skills are then acquired over time.

An increasing number of dental assistants are acquiring their training in formal programs at junior and community colleges and vocational and technical schools. Most of these programs require one year or less to complete. Two-year programs include some liberal arts courses and offer an associate degree upon completion. Some private schools offer four- to six-month courses in dental assisting, but these are not accredited by the Commission on Dental Accreditation. Dental assistants who receive their training in the armed forces usually qualify for civilian jobs.

Graduates of accredited programs may receive professional recognition by completing an examination given by the Dental Assisting National Board, having two years' experience, and earning CPR certification. They are then designated as certified dental assistants.

Potential and advancement

There are about 229,000 people working as dental assistants across the country; 30 percent work part-time. Job opportunities should be excellent for the future, especially for graduates of formal training programs.

Dental assistants in large dental offices or clinics are sometimes promoted to supervisory positions. Some advance by fulfilling the educational requirements necessary to become dental hygienists. Others teach in or administer dental assisting education programs.

Income

Salaries vary widely from community to community and depend on training and experience, job responsibilities and duties, and size of the dental practice.

The average income for full-time dental assistants is about $10.88 per hour.

Additional sources of information

American Dental Assistants Association
203 North LaSalle Street, Suite 1320
Chicago, IL 60601-1225

Dental Assisting National Board
676 North Saint Clair, Suite 1880
Chicago, IL 60611
www.dentalassisting.com

DENTAL HYGIENIST

The job

Dental hygienists are involved in both clinical dental work and education, with specific responsibilities governed by the state in which the hygienist is employed.

Working as part of a dental health team under the supervision of a dentist, a dental hygienist may clean and polish a patient's teeth, removing deposits and stains at the same time; apply medication for the prevention of tooth decay; take and develop x-rays; make model impressions of teeth; take medical and dental histories; and provide instruction for patient self-care, diet, and nutrition. In some states, dental hygienists also perform pain control and restorative procedures.

Some dental hygienists work in school systems, where they examine students' teeth, assist dentists in determining necessary treatment, and report their findings to parents. They give instruction in proper mouth care and develop classroom or assembly programs on oral health.

Most dental hygienists are employed in private dental offices; many are employed part-time.

Other employers are public health agencies, industrial plants, clinics and hospitals, dental hygienist schools, the federal government, and the U.S. armed forces (dental hygienists with a bachelor's degree are commissioned officers). A few dental hygienists are involved in research projects.

Places of employment and working conditions

Dental hygienists work in communities of all sizes.

They usually maintain a 35- to 40-hour workweek; those employed by a dentist in private practice usually have some weekend and evening hours. The nature of the job requires dental hygienists to stand for a major part of the working day.

Certain health protection procedures are important for anyone working in this field. These include regular medical checkups and strict adherence to established procedures for disinfection and use of x-ray equipment.

Qualifications, education, and training

An enjoyment of people and the ability to put a patient at ease are strong assets. Manual dexterity is necessary. Good health, personal cleanliness and neatness, and stamina are likewise important.

High school courses recommended for anyone interested in a career in this field include biology, chemistry, health, and mathematics.

Requirements for admission to dental hygienist schools vary. Some hygienist schools that offer a bachelor's degree require one or two prior years of college.

There are 250 programs in dental hygiene in the United States that are accredited by the Commission on Dental Accreditation. Students in dental hygienist programs study anatomy, physiology, chemistry, pharmacology, nutrition, tissue structure, gum diseases, dental materials, and clinical dental hygiene. Liberal arts courses are also part of the program. Most programs grant an associate degree, which is sufficient for working in private dental practice. Some schools award a bachelor's degree. Several schools offer master's-degree programs in dental hygiene or related fields. Advanced degrees are required for some teaching and research positions.

Licensing is required for all dental hygienists; all states require graduation from an accredited dental hygienist school as well as written and clinical examination. To pass the clinical examination, the applicant for licensing is tested on proficiency in performing dental hygiene procedures. Most states will accept a passing grade on the written examination given by the American Dental Association Joint Commission on National Dental Examinations as part of the licensing requirement.

Potential and advancement

The United States has about 143,000 dental hygienists.

This is a field in which current job openings outnumber qualified graduates, and the employment outlook for potential dental hygienists is excellent. An expanding population and increased use of hygienists will contribute to strong demand through 2008. There will also be many opportunities for dental hygienists who desire part-time work and for those willing to work in rural areas.

Income

Dental hygienists working in private dental offices are paid on an hourly, daily, salary, or commission basis.

Full-time dental hygienists' average hourly pay is $22.06.

Additional source of information

American Dental Hygienists' Association
Commission on Dental Accreditation
211 East Chicago Avenue, Suite 1814
Chicago, IL 60611

DENTIST

The job

Graduates of approved dental schools are entitled to use the designations D.D.S. (doctor of dental surgery) or D.M.D. (doctor of dental medicine).

Most dentists are general practitioners who provide many types of dental care. They examine teeth and mouth tissues to diagnose and treat any diseases or abnormalities of the teeth, gums, supporting bones, and surrounding tissues. They extract teeth, fill cavities, design and insert dentures and inlays, and perform surgery. The dentist, or someone on his or her staff, takes dental and medical histories, cleans teeth, and provides instructions on proper diet and cleanliness to preserve dental health.

Some dentists are specialists. The two largest branches comprise *orthodontists*, who straighten teeth, and *oral surgeons*, who operate on the mouth and jaws. Other specialties are pediatric dentistry (dentistry for children), periodontics (treatment of the gums), prosthodontics (artificial teeth and dentures), endodontics (root canal therapy), oral pathology (diseases of the mouth), and public health dentistry.

Places of employment and working conditions

Dentists nationwide currently hold about 160,000 jobs. Most work in private practice, which includes a wide variety of work settings and payment systems. The dentists who work outside private practice include researchers, teachers, and administrators in dental schools. Others work in hospitals and clinics. The federal government also employs dentists, primarily in the hospitals and clinics of the Department of Veterans Affairs and the U.S. Public Health Service.

Most dentists' offices are open five days a week, and some dentists work weekend and evening hours to accommodate their patients' needs. Dentists usually work about 40 hours a week, with those who are just starting up working fewer hours until the practice is established.

Qualifications, education, and training

Students interested in dentistry as a career should possess a high degree of manual dexterity and scientific ability and have good visual memory and excellent judgment of space and shape.

High school courses should include biology, chemistry, health, and mathematics.

Dental education is expensive because of the length of time required to earn a degree. From two to four years of predental college work in the sciences and humanities is required by dental schools, with most successful applicants having a bachelor's or master's degree. Competition for admission is stiff; dental schools give considerable weight to the amount of predental education and to college grades. Schools also require personal interviews and recommendations as well as completion of the Dental Admissions Test. In addition, state-supported dental schools usually give preference to residents of the state.

Dental school training lasts four academic years after college or, in some dental colleges, three calendar years. The first two years consist of classroom instruction and laboratory work in anatomy, microbiology, biochemistry, physiology, clinical sciences, and preclinical technique. The remainder of the training period is spent in actual treatment of patients.

A license to practice is required by all states and the District of Columbia. Requirements include a degree from a dental school approved by the Commission on Dental Accreditation and written and practical examinations. A passing grade on the written examination given by the National Board of Dental Examiners is accepted by most states as fulfilling part of the licensing requirements; many states require additional written and/or skills tests.

In 17 states, dentists who wish to specialize must have two or four years of graduate training and, in some cases, pass an additional state examination. In the remaining states, a licensed dentist may engage in general or specialized dentistry.

In these states, the additional education is also necessary to specialize; however, specialists are regulated by the state dental profession rather than by state licensing.

Potential and advancement

There are about 160,000 dentists in America, 90 percent of them in private practice. The demand for dentists is expected to rise because of population gains, increased awareness of the necessity of dental health, and the growing elderly population. Although the employment of dentists is expected to grow more slowly than the average for all occupations, many dentists are projected to retire.

Income

Dentists setting up a new practice can anticipate a few lean years in the beginning. As the practice develops, income will rise rapidly, with average yearly earnings around $110,160.

Additional sources of information

American Association of Dental Schools
1625 Massachusetts Avenue NW
Washington, DC 20036

American Dental Association
Commission on Dental Accreditation
211 East Chicago Avenue
Chicago, IL 60611

DIETITIAN

The job

Depending on the setting, dietitians plan nutritious and appetizing meals, supervise the preparation and service of food, and manage the purchasing and accounting for their respective units or departments. Some are involved in research and education.

More than half of all dietitians are employed in hospitals, nursing homes, and other health care facilities. Colleges, universities, school systems, restaurants and cafeterias, companies that provide food service for their employees, and food processors and manufacturers also employ dietitians.

Some serve as commissioned officers in the armed forces. The federal government also employs dietitians in veterans' hospitals and in the U.S. Public Health Service.

Clinical dietitians form the largest group. They plan diets and supervise the service of meals to meet the various nutritional needs of patients in hospitals, nursing homes, and clinics. They confer with doctors and instruct patients and their families on diet requirements and food preparation.

Management dietitians are responsible for large-scale meal planning and preparation. They purchase food, equipment, and supplies; enforce safety and sanitary regulations; and train and direct food-service and supervisory workers. If they are directors of a dietetic department, they may also manage a budget, coordinate dietetic service activities with other departments, and set department policy. In a small institution, the duties of administrative and clinical dietitians are usually combined into one position.

Research dietitians evaluate the dietary requirements of specific groups such as elderly people, people with a chronic disease, or even astronauts. They also conduct research in food management and service systems and equipment.

Dietetic educators teach in medical, dental, and nursing schools.

Nutritionists provide counseling in proper nutrition practices. They work in food industries, educational and health facilities, agricultural agencies, welfare agencies, and community health programs.

Places of employment and working conditions

Dietitians are employed throughout the country, with most job opportunities in large metropolitan regions and in areas with large colleges and universities.

Most dietitians work a 40-hour week, but this usually includes some weekend hours. There are many part-time opportunities for dietitians.

Qualifications, education, and training

Anyone interested in pursuing this career field should have scientific aptitude, organizational and administrative skills, and the ability to work well with people.

High school courses should include biology, chemistry, home economics, mathematics, and some business courses, if possible.

A bachelor's degree in the home economics department with a major in foods and nutrition or institutional management is the basic requirement for a dietitian. Currently, 235 schools offer undergraduate or graduate programs accredited by the American Dietetic Association.

A 9- to 12-month internship or a preprofessional practice program should also be completed by any dietitian who wants professional recognition. These programs consist primarily of clinical experience under the direction of a qualified dietitian. Some colleges and universities have coordinated undergraduate programs that enable students to complete both the clinical and bachelor's-degree requirements in four years.

The American Dietetic Association registers dietitians who meet its established qualifications. The designation RD (registered dietitian) is an acknowledgment of a dietitian's competence and professional status. At present, 27 states require licensure.

Potential and advancement

Countrywide, about 54,000 people work as dietitians. Job opportunities, both full- and part-time, should grow at an average rate through 2008.

Dietitians usually advance by moving to larger institutions. In a large institution, they may advance to director of the dietetic department. Some advance by entering an area of clinical specialization. Others become consultants or opt for careers in business and management. Advancement in research and teaching positions usually requires a graduate degree.

Income

Experienced dietitians earn about $28,010 to $42,720 a year.

Additional source of information

American Dietetic Association
216 West Jackson Boulevard, Suite 800
Chicago, IL 60606-6995
www.eatright.org

DRAFTER

The job

Drafters prepare detailed drawings from rough sketches, specifications, and calculations made by engineers, architects, designers, and scientists. Work completed by a drafter usually includes a detailed view of the object from all sides, specifications for materials to be used, and procedures to be followed. Any other information necessary to carry out the job is also included by the drafter. Most drafters now use computer-aided design and drafting (CADD) systems to create drawings.

Drafters usually specialize in a particular field, such as mechanical, electronic, structural, architectural, electrical, or aeronautical drafting. They are classified according to the work they do and their level of responsibility. *Senior drafters* translate preliminary drawings and plans into design layouts—scale drawings of the object to be built. *Detailers* draw each part shown on the layout, giving dimensions, materials, and other information. *Checkers* examine drawings and specifications for errors. Supervised by experienced drafters, *tracers* make minor corrections and trace drawings for reproduction on paper or plastic film. Beginners usually start as tracers or junior drafters and work their way up through checker and detailer positions.

Places of employment and working conditions

Most drafters work in private industry. Engineering, architectural, design, and construction firms employ 35 percent; 29 percent work for fabricated metals, electrical equipment, and machinery firms. Others work for federal, state, and local government agencies. About 17,600 (6.2 percent) are self-employed.

Drafters work in all areas of the country, with the largest concentrations in industrialized areas.

Working areas are usually pleasant, but drafters do highly detailed work at drawing boards or computer terminals and must often sit for long periods.

Qualifications, education, and training

Drafters need good eyesight, manual dexterity, and drawing ability and must be able to do accurate, detailed work. They must have the ability to work as part of a team. In some specialized fields, artistic ability is also necessary.

High school courses should include mechanical drawing, science, computers, and mathematics. Shop skills are also helpful.

Drafting skills may be acquired in several ways. Vocational and technical high schools provide enough training for entry-level jobs at companies with on-the-job training programs. Technical institutes, junior and community colleges, and extension divisions of universities provide training for full-time and evening students. The armed forces also train drafters.

Due to the increasing use of CADD systems, persons trained in electronic drafting will have the best prospects for employment.

Potential and advancement

There are about 283,000 drafters employed in the United States, and the size of the field is expected to grow slowly through 2008. Expanded use of CADD equipment will offset increased demand for service.

Experienced drafters can advance to senior drafter and supervisory positions. Some become independent designers or continue their education to transfer to engineering or architectural positions.

Income

In private industry, drafters earn between $10.19 and $24.80 per hour, depending on their level of experience.

Additional sources of information

American Design Drafting Association
P.O. Box 11937
Columbia, SC 29211

International Federation of Professional and Technical
    Engineers
8630 Fenton Street, No. 400
Silver Spring, MD 20910-3803

ECONOMIST

The job

Economists study and analyze the relationship between supply and demand of goods and services and how they are produced, distributed, and consumed.

Eighty percent of all economists work in private industry for manufacturing firms, banks, insurance companies, securities and investment firms, and management consulting firms. They provide information to management that affects decisions on marketing and pricing of company products, long- and short-term economic forecasts, and the effect of government policies on business.

Many economists are employed by colleges and universities, where they teach or are engaged in research and writing. These economists are often called on to act as consultants to business firms and government agencies.

Economists employed in government prepare studies to assess economic conditions and the need for changes in government policies. They usually work in the fields of agriculture, forestry, business, finance, labor, transportation, and international trade and development.

A related job is credit manager.

Places of employment and working conditions

Economists work in all large cities and in university towns. The highest concentrations are in the New York City, Washington, D.C., and Chicago metropolitan areas.

Qualifications, education, and training

Anyone interested in pursuing this career field should be able to work accurately and in detail because economics entails careful analysis of data. Good communication skills are also necessary.

High school should include as many mathematics and computer science courses as possible.

A college major in economics is the basic preparation for a career as an economist. Students should also study political science, psychology, sociology, finance, business law, and international relations. A bachelor's degree is sufficient for some beginning research, administrative, management trainee, and sales jobs; however, graduate school is increasingly necessary, especially for advancement.

Graduate training in a specialty area such as advanced economic theory, labor economics, or international economics is necessary for college teaching positions. The larger colleges and universities require a Ph.D.

Potential and advancement

There are about 70,000 economists in the United States. Growth in the economics field is expected to be as fast as the average for all occupations through 2008. Most opportunities will occur as incumbents transfer to other occupations or leave the labor force.

The best opportunities will be with testing facilities, research organizations, and consulting firms. Nonprofit organizations and trade associations will provide other opportunities. Employment of economists in the federal government is expected to decline more slowly than other federal jobs, and employment of economists in state and local government is expected to grow slowly.

Advancement in this field usually requires higher levels of education.

Income

The average starting salary for economists with a bachelor's degree is $20,600. Experienced economists earn $48,330 to $94,810, depending on specialization and level of education. Economists employed by the federal government earn an average of $65,300.

Additional sources of information

American Economists Association
1313 21st Avenue, South
Nashville, TN 37212

National Association for Business Economics
1233 20th Street NW, Suite 505
Washington, DC 20036

EDITOR, BOOK PUBLISHING

The job

An editor has two basic functions: to work with the author in the preparation of the author's work for publication and to prepare the manuscript for the various phases of the production process. Because no one person could efficiently manage all the editorial details involved in publication, specific areas of responsibility are usually assigned to individual members of an editorial staff.

The *editor in chief*, sometimes called the *editorial director*, manages the editorial department, organizes the editorial staff, sets the budget, and makes key decisions on editorial policy. Editors function within the financial and policy goals of the publisher and editor in chief. They work with authors, agents, and other publishers; develop authors and manuscripts; and prepare contracts. Editors have titles in accordance with their seniority. After the editor in chief and editorial director, *senior editors* have the most seniority, followed by *full editors*, *associate editors*, and *assistant editors*.

In some publishing houses, there is an added distinction between *acquisitions editors* and *production editors* or *project editors*. Acquisitions editors scout for manuscripts and read and evaluate submissions. Production or project editors edit the manuscript and work with production and art department personnel to turn the manuscript into a finished book.

A *managing editor* coordinates all editorial functions on each project and acts as a traffic manager, verifying that all production schedules are met.

A *copyeditor* does a careful reading of the manuscript with attention to grammar, spelling, and punctuation as well as to coherence, arrangement, and accuracy. The copyeditor marks all necessary directions for the typesetter and may query (question) the author on any material that is not clear.

Editorial assistants process incoming manuscripts, give a first reading to unsolicited ones, return rejected manuscripts, and perform clerical duties.

Another important job in the editorial and production processes is that of the *proofreader*, who checks material after it has been set into type. The proofreader checks the typeset copy against the copyedited manuscript to make sure that the typesetter has set the material exactly as indicated. The proofreader is expected to catch any mistakes in spelling, nonconformity with design specifications, or other errors, as introduced by the typesetter, as well as any errors of grammar or discrepancies overlooked by the copyeditor. Although proofreading is a specialty in itself, most editors have done their share of it at some point in their careers.

Places of employment and working conditions

Every city has some job opportunities for editors. The biggest publishing center is New York City, followed by Philadelphia, Boston, Chicago, Los Angeles, San Francisco, and Washington, D.C. Most college communities also provide job openings in this field.

The usual workweek is 40 hours, but production deadlines and large workloads frequently make overtime necessary.

Qualifications, education, and training

Facility in working with people, tact, an ability to recognize not only what is well written but also what will sell, attention to detail, good judgment, and excellent communication skills are necessary.

High school courses in English are fundamental, but a student interested in this profession should also get a well-rounded education to prepare for college. Keyboarding is a must, and mastery of computer and word processing techniques is becoming increasingly important.

Liberal arts with a major in English or a bachelor's degree in journalism is the usual preparation for this field. Textbook, scientific, and technical publishers usually require a background in specific subject areas as well as proficiency in English.

Potential and advancement

There are thousands of U.S. book publishers that employ editors. Because there is always an overabundance of English and journalism majors seeking jobs in this field, the best job prospects are with small publishers, especially for beginners.

Promotion up through various editorial positions occurs as an editor gains experience, but career advancement often takes the form of moving to a larger company.

Income

Publishing is not a well-paid profession on the whole. Salaries are low compared with other fields that require comparable education and experience.

Beginning editorial positions pay an average of $20,920 a year. Most experienced editors earn about $35,200 a year. Some executive editors earn more than $76,660 yearly.

Additional source of information

Association of American Publishers
71 Fifth Avenue
New York, NY 10003-3004

EDITOR, NEWSPAPER AND MAGAZINE

The job

The editorial positions and responsibilities on a newspaper differ in many respects from those in book publishing; those in magazine publishing cover aspects of both publishing fields.

The editor or *editor in chief* of a magazine or newspaper sets general editorial policy in accordance with the wishes of the publisher, who may also be the editor. The editor may write some or all of the editorials and may be involved to varying degrees in the daily operation of the paper or magazine.

A *managing editor* directs and supervises the day-to-day operation of the publication. On a newspaper, the managing editor usually has the responsibility of selecting the news stories that will receive top play. Some newspapers and magazines also have an *executive editor* whose responsibilities lie between those of the editor and the managing editor, taking some of the workload from each job.

On a newspaper, the *city editor* directs local and area news coverage. He or she schedules reporters and assigns the news stories they are to cover. The city editor also supervises the rewrite staff. The *wire editor* handles the national and foreign news. On some papers, a *news editor* rather than the managing editor decides on the final mix of local, national, and foreign news and which stories will receive top play. Weekly news magazines also have foreign and news editors.

The *makeup editor* on a newspaper or magazine is responsible for page layout. On a newspaper, the makeup editor must be able to work swiftly to meet deadlines and may have to remake pages at the last minute when late-breaking news bumps previously positioned stories.

Both magazines and newspapers employ *copyeditors*, or *copyreaders*, who prepare all material for typesetting. They correct grammar, spelling, and punctuation; check names, dates, and other facts; and write headlines to go with each item or article. Some copyeditors also perform page layout and photo editing. On a daily newspaper, all of this must be done quickly to meet production deadlines.

Various special editorial positions may include women's editor, sports editor, financial editor, food editor, and many others. These editors have responsibility for news and features in their specialty areas and sometimes supervise large staffs.

Places of employment and working conditions

Large metropolitan areas provide the most opportunities for newspaper and magazine editors, but opportunities exist throughout the country in communities of all sizes.

Constant deadline pressure is a fact of life for newspaper editors and, to a lesser extent, magazine editors. For newspaper and news magazine editors, personal plans must often be subordinated to the demands of the job. The pace and pressure can be physically and emotionally wearing.

Although the workweek is supposed to be about 40 hours, often this is not the case because important news stories can mean longer hours and irregular schedules. Those who work on morning papers usually work evening hours.

Qualifications, education, and training

A newspaper or magazine editor needs a sense of what is important and interesting to the reader. An excellent command of the English language, management skills, sound judgment, and the ability to motivate people are also necessary.

A broad high school curriculum with emphasis on the development of communication skills is important. Experience on school publications or as a stringer (covering local events such as sports for several newspapers) can provide valuable background. Computer literacy is a must.

College is a standard prerequisite for anyone interested in working as an editor. A liberal arts degree or a degree in journalism is the usual preparation, with employers about evenly divided on which they prefer.

Potential and advancement

There are thousands of newspapers in the United States as well as consumer magazines, business publications, and house organs (internal publications of a business) that employ editors. Competition for all editorial jobs on large newspapers and magazines is the norm; publications in smaller communities and in areas away from large metropolitan areas offer the best employment opportunities. For beginners, the best opportunities are on small magazines and weekly newspapers, where they can accumulate experience in a variety of editorial functions.

Promotion in this field is usually up through the ranks, with many editors starting as reporters, feature writers, and rewriters. Advancement also takes the form of movement to larger publications or larger cities.

Income

Salaries for newspaper employees vary greatly and depend on the person's level of experience and the size and scope of the paper.

Beginners earn a median starting salary of $20,920. Employees with experience average about $28,500.

Salaries are higher for employees of newspapers that have a contract with the Newspaper Guild, the union for newspaper employees.

Most senior editors ar large newspapers earn more than $76,600 per year.

Additional source of information

Newsletter Association of America Foundation
The Newspaper Center
11600 Sunrise Valley Drive
Reston, VA 22091

ELECTRICAL/ELECTRONICS ENGINEER

The job

Electrical and electronics engineering is the largest branch of engineering. These engineers design and develop electrical and electronic equipment and products. They may work in power generation and transmission; machinery controls; lighting and wiring for buildings, automobiles, and aircraft; computers; radar; communications equipment; missile guidance systems; or consumer goods such as television sets and appliances.

Engineers in this field usually specialize in a major area such as communications, computers, or power distribution equipment or in a subdivision such as aviation electronic systems. Many are involved in research, development, and design of new products; others are in manufacturing and sales.

Places of employment and working conditions

Engineers are employed in all areas of the country, in towns and cities of all sizes as well as rural areas, with some specialties concentrated in certain areas.

The main employers of electrical engineers are companies that manufacture electrical and electronic equipment, aircraft and parts, computers and other business machines, and professional and scientific equipment. Telephone, telegraph, and electric light and power companies also employ many electrical engineers. Others work for construction firms, engineering consulting firms, and government agencies. Some also work in the field of nuclear energy.

Qualifications, education, and training

The ability to think analytically, a capacity for details, and the ability to work as part of a team are all necessary. Good communication skills are also important.

Mathematics and the sciences must be emphasized in high school.

A bachelor's degree in engineering is the minimum requirement in this field. In a typical curriculum, the first two years are spent in the study of basic sciences such as physics and chemistry, mathematics, introductory engineering, and liberal arts. The remaining years are usually devoted to specialized engineering courses.

Engineering programs can last from four to six years. Those requiring five or six years to complete may award a master's degree or may provide a cooperative plan of study plus practical work experience.

Because of rapid changes in technology, many engineers continue their education throughout their careers. A graduate degree is necessary for most teaching and research positions and for many management jobs. Some persons obtain graduate degrees in business administration.

Engineering graduates usually work under the supervision of an experienced engineer or in a company training program until they become acquainted with the requirements of a particular company or industry.

All states require licensing of engineers whose work may affect life, health, or property or who offer their services to the public. Those who are licensed are called registered engineers. Requirements for licensing include graduation from an accredited engineering school, four years of experience, and passing a written examination.

Constant advances in technology make continuing education necessary.

Potential and advancement

There are about 357,000 electrical engineers nationwide. Increased demand for computers and communications equipment is expected to provide ample job opportunities for electrical engineers through 2008. A sharp rise or fall in government spending for defense could change this picture in either direction.

Income

Starting annual salaries in private industry average $45,200 for someone with a bachelor's degree; $57,200 with a master's degree; and $70,800 or more with a Ph.D.

Experienced engineers average $62,660, but those in the private sector can earn $91,490 or more. Those employed by the federal government average $68,000.

Additional sources of information

Accreditation Board for Engineering and Technology
111 Market Place, Suite 1050
Baltimore, MD 21202-4012
www.abet.org

Institute of Electrical and Electronics Engineers
1828 L Street NW, Suite 1202
Washington, DC 20036

Junior Engineering Technical Society
1420 King Street, Suite 405
Alexandria, VA 22314-2794
www.jets.org

National Society of Professional Engineers
1420 King Street
Alexandria, VA 22314-2794
www.nspe.org

Society of Women Engineers
120 Wall Street, 11th Floor
New York, NY 10005
www.swe.org

ELECTRICIAN

The job

The installation and maintenance of electrical systems and equipment are handled by electricians. They follow National Electrical Code specifications and any state and local electrical codes. Observance of safety practices is vital in this field, and electricians often use protective equipment and clothing.

Construction electricians, following blueprints and specifications, install wiring systems in newly constructed or renovated homes, offices, and factories. They also install electrical machinery, electronic equipment and controls, and signal and communications systems. Most construction electricians are employed by electrical contractors; some are self-employed.

Maintenance electricians maintain the electrical systems installed by construction electricians and usually work in factories or other large buildings such as office complexes and apartment houses. They also install new electrical equipment and keep lighting systems, generators, and transformers in working order. Maintenance electricians spend much of their time doing preventive maintenance, inspecting equipment to locate and correct problems before breakdown can occur. More than half of all maintenance electricians are employed in manufacturing industries. Others are employed by public utilities, mines, and railroads and by federal, state, and local governments.

Electricians usually furnish their own hand tools (screwdrivers, pliers, knives, hacksaws), while employers furnish heavier tools (pipe threaders, conduit benders) as well as most test meters and power tools.

The majority of construction electricians are members of the International Brotherhood of Electrical Workers.

Places of employment and working conditions

Electricians are employed throughout the country, with the greatest numbers in industrialized and urban areas. The heavily industrialized states such as California, New York, Pennsylvania, Illinois, and Ohio employ many maintenance electricians.

Electricians do not need superior physical strength, but they must be in good physical condition because they must stand for long periods and often work in cramped spaces. Because they usually work indoors, they are not exposed to bad weather as much as other workers in the building trades; however, they do risk injury from falls, electrical shock, and falling objects. Maintenance electricians work near high-voltage industrial equipment and are exposed to noise and the grease and oil of machinery.

Qualifications, education, and training

Electricians need at least average physical strength, agility, and dexterity. Good color vision is important because electrical wires are often identified by color.

High school or vocational school courses in electricity, electronics, mechanical drawing, science, and electrical shop are suitable background for someone interested in becoming an electrician. Because completion of a formal apprenticeship program is considered the best way to become an electrician, this trade has a higher percentage of apprenticeship-trained workers than most other construction trades. A local union-management commission sponsors and supervises each program. Those who complete an apprenticeship program can usually qualify as either a construction or maintenance electrician.

Applicants for apprenticeship should be in good health and at least 18 years of age. Most programs require a high school or vocational school diploma. Typically, programs last four or five years and include up to 8,000 hours of comprehensive on-the-job training as well as 144 hours per year of classroom instruction. Classroom courses include blueprint reading, electrical theory, electronics, mathematics, and safety and first-aid training.

Some people learn the trade informally by working as electricians' helpers in construction or maintenance jobs. They can gain additional knowledge through trade schools, correspondence courses, or special training in the armed forces. This method, however, often takes longer than a formal apprenticeship program.

In most areas, electricians must be licensed. The examination for licensing requires a thorough knowledge of the craft, state and local building codes, and the National Electrical Code.

Potential and advancement

There are approximately 656,000 electricians in the country. Job opportunities are expected to be good through 2008. Electricians will be needed to install and repair electrical devices and wiring in homes, factories, offices, and other building structures. New automated manufacturing technologies and increased use of computers and telecommunications equipment should keep electricians in demand.

Employment of electricians varies with the economy, the geographic area, and the cyclical nature of construction work. Construction electricians may experience periods of unemployment between construction projects and during times when the weather does not allow construction work. Maintenance electricians working for industries that are sensitive to shifts in the economy, such as automotives, may be laid off during recessions.

Experienced construction electricians can be promoted to supervisory jobs or become estimators for contractors. Many start their own contracting businesses, which may require obtaining an electrical contractor's license. Maintenance electricians can become supervisors and occasionally advance to jobs such as plant electrical superintendent or plant maintenance superintendent.

Income

Electricians who are not self-employed earn an hourly average of $16.98. Those at the low end of the pay scale earn less than $10.07, and those at the high end earn more than $30.99.

Apprentices usually have beginning salaries that are 30 to 50 percent of those paid to experienced electricians.

Additional sources of information

International Association of Machinists and Aerospace Workers
9000 Machinists Place
Upper Marlboro, MD 20772

International Brotherhood of Electrical Workers
1125 15th Street NW
Washington, DC 20005

International Union of Electronic, Electrical, Salaried,
    Machine, and Furniture Workers
1126 16th Street NW
Washington, DC 20036

National Electrical Contractors Association
3 Metro Center, Suite 1100
Bethesda, MD 20814

United Steelworkers of America
5 Gateway Center
Pittsburgh, PA 15222

EMERGENCY MEDICAL TECHNICIAN

The job

Emergency medical technicians, or EMTs, are usually the first caregivers to arrive on the scene of a medical emergency. Their ability to provide medical care quickly and accurately may save a victim's life.

Upon arrival at the scene, EMTs assess the situation and decide which emergency services must be given first. They must determine the victim's condition as well as whether he or she has any preexisting medical conditions, such as epilepsy or diabetes, that will affect the type of treatment given. The medical treatments EMTs are trained to give include opening airways, restoring breathing, controlling bleeding, treating for shock, administering oxygen, assisting in childbirth, and treating and resuscitating heart-attack victims.

When a situation is especially serious, EMTs may report directly to the hospital by radio, transmitting vital signs and other information so that the hospital can provide instructions for treatment.

Another difficulty EMTs sometimes face is coming to the aid of trapped victims, as in a car accident or a collapsed building. They must try to free the victims while making sure that they are not injured further.

If victims must be transported to a hospital, EMTs put them on stretchers, carry them to the ambulance, and place them inside, making sure that the stretcher is secure. One EMT drives the ambulance while the other stays with the victim and continues medical treatment. After the ambulance arrives at the hospital, the EMTs help get the victim into the emergency room and inform the physicians and nurses of their observations and the treatment they have given.

It is also the EMTs' responsibility to make sure that the ambulance is properly equipped and maintained. They must be certain that any supplies that have been used are either replaced or cleaned and sterilized and must check the equipment to ensure that it is working properly. They also must see that the ambulance is in good working condition.

There are four classifications for EMTs: First Responder, EMT-Basic, EMT-Intermediate, and EMT-Paramedic. First Responders provide basic emergency care; many firefighters and police officers have this training. An EMT-Basic can care for patients on the scene and in transit to the hospital under medical direction. EMT-Intermediates and EMT-Paramedics have received more training and are capable of giving additional types of medical treatment. These EMTs are trained in using electrical defibrillation to resuscitate heart-attack victims.

Places of employment and working conditions

EMTs are employed by private ambulance services; hospitals; and municipal police, fire, and rescue squad departments.

EMTs work inside and outside, sometimes in poor weather conditions. EMTs' services are needed 24 hours a day, so they are often required to work evenings, weekends, and holidays. This job is physically strenuous; it involves a great deal of lifting. There is also much pressure in this field because EMTs must make life-and-death decisions.

Qualifications, education, and training

EMTs must be physically strong and healthy. They must be able to make sound decisions quickly in stressful situations. In addition, they should be emotionally stable and have leadership abilities as well as a neat and clean appearance and a pleasant personality.

EMTs are required to undergo instruction in emergency medical-care techniques. The course for EMT-Basic is 110 hours long and explains basic life-support techniques. It is offered in all 50 states and the District of Columbia. The course is administered by police, fire, and health departments; hospitals; and medical schools, colleges, and universities.

Those taking the course learn how to respond to emergencies such as bleeding, fractures, lack of oxygen, airway obstruction, cardiac arrest, and emergency childbirth.

To become an EMT-Intermediate, EMT-Basics must take additional courses and learn more medical procedures. EMT-Paramedic programs last up to two years and result in an associate degree in applied science.

Applicants to EMT training courses must be at least 18 years old, have a high school diploma or its equivalent, and have a valid driver's license.

The National Registry of Emergency Medical Technicians registers EMT-Paramedics who meet its standards. While registration is not a requirement, it does give greater credibility to EMTs who have earned it.

All 50 states have certification procedures.

Potential and advancement

Nationwide, there are currently 150,000 EMTs. This field is expected to grow much faster than the average for all occupations through 2008. The rapid growth in the number of senior citizens and developments in the field of emergency medicine will fuel demand for EMTs. However, competition for jobs with police, fire, and rescue squads will be keen, as these positions are more secure and more highly paid than those with hospitals and private ambulance services.

EMTs who have risen through the ranks to become EMT-Paramedics must leave fieldwork to advance any further. They may become field supervisor, operations supervisor, operations manager, administrative director, and then executive director.

Another advancement route for EMTs is to become an instructor, but this option usually requires a bachelor's degree in education.

Other EMTs become sales representatives for emergency medical equipment manufacturers; some become police officers or firefighters. By getting more education, some are able to move into clinical or management careers in health or related fields.

Income

Earnings for EMTs depend on an individual's level of experience and training, the employer, and the geographic area.

The average salary for an EMT-Basic is from $15,660 to $26,240 a year.

Additional source of information

National Association of Emergency Medical Technicians
408 Monroe Street
Clinton, MS 39056
www.naemt.org

National Registry of Emergency Medical Technicians
P.O. Box 29233
Columbus, OH 43229
www.nremt.org

EMPLOYMENT COUNSELOR

The job

Employment counselors, also called vocational counselors, help job seekers who have difficulties finding jobs. They provide services to experienced workers who have been displaced by automation or who are unhappy in their present jobs and to returning veterans, school dropouts, disabled and older workers, ex-prisoners, and people with minimal job skills.

In-depth interviews with job seekers, aptitude tests, and other background information help the counselor evaluate the capabilities of each person. The counselor then helps the job seeker develop a vocational plan and a job goal that will be implemented, using whatever remedial action is necessary. This could include education or retraining, physical rehabilitation or psychological counseling, specific work experience, or development of appropriate work skills. Once the job seeker obtains a position, the counselor usually provides follow-up counseling for a period of time.

Counselors must be familiar with the local labor market and with the job-related resources of the community. Some employment counselors contact local employers and keep abreast of job openings within local industries to refer job seekers to specific jobs.

Most employment counselors work for state employment centers or community agencies. Others work for private agencies, prisons, training schools, and hospitals. The federal government offers positions for employment counselors in the Department of Veterans Affairs and the Bureau of Indian Affairs.

Places of employment and working conditions

Employment counselors work throughout the country in communities of all sizes.

Counselors usually work a 40-hour week. Those in community agencies may work overtime or some evening and weekend hours.

Qualifications, education, and training

Anyone pursuing this field should have a strong interest in helping others, should be able to work independently and keep detailed records, and should possess patience.

Graduate work beyond a bachelor's degree or equivalent counseling-related experience is necessary for even entry-level jobs in employment counseling. Undergraduate work should include courses in psychology and sociology; graduate work includes actual counseling experience under the supervision of an instructor.

Employment counselors working for state and local government agencies must fulfill local civil service requirements, which include specific education and experience requirements and a written examination.

Potential and advancement

The employment outlook for this field should be good through 2008, especially in private business. Employment opportunities in federal and state agencies will depend on the availability of government funding.

Employment counselors in federal and state agencies may advance to supervisor or administrative positions. Those working in private business may move into personnel and management positions.

Income

Earnings for employment counselors vary widely. Counselors in private practice have the highest earnings. Salaries vary from $28,400 to $49,960.

Additional source of information

National Employment Counselors Association
5999 Stevenson Avenue
Alexandria, VA 22304

ENGINEER

The job

Engineers apply the theories and principles of science and mathematics to technical problems. This is one of the largest professions in the country.

Most engineers specialize in one of the more than 25 major branches of engineering. Within these branches, there are numerous subdivisions, and engineers may further specialize in one industry, such as motor vehicles, or one field of technology, such as propulsion or guidance systems. This job description provides an overall picture of engineering as a career. Information on 12 major branches of this profession appears elsewhere in this book.

In general, engineers in a particular field may be involved in research, design, and development; production and operation; maintenance; time and cost estimation; sales and technical assistance; or administration and management. Engineers usually work as part of a team and, regardless of specialty, may apply their knowledge across several fields. For example, an *electrical engineer* can work in the medical field, computers, missile guidance systems, or electrical power distribution. An *agricultural engineer* may design farm equipment, manage water resources, or work in soil conservation.

There are about 1.5 million engineers in the country. Engineers work for manufacturing industries and in nonmanufacturing industries such as construction, public utilities, engineering and architectural services, and business and consulting services.

Federal, state, and local government agencies employ about 166,000 engineers. Federally employed engineers work mainly for the Departments of Defense, Interior, Agriculture, Transportation, and Energy and for the National Aeronautics and Space Administration. In state and local governments, engineers usually work for highway and public works departments.

Some engineers teach and do research.

Related jobs are mathematician, engineering and science technician, and architect.

Places of employment and working conditions

Engineers are employed in all areas of the country, in towns and cities of all sizes as well as rural areas, with some specialties concentrated in certain areas.

Most engineers work indoors, but some, depending on specialty, work outdoors or at remote locations.

Qualifications, education, and training

The ability to think analytically, a capacity for details, and the ability to work as part of a team are necessary. Good communication skills are also important.

Mathematics and the sciences must be emphasized in high school.

A bachelor's degree in engineering is the minimum requirement in this field. In a typical curriculum, the first two years are spent in the study of basic sciences such as physics and chemistry, mathematics, introductory engineering, and some liberal arts courses. The remaining years are usually devoted to specialized engineering courses.

Engineering programs can last from four to six years. Those requiring five or six years to complete may award a master's degree or may provide a cooperative plan of study plus practical work experience.

Because of rapid changes in technology, many engineers continue their education throughout their careers. A graduate degree is necessary for most teaching and research positions and for any management jobs. Some specialties, such as nuclear engineering, are taught only at the graduate level. Some persons obtain graduate degrees in business administration or in a field such as law (for patent attorneys).

Engineering graduates usually work under the supervision of an experienced engineer or in a company training program until they become acquainted with the requirements of a particular company or industry.

All states require licensing of engineers whose work may affect life, health, or property or who offer their services to the public. Those who are licensed are called registered engineers. Requirements for licensing include graduation from an accredited engineering school, four years of experience, and passing a written examination.

Potential and advancement

The employment outlook for engineers is good for the foreseeable future, with some specialties more in demand than others. The field will continue to grow, while the number of degrees granted in engineering is expected to decline.

Experienced engineers may advance to administrative and management positions. Many of the highest-level executives in private industry started their careers as engineers.

Income

Salaries vary by industry. Civil engineers tend to earn the least; they average $53,450. Petroleum engineers, averaging $74,260, are among the most highly paid.

Additional sources of information

Accreditation Board for Engineering and Technology
111 Market Place, Suite 1050
Baltimore, MD 21202-4012
www.abet.org

Junior Engineering Technical Society
1420 King Street, Suite 405
Alexandria, VA 22314-2794
www.jets.org

National Society of Professional Engineers
1420 King Street
Alexandria, VA 22314-2794
www.nspe.org

Society of Women Engineers
120 Wall Street, 11th Floor
New York, NY 10005
www.swe.org

ENVIRONMENTALIST

The job

Pollution is one of the major problems of modern society. Environmentalists find ways to control and prevent water, air, and land pollution. They must keep in mind the needs of the environment as well as the economic needs of industries.

Areas of specialization for environmentalists include land conservation, acid rain, toxic-waste removal and disposal, wildlife preservation, and groundwater contamination. Environmentalists conduct research, perform environmental impact studies, and develop systems to monitor pollution. Some work with community groups and leaders to solve environmental problems in a particular area. They may attend public meetings or appear before legislative committees or in court.

Some environmentalists work as consultants. They are hired by the government or a private company to study a problem and then advise the employer on how best to deal with it to protect the environment and not suffer financial loss.

Other environmentalists work with members of Congress and state legislatures to see that laws are written and passed that protect the environment.

Places of employment and working conditions

Environmentalists may work for the federal government, usually in the Environmental Protection Agency or the Department of the Interior. Others work for state and local governments. Employers hiring environmentalists also include environmental consulting firms, nonprofit environmental organizations, chemical and oil companies, and mining companies.

Environmentalists work indoors, in an office, and outdoors. They often have to travel to problem sites to perform research and studies. Their work hours may be irregular.

Qualifications, education, and training

Environmentalists must be able to work well with people. They should be good communicators and have an interest in the outdoors and science.

Environmentalists usually must have a bachelor's degree in one of the environmental or natural sciences. Some have degrees in engineering or political science. Most environmentalists continue to take courses to stay aware of the latest developments in the field.

Potential and advancement

Environmentalists will be in demand through 2008. Because of current awareness of environmental problems and the subsequent laws that are being passed to regulate environmental quality, companies will need the advice of experts in the field. This should result in good opportunities for environmentalists.

Environmentalists usually begin as researchers or interns. They advance by becoming project directors or managers. Those with experience often become consultants.

Income

Salaries for environmentalists range from $31,600 to more than $80,000 annually.

Additional sources of information

Association of Environmental Scientists and Administrators
3433 Southwest McNary Parkway
Lake Oswego, OR 97035

National Association of Environmental Professionals
P.O. Box 9400
Washington, DC 20016

FARMER

The job

Farmers today are businesspeople. They buy seed, fertilizer, and equipment; plant only a few crops or even one crop; follow scientific production methods; and sell all they grow or raise.

The dwindling supply and high cost of available farmland, plus the cost of the equipment necessary to run a farm using today's agricultural technology, are leading to an increase in some alternative styles of farming. Given their working conditions, farmers in areas with long winters often take jobs in nearby cities during the cold months, working their farms through the spring, summer, and fall.

Tenant farmers rent their land from farm owners, usually in return for a percentage of the crop. Some owners also supply machinery, seed, and fertilizer.

Large corporate and partnership farms are usually operated by *farm managers*, who handle all the day-to-day responsibilities as well as decisions on what crops to plant. These managers now use computers for inventory and record keeping, and as a source of information about prices of farm products.

Firms that supply seed, feed, fertilizer, and farm equipment also attract experienced farmers to work as salespeople and dealers for their products. Some farmers use their accumulated knowledge in other areas related to farming such as farm insurance, banking and credit, real estate sales, and appraisals.

Related jobs are agricultural engineer, soil scientist, and range manager.

Places of employment and working conditions

Some farming is done in just about every county in the United States. The eastern and southern states have smaller farms than the midwestern and western states. Many of the larger or corporate farms employ many laborers.

The workweek for a farmer during the planting, growing, and harvesting seasons is often six or seven days and much longer than eight hours a day. Farmers who raise livestock and poultry have a more even work schedule year-round, but their work is always seven days a week because animals must be cared for every day.

Farmers face constant financial risk due to the uncertainties of weather, which can ruin a crop and eliminate an entire year's income.

Qualifications, education, and training

To successfully run a modern farm, a farmer needs managerial and business skills, mechanical ability, physical stamina, patience, and an affinity for working outdoors.

Probably the best background is growing up on a farm or working for a farmer. Organizations such as the 4-H clubs and Future Farmers of America provide valuable preparation for young people interested in farming.

The complexities of modern scientific farming make formal training in a two- or four-year agricultural college almost a necessity. Most such colleges offer majors in areas such as dairy science, crop science, agricultural economics, horticulture, and animal science, plus special course work in the products produced in the area in which the college is located.

Colleges that offer degrees in agricultural engineering sometimes offer degrees or course work in mechanized agriculture. These programs provide broad basic agricultural training, practical application of farm machinery and equipment to agricultural production, and economics and management courses.

Other useful areas of study include veterinary medicine and bookkeeping. Continuing education and research keep farmers informed of advances in farming methods.

Potential and advancement

In America, there are about 1.5 million people employed as farmers or farm managers. Although the rapidly increasing world population demands more food and fiber, the employment of farmers is expected to decrease through 2008 because the extremely efficient agricultural sector is expected to meet domestic and export needs. The trend is toward fewer and larger farms. The great expense of purchasing and operating a farm puts farming out of the reach of many people.

There are a growing number of horticultural farms, and these are expected to produce some new job opportunities. Aquaculture should also create new jobs.

Income

Earnings for farmers vary from year to year. Weather conditions, which are for the most part unpredictable, determine the amount and quality of farm products and, thus, their price. A farm that achieves a hefty profit one year might show a loss the next.

Most farmers and farm managers earn from $302 to $619 a week, depending on the size or number of farms managed.

Additional sources of information

American Farm Bureau Federation
225 Touhy Avenue
Park Ridge, IL 60068

Higher Education Program
Cooperative State Research Service
U.S. Department of Agriculture
14th and Independence Avenue SW
Washington, DC 20250

National Future Farmers of America
Box 15160
5632 Mt. Vernon Memorial Highway
Alexandria, VA 22309-0160

FASHION DESIGNER

The job

Fashion and clothing designers create new styles or adjust and change existing styles. They may work in men's, women's, or children's clothing design.

Designers work with sketches or directly with fabric in creating a design. They must understand color, fabrics, production processes, and costs as well as the public's tastes and preferences. Many designers work on one type of apparel such as sports clothes or evening wear.

People who want a career in designing often take any job they can in the fashion field to get a start. The field is popular and always has more new talent than it can adequately support.

Places of employment and working conditions

New York City is the center of the fashion industry; Los Angeles is an important swimsuit and casual clothes fashion center, and other cities produce limited fashion trends.

Fashion is a hectic and fast-paced field with seasonal peaks that often require long hours.

Qualifications, education, and training

Fashion designers must have a flair for clothes, a sense of style, a keen sense of color, and the ability to turn their ideas into reality.

High school courses in art, merchandising, and business are helpful. Sewing experience is important.

Apparel firms prefer to hire designers with formal training, and they often recruit designers from colleges and schools that provide specialized training in fashion design. They seek workers who are knowledgeable about textiles, fabrics, ornamentation, and trends in the fashion world. A few designers work their way up through the ranks from tailoring or cutting jobs.

Beginners should be prepared to serve as sample makers or assistant designers or even work in clerical jobs for their first few years.

Potential and advancement

Fashion is a crowded, popular, and often cutthroat career field. Although the demand for fashion designers is increasing, eager job seekers always outnumber job openings, and there will be stiff competition for all designer positions.

Income

Average annual earnings for experienced, full-time designers are about $38,400. Those at the bottom of the range earn annual salaries of less than $18,420, while those at the top earn more than $68,310. Well-known designers with their own clothing lines earn considerably more.

Additional sources of information

American Apparel Manufacturers Association
2500 Wilson Boulevard, Suite 301
Arlington, VA 22201

National Association of Schools of Art and Design
11250 Roger Bacon Drive, Suite 21
Reston, VA 20190

FBI SPECIAL AGENT

The job

Special agents for the Federal Bureau of Investigation (FBI) investigate violations of federal laws in connection with bank robberies, kidnappings, white-color crime, thefts of government property, organized crime, espionage, and sabotage. The FBI, which is part of the U.S. Department of Justice, has jurisdiction over many federal investigative matters. Special agents, therefore, may be assigned to any type of case, although those with specialized training usually work on cases related to their backgrounds. Agents with an accounting background, for example, may investigate white-color crimes such as bank embezzlements or fraudulent bankruptcies or land deals.

Because the FBI is a fact-gathering agency, its special agents function strictly as investigators, collecting evidence in cases in which the U.S. government is, or may be, an interested party. In their casework, special agents conduct interviews, examine records, observe the activities of suspects, and participate in raids. Because the FBI's work is highly confidential, special agents may not disclose any of the information gathered in the course of their official duties to unauthorized persons, including members of their families. Frequently, agents must testify in court about cases that they investigate.

Although they usually work alone on most assignments, two agents or more are assigned to work together when performing potentially dangerous duties such as arrests and raids. Agents communicate with their supervisors by radio or telephone as the circumstances dictate.

Places of employment and working conditions

Most agents are assigned to the FBI's field offices located throughout the nation and in Puerto Rico. They work in cities where field office headquarters are located or in resident agencies (suboffices) established under field office supervision to provide prompt and efficient response to investigative matters arising throughout the field office territory. Some agents are assigned to the Bureau headquarters in Washington, D.C., which supervises all FBI activities.

Special agents are subject to call 24 hours a day and must be available for assignment at all times. Their duties call for some travel, since they are assigned wherever they are needed in the United States or Puerto Rico. They frequently work longer than the customary 40-hour week.

Qualifications, education, and training

To be considered for appointment as an FBI special agent, an applicant usually must be either a graduate of a state-accredited law school; a college graduate with a major in accounting; or a college graduate who is fluent in a foreign language or has three years of full-time job experience.

Applicants for the position of FBI special agent must be U.S. citizens, between 23 and 37 years old, and willing to serve anywhere in the United States and Puerto Rico. They must be capable of strenuous physical exertion and have excellent hearing and vision, normal color perception, and no physical defects that would prevent their using firearms or participating in dangerous assignments. All applicants must pass a rigid physical examination as well as written and oral examinations testing their aptitude for meeting the public and conducting investigations. All of the tests except the physical examinations are administered by the

FBI at its facilities. Background and character investigations are made of all applicants. Appointments are made on a probationary basis and become permanent after one year of satisfactory service.

Each newly appointed special agent is given about 16 weeks of training at the FBI Academy at the U.S. Marine Corps base in Quantico, Virginia, before assignment to a field office. During this period, agents receive intensive training in defensive tactics and the use of firearms. In addition, they are thoroughly schooled in federal criminal law and procedures, FBI rules and regulations, fingerprinting, and investigative work. After assignment to a field office, the new agent usually works closely with an experienced agent for about two weeks before handling any assignments independently.

Potential and advancement

The jurisdiction of the FBI has expanded greatly over the years. Although it is impossible to forecast personnel requirements, employment may be expected to increase with growing FBI responsibilities. The federal budget ultimately determines the number of job openings for special agents.

The FBI provides a career service, and its rate of turnover is traditionally low. Nevertheless, the Bureau is always interested in applications from qualified persons who would like to be considered for the position of special agent.

All administrative and supervisory jobs are filled from within the ranks by selection of those agents who have demonstrated the capacity and talent to assume more responsibility.

Income

The entrance salary for FBI special agents is about $43,000, including payment for overtime. Experienced agents can earn $67,300 a year for nonsupervisory positions. Those who advance to management and executive positions may earn as much as $93,500 per year.

Additional source of information

For information on opportunities for FBI special agents, check your local telephone directory for the nearest state FBI office. You can also research on-line at www.fbi.gov.

FIREFIGHTER

The job

Firefighters must be prepared to respond to a fire and manage any emergency that arises. This is dangerous work that requires courage and expert training.

Fire fighting demands organization and teamwork. Each firefighter at the scene of a fire has specific duties assigned by a company officer, but each must also be ready to perform any of the duties—such as connecting hoses to hydrants, positioning ladders, or operating pumps—at any time because duties change in the course of a fire. Firefighters may also be called on to rescue people or to administer first aid.

Between calls, firefighters spend their time cleaning and servicing equipment, carrying out practice drills, and maintaining their living quarters. They also take part in fire-prevention activities such as building inspections and educational programs for schools and civic groups.

Most firefighters work for municipal fire departments. The remainder work on federal and state installations or in private fire-fighting companies.

Most firefighters are members of the International Association of Firefighters.

Places of employment and working conditions

In some cities, firefighters are on duty for 24 hours and then off for 48 hours. In other cities, they work a 10-hour day shift or a 14-hour night shift, with shifts rotated frequently. The average workweek varies, but many firefighters work more than 50 hours a week. These duty hours usually include free time, which can be used for personal interests or study.

Firefighters face the risk of injury or death in the course of their work and must work outdoors in all kinds of conditions and weather.

Qualifications, education, and training

A firefighter must have courage, mental alertness, physical stamina, mechanical aptitude, and a sense of public service. Initiative, good judgment, and dependability also are essential. Because firefighters live together as well as work together, they should be able to get along with others.

Applicants for municipal fire-fighting jobs may have to pass a written test and medical examination that includes a screen for drug use and tests of strength, stamina, and agility. They must meet other local regulations as to height and weight, have a high school education or equivalent, and be at least 18 years old. Experience as a volunteer firefighter or fire-fighting training received in the armed forces improves the applicant's chances for appointment to a job, and some communities also give extra credit to veterans of the armed forces.

Beginners are usually trained at the city's fire school for several weeks and then assigned to a fire company for a probationary period.

Fire departments frequently conduct training programs to help firefighters upgrade their skills, and many colleges offer courses such as fire engineering and fire science that are helpful to firefighters. An increasing number of firefighters have some postsecondary training—either a two- or four-year college degree or a three- or four-year apprenticeship. Experienced firefighters also continue to study to prepare for promotional examinations.

Potential and advancement

There are about 314,000 firefighters nationwide. Employment of firefighters is expected to grow slowly through 2008. Competition for jobs is stiff, and interested candidates continually outnumber job openings.

Opportunities for promotions are good in most fire departments. Promotion to lieutenant, captain, battalion chief, assistant chief, deputy chief, and finally chief depends on written examinations, seniority, and rating by supervisors. Advanced degrees and certification from the National Fire Academy are advantageous for those seeking promotion.

Income

Earnings for firefighters depend on experience, city size, and region of the country. Annual salaries range from $22,370 to $40,840, with the average being about $31,170. Firefighters in supervisory positions may earn significantly more.

Most fire departments provide allowances to pay for protective clothing such as helmets, boots, and rubber coats, and many also provide dress uniforms.

Firefighters are usually covered by liberal pension plans that often provide retirement at half pay at age 50 after 25 years of service or at any age if the person is disabled in the line of duty. Generous sick leave and compensation are usually provided for any firefighter injured in the line of duty.

Additional sources of information

Information is available from local civil service commission offices or fire departments as well as the following sources:

International Association of Fire Chiefs
1750 New York Avenue NW
Washington, DC 20006

International Associaton of Firefighters
1750 New York Avenue NW
Washington, DC 20006
www.iaff.org

FLIGHT ATTENDANT

The job

Few other occupations appear as glamorous as that of flight attendant. The lure of travel and the opportunity to meet all kinds of people appeal to many job seekers.

Formerly called stewardesses and stewards, flight attendants are aboard almost every commercial passenger plane to meet the needs of passenger safety and comfort. Before each flight, attendants check supplies such as food, beverages, blankets, reading material, first-aid kits, and emergency equipment. During flight, they instruct passengers in the use of emergency equipment; check seat belts before takeoff or landing; and help care for small children, elderly people, and people with disabilities. They also distribute reading material and serve food and beverages.

The main reason planes carry flight attendants is to provide assistance to passengers in the event of an emergency. A calm and reassuring manner is important, whether the emergency is a sick passenger or an emergency landing. Flight attendants are trained to handle many situations, including evacuation of the plane.

Most flight attendants are members of either the Transport Workers Union of America or the Association of Flight Attendants.

Places of employment and working conditions

Most flight attendants work out of a large city, such as Chicago, Dallas, Los Angeles, Miami, New York City, or San Francisco. The remainder are assigned to other cities where airlines maintain facilities.

Airlines operate around the clock for 365 days a year, so flight attendants must be prepared to work nights, weekends, and holidays. They usually fly 75 to 85 hours a month, with about 75 to 85 additional hours of ground duties. Their workweek is not divided into neat segments, and because of scheduling and limitations on flying time, many have 11 or 12 days or more off each month. At least one-third of their time may be spent away from the home base. Airlines provide hotel accommodations and meal allowances for these periods.

Flight attendants are on their feet during most of a flight. Poor weather can cause difficulties, as can sick or frightened passengers. Flight attendants are expected to be pleasant and efficient under all circumstances and with even the most difficult passengers.

Qualifications, education, and training

Anyone considering this career field should be poised and tactful, enjoy working with people, and be able to speak clearly and comfortably with strangers. Excellent health is a must, as is good vision. All flight attendants must be at least 18 to 21 years old and have a high school diploma.

Airlines give preference to applicants with several years of college, nurse's training, or experience in dealing with the public. Fluency in a foreign language is required on international airlines.

Large airlines provide about four to seven weeks of training in their own schools. Some also provide transportation to the training center and an allowance while training. Instruction includes emergency procedures, evacuation of a plane, operation of emergency equipment, first aid, flight regulations and duties, and company operations and policies. On international airlines, flight attendants also study passport and customs regulations. Practice flights complete the training. After assignment to a home base, new flight attendants begin their careers by "filling in" on extra flights or replacing attendants who are sick or on vacation.

Potential and advancement

There are about 99,000 flight attendants working for airlines in the United States. Employment of flight attendants is expected to rise as growth in population and income increases the use of air transportation. Air travel, however, is sensitive to the ups and downs of the economy, and job opportunities may vary from year to year. Overall, job opportunities should be favorable; the number of applicants is expected to roughly equal the number of job openings.

As flight attendants gain seniority, they earn the right to choose their flight assignments and home base. A few attendants advance to positions as flight service instructors, customer service directors, or recruiting representatives.

Income

Salaries for beginners average about $13,700 a year. Flight attendants with six years of flying experience earn about $20,000 a year, while some senior flight attendants earn as much as $50,000 a year. Flight attendants earn compensation for overtime and night and international flights.

An attractive employee benefit is the reduced airfare for flight attendants and their families on the airline for which the attendant works and on most other airlines as well.

Additional sources of information

Information about job opportunities and requirements for a particular airline may be obtained by writing to the personnel manager of the company. Addresses are available from:

Air Transport Association of America
1301 Pennsylvania Avenue, Suite 1100
Washington, DC 20004-7017

FLORAL DESIGNER

The job

Floral designers, also called *florists*, combine a knowledge of flowers and plants with design techniques to produce floral and plant gifts and decorations.

Just about all floral designers work in retail flower shops, many of which are small and employ only a few people. Many of the shops are owner operated.

Floral designers must know the seasonal availability and lasting qualities of many flowers and have a sense of form, color harmony, and depth. They prepare bouquets; corsages; funeral pieces; dried arrangements; and decorations for weddings, parties, and other events.

Places of employment and working conditions

Flower shops are located throughout the country, with at least one in nearly every city and town.

Floral designers stand during much of the workday. Work areas are kept cool and humid to preserve the flowers, and designers are subject to sudden temperature changes when entering or leaving refrigerated storage areas.

A 40-hour workweek is usual, but this often includes Saturday hours. Floral designers work long hours around certain holidays such as Valentine's Day and Mother's Day.

Qualifications, education, and training

Creativity, good color vision, and manual dexterity are necessary for a floral designer. Business and selling skills are important for those who operate their own shops.

High school courses in business arithmetic, art, and bookkeeping are helpful. Part-time or summer jobs in a plant nursery or flower shop can provide valuable experience.

Many floral designers acquire their skills through on-the-job training. They work under the guidance of an experienced floral designer for about two years to become fully qualified.

The trend in recent years, however, is toward more formal training. Vocational schools offer programs lasting up to one year, while junior colleges and universities offer wider training. The longer programs provide instruction in basic horticulture, ornamental horticulture, floriculture, and floral design. This curriculum is especially useful for floral designers who intend to open their own shops.

Potential and advancement

The field is expected to grow as the population increases. Ups and downs in the economy may cause temporary slow periods, but over the long run the outlook is good.

Income

In large flower shops, floral designers may advance to shop manager or to design supervisor. Others advance by opening their own businesses. A new flower shop in an area with many other florists faces stiff competition and must establish a reputation by efficient operation and outstanding work if the business is to succeed. Floral designers who can provide such service are always in demand.

Floral designers receive relatively low pay. Beginners earn about $13,780 a year. Designers with experience earn $18,420 to $29,200.

The earnings of shop owners vary greatly, depending mainly on locality and the size of the community being served.

Additional source of information

Society of American Florists
1601 Duke Street
Alexandria, VA 22314

FORESTER

The job

The forest lands of the United States—whether publicly or privately owned—must be carefully and efficiently managed if they are to survive. It is the work of the professional forester to develop, manage, and protect forest lands and their resources of timber, water, wildlife, forage, and recreation areas. If properly protected and managed, these resources can be used repeatedly without being destroyed.

Foresters often specialize in one type of work, such as timber management, outdoor recreation, or forest economics. In these capacities, they might plan and supervise the planting and cutting of trees or devote themselves to watershed management, wildlife protection, disease and insect control, fire prevention, or the development and supervision of recreation areas.

Many foresters work for private industries such as pulp and paper, lumber, logging, and milling companies. The federal government employs about 30 percent of all foresters, most of them in the Forest Service and Natural Resource Conservation Service of the Department of Agriculture. Others conduct research, teach at the college and university level, or work as consultants. State and local governments also employ foresters.

Related jobs are environmentalist, soil scientist, and soil conservationist.

Places of employment and working conditions

Foresters are employed in just about every state, but the largest numbers are in the heavily forested areas of the western and southeastern states.

Although some foresters work in offices or labs, many, especially beginners, spend a great deal of time outdoors in all kinds of weather and often at remote locations. During emergencies such as fires and rescue missions, they may work long hours under difficult and dangerous conditions.

Qualifications, education, and training

Anyone interested in forestry as a career should be physically hardy, enjoy working outdoors, and be willing to work in remote areas.

A bachelor's degree with a major in forestry is the minimum requirement; research and teaching positions require advanced degrees. About 48 colleges offer degrees in forestry, most of them accredited by the Society of American Foresters. Scientific and technical forestry subjects, liberal arts, and communication skills are emphasized along with courses in forest economics and business administration. All schools encourage work experience in forestry or conservation, and many require at least one summer at a college-operated field camp.

Some states have either mandatory licensing or voluntary registration for professional foresters.

Potential and advancement

Employment opportunities are expected to grow at an average rate. Job opportunities will probably be greatest with state and local governments and with research and testing services. Federal government opportunities will be limited because of reduced budgets.

Advancement in this field depends on experience, with federally employed foresters able to advance through local supervisory positions to regional forest supervisory or top administrative positions. In private industry, experienced foresters may advance to top managerial positions within a company.

Income

Starting salaries for federally employed foresters vary: those having a master's degree or equivalent experience receive about $25,500 to $31,200 a year; Ph.D.s start at $37,700 to $45,200; with a bachelor's degree, the salary is about $20,600 to $25,500. Salaries in state and local governments are generally lower, but salaries in private industry are comparable.

Additional sources of information

American Forests
1516 P Street NW
P.O. Box 2000
Washington, DC 20005

Society of American Foresters
5400 Grosvenor Lane
Bethesda, MD 20814
www.safnet.org

U.S. Forest Service
U.S. Department of Agriculture
14th Street and Independence Avenue SW
Washington, DC 20013

FORESTRY TECHNICIAN

The job

Forestry technicians assist foresters in the care and management of forest lands and their resources. They estimate timber production; inspect for insect damage; supervise surveying and road-building crews; work in flood-control and water-quality programs; supervise fire-fighting crews; supervise planting and reforestation programs; and maintain forest areas for hunting, camping, and other recreational uses.

About half of all forestry technicians work for private logging, lumber, paper, mining, and railroad companies. The federal government employs about an equal number. Many of the technicians employed by federal and state governments work only during summer or during the spring and fall fire seasons.

A related job is landscape architect.

Places of employment and working conditions

Forestry technicians work throughout the country in just about every state.

Outdoor work in all kinds of weather is the norm for this field. In emergencies such as forest fires and floods, the working hours are long and the work can be dangerous. In many areas, the work is seasonal.

Qualifications, education, and training

Good physical condition, stamina, affinity for the outdoors, and ability to perform with or without supervision and to interact with a variety of people are all necessary for a forestry technician.

High school should include as many science courses as possible.

Some technicians acquire their training through experience on fire-fighting crews, in recreation work, or in tree nurseries. Nevertheless, because this is a competitive job field, those with specialized training in forestry have better opportunities for full-time employment.

One- and two-year courses for forestry technicians are available in technical institutes, junior colleges, and four-year colleges and universities. Subjects studied include mathematics, biology and botany, land surveying, tree identification, aerial photography interpretation, and timber harvesting.

Potential and advancement

This field is expected to decline slightly through 2008. A tight federal budget will limit the number of government jobs. Meanwhile, conservation efforts and mechanization of timber cutting will limit the number of workers required in the private sector. Some openings will exist because of replacement needs.

Income

Forestry technicians who work for the federal government earn about $31,300 per year.

Additional sources of information

American Forests
1516 P Street NW
P.O. Box 2000
Washington, DC 20005

Society of American Foresters
5400 Grosvenor Lane
Bethesda, MD 20814
www.safnet.org

U.S. Forest Service
U.S. Department of Agriculture
14th Street and Independence Avenue SW
Washington, DC 20013

FUNERAL DIRECTOR

The job

While this job field does not appeal to everyone, persons involved in funeral directing take pride in the fact that they provide efficient and appropriate service to their customers. Probably more than in any other job situation, personal qualities of tact, compassion, and the ability to deal with people under difficult circumstances come into play. A funeral director arranges for the transportation of the deceased to the funeral home, obtains information for the death certificate and obituary notices, and arranges all details of the funeral and burial as decided on by the family. The funeral director must be familiar with the funeral and burial customs of many faiths, ethnic groups, and fraternal organizations. Even after the funeral, the funeral director assists the family in filing Social Security insurance and veteran's claims.

An *embalmer* prepares the body for viewing and burial. Embalming is a sanitary, cosmetic, and preservative process and is required by law in most states. The body is washed with germicidal soap, blood is replaced with embalming fluid, cosmetics are applied to provide a natural appearance or to restore disfigured features, and the body is placed in the casket.

In small funeral homes, the duties of funeral director and embalmer may be handled by one person; in large funeral homes, a staff of one or more embalmers plus several apprentices may be employed. Embalmers are also employed by hospitals and morgues.

In most funeral homes, one of the funeral directors is also the owner. The staff may consist of from one to more than a dozen funeral directors, embalmers, and apprentices. In some communities, it is customary for a prospective embalmer or funeral director to obtain a promise of employment from a local funeral home before starting mortuary training.

Places of employment and working conditions

There is at least one funeral home in every community in the United States, so job opportunities are everywhere.

In smaller funeral homes, working hours may vary, but in larger homes employees work eight hours a day, five or six days a week. Shift work is sometimes necessary because funeral home hours include evenings.

Embalmers occasionally come into contact with contagious diseases but are not likely to become ill because of strict observance of sanitary procedures.

Qualifications, education, and training

High school courses in biology, chemistry, computer science, and public speaking are helpful, and a part-time or summer job at a funeral home can provide exposure to the profession for anyone considering the field.

There are more than 40 mortuary science programs that are accredited by the American Board of Funeral Service Education. They usually take from one to two years to complete. A few colleges also offer two- or four-year programs in mortuary science.

A period of apprenticeship must be completed under the guidance of an experienced funeral director or embalmer. Depending on state regulations, this apprenticeship consists of from one to two years and may be served during or after mortuary school.

All states require emblamers to be licensed, and most states also require funeral directors to be licensed.

State board licensing examinations vary but usually consist of written and oral tests as well as a demonstration of skills. Other state licensing standards usually require the applicant to be at least 21 years old, have a high school diploma or its equivalent, and complete a mortuary science program and an apprenticeship.

Some states issue a single license to funeral directors and embalmers. In states that have separate licensing and apprenticeship requirements for the two positions, most people in the field obtain both licenses. Some states will accept the credentials of those licensed by another state without further examination.

Potential and advancement

Employment opportunities in this field likely will increase at an average rate through 2008 as the number of jobs available exceeds the number of graduates from mortuary science programs.

Advancement opportunities are best in large funeral homes where better-paying positions such as general manager or personnel manager exist. Directors and embalmers who accumulate enough capital and experience often establish their own businesses.

Income

Funeral directors earn average salaries of about $35,040 to $48,260 a year. Owners of funeral homes earn $78,550 or more annually.

Additional sources of information

Information on licensing requirements is available from the appropriate state office of occupational licensing. You can also request information from the following organizations:

American Board of Funeral Service Education
38 Florida Avenue
Portland, ME 04103

National Funeral Directors Association
13625 Bishop's Drive
Brookfield, WI 53005

GEOGRAPHER

The job

Geographers study and analyze the distribution of land forms; climate; soils; vegetation; and mineral, water, and human resources. These studies help to explain the patterns of human settlement.

Many geographers are employed by colleges and universities. The federal government also employs many geographers for mapping, intelligence work, and remote sensing interpretation. State and local governments employ geographers on planning and development commissions.

Textbook and map publishers; travel agencies; manufacturing firms; real estate developers; and insurance, communications, and transportation companies are other employers. People with additional training in another discipline such as economics, sociology, or urban planning have a wider range of job opportunities and can work in many other fields.

Cartographers design and construct maps and charts. They also conduct research in surveying and mapping procedures. They work with aerial photographs and analyze data from remote sensing equipment on satellites.

Places of employment and working conditions

Geographers are employed throughout the country and on foreign assignment as well. The largest single concentration of geographers is in the Washington, D.C., area.

Fieldwork sometimes entails assignment to remote areas and less developed regions of the world. A geographer should be prepared for the physical and social hardships that such relocation may require.

Qualifications, education, and training

Anyone intending to pursue this field should enjoy reading, studying, and conducting research and be able to work independently. Good communication skills are also necessary.

High school should include as many mathematics and science courses as possible.

A bachelor's degree with a major in geography is the first step for an aspiring geographer. Course work should also include some specialty fields such as cartography, aerial photography, or statistical analysis.

Advanced degrees are required for most teaching positions and for advancement in business and government; a Ph.D. is necessary for the top jobs. Mathematics, statistics, and computer science are of increasing importance in graduate studies; students interested in foreign regional geography are usually required to take a foreign language as well.

Potential and advancement

In general, this field will experience average growth, with most job openings created by replacement needs. There will be a demand for geographers who specialize in geographic information systems, which combine computer graphics, artificial intelligence, and high-speed communication to store, retrieve, manipulate, and map geographic data. Persons with only a bachelor's degree will face competition for jobs.

Advancement in this field depends on experience and additional education.

Income

Geographers employed by the federal government have average annual earnings of $53,700.

Additional source of information

Association of American Geographers
1710 16th Street NW
Washington, DC 20009

GEOLOGIST

The job

By examining surface rocks and rock samples drilled from beneath the surface, geologists study the structure, composition, and history of the earth's crust. Their work is important in the search for mineral resources and oil and in the study of predicting earthquakes. Geologists are also employed to advise on the construction of buildings, dams, and highways.

Geologists study plant and animal fossils as well as minerals and rocks. Some specialize in the study of the ocean floor or the composition of other plants. *Vulcanologists* study active and inactive volcanoes and lava flows. *Mineralogists* analyze and classify minerals and precious stones.

Many geologists work in private industry, mainly for petroleum and mining companies. The federal government employs about 5,800 geologists in the U.S. Geological Survey and other departments. State and local governments employ geologists in survey and conservation work.

Colleges and universities, nonprofit research institutions, and museums also employ geologists.

Related jobs are geophysicist, meteorologist, and oceanographer.

Places of employment and working conditions

States with large oil and mineral deposits provide job opportunities. American companies often send their geologists to overseas locations for varying periods.

Some geologists work in offices or labs, but much of the work done by geologists is out-of-doors, often at remote locations. Geologists also cover many miles on foot. Those involved in mining often work underground; geologists in petroleum research often work on offshore oil rigs.

Qualifications, education, and training

Curiosity, analytical thinking, and physical stamina are all necessary for a geologist.

High school work should include as much science, computer science, and mathematics as possible.

A bachelor's degree in geology or a related field is the basic preparation but is adequate only for some entry-level jobs. Teaching and research positions require advanced degrees with specialization in one particular branch of geology. Education beyond the bachelor's level is essential for advancement in all areas of this field.

Potential and advancement

Job opportunities in the petroleum industry have declined sharply, but opportunities in environmental protection remain positive.

The number of job openings will depend on the number of graduates and on the economy. Candidates with advanced degrees will have the most job opportunities and the best chances for promotion.

Income

Beginners with a bachelor's degree earn about $34,900 a year, although those who work in the oil and gas industry earn more. The average annual salary for all geologists employed by the federal government is about $64,400.

Additional sources of information

American Geological Institute
4220 King Street
Alexandria, VA 22302-1502
www.agiweb.org

Geological Society of America
P.O. Box 9140
3300 Penrose Place
Boulder, CO 80301-9140
www.geosociety.org

GEOPHYSICIST

The job

In general terms, geophysicists study the earth—its composition and physical aspects and its electric, magnetic, and gravitational fields. They usually specialize in one of three general phases of the science—solid earth, fluid earth, or upper atmosphere—and some also study other planets.

Solid earth geophysicists search for oil and mineral deposits, map the planet's surface, and study earthquakes. This field includes *exploration geophysicists*, who use seismic prospecting techniques (sound waves) to locate oil and mineral deposits; *seismologists*, who study the earth's interior and vibrations caused by earthquakes and human-engineered explosions, explore for oil and minerals, and provide information for use in constructing bridges, dams, and large buildings (by determining where bedrock is located in relation to the surface); and *geodesists*, who study the size, shape, and gravitational field of the earth and other planets and whose principal task is the precise measurement of the earth's surface.

Hydrologists are concerned with the fluid earth. They study the distribution, circulation, and physical properties of underground and surface waters, including glaciers, snow, and permafrost. Those who are concerned with water supplies, irrigation, flood control, and soil erosion study rainfall and its rate of infiltration into the soil. *Oceanographers* are also sometimes classified as geophysical scientists.

Geophysicists who study the earth's atmosphere and electric and magnetic fields and compare them with those of other planets include *geomagneticians*, who study the earth's magnetic field; *paleomagneticians*, who study rocks and lava flows to learn about past magnetic fields; and *planetologists*, who study the composition and atmosphere of the moon, planets, and other bodies in the solar system. They gather data from geophysical instruments placed on interplanetary space probes or from equipment used by astronauts during the Apollo missions. *Meteorologists* are also sometimes classified as geophysical scientists.

Most geophysicists work in private industry, chiefly for petroleum and natural gas companies. Others are in mining, exploration, and consulting firms or in research institutes. A few are independent consultants doing geophysical prospecting on a fee or contract basis.

In addition, geophysicists work for the federal government, mainly in the U.S. Geological Survey, the National Oceanic and Atmospheric Administration, and the Department of Defense. Other employers are colleges and universities, state governments, and research institutions. Some geophysicists are also employed by American firms overseas.

New geophysicists usually begin their careers doing field mapping or exploration. Some assist senior geophysicists in research work.

Places of employment and working conditions

In the United States, geophysicists are employed in southwestern and western states and along the Gulf Coast where large oil and natural gas fields are located.

Many geophysicists work outdoors and must be willing to travel for extended periods. Some work at research stations in remote areas or aboard ships and aircraft. When not in the field, geophysicists generally work in modern, well-equipped laboratories and offices.

Qualifications, education, and training

Geophysicists should be curious, analytical, and able to communicate effectively and should like to work as part of a team.

High school courses should include as many science courses as possible and mathematics. Computer-modeling skills are increasingly in demand, so courses in computer science are also useful.

A bachelor's degree in geophysics or in a geophysical specialty is acceptable for some beginning jobs. A bachelor's degree in a related field of science or engineering is also adequate, provided courses in geophysics, physics, geology, mathematics, chemistry, and engineering have been included.

Hundreds of colleges and universities award a bachelor's degree in geophysics, geology, oceanography, or another geoscience. Other training programs offered include geophysical technology, geophysical engineering, engineering geology, petroleum geology, and geodesy.

Several hundred universities grant master's and Ph.D. degrees in geophysics or geology. Geophysicists doing research or supervising exploration should have graduate training in geophysics or a related science, and those planning to do basic research or teach at the college level need a Ph.D. degree.

Potential and advancement

Employment of geophysicists is expected to grow at an average pace through 2008. The need to replace those who retire will create openings during the next decade. However, petroleum and mining companies are expected to hire fewer geophysicists than in the past. Federal agencies also are expected to hire fewer people, unless their budgets increase. Energy exploration and efforts by private companies to comply with environmental regulations will contribute, in a limited way, to growth.

Income

Geophysicists earn relatively high salaries. The average starting salary for graduates with a bachelor's degree is $34,900 a year. Those working in the oil and gas industry earn more.

The average salary for all geophysicists employed by the federal government is about $64,400 a year.

Additional sources of information

American Geophysical Union
2000 Florida Avenue NW
Washington, DC 20009
www.agu.org

Society of Exploration Geophysicists
8801 South Yale
Tulsa, OK 74137
www.seg.org

GRAPHIC DESIGNER

The job

Graphic designers use a variety of methods and materials to produce art for their clients: corporations, advertising agencies, and publishers. *Graphic artists* design logos, product packaging, corporate publications, magazine layouts, book covers, and television graphics.

Illustrators create drawings or paintings used for books, magazines, or greeting cards. Some illustrators specialize in a particular aspect of the field, such as illustrating children's books or creating storyboards for television commercials. Others pursue fashion illustration or medical illustration. A talented few become cartoonists or animators.

Art directors manage the visual aspect of printed media. They select photographs, artwork, typefaces, and layouts for magazines, newspapers, and books.

All graphic designers depend increasingly on sophisticated computer software for assistance with layouts and creation of images.

Places of employment and working conditions

Opportunities exist in all parts of the country, but the majority are in large cities such as Boston, Chicago, Los Angeles, New York City, and San Francisco.

The workweek for salaried artists and designers is usually 40 hours. They sometimes put in additional hours, often under considerable pressure, to meet deadlines.

Many graphic designers are freelancers.

Qualifications, education, and training

Artistic talent, imagination and style, manual dexterity, computer skills, and the ability to transform ideas into visual concepts are all necessary for anyone interested in joining this field.

Prospective graphic designers should tailor their high school work to the requirements of the art school or college they wish to attend. Any training in art is valuable, and students should begin to accumulate a portfolio of their work because art schools and colleges usually require a sample of the applicant's work as well as an aptitude test.

Art schools, trade schools, junior colleges, and other colleges and universities offer two- and four-year courses in commercial art or graphic design; some offer fine arts with some course work in commercial art. Art directors especially need a broad background in art plus experience and training in business, photography, typography, printing production methods, and computer science.

The continued accumulation of a portfolio representative of the artist's talents and abilities is necessary for employment. Freelance artists in particular must be prepared to display their work for prospective clients.

Potential and advancement

Nationwide, there are about 308,000 people working in graphic design. The field is expected to grow at a faster-than-average rate through 2008. Competition for all jobs is the norm, and beginners with little specialized training or experience face the stiffest competition. Beginners are usually willing to take any design job they can get just to break in to the field and gain some experience.

Some jobs will be more in demand than others. Most new jobs will be in advertising agencies and graphic art studios. This field is also sensitive to changes in general economic conditions.

Advancement in commercial art usually depends on talent and development of a strong reputation and specialized skills.

Income

The average annual salary for graphic designers who are full-time employees is about $31,690. The top 10 percent earn more than $64,580 a year, and the bottom 10 percent earn less than $17,910.

Earnings for freelance graphic designers vary widely.

Additional source of information

American Institute of Graphic Arts
164 Fifth Avenue
New York, NY 10010

GUARD

The job

Valuable properties need to be protected from theft, fire, vandalism, and trespassers. It is the duty of guards, sometimes called *security officers*, to maintain the security of properties and prevent any of these damaging situations.

Guards have a variety of duties, depending on the type, size, and location of the employer. Most guards usually make their rounds on foot, but some who watch over larger properties may patrol by car or motor scooter. Very large organizations may have a managing security officer who oversees a guard force.

Some guards are responsible for the protection of records, merchandise, money, equipment, and, in museums and other public buildings, art and exhibits. Other guards must keep unauthorized people from entering restricted areas; usually this is the case when the employer is trying to maintain the security of new products, computer codes, or defense secrets. At airports, railroad stations, and public events, guards must make sure that order is maintained and watch for people who may try to cause trouble. Guards are also needed to protect money and valuable items being transported in armored cars. Bodyguards are hired to protect people who are at risk of injury, kidnapping, or invasion of privacy.

Guards usually wear uniforms and carry nightsticks and sometimes guns. Other equipment they use in performing their duties includes computers, flashlights, two-way radios, and watch clocks.

Places of employment and working conditions

Guards work throughout the country, but most are in urban areas. Organizations employing guards include security firms and guard agencies; banks; building management companies; hotels; hospitals; retail stores; restaurants and bars; schools, colleges, and universities; and federal, state, and local governments.

Guards work both indoors and outdoors. Those who work outdoors must carry out patrols in all types of weather. While the work is usually routine, guards may find themselves in dangerous situations when either they or the property they protect is threatened. Many guards have to work alone at night and have little contact with people. They are also sometimes required to work weekends and holidays.

Qualifications, education, and training

There are few formal requirements for becoming a guard. Most employers prefer to hire high school graduates, and some prefer to hire workers with experience in the military police or in local and state police departments. Some jobs require a driver's license.

Applicants should be honest and responsible and have solid character references and good health. Employers check for police records and often require applicants to take polygraph and drug-screening tests.

Guards who work for contract security agencies are required to be licensed or registered in most states. To become registered, they must be at least 18 years old; have no convictions for perjury or violence; pass an exam; and complete training in property rights, emergency procedures, and seizure of suspected criminals.

Training varies. Most guards receive some training before they begin their jobs and then get more instruction on the job. Employers with complex security systems may give more-extensive formal training. Many states now require continued training, especially for armed guards.

Potential and advancement

There are currently more than a million guards in the United States. Job opportunities should be plentiful through 2008 as concern about crime, vandalism, and terrorism mounts. There will be more competition for in-house positions because they usually offer higher pay, better benefits, and more opportunities for training and advancement.

Advancement for guards is limited. Some workers with guard experience take training and move on to police work. Guards with some college education may advance to jobs that involve administrative tasks or preventing espionage and sabotage. Some guards advance by owning their own contract security agencies.

Income

Earnings vary by type of employer. The average annual salary for guards is $16,400. Guards with specialized training or experience may earn $26,640 or more.

Additional sources of information

More information about employment as a guard can be obtained from local employers and the state employment service office. Registration and licensing information is offered by state licensing commissions or police departments.

GUIDANCE COUNSELOR

The job

Although their services are used in a wide variety of ways, the main function of school guidance counselors is to assist individual students with their problems, whether the problems are educational, social, or personal. To accomplish this, the counselors work closely with the school staff, parents, and the community.

Most guidance counselors are employed in secondary schools, where they assist students in making career choices and work with them in selecting courses and meeting college requirements. Counselors also test and assess students' abilities. A counselor's involvement in social problems includes work with drug and alcohol abuse, criminal behavior, and pregnancy. A student's personal problems can also require that the counselor help the student find a job or obtain medical or psychiatric help. In some schools, guidance counselors also teach some classes or supervise extracurricular activities.

The number of counselors in elementary schools is growing. At this educational level, counselors concentrate on the early detection of learning and personality problems because treatment and counseling can be most effective when started at an early age.

Most guidance counselors work in school buildings. A typical workday might include individual counseling sessions; meetings with small groups; or large meetings with students, parents, and community groups. Counselors may also be required to meet with law enforcement officers or agencies and with parents—sometimes in emotionally charged or difficult situations.

Places of employment and working conditions

Guidance counselors work in all areas of the United States in communities and schools of all sizes.

This is an active job, not always limited to an office atmosphere. There can be unpleasant and highly emotional confrontations from time to time, and a counselor must be careful not to become overinvolved in the lives and problems of individual students.

Qualifications, education, and training

A sincere desire to help young people is the most important characteristic for potential guidance counselors. In addition, the ability to work not only with students but also with all members of the educational team is essential. Guidance counselors should also have a thorough background in the study of human behavior.

Many guidance counselors come from the teaching profession, and some states require teacher certification as well as counseling certification for school counselors. College courses leading to teacher certification, with additional courses in psychology and sociology, are the best preparation.

One or two years of additional study is usually necessary to obtain the master's degree needed for counseling certification. Graduate courses usually include student appraisal, individual and group counseling, career information services, professional relations, ethics, statistics, and research. Depending on the state, from one to five years of teaching experience is also required.

Some states allow other types of education and experience, and requirements have been changing rapidly in recent years. A prospective counselor should check with the appropriate state department of education before selecting a graduate program.

Potential and advancement

Employment opportunities for school guidance counselors should be favorable through 2008, with faster-than-average growth. Renewed emphasis on quality education has encouraged expanded counseling programs. Many schools will expand existing programs and initiate new ones in the coming years. However, economic downturns may have a dramatic effect on counseling opportunities because these positions are usually cut before teaching jobs when school budgets tighten.

School counselors may advance to supervisory positions or administrative posts in larger schools or school districts. With additional education and experience, they can become educational psychologists or college counselors, positions that require a Ph.D.

Income

School counselors usually earn more than classroom teachers in the same school. Salaries average about $49,960 a year, with increases usually granted for additional education and experience. Some counselors supplement this income with work for government, private, or industrial counseling units.

Additional source of information

American School Counselor Association
5999 Stevenson Avenue
Alexandria, VA 22304-3300

HEALTH SERVICES MANAGER

The job

The exact title may vary from institution to institution, but the responsibilities are the same: to plan, organize, coordinate, and supervise the delivery of health care. There are two types of health services managers: *generalists*, who manage or help to manage an entire facility; and *health specialists*, who manage specific clinical departments or services found only in the health industry.

The top administrator must staff the hospital with medical and nonmedical personnel; provide all aspects of patient care services; purchase supplies and equipment; plan space allocations; and arrange for housekeeping items such as laundry, security, and maintenance. The administrator must also provide and work within a budget; act as liaison between the directors of the hospital and the medical staff; keep up with developments in the health care field, including government regulations; handle hospital community relations; and sometimes act as a fund-raiser.

In large facilities, the administrator has a staff of assistants with expertise in a variety of fields, but in small and medium-size institutions, the administrator is responsible for all of these areas.

Health specialists manage the daily operations of individual, specialized departments such as surgery, rehabilitation therapy, nursing, and medical records. These workers have more narrowly defined responsibilities than generalists. They also receive more specialized training and experience in the specific field.

In addition to working in hospitals, health services managers are employed by nursing homes and extended-care facilities, community health centers, mental health centers, outreach clinics, city or county health departments, and health maintenance organizations. Others are employed as advisers and specialists by insurance companies, government regulatory agencies, and professional standards organizations such as the American Cancer Society and the American Heart Association. Some serve as commissioned officers in the medical service and hospitals for the various armed forces or work for the U.S. Public Health Service or Veterans Administration.

Depending on the size of the institution, a new graduate might start as an administrative assistant, an assistant administrator, a specialist in a specific management area, a department head, or an assistant department head. In a small health care facility, the new graduate typically would start in a position with broad responsibilities, whereas in a large hospital, the position might be narrow in scope, with rotating work in several departments necessary to gain broad experience.

Places of employment and working conditions

Health services managers work throughout the country in hospitals and health care facilities of all sizes.

Health services managers put in long hours. They are on call at all times for emergency situations that affect the functioning of the institutions. They have heavy workloads and are constantly under considerable pressure.

Qualifications, education, and training

Health services managers should have good health and vitality, maturity, sound judgment, tact, patience, the ability to motivate others, solid communication skills, and sensitivity for people.

Good grades in high school are important. Courses should include English, science, mathematics, business, public speaking, and social studies. Volunteer work or a part-time job in a hospital is helpful.

Preparation for this career includes the completion of an academic program in health administration that leads to a bachelor's, master's, or Ph.D. degree. The various levels of degree programs offer different levels of career preparation. Most health care organizations prefer to hire administrators with at least a master's degree in health administration, hospital administration, public health, or business administration. Usually, larger organizations require more academic preparation for their administrative positions. Teaching and research positions require a Ph.D.

The administrators of nursing homes must be licensed. Licensing requirements vary from state to state, but all include a specific level of education and experience.

Potential and advancement

There are about 222,000 people across the country working in some phase of health care administration. Significant growth is projected for this field through 2008 as the increasing number of people aged 85 and older creates a greater demand for health services.

The most opportunities will be in home health care, long-term care, and managed-care organizations. Fewer jobs will be available in hospitals as they continue to consolidate and shift away from some long-term and primary-care functions now assumed by other sectors of the industry.

In spite of the tremendous growth in this field, there will be active competition for upper-level management jobs in hospitals.

Health services managers advance as they move into higher-paying positions with more responsibilities. They also may advance by transferring to another health care facility or organization.

Income

Salaries depend on the manager's level of experience and expertise, the type and size of health facility, the geographic location, and the type of ownership. Administrators in group practices earn salaries of $76,700 per year, on average. Clinical departments pay between $57,700 and $100,200, depending on the specialization. People managing nursing and rehabilitative services earn the most. Nursing home administrators average $52,800 per year.

Additional sources of information

American College of Health Care Administrators
325 South Patrick Street
Alexandria, VA 22314

American College of Healthcare Executives
One North Franklin Street, Suite 1700
Chicago, IL 60606
www.ache.org

Association of University Programs in Health Administration
730 11th Street NW
Washington, DC 20001-4510
www.aupha.org

HISTORIAN

The job

The description and analysis of events of the past through writing, teaching, and research is the work of historians. Historians usually specialize in the history of an era—ancient, medieval, or modern—or in a specific country or area. They may also specialize in the history of a field such as economics, the labor movement, architecture, or business.

In the United States, many historians specialize in the social or political history of either the United States or modern Europe. The fields of African, Latin American, Asian, and Near Eastern history are becoming popular as well.

Most historians are employed in colleges and universities, where they lecture, write, and do research in addition to teaching. Historians are also employed by libraries, museums, research organizations, historical societies, publishing firms, corporations, and state and local government agencies.

The federal government employs historians primarily in the National Archives, the Smithsonian Institution, and the Departments of Defense, Interior, and State.

Archivists collect historical objects and documents, prepare historical exhibits, and edit and classify historical materials for use in research and other activities. They are employed by museums, special libraries, and historical societies.

Places of employment and working conditions

Historians are employed in just about every college and university, and most cities have at least one museum. Those who work for the federal government work mostly in Washington, D.C.

Qualifications, education, and training

Anyone considering a career in this field should have an interest in reading, studying, and research and should have the ability and desire to write papers and reports. A historian also needs analytical skills and should be able to work both independently and as part of a group.

High school should include as many social science courses as possible. Summer or part-time jobs in museums or libraries are helpful.

Although a bachelor's degree with a major in history is sufficient for a few entry-level jobs, almost all jobs in this profession require advanced degrees. A master's degree is the minimum requirement for college instructors, with a Ph.D. necessary for a professorship and administrative positions.

History curricula vary, but all provide training in the basic skills of research methods, writing, and speaking, which are needed by historians. Also important is training in archival work and quantitative methods of analysis, including statistical and computer techniques.

Potential and advancement

Competition will continue despite average growth in this field. Most openings will occur to replace those who retire or leave the field. People graduating from prestigious universities and those well trained in quantitative methods of historical research will have the best job opportunities.

Historians with a master's degree will find teaching positions in community and junior colleges or high schools, but these jobs may also require state teaching certification.

Those with only a bachelor's degree will find limited opportunities, but a major in history can be an excellent background for a career in journalism, politics, and other fields or for continuing education in law, business administration, or other related disciplines.

Income

The average annual starting salary for professional historians is $38,990.

The starting salary for historians employed by the federal government averages between $20,600 and $25,500 a year. Experienced historians employed by the federal government earn more. Those with an advanced degree earn starting salaries of $45,200.

Many professional historians supplement their salaries by consulting, writing, and lecturing.

Additional sources of information

American Historical Association
400 A Street SE
Washington, DC 20003
www.theaha.org

National Trust for Historic Preservation
1785 Massachusetts Avenue NW
Washington, DC 20036

Organization of American Historians
112 North Bryan Street
Bloomington, IN 47408
www.oah.org

HOME ECONOMIST

The job

The comfort and well-being of the family and the products, services, and practices that affect them are the concern of home economists. Some have a broad knowledge of the whole professional field, while others specialize in consumer affairs, housing, home management, home furnishings and equipment, food and nutrition, clothing and textiles, or child development and family relations.

Many home economists teach. Those who teach in secondary schools provide instruction in foods and nutrition, child development, clothing selection and care, sewing, consumer education, and other homemaking subjects. Others teach in adult-education programs and present material on improving family relations and homemaking skills; some teach people with disabilities and disadvantaged populations. College teachers often combine research and teaching duties.

Home economists who are employed by private business firms and trade associations conduct research, test products, and prepare advertising and instructional materials. Some study consumer needs and advise manufacturers on products to serve those markets.

The federal government employs home economists in the U.S. Department of Agriculture to research the buying and spending habits of families in all socioeconomic groups and to develop budget guides for them. Federal, state, and local governments, as well as private agencies, employ home economists in social welfare programs to instruct clients in homemaking skills and family living.

Some home economists work as extension service agents and provide adult-education programs for rural communities and farmers. They also provide youth programs such as 4-H clubs and train and supervise volunteer leaders for these programs.

Most home economists are women, although a growing number of men have entered the field in recent years.

Related jobs are agricultural extension service worker and dietitian.

Places of employment and working conditions

A 40-hour workweek is the norm in this field, but people in teaching positions usually work some evening hours.

Qualifications, education, and training

Leadership, poise, communication skills, the ability to work with people of many cultures and levels of income, and an interest in the welfare of the family are necessary for this work.

High school courses should include English, home economics, health, mathematics, chemistry, and the social sciences. Part-time or summer jobs in children's camps or day nurseries provide valuable experience.

A bachelor's degree in home economics qualifies graduates for most entry-level positions. A master's degree or Ph.D. is required for college teaching, some research and supervisory positions, extension-service specialists, and most jobs in nutrition.

Students who intend to teach at the secondary level must complete courses required for teaching certification. Those who intend to specialize in a particular area of home economics need the appropriate advanced courses: chemistry and nutrition for work in foods and nutrition; science and statistics for research work; journalism for advertising and public relations; art and design for clothing and textiles.

Potential and advancement

Job competition for home economics teachers is projected to be stiff through 2008, with many more qualified home economics teachers than openings. The best opportunities will be for college-level and adult-education teachers and for those who work with people with disabilities.

Concern over product quality and environmental issues will bring about a slight increase in job opportunities for home economists who work in research. The best jobs will go to those with advanced degrees or experience.

Home economics teachers advance by becoming head of the school's home economics department or by overseeing the home economics program of an entire school system. Research home economists advance by becoming the head of a department or team. They can also become administrators or executives in government agencies.

Income

Starting salaries for home economics teachers in secondary schools average $34,100 to $37,000 a year. Those who teach at the college level receive average annual salaries of $46,630.

Home economists who work for the federal government have starting salaries of about $45,300.

Additional source of information

American Association of Family and Consumer Sciences
1555 King Street
Alexandria, VA 22314

HOTEL/MOTEL MANAGER

The job

The manager of a hotel or motel is charged with the profitable operation of the facility and the comfort and satisfaction of the guests.

The manager is responsible for room rates and credit policies; the operation of the kitchen and dining rooms; and the housekeeping, accounting, and maintenance departments. In a large hotel or motel, the manager may have several assistants who direct some parts of the operation; in small facilities, the manager may handle all aspects of the business personally, including front-desk clerical work such as taking reservations. This is especially true in owner-operated facilities.

Hotels and motels that have a restaurant and/or cocktail lounge usually employ a *restaurant manager* or *food and beverage manager* to oversee these functions because this is usually an important part of the hotel's business.

Some hotel and motel managers are self-employed. Others work for large chains.

Places of employment and working conditions

Managers and their families often live in the hotel or motel, and managers are on call at all times. Owner-operators often work long hours.

Qualifications, education, and training

Initiative, self-discipline, and a knack for organization are necessary in this field. Summer or part-time work in a hotel, motel, or restaurant is helpful. Computer skills are also important.

Although small hotels, motels, and restaurants generally do not have specific educational requirements, they do require experience for manager positions. Some employers, especially in larger facilities, require a bachelor's degree in hotel and restaurant administration.

Training is also available at many junior and community colleges, technical institutes, vocational and trade schools, and other academic institutions.

Some large hotels have on-the-job management programs in which trainees rotate among various departments to acquire a thorough knowledge of the hotel's operation.

Potential and advancement

There are about 76,000 hotel and motel managers nationwide holding wage and salary jobs. The field is expected to grow more slowly than the average through 2008. Increases in business travel and in domestic and foreign tourism will create some growth. Most of this gain will come from economy hotels, which are increasingly popular, and from the need to replace managers who leave the field or retire.

Assistant managers can advance to manager positions, but they often do so by moving to a larger hotel. Hotel and motel chains usually provide better opportunities for advancement than independent hotels because employees can transfer to another site in the chain or to the central office.

Income

Salaries of hotel and motel managers and assistants depend on the size, location, and sales volume of the facility, and on which departments they manage.

Annual salaries average $26,700, but some people earn $45,420 and more. Managers earn bonuses of up to 25 percent of base salary at some hotels.

Additional sources of information

American Hotel and Motel Association
1201 New York Avenue NW
Washington, DC 20005-3931

Council on Hotel, Restaurant, and Institutional Education
1200 17th Street NW
Washington, DC 20036-3097

Educational Institute of the American Hotel and Motel
    Association
P.O. Box 531126
Orlando, FL 32853-1126
www.ei-ahma.org

INDUSTRIAL DESIGNER

The job

Industrial designers develop new styles and designs for products ranging from pencil sharpeners and dishwashers to automobiles. Some specialize in package design or the creation of trademarks; others plan the entire layout of commercial buildings such as supermarkets.

Industrial designers combine artistic talent with knowledge of materials and production methods. Teamwork is necessary in this field, and input from many people goes into a finished product. Working closely with engineers, production personnel, and sales and marketing experts, industrial designers thoroughly research a product. They prepare detailed drawings and then a scale model of a new design. After approval of a design, a full-scale working model is built and tested before production begins.

Most industrial designers work for large manufacturing firms, where they fill day-to-day design needs and work on long-range planning of new products, or for design consulting firms that service a number of industrial companies. Some do freelance work or work for architectural and interior design firms. A few teach in colleges and universities or art schools.

Places of employment and working conditions

Industrial designers work for manufacturing firms in all parts of the United States. Industrial design consultants work mainly in New York City, Chicago, Los Angeles, and San Francisco.

A five-day, 35- to 40-hour week is usual, with occasional overtime necessary to meet deadlines.

Qualifications, education, and training

Creativity, artistic talent and drawing skills, the ability to see familiar objects in new ways, and communication skills are necessary. An industrial designer must be able to design to meet the needs and tastes of the public, not just to suit his or her artistic ideas.

High school should include courses in art, mechanical drawing, mathematics, and computer science.

Four- to five-year programs in industrial design are offered by art schools, technical schools, and colleges and universities. Most large manufacturing firms require a bachelor's degree in industrial design.

Some schools require the submission of samples of artistic ability before acceptance into their industrial design programs. After graduation, job applicants are expected to show a portfolio of their work to demonstrate their creativity and design ability.

Those who plan to pursue a career in industrial design need to develop strong computer skills. Computer-aided design and drafting is used extensively by industrial designers, especially in the aerospace, automotive, and electronics industries.

Potential and advancement

This is a relatively competitive field, and job opportunities will be best for college graduates with degrees in industrial design.

The field is expected to grow faster than the average for all occupations through 2008. Continued demand for safer, less expensive, and more efficient products will spur growth in the field. Advances in high technology and global competition will also increase the need for talented industrial designers.

Industrial designers may be promoted to supervisory positions with major responsibility for design of a specific product or group of products. Those with an established reputation sometimes start their own consulting firms.

Income

Beginners in this field earn about $31,000 a year. Experienced designers earn from $39,000 to $51,000, depending on their talent and the size of the firm. Industrial designers in executive positions may earn $75,000 to $100,000 or more a year.

Additional source of information

Industrial Designers Society of America
1142-E East Walker Road
Great Falls, VA 22066
www.idsa.org

INDUSTRIAL ENGINEER

The job

Industrial engineers are concerned with people and methods, while other engineers may usually be concerned with a product or process. Industrial engineers determine the most efficient and effective way for a company to use the basic components of production—people, machines, and materials.

Industrial engineers develop management control systems for financial planning and cost analysis; design production planning and control systems; design time-study and quality-control programs; and survey possible plant locations for the best combination of raw materials, transportation, labor supply, and taxes.

More than 70 percent of all industrial engineers are employed by manufacturing industries, but because their skills can be used in almost any type of company, industrial engineers work in many industries that don't employ other types of engineers. They may work for insurance companies, banks, hospitals, retail organizations, and other large business firms as well as for more traditional engineering employers such as construction companies, mining firms, and utility companies.

Related jobs are office manager, interior designer, and systems analyst.

Places of employment and working conditions

Industrial engineers work in all parts of the country but are concentrated in industrialized and commercial areas.

This is a physically active engineering specialty involving daily visits to departments within the plants, offices, and grounds of the employer as well as travel to possible plant locations.

Qualifications, education, and training

The ability to think analytically, a capacity for details, and the ability to work as part of a team are necessary. Good communication and strong computer skills are also important.

Mathematics and the sciences must be emphasized in high school.

A bachelor's degree in engineering is the minimum requirement in this field. In a typical curriculum, the first two years are spent in the study of basic sciences such as physics and chemistry, mathematics, introductory engineering, and some liberal arts courses. The remaining years are usually devoted to specialized engineering courses.

Engineering programs can last from four to six years. Those that require five or six years to complete may award a master's degree or may provide a cooperative plan of study plus practical work experience with a nearby industry.

Because of rapid changes in technology, many engineers continue their education throughout their careers. A graduate degree is necessary for most teaching and research positions and for many management jobs. Some persons obtain graduate degrees in business administration.

Engineering graduates usually work under the supervision of an experienced engineer or in a company training program until they become acquainted with the requirements of a particular company or industry.

All states require licensing of engineers whose work may affect life, health, or property or who offer their services to the public. Those who are licensed, about one-third of all engineers, are called registered engineers. Requirements for licensing include graduation from an accredited engineering school, four years of experience, and passing a written examination.

Potential and advancement

There are about 126,000 industrial engineers in the United States. Job opportunities in this field are expected to increase at an average rate through 2008. Some gains will result from the increased complexity and expanding use of automated processes and the growing recognition of the importance of scientific management and safety engineering in reducing costs and improving productivity. Most new jobs, however, will result from replacement needs.

Income

Starting annual salaries in private industry average $43,100 for engineers with a bachelor's degree and $49,900 for those with a master's degree. The median salary for all industrial engineers is about $52,610.

Additional sources of information

Accreditation Board for Engineering and Technology
111 Market Place, Suite 1050
Baltimore, MD 21202-4012
www.abet.org

Institute of Industrial Engineers
25 Technology Park/Atlanta
Norcross, GA 30092
www.iienet.org

Junior Engineering Technical Society
1420 King Street, Suite 405
Alexandria, VA 22314-2794
www.jets.org

National Society of Professional Engineers
1420 King Street
Alexandria, VA 22314-2794
www.nspe.org

Society of Women Engineers
120 Wall Street, 11th Floor
New York, NY 10005
www.swe.org

INSURANCE AGENT AND BROKER

The job

Insurance agents and brokers sell insurance policies to individuals and businesses to protect against financial losses and to provide for future financial needs. They sell one or more of the three basic types of insurance: life, property-liability (casualty), and health.

An *agent* may be either the employee of an insurance company or an independent representative of one or more insurance companies. A *broker* is not under contract to a specific insurance company or companies but places policies directly with whichever company can best serve the needs of a client. Agents and brokers spend the largest part of their time discussing insurance needs with prospective customers and designing insurance programs to fill each customer's individual needs.

Life insurance agents and brokers (life underwriters) sell policies that provide payment to survivors (beneficiaries) when the policyholder dies. A life policy can also be designed to provide retirement income, educational funds for surviving children, or other benefits.

Casualty insurance agents and brokers sell policies that protect against financial losses from such events as fire, theft, and automobile accidents. They also sell commercial and industrial insurance such as workers' compensation, product liability, and medical malpractice.

Health insurance policies offer protection against the cost of hospital and medical care as well as loss of income due to illness or injury and are sold by life and casualty agents and by brokers.

More and more agents and brokers are becoming multiline agents, offering both life and property-liability policies to their clients. Some agents and brokers also sell securities such as mutual funds and variable annuities or combine a real estate business with insurance selling. Successful insurance agents or brokers are highly self-motivated. Anyone interested in this work as a career should be aware that many beginners leave the field because they are unable to establish a large enough clientele. For those who succeed, the financial rewards are usually very good.

Recognizing that professional working women now represent a significant market, the insurance industry has recently been designing insurance programs to meet the special needs of this segment. In turn, the need for women insurance agents and brokers to service these clients has expanded, and some insurance companies are actively recruiting women for their sales forces. While some companies hire only college graduates, others are seeking women with experience in sales, business, and finance.

Related jobs are actuary, claim representative, and underwriter.

Places of employment and working conditions

Insurance agents and brokers are employed throughout the country, in all locations and communities, but the largest number work in or near major population centers.

Agents and brokers are free to schedule their own working hours but often work evenings and weekends for the convenience of their clients. Additional time devoted to paperwork and continuing education often extends the workweek beyond 40 hours.

Agents and brokers usually pay their own automobile and travel expenses. If they own and operate an agency, they also pay clerical salaries, office rental, and operating expenses out of their income.

Qualifications, education, and training

Agents and brokers should be enthusiastic, self-confident, and able to communicate effectively. They need initiative and sales ability to build a clientele and must be able to work without supervision.

Many insurance companies prefer a college degree but will hire high school graduates with proven ability or other potential. Courses in accounting, economics, finance, business law, and insurance subjects are the most useful, whether the agent works for an insurance company or is self-employed.

New agents receive training at the agency or at the home office of the insurance company for which they work. Much of this training involves home-study courses.

All states require agents and most brokers to be licensed. Anyone who plans to sell securities or mutual funds needs a separate securities license. In most states, licensing takes the form of a written examination covering state insurance laws. Insurance companies often sponsor classes to prepare their new agents for the licensing exam, while other new agents study on their own.

Agents and brokers who are committed to succeed in this field are constantly studying to increase their skills. They take college courses and attend educational programs sponsored by their employers or by insurance organizations.

Specialized professional designations are awarded by insurance organizations. These groups also sponsor continuing education courses, which in most states are mandatory to maintain an insurance license.

Potential and advancement

The United States has approximately 387,000 full-time insurance agents and brokers, with many more working part-time.

Employment of insurance agents and brokers is expected to grow more slowly than the average for all occupations through 2008. Although sales volume should increase rapidly as a larger proportion of the population enters the period of peak earnings and family responsibilities, employment of agents and brokers will not keep pace. This is because more policies will be sold to groups and by multiline agents and because more of an agent's time-consuming paperwork will be done by computer, releasing agents to spend more time in actual selling and client contact.

Promotion to positions such as sales manager in a local office or to management positions in a home office or agency is open to agents with exceptional sales ability and leadership. However, many agents who have a good client base prefer to remain in sales, with some establishing independent agencies or brokerage firms.

Income

Insurance agents and brokers usually work on a commission basis. Beginners are often provided with a moderate salary for about six months until they complete their training and begin to build a clientele.

Average annual earnings for insurance agents and brokers are about $34,370. Those at the bottom of the pay scale earn $17,870 or less, while those at the top earn about $91,890. Earnings usually increase rapidly as an agent gains experience.

Additional sources of information

General occupational information about insurance agents and brokers is available from the home office of many insurance companies. Information on state licensing requirements may be obtained from the department of insurance at any state capital. Additional sources are:

American Society of Chartered Life Underwriters (CLU) and
    Chartered Financial Consultants (ChFC)
270 Bryn Mawr Avenue
Bryn Mawr, PA 19010-2195

Independent Insurance Agents of America
127 South Peyton Street
Alexandria, VA 22314
www.iiaa.org

National Association of Professional Insurance Agents
400 North Washington Street
Alexandria, VA 22314

INTERIOR DESIGNER

The job

Interior designers plan and supervise the design and arrangement of building interiors and furnishings. Some work on private residences; others specialize in large commercial and public buildings.

The work of an interior designer is guided by the purpose of the area and the client's budget and taste. Sketches are prepared for the client's approval, and changes are made as required. In some cases, plans and sketches must be prepared several times before a client is satisfied. Once the plans and the cost are approved, the designer shops for and buys furnishings and accessories; supervises the work of painters, carpet layers, and others; and makes sure furnishings are delivered and properly arranged.

Some designers specialize in nonresidential work, such as entire office buildings or public buildings, such as libraries or hospitals. These designers plan the complete layout of the interior, working with the architect. In some instances, they also design the furnishings and arrange for their manufacture.

Most interior designers work for large design firms that provide design services to multiple clients. Others work for department or furniture stores, furniture and textile manufacturers, and antique dealers. A few have permanent jobs with hotel and restaurant chains.

A few interior designers design stage sets for motion pictures and television or work for home furnishing magazines.

Places of employment and working conditions

Interior designers work throughout the country, mostly in larger communities.

The work setting is usually a comfortable, pleasant studio or store. The work may require some travel to visit homes, buildings being constructed, and warehouses. The workweek is usually long in this field, and the hours are often irregular.

Qualifications, education, and training

Artistic talent, color sense, good taste, imagination, and the ability to work well with people are necessary.

High school courses should include art, business, and computer science. Part-time or summer jobs in a home furnishings department or store are helpful.

Formal training in interior design is necessary for all the better jobs with architectural firms, well-established design firms, department and furniture stores, and other major employers. Programs are available at professional schools of interior design (three-year programs); colleges and universities, which award a bachelor's degree; or in graduate programs leading to a master's degree or Ph.D. Courses in sales and business subjects are also valuable. An understanding of computer-aided design and drafting techniques is also an asset.

Regardless of education, beginners almost always go through a training period with the company that hires them. They may function as shoppers, stockroom assistants, sales associates, assistant decorators, or junior designers. This trainee period generally lasts from one to three years.

Some states license interior designers. In others, membership in a recognized professional association is the standard mark of achievement for interior designers. The usual requirements for professional membership are a postsecondary degree, two years of experience, and completion of a qualifying exam sponsored by the National Council for Interior Design.

Potential and advancement

Even though growth is expected in this field, its popularity means competition for just about all job openings. The field is also affected by changing conditions in the economy.

After considerable experience, designers may advance to supervisory positions. Some launch their own businesses.

Income

Beginners may be paid anywhere from minimum wage plus commission to salaries of $19,000 to $23,580 a year.

Experienced interior designers may work for commission, salary plus commission, or straight salary. They have annual salaries ranging from $31,760 to $75,000 a year. Good designers with an established reputation can earn well over $85,000 a year.

Additional source of information

American Society of Interior Designers
608 Massachusetts Avenue NE
Washington, DC 20002-6006

INTERPRETER

The job

Oral interpretation is needed whenever a difference in language creates a barrier among people of different cultures. Interpreters can be found escorting foreign visitors and businesspeople, interpreting highly technical speeches and discussions at international medical or scientific meetings, or appearing in a courtroom when the proceedings involve parties who do not speak or understand English.

There are two basic types of interpretation: simultaneous and consecutive. In simultaneous interpretation, the interpreter translates what is being said in one language as the speaker continues to speak in another. This requires fluency and speed on the part of the interpreter and is made possible by the use of electronic equipment that allows the transmission of simultaneous speeches. Simultaneous interpretation is preferred for conferences and meetings. Conference interpreters often work in a glass-enclosed booth, using earphones and a microphone. Those attending the conference can tune in to a preferred language by turning a dial or pushing a button.

In consecutive interpretation, the speaker and the interpreter take turns speaking. In addition to having fluency in the language, a consecutive interpreter must have a good memory and usually takes notes to give a full and accurate translation. This method is time consuming but is the usual practice with person-to-person interpretation.

The United Nations (UN) employs full-time interpreters. Full-time staff interpreters are also employed by the Organization of American States, the International Monetary Fund, the Pan American Health Organization, and the World Bank. The U.S. Department of State and the U.S. Department of Justice are the major employers of full-time interpreters in the federal government.

Freelance interpreters usually work on short-term contracts, although some assignments can be of longer duration. The greatest number of freelance interpreters work under contract for the U.S. Department of State and the Agency of International Development, serving as escort interpreters for foreign visitors to the United States. The next largest group of freelance interpreters works in the conference field.

A related job is translator.

Places of employment and working conditions

This is a relatively small job field, with the largest concentrations of interpreters in New York City and Washington, D.C.

The conditions under which interpreters work vary widely. Freelance interpreters have little job security because of the fluctuations in demand for their service. Freelance assignments can last from a few days for a typical conference to several weeks on some escort assignments. Although interpreters do not necessarily work long hours, they may work irregular hours, with escort interpreters often required to do considerable traveling.

Qualifications, education, and training

Anyone interested in becoming an interpreter should be an articulate speaker and have good hearing. This work requires quickness, accuracy, tact, and emotional stamina to withstand the tensions of the job. Interpreters must be dependable as to the honesty of their interpretations and have a sense of responsibility regarding the confidentiality of their work.

A complete command of two or more languages is the usual requirement for an interpreter. Interpreters at the UN must know at least three of the six official UN languages: Arabic, Chinese, English, French, Russian, and Spanish.

An extensive and up-to-date working vocabulary and ease in making the transition from one language structure to another are necessary, as is the ability to instantly call to mind appropriate words or idioms of the language.

Many individuals may qualify on the basis of their own foreign backgrounds, and the experience of living abroad is also important. Interpreters should be generally well informed and, in the case of conference interpretation, well grounded in technical subjects such as medicine or scientific and industrial technology.

Interpreters who speak Portuguese, Japanese, and German are also widely in demand in the United States.

Although there is no standard requirement for entry into this profession, a university education generally is essential. In the United States, two schools offer special programs for interpreters. Foreign language proficiency is an entry requirement in both.

Applicants to Georgetown University School of Languages and Linguistics in Washington, D.C., must qualify on the basis of an entrance examination and previous studies at the university level; they usually hold a bachelor's degree and often a master's degree. The school awards a certificate of proficiency as a conference interpreter upon successful completion of a one- or two-year course of study. The certificate is recognized by the International Association of Conference Interpreters.

The Department of Translation and Interpretation at the Monterey Institute of Foreign Studies in Monterey, California, offers a two-year graduate program leading to a master's degree in intercultural communication and a graduate certificate in either translation, translation/interpretation, or conference interpretation. School entrance requirements include a bachelor's degree, an aptitude test, and fluency in English plus one other language if studying translation, or two other languages for the interpretation field. After two semesters of basic courses in translating and interpreting, applicants must pass a qualifying examination for entrance into the translation or interpretation programs.

Potential and advancement

There are about 1,000 interpreters working full-time in the United States. Many others do some interpretation work in the course of their jobs. Secretaries with foreign-language abilities are in demand by companies with foreign subsidiaries or customers.

Only highly qualified applicants will find jobs in this field. There is stiff competition for the limited number of openings, and the level of openings is not expected to rise through 2008. Some hirings will occur to replace interpreters who retire, die, or leave the field for other reasons. In the past, any increase in the demand for full-time interpreters has been slight and usually temporary and has been met by the existing pool of freelance interpreters.

Income

Salaries vary. Full-time interpreters working for large corporations earn more than $50,000 per year. Freelance interpreters are paid on a daily basis, with conference interpreters earning about $350 a day and courtroom interpreters receiving $250 per day.

Additional sources of information

American Association of Language Specialists
1000 Connecticut Avenue NW, Suite 9
Washington, DC 20036

Department of Translation and Interpretation
Monterey Institute of Foreign Studies
P.O. Box 1978
Monterey, CA 93940

Division of Interpretation and Translation
School of Languages and Linguistics
Georgetown University
Washington, DC 20057

Language Services Division
U.S. Department of State
Washington, DC 20520

Secretariat Recruitment Service
United Nations
New York, NY 10017

INVESTMENT MANAGER

The job

An investment manager's function is to manage a company's or an institution's investment positions. Investment decisions involve such questions as what to buy in the way of securities, investment property, or other items, and whether and when to sell any existing holdings for maximum return.

Also called *financial analysts* and *securities analysts*, investment specialists work for banks (where they are usually officers), insurance companies, brokerage firms, and pension plan investment firms and mutual funds. They may function as trustees for institutions or individuals with large holdings or for colleges that have endowment funds to manage. Some use their expertise as financial journalists, analyzing the market for financial publications, newspapers, and magazines. (For a detailed description of the work of people involved in this field, see the job description for **market analyst**.)

Places of employment and working conditions

Investment managers work in all parts of the country but are concentrated in Boston, Chicago, New York City, and San Francisco.

The work is time consuming because investment specialists must read constantly—newspapers, annual reports, trade publications—to keep abreast of developments and changes in the market.

Qualifications, education, and training

Facility in mathematics; the ability to digest, analyze, and interpret large amounts of material; an inquiring mind; and good communication skills are important in this occupation.

A college degree in economics, political science, business administration, finance, or marketing is preferred. Engineering or law, especially if combined with graduate work in business administration, can also provide an excellent background. Training in mathematics, statistics, and computers is becoming increasingly important.

The mark of professionalism in this field is the chartered financial analyst (CFA) degree, which is comparable to the certified public accountant (CPA) designation for accounting professionals. To earn it, the applicant must fulfill the membership requirements of one of the financial analyst societies and complete three examination programs. Five or more years of experience as a financial analyst must be attained before the third examination can be taken.

Potential and advancement

Job opportunities will be good into 2008 for candidates with the appropriate degrees and experience.

Since this is already a high-level position in most organizations, further advancement would usually take the form of moving to a larger institution or organization for an investment manager who has achieved a reputation for accurate analysis and wise management of investments.

Income

Investment managers who work in banking or for large institutions such as colleges reach salary levels of $55,070 or more a year.

The range for all analysts in this field is about $38,240 to $83,800. Some with excellent reputations earn considerably more.

Additional sources of information

Institute of Chartered Financial Analysts
P.O. Box 3668
Charlottesville, VA 22903

New York Stock Exchange
11 Wall Street
New York, NY 10005

Securities Industry Association
120 Broadway
New York, NY 10271

JANITOR

The job

Janitors, or *building custodians*, clean and maintain many types of buildings, including offices, hotels, stores, homes, apartments, and hospitals.

Janitors have a variety of duties, depending on the employer and the extent of their responsibilities. Some janitors are responsible only for cleaning, while others have maintenance responsibilities as well. Typical janitorial duties include mopping floors, vacuuming carpets, emptying garbage cans, cleaning bathrooms, making beds, and dusting furniture. Light maintenance work may include changing lightbulbs, painting, carpentry, and repairing leaky faucets.

Janitors use tools and cleaning equipment to perform their tasks.

Places of employment and working conditions

Janitors are employed throughout the United States. Most janitors work in the evenings when buildings are empty. Some work during the day, especially in schools, hotels, and hospitals.

Janitors usually work indoors, but they sometimes have to shovel sidewalks and mow lawns. Some tasks that a janitor may be required to perform are dirty and unpleasant. Janitors spend most of their working hours on their feet and may have to move heavy objects or cleaning equipment.

Many janitors are employed part-time.

Qualifications, education, and training

There are no formal educational requirements for this position. Janitors need to know simple arithmetic and must be able to follow directions.

Most janitors receive on-the-job training. Beginners usually work with a more experienced person to learn efficient methods of performing tasks.

Potential and advancement

Janitors and cleaners hold about 3.3 million jobs nationwide. An average number of openings in this field is projected through 2008.

Advancement opportunities for janitors are generally limited. Where there are large maintenance staffs, some janitors may become supervisors. Others advance by owning a cleaning business.

Income

Janitors earn an average of $15,340 a year. Those in the middle of the salary range earn between $12,560 and $19,110, those at the bottom earn less than $11,620, and those at the top earn more than $25,060.

Additional source of information

Building Service Contractors Association International
10201 Lee Highway, Suite 225
Fairfax, VA 22030

LABOR RELATIONS SPECIALIST

The job

The field of labor relations covers the relationship between the management of a company and the company's unionized employees. More and more government employees are becoming unionized, so specialists in the field of labor relations are now employed in government agencies as well as in private industry.

The day-to-day administration of the provisions of a union contract is usually the responsibility of a company's personnel department or, in a large company, the industrial relations department. In a small or medium-size company, the personnel manager might handle union matters as part of his or her responsibilities, whereas a large company would likely have one or more labor relations specialists. Their responsibilities include handling grievances, preparing for collective bargaining sessions, and participating in contract negotiations. In some companies, labor relations specialists are also involved in accident prevention and industrial safety programs.

A labor relations specialist must stay abreast of developments in labor law and of wages and benefits in local companies and within the industry and serves as constant liaison between the company and union officials. An effective labor relations specialist must be able to work with union representatives in an atmosphere of mutual respect and cooperation.

In companies, usually large ones, that have both union and nonunion employees, labor relations and personnel management are functions of the industrial relations department.

Labor relations specialists employed by government agencies perform much the same duties as those employed in private industry.

Labor unions do not employ many professionally trained labor relations specialists. At the company and local levels, elected union officials handle all union-management matters. At national and international union headquarters, however, research and education staffs usually include specialists with degrees in industrial and labor relations, economics, or law.

Related jobs are personnel manager and employment counselor.

Places of employment and working conditions

Labor relations specialists work throughout the United States, with the largest concentrations in heavily industrialized areas.

A 40-hour workweek is usual in this field, but longer hours may be necessary during contract negotiations or periods of labor problems.

Qualifications, education, and training

The ability to see opposing viewpoints is important for a labor relations specialist. Integrity, a sense of fairness, and the ability to work with people of various educational levels and social backgrounds are also necessary qualities. Communication skills are another major requirement.

High school courses should include social studies, English, and any class work or extracurricular activities available in public speaking and debating.

Most labor relations specialists begin their careers in personnel work and move into labor relations as they gain experience. (Educational requirements for personnel workers are listed under the **personnel manager** job description.) People who enter the field of labor relations directly are usually graduates of master's-degree programs in industrial or labor relations or have a law degree with course work in industrial relations. Courses in labor law, collective bargaining, labor economics and history, and industrial psychology should be included in either under-graduate or graduate study.

Potential and advancement

Average growth is expected in this field, with the most job opportunities in private business as employers try to provide effective training and employee relations programs for a rapidly growing workforce. In spite of the projected growth in the field, there will be competition for available job openings because of the abundance of qualified workers and college graduates with degrees in labor relations.

Advancement often takes the form of moving to a larger company. Others advance by moving from middle-level positions in large companies to top-level positions in smaller companies.

Labor relations specialists who gain substantial experience and establish a wide reputation sometimes work as federal mediators. Their services are made available to companies or industries that have arrived at a stalemate in contract negotiations with a union.

Income

The annual salary for labor relations specialists depends on the employer and the field of specialization. Personnel managers earn about $35,400 to $73,830. Equal employment opportunity/affirmative action specialists average $44,800. The federal government pays labor relations specialists entry-level salaries of $28,000 to $44,500, depending on the amount of higher education completed.

Additional sources of information

American Arbitration Association
140 West 51st Street
New York, NY 10020

International Personnel Management Association
1617 Duke Street
Alexandria, VA 22314

Society for Human Resource Management
606 North Washington Street
Alexandria, VA 22314

LANDSCAPE ARCHITECT

The job

Landscape architects design the outdoor areas of commercial buildings and private homes, public parks and playgrounds, real estate developments, airports, shopping centers, hotels and resorts, and public housing. Their work not only beautifies these areas but helps them to function efficiently as well.

A landscape architect prepares detailed maps and plans showing all existing and anticipated features and, once the plans are approved, may accept bids from landscape contractors on the work to be done. In addition to planning the placement of trees, shrubs, and walkways, the landscape architect supervises any necessary grading, construction, and planting.

Most landscape architects now use computer-aided design and drafting (CADD) technology to create designs. Some also use video simulation to help clients visualize proposed plans. Some larger projects require geographic information systems technology, a computer-mapping system.

Most landscape architects either are self-employed or work for architectural, landscape architectural, or engineering firms. State and local government agencies also employ landscape architects for projects involving forest management, water storage, public housing, city planning and urban renewal, highways, parks, and recreation areas. The federal government offers positions in the Departments of Agriculture, Defense, and Interior. A few are employed by landscape contractors.

Beginners in this field are given simple drafting assignments, working their way up by preparing specifications and construction details and other aspects of project design. It is usually two or three years before they are allowed to oversee a design through all stages of development.

Related jobs are environmentalist, farmer, floral designer, forester, forestry technician, urban planner, nursery worker, and architect.

Places of employment and working conditions

Landscape architects work throughout the United States, but most job opportunities exist in areas with favorable weather conditions, such as Florida, California, and Texas.

Salaried employees in this field usually work a 40-hour week; self-employed landscape architects often work much longer hours. Although much of an architect's time is spent outdoors, a substantial number of hours are spent indoors in planning and mapping activities.

Qualifications, education, and training

Creative ability, appreciation of nature, talent in art and design, and the ability to work in detail are basic requirements. Business ability is necessary for those who intend to open their own landscape architectural firms. Strong computer skills are also important, as CADD systems are becoming an integral design tool.

High school should include courses in biology, botany, art, mathematics, and mechanical drawing. Summer jobs for landscaping contractors or plant nurseries provide relevant experience.

Fifty-eight colleges offer bachelor's- or master's-degree programs in landscape architecture that are approved by the American Society of Landscape Architects. Bachelor-level programs take four or five years to complete, and master's programs take two to three years.

A license is required in 46 states for the independent practice of landscape architecture. Qualifications usually include a degree from an accredited school of landscape architecture, one to four years of experience, and a passing grade on a uniform national licensing examination.

Potential and advancement

There are about 22,000 practicing professional landscape architects in the country. The outlook is for average growth in this field through 2008, although any downturns in the construction industry could cause temporary slow periods.

Landscape architecture is a popular field, and job seekers can expect to encounter considerable competition. Those with strong computer skills and an understanding of environmental issues and regulations will have the best job prospects.

Landscape architects usually advance by moving to a larger firm, by becoming associates in the firm, or by opening their own businesses.

Income

Landscape architects earn about $37,930 to $50,550 annually, with some earning $78,920 or more. Average earnings for landscape architects employed by the federal government are about $57,500.

Additional source of information

American Society of Landscape Architects
Career Information
636 Eye Street NW
Washington, DC 20001-3736
www.asla.org

LAWYER

The job

The basic work of a lawyer involves interpreting the law and applying it to the needs of a particular case or client.

Lawyers, also called *attorneys*, who have a general practice handle a variety of legal matters—making wills, settling estates, preparing property deeds, and drawing up contracts. Others specialize in criminal, corporate, labor, tax, real estate, or international law.

About three-fifths of all lawyers are in private practice, either alone or in a law firm. Business firms employ lawyers as salaried in-house counselors to handle company legal matters. The federal government employs lawyers in the Department of Justice and other regulatory agencies; state and local governments employ even more. Some lawyers teach full- or part-time in law schools.

Many people with legal training do not practice law but use their legal knowledge as a background for careers in financial analysis, insurance claim adjusting, tax collection, or management consulting. Others work as parole officers or law enforcement officers. Many elected public officials also have a background in law.

Places of employment and working conditions

Lawyers are needed in every community and by businesses and government agencies throughout the country.

Lawyers often work long hours and are under considerable pressure when a case is being tried. Those in private practice, however, can determine their own hours and caseloads and are usually able to work past the usual retirement age.

Qualifications, education, and training

Assertiveness, an interest in people and ideas, the ability to inspire trust and confidence, and top-notch debating and writing skills are necessary for this field. A successful lawyer must be able to research and analyze a case and to think conceptually and logically. Computers are an increasingly commonplace research tool for lawyers.

High school courses that develop language and verbal skills are important. Computer science, American history, civics and government, and any training in debating, public speaking, or acting will prove useful.

Obtaining a law degree requires at least seven years of full-time study beyond high school. This study includes four years of college and three years of law school.

Although there is no specific "prelaw" college program, the best undergraduate training is one that gives the student a broad educational background while developing the writing, speaking, and thinking skills necessary for a legal career. Majors in the social sciences, natural sciences, and humanities are suitable and should include courses in economics, philosophy, logic, history, and government. Good grades are key.

To help gauge individuals' aptitude for the study of law, most law schools require the applicants to take the Law School Admission Test. Competition for admission to law school is intense. Although the number of applicants has dropped from recent highs, stiff competition for entrance will remain for the foreseeable future, particularly for the more prestigious law schools.

Students should attend a law school that is approved by the American Bar Association (ABA) or by an individual state. ABA approval indicates that the school meets the minimum standards of education necessary for practice in any state; state-approved law schools that lack ABA approval prepare graduates for practice in that particular state only. A few states recognize the study of law done entirely in a law office or a combination of law office and law school study. California will accept the study of law by correspondence course if all other qualifications are met. Several states require the registration and approval of law students by the state board of law examiners before students enter law school or during the early years of legal study.

The first part of law school is devoted to fundamental courses such as constitutional law, contracts, property law, and judicial procedure. Specialized courses in such fields as tax, labor, or corporate law are also offered. The second part of law school consists of practical training through participation in school-sponsored legal aid activities, courtroom practice in the school's practice court under the supervision of experienced lawyers, and writing on legal issues for the school's law journal.

Upon successful completion of law school, graduates usually receive the degree of doctor of laws (J.D.) or bachelor of laws (L.L.B.). Those who intend to teach, do research, or specialize usually continue with advanced study.

All states require a lawyer to be admitted to the state bar before practicing law. Requirements include a written examination, at least three years of college, and graduation from an ABA- or state-approved law school. An increasing number of states require Multistate Performance Testing as a one-time test of practical skills for new lawyers.

Potential and advancement

There are about 681,000 lawyers practicing in the United States. Although this field is expected to grow steadily, a rapid increase in the number of law school graduates in recent years has created keen competition for available jobs. This situation will probably continue. Graduates of prestigious law schools and those who rank high in their graduating class will have the best odds of securing salaried positions with law firms, corporations, and government agencies and as law clerks (research assistants) for judges. Lawyers who wish to establish a new practice will find the best opportunities in small towns and in expanding suburban areas.

Lawyers advance from positions as law clerks to experienced lawyers through assuming progressively more responsible work. Many establish their own practices. After years of experience, some lawyers become judges.

Income

Lawyers who establish their own practices usually earn little more than expenses during the first few years, but income increases rapidly as the practice develops. Private practitioners who are partners in a law firm generally earn more than those who practice alone.

Lawyers starting in salaried positions earn about $45,500 a year. Experienced lawyers earn an average of $115,000 or more in private practice and $78,200 working for the federal government.

Additional sources of information

Association of American Law Schools
1201 Connecticut Avenue NW, Suite 800
Washington, DC 20036-2605

Information Services
American Bar Association
750 North Lake Shore Drive
Chicago, IL 60611
www.abanet.org

LIBRARIAN

The job

Librarians select and organize books and other publications and materials and assist readers in their use. Their work is divided into three areas: librarians in user services deal directly with the public, helping patrons to find the information and materials they need; those in technical services order, classify, and catalog materials and do not usually interact with the public; and those in administrative services prepare budgets, supervise employees, purchase equipment, and direct long-term planning. A librarian in a small or medium-size library does all three types of work.

Librarians are usually classified by the type of institution in which they work—public, school, college and university, or special library.

Public librarians work in community libraries and provide a full range of library services for local citizens. Depending on the budget and size of the community, the library staff may include *acquisition librarians*, who purchase books and other materials and help users find what they need; *reference librarians*, who help with specific questions and suggest information sources; and *extension* or *outreach librarians*, who staff bookmobiles. *Children's librarians* and *adult services librarians* may be in charge of services for those particular age groups.

School librarians in elementary and secondary schools instruct students in the use of school library facilities, work with teachers to provide materials that interest students and supplement their classroom work, sometimes participate in team-teaching activities, and develop audiovisual programs.

College and university librarians provide services to students, faculty members, and researchers. Some operate documentation centers that record, store, and retrieve specialized information for university research projects or work in a special field such as law, medicine, or music.

Special librarians work in libraries maintained by government agencies and by commercial and business firms. They build and arrange the organization's information resources and provide materials and services covering subjects of special interest or use to the organization. They may be called on to conduct a literature search or compile a bibliography on a specific subject.

Information science specialists work in much the same way as special librarians, but they have a more extensive technical and scientific background and greater knowledge of new information-handling techniques. They condense complicated information into readable form and interpret and analyze data for a highly specialized clientele. They develop classification systems, prepare coding and programming techniques for computer information storage and retrieval, and develop microfilm technology.

Most librarians work in school and academic libraries. Others work in special and public libraries.

Librarians are increasingly making use of remote databases, electronic mail, the Internet, and other worldwide computer systems to expand the information they can make available to users. Strong computer skills are therefore an asset in this field.

Places of employment and working conditions

Librarians work in communities of all sizes.

A typical workweek is 35 to 40 hours. In public libraries and college and university libraries, this usually includes some evening and weekend work.

Because many opportunities for part-time work exist in public libraries and because elementary and secondary school librarians work a nine-month year, this is a suitable field for people with family responsibilities.

Qualifications, education, and training

Intellectual curiosity and an interest in helping others are necessary characteristics for a librarian. A knack for organization and a retentive memory are also important.

High school should include courses and activities that develop verbal and language skills in a broad college preparatory program.

A liberal arts degree is required for entrance into a graduate program in library science. The one- or two-year program leads to a master of library science degree (M.L.S.). Those who intend to work as special librarians usually earn a bachelor's degree in the specialty plus a master's or Ph.D. degree in library or information science.

Both undergraduate and graduate programs offer course work in such library specialties as data processing fundamentals, computer languages, and the use and development of audiovisual materials. Librarians who intend to work as public school librarians must have an M.L.S. and complete teaching certification requirements in most states.

A Ph.D. degree is usually necessary for administrative positions in large public library systems and in college and university libraries.

Potential and advancement

There are about 152,000 professional librarians in the country. Slow growth for employment in this field is projected through 2008. Limited budgets, the high number of recent graduates in the field, and the increased efficiency provided by computer technology will lessen the demand for public librarians. Some openings will occur as librarians retire, and job seekers may have better odds for success in rural areas. Others will find opportunities in the corporate sector as researchers or systems analysts.

Experienced librarians with graduate training can advance to administrative positions. Those who acquire specialized training can advance to special librarian positions or to jobs in specialized libraries in government agencies or businesses.

Income

Earnings for librarians depend on individual qualifications and the type, size, and location of the library.

Salaries average $38,470 a year for all librarians. Experienced librarians earn between $30,440 and $48,130, with library directors earning the highest salaries of $67,810 or more.

The average salary for those employed by the federal government is $56,400.

Additional sources of information

American Library Association
50 East Huron Street
Chicago, IL 60611
www.ala.org

American Society for Information Science Education
P.O. Box 7640
Arlington, VA 22207
www.sils.umich.edu/ALISE

Office of Educational Research and Improvement
Library Programs
Library Development Staff
U.S. Department of Education
555 New Jersey Avenue NW, Room 402
Washington, DC 20208-5571

Special Libraries Association
1700 18th Street NW
Washington, DC 20009

LIFE SCIENTIST

The job

From the smallest living cell to the largest animals and plants, life scientists study living organisms and their life processes. Life scientists usually work in one of three broad areas: agriculture, biology, or medicine.

Many life scientists are involved in research and development—doing basic research or applying it in medicine, increasing agricultural yields, and improving the environment. Others hold management and administrative positions in zoos and botanical gardens and in programs involving the testing of foods and drugs. Some work in technical sales and service jobs for industrial firms or as consultants to business and government.

Some life scientists call themselves *biologists*, but the usual method of classification is according to type of organism studied or the specific activity performed. *Botanists* deal with plants—studying, classifying, and developing cures for plant disease. *Agronomists* work with food crops to increase yields; control disease, pests, and weeds; and prevent soil erosion. *Horticulturists* are concerned with orchard and garden plants such as fruit and nut trees, vegetables, and flowers.

Zoologists, who study animal life, have titles that reflect the group they study: *ornithologists* study birds, *entomologists* study insects, and *mammalogists* study mammals. *Animal husbandry specialists* are involved in breeding, feeding, and controlling disease in domestic animals. *Embryologists* study the development of animals from fertilized egg through the birth or hatching process.

Microbiologists investigate the growth and characteristics of microscopic organisms such as bacteria, viruses, and molds. *Medical microbiologists* study the relationship between bacteria and disease and the effects of antibiotics on bacteria.

Pathologists study the effect of diseases, parasites, insects, or drugs on human cells and tissue. *Pharmacologists* test the effect of drugs, gases, poisons, and other substances on animals and use the results of their research to develop new or improved drugs and medicines.

Anatomists, ecologists, geneticists, and *nutritionists* are also life scientists. Many of these life scientists work in colleges and universities, usually in medical schools and state agricultural colleges. Some also are employed by the federal government, almost all of them in the Department of Agriculture. The remainder hold private-sector positions in drug, food products, and agricultural-related industries.

Related jobs are biochemist, environmentalist, oceanographer, soil scientist, and veterinarian.

Places of employment and working conditions

Life scientists work throughout the United States, with the largest concentrations in metropolitan areas.

Most life scientists work in laboratories; some jobs, however, require outdoor work and strenuous physical labor. Working hours may be irregular in some specialties due to the nature of the research or activity under way.

Qualifications, education, and training

The ability to work independently as well as to function as part of a team is necessary for a career in the life sciences. Good communication skills are also needed. Physical stamina is necessary in some of the specialty areas that require outdoor work.

High school courses should include as much science and mathematics as possible.

Almost all liberal arts programs include a biology major, and life science students should also take chemistry and physics courses. Some colleges offer bachelor's degrees in specific life sciences; many state universities offer programs in agricultural specialties. A bachelor's degree is adequate preparation for testing and inspection jobs and for advanced technician jobs in the medical field. With courses in education, it is also adequate background for high school teaching positions.

An advanced degree is required for most jobs in the life sciences. A master's degree is sufficient for some jobs in applied research and college teaching, but a Ph.D. is mandatory for most teaching positions at the college level, for independent research, and for many administration jobs. Medical scientists need a Ph.D. as well; some also have a medical degree.

Requirements for advanced degrees usually include fieldwork and laboratory research.

Potential and advancement

There are approximately 112,000 life scientists in the United States. Job opportunities in the life sciences will increase, but some fields will be better than others. Environmental science and medical research will account for most of the growth. Federal funding, the overall health of the economy, and the number of new graduates in life science will influence the number of openings.

Advancement in this field depends on experience and is usually limited to those with higher academic degrees.

Income

Life scientists earn an average of $46,140 in private industry; the rate is about $48,600 in the federal government. Medical scientists tend to earn more, about $52,200 on average.

Additional sources of information

American Institute of Biological Sciences
1444 I Street NW, Suite 200
Washington, DC 20005
www.aibs.org

American Physiological Society
Education Office
9650 Rockville Pike
Bethesda, MD 20814
www.faseb.org/aps

American Society for Microbiology
Office of Education and Training—Career Information
1325 Massachusetts Avenue NW
Washington, DC 20005
www.asmusa.org

LOBBYIST

The job

Lobbying is an effort by an interested person or organization to influence legislation. On one hand, lobbying provides information relative to the target legislation and lets the legislator know the feelings of a particular group of constituents. On the other hand, lobbying may also have the negative reputation of applying pressure.

Lobbyists may take the form of individual citizens who write to members of Congress or to state legislators about a particular matter. Groups of citizens who band together in demonstrations, telephone campaigns, or other efforts to influence lawmakers and regulatory agencies are also lobbying.

At the professional level, full-time officials of powerful organizations and industries are paid to present the employer's side of a controversial question to the appropriate member of Congress or committee. Their titles may signify legislative liaison or public relations duties, but their actual work is lobbying. Some professional lobbyists represent several clients simultaneously.

Some of the most effective lobbyists are former members of Congress, state legislators, and other administrative officials who are no longer active politically but who know their way around state capitals or federal agencies.

The most active lobbying groups at all levels are those from business, labor, farming, education, churches, and citizens' groups.

Places of employment and working conditions

Lobbyists operate at all levels of government in all parts of the country.

Although some lobbyists are involved in "wining-and-dining" activities, a lot of hard work accompanies the more glamorous duties. Long hours are normal, and it is often necessary to work irregular hours to get to see important congresspersons and state officials.

Qualifications, education, and training

Personal integrity, sound judgment, persistence, resourcefulness, patience, tact, the ability to get along with people, good communication skills, and physical stamina are necessary.

There are no specific educational requirements for a lobbyist. Thorough training or experience in a particular field of interest plus a knowledge of how the government works and of which people can make a difference are what make an effective lobbyist.

Potential and advancement

So long as there is legislation being considered, there will be lobbyists employed to influence the legislators. Active participation in a professional or political organization can provide opportunities for lobbying, and membership in nationally active groups can lead to federal-level lobbying.

Income

Earnings for this occupation are difficult to establish. Many lobbyists are people who work without pay for organizations or causes in which they have an interest. Others, although registered as lobbyists, earn the bulk of their income in some other line of work. An example is public relations directors for large organizations who spend a small percentage of their time as lobbyists, representing their companies' interests on a particular piece of pending legislation.

Additional source of information

American Association of Political Consultants
1211 Connecticut Avenue NW
Washington, DC 20036

MACHINIST

The job

Machinists are skilled metalworkers who know the working properties of a variety of metals and use this knowledge to turn a block of metal into a precisely machined part. In addition to making parts for automobiles, machines, and other equipment, machinists repair or make parts for factory machinery.

Machinists work from blueprints or written specifications and use a variety of machine tools, precision instruments such as micrometers, and hand tools. Machine tools are becoming more technologically advanced. Many metal parts are now produced by machine tools that are computer numerically controlled (CNC). These machine tools contain a controller that reads a program and runs the tool's mechanism through the coded steps. Tool programmers, who begin their careers as machinists, write the programs, sometimes with the assistance of computer-aided manufacturing technology.

All factories employ machinists to perform repairs and maintenance on equipment and machinery. Others are employed in industries that manufacture large numbers of metal parts, such as the auto industry. Independent machine shops of all sizes also employ many machinists; the federal government employs many more in navy yards and other installations.

Machinists are usually union members, with most belonging to either the International Association of Machinists and Aerospace Workers; United Automobile, Aerospace, and Agricultural Implement Workers of America; United Electrical, Radio, and Machine Workers of America; International Brotherhood of Electrical Workers; or United Steelworkers of America. A related job is tool-and-die maker.

Places of employment and working conditions

Machinists work in all parts of the United States but mainly in large industrial areas such as Boston, Chicago, New York City, Philadelphia, San Francisco, and Houston.

Machinists work in well-lighted areas, but the work is often noisy and can be tedious and repetitive. They use grease and oil in the course of their work and often stand most of the day. Finger, hand, and eye injuries are possible from flying metal particles, and safety rules usually require the use of specially fitted eyeglasses, protective aprons, and short-sleeve shirts.

Qualifications, education, and training

Anyone who wants to be a machinist should be mechanically inclined and temperamentally suited to doing work that requires concentration, precision, and physical effort. A machinist must also be able to work independently.

High school or vocational courses should include mathematics, physics, machine shop classes, computer courses, drafting, and electronics, if possible.

A formal apprenticeship is the best training for an all-around machinist. Some companies offer shorter courses for machinists who will work on single-purpose machines, and some machinists learn through on-the-job training, but those who complete a formal apprenticeship program usually have the best opportunities for advancement because they are capable of handling a wider variety of jobs.

A typical apprentice program consists of shop training and related classroom instruction in blueprint reading, mechanical drawing, and shop mathematics.

Some companies require experienced machinists to take additional courses in mathematics and electronics, at company expense, so that they qualify to service and operate CNC machine tools.

Many training programs have incorporated skills standards developed by the National Institute of Metalworking Skills. Those who complete such a curriculum and pass an exam receive the NIMS credential.

Potential and advancement

There are about 434,000 machinists currently in the United States, but the number is expected to decline slightly through 2008. Job opportunities should be good, as employers report difficulty attracting people to the field.

Advancement in this occupation is to supervisory positions. With additional training, machinists can also become tool-and-die makers or instrument makers. Some experienced machinists open their own machine shops or take technical jobs in machine tooling and programming.

Income

Average annual earnings for machinists are $28,860. Most earn between $22,670 and $36,100, with the bottom 10 percent earning less than $17,800 and the top 10 percent earning more than $42,480.

Additional sources of information

International Association of Machinists and Aerospace Workers
9000 Machinists Place
Upper Marlboro, MD 20772

International Union of Electronic, Electrical, Salaried,
   Machine, and Furniture Workers
1126 16th Street NW
Washington, DC 20036

National Tooling and Machining Association
9300 Livingston Road
Fort Washington, MD 20744
www.ntma.org

United Automobile, Aerospace, and Agricultural Implement
   Workers of America
Skilled Trades Department
8000 East Jefferson Avenue
Detroit, MI 48214

MANAGEMENT CONSULTANT

The job

Management consultants help managers analyze the administrative and operating problems of an organization. They recommend solutions to problems concerning the objectives, policies, functions, and staffing of the organization. They may also help with implementation of any recommended programs.

Many management consultants are self-employed. The rest work for general management consulting and accounting firms, and for federal, state, and local governments.

Businesses and industries of all kinds use the services of management consultants, as do government agencies, nonprofit organizations, and institutions such as hospitals.

Related jobs are systems analyst, operations research analyst, industrial engineer, and office manager.

Places of employment and working conditions

Management consultants are employed in all areas of the country. Some jobs may necessitate temporary overseas assignment if multinational corporations are involved.

Management consultants work a 40-hour week. Overtime is common. Travel plays a large part in the consultant's work; some estimates say 20 to 35 percent of a consultant's time is taken up in traveling to a client's location or between branches of a client's organization.

Qualifications, education, and training

An analytical mind, sound judgment, objectivity, tact, good communication skills, and the ability to work as part of a team are necessary.

High school should provide a solid college preparatory course with emphasis in mathematics, social sciences, and communication skills.

A college degree in engineering, business administration, accounting, or other related fields should be followed by graduate study in business administration or public administration.

The Institute of Management Consultants offers an examination leading to the certified management consultant (CMC) designation, a useful credential, especially for self-employed consultants.

Potential and advancement

Nationwide there are about 344,000 people engaged in management consulting. This field is expected to grow rapidly through 2008 as companies strive to improve their performance. Job competition will be keen, however, because of the high number of qualified candidates.

Management consultants can advance to positions as project directors in a firm and, with extensive experience, may become associates or partners. Some advance by going into business for themselves or take a high-level job with a large corporation.

Income

The income of management consultants depends on the individual's experience, qualifications, and employer. Those who are wage and salary workers earn an average starting salary of about $38,900; senior consultants average $96,800; junior partners, $151,100; and senior partners, $266,700.

Additional source of information

Institute of Management Consultants
1200 19th Street NW, Suite 300
Washington, DC 20036
www.imcusa.org

MANUFACTURER'S SALES REPRESENTATIVE

The job

Most manufacturing firms sell their products to businesses, other industrial firms, and retail outlets through their own sales representatives. Familiarly known as *sales reps* or *manufacturer's reps*, these sales workers are thoroughly familiar with the employer's product and often provide advice, marketing strategies, and technical expertise to their customers.

When the product sold is highly technical, such as computers or industrial equipment, a manufacturer usually employs engineers or other technically trained people for sales. These *sales engineers* or *technical sales workers* may design systems for the client, supervise installation, and provide training for the client's employees who will use the product.

Related jobs are sales manager, engineer, and wholesaler.

Places of employment and working conditions

Some sales reps work out of local or regional offices, which keeps them fairly close to home. Others cover large territories and travel extensively. Because they almost always work on commission, successful sales reps spend as much time as possible calling on customers during business hours and do any necessary traveling during evenings and weekends.

Qualifications, education, and training

Selling skills, assertiveness, a pleasant personality, physical stamina, and the ability to get along with all kinds of people are necessary for this job.

A college preparatory course should be pursued in high school. Part-time or summer job experience in selling is valuable experience.

A college degree is becoming increasingly important for those who wish to work as a manufacturer's sales representative. Manufacturers of nontechnical products often prefer a liberal arts, business administration, or marketing degree. Other employers have specific educational requirements. Pharmaceutical retailers sometimes need training at a college of pharmacy; chemical manufacturers often require a degree in chemistry; a computer manufacturer might hire only electronics engineers for its sales positions.

Regardless of the field, employers usually provide a training period of up to two years for new employees. Some programs consist of classroom instruction plus on-the-job training in a branch office under the supervision of a field sales manager. In other programs, trainees are rotated through several jobs and departments to learn all phases of production, installation, and service of the employer's product. New employees sometimes accompany experienced salespeople for a time before being assigned to a sales territory. Certification courses are also available, and those who complete them become certified professional manufacturer's representatives (CPMRs).

Potential and advancement

There are about 1.5 million manufacturer's sales representatives in the country. This field is expected to grow slowly through 2008, with the greatest demand being for technically trained sales workers. Employers are expected to be very selective, and candidates with solid educational backgrounds will get the choice jobs.

Experienced and hard-working sales reps can advance to branch manager and district manager positions and to executive-level positions such as sales manager. Many of the top-level corporate positions in industry are filled by people who started out in sales.

Income

Manufacturer's sales representatives may be paid in a number of ways: a salary (usually for trainees), salary plus commission, or straight commission. Many companies also provide bonuses based on sales performance.

Earnings for sales reps average about $36,540 a year.

Additional sources of information

Manufacturers' Agents National Association
P.O. Box 3467
Laguna Hills, CA 92654-3467
www.manaonline.org

National Association of Wholesaler-Distributors
1725 K Street NW
Washington, DC 20006

Sales and Marketing Executives International
5500 Interstate North Parkway, No. 545
Atlanta, GA 30328
www.smei.org

MARKET ANALYST

The job

An individual's decision to buy, hold, or sell securities is sometimes based on personal knowledge, but most people consult their stockbrokers for advice. The stockbroker, in turn, depends on the expertise of the company's research department to provide the necessary information. These experts are called market analysts or *securities analysts.*

In addition to working for brokerage houses, market analysts and securities analysts are employed by investment banking firms, bank trust departments, insurance companies, pension and mutual funds, investment advisory firms, and institutions such as colleges that have endowment funds to manage. All these organizations expect the same service: expert advice that will help them to invest wisely with the best return on their money.

Market analysts evaluate the market as a whole. They study information on changes in the gross national product, cost of living, personal income, rate of employment, construction starts, fiscal plans of the federal government, growth and inflation rates, balance of payments, market trends, and indexes of common stocks. They also monitor events that might produce a psychological reaction in the market: international crisis, war, political activity, or a tragedy large enough to cause the market to change direction. In addition, market analysts keep an eye on business and industry developments and actions of the Federal Reserve to loosen or tighten credit.

Securities analysts study and analyze individual companies or industries, relating knowledge of the current and future state of the economy to predict the future performance of the company or industry. Analysts may specialize in a specific area, such as companies involved in energy production or the aircraft manufacturing industry. The analyst studies all available material on an individual company, including annual reports and details of company management, and sometimes travels to the company to take a closer look in person.

An investor who has a portfolio containing a variety of securities needs advice not only on the individual securities but also on the makeup of the entire portfolio. A *portfolio analyst* has the broad general knowledge to give advice on the market and its relationship to the objectives of the investor. The accumulation of a balanced portfolio can then be accomplished.

Analysts who deal in securities actually combine elements of all three areas within the scope of their work, but in organizations that employ many researchers, the jobs are often separate.

Related jobs are actuary, economist, insurance agent and broker, investment manager, statistician, and securities sales worker (stockbroker).

Places of employment and working conditions

Analysts work in all parts of the country but are concentrated in Boston, Chicago, New York City, and San Francisco. Major brokerage houses have branch offices in about 800 cities.

Analysts find their work fascinating but time consuming. They must read constantly—newspapers, annual reports, trade publications—to keep abreast of developments and changes in the market. Their advancement depends on the reputation they achieve for accurate analysis and predictions. They are sometimes required to make decisions quickly on securities worth thousands, or even millions, of dollars.

Qualifications, education, and training

The ability to interpret and analyze large amounts of material, an inquiring mind, and facility in mathematics are absolutely necessary. Good communication skills are also important.

A high school background with plenty of mathematics and preparation for college is essential. Some type of selling experience is usually necessary as well.

A college degree is required by just about all employers. Economics, political science, and business administration are the preferred degrees. Engineering, law, finance, and marketing, especially when combined with graduate work in business administration, are also accepted. The growing use of computers in this field requires the addition of research staffs trained in mathematics and statistics.

The mark of professionalism among analysts is the chartered financial analyst (CFA) degree, comparable to the CPA for an accountant. To earn this degree, an analyst must fulfill the membership requirements of one of the financial analyst societies in the United States and complete three examination programs. Analysts must have five or more years of experience before taking the third examination.

Potential and advancement

Job opportunities in this field will be average through 2008 for candidates with appropriate degrees and knowledge of computers. However, opportunities fluctuate along with trends in the economy.

In the securities field, research departments are considered the best springboard to advancement, since analysts acquire in-depth knowledge of the economy and the market. Within research, the career path is usually junior analyst; analyst, sometimes in a specialty field; then senior analyst. Advancement to management positions in branch offices is also possible.

Income

Analysts earn $34,650 to $74,500 a year. Senior analysts who acquire a reputation for accuracy can earn more than $120,000 a year.

Additional sources of information

Institute of Chartered Financial Analysts
P.O. Box 3668
Charlottesville, VA 22903

Securities Industry Association
120 Broadway
New York, NY 10271

MARKETING MANAGER

The job

For a company to stay in business, it must be able to sell its goods or services at a profit. It is the responsibility of the marketing manager to coordinate and oversee the workers and strategies that will enable a company to identify potential customers and sell its goods or services to them successfully.

Marketing managers develop a business's marketing strategy. They work closely with product development managers and market research managers to determine the demand for the company's goods or services and to identify competitors and customers. These strategies are then developed based on researchers' findings regarding the best markets for the goods or services by geographic region, age, income, and lifestyle.

Marketing managers are also responsible for setting prices that will allow the business to make a profit while at the same time dominating the market for its particular goods or services.

By working with sales and product development managers, marketing managers follow sales trends and generate ideas for new products.

Marketing managers also work closely with advertising and publicity departments to assure that products are promoted adequately to attract customers.

Places of employment and working conditions

This position can be found in nearly every industry.

Marketing managers are considered to be among top management and face a great deal of pressure. They often work long hours, including evenings and weekends. They frequently have to travel to attend meetings and meet with customers.

Qualifications, education, and training

Marketing managers must be creative, aggressive, responsible, and hard working. Usually, marketing managers have been promoted from other positions where they have gained experience, decision-making skills, and leadership ability.

Educational backgrounds for marketing managers vary, but most employers require a college degree in either liberal arts or business administration with an emphasis on marketing. Highly technical industries, such as computer and electronics manufacturing, often require a degree in engineering or science.

Some large firms have management training programs. Others offer continuing education opportunities either in-house or at local colleges and universities. Companies often encourage their employees to attend seminars and conferences given by professional organizations by paying their costs. Certification is also available from several professional associations.

Potential and advancement

Growing competition between foreign and domestic companies for control of their markets will result in many opportunities for marketing managers. Open positions will also occur as some managers are promoted to top executive positions and others leave the workforce.

Some industries will offer better opportunities than others. Faster growth is expected in data processing services and in radio and television broadcasting. Growth will be slower in some manufacturing industries.

Income

The median salary for marketing managers is $57,300 a year. Those with the lowest salaries earn $28,190 or less, and those with the highest salaries earn $116,160 or more. Marketing managers with experience and higher levels of responsibility can earn annual salaries of $116,160 or more.

Additional sources of information

American Marketing Association
250 South Wacker Drive, Suite 200
Chicago, IL 60606

Sales and Marketing Executives, International
977 Statler Office Tower
Cleveland, OH 44115

MARKETING RESEARCHER

The job

Marketing researchers plan and design research projects, conduct interviews and other fact-gathering operations, and tabulate and analyze the resulting material.

The information a marketing researcher provides may help a company to decide on brand names, product and packaging design, business locations, and the type of advertising to use.

A *marketing research director* designs a research project after studying a company's sales records, its competitors, and the consumer market that uses the type of product or service the company offers. He or she then assigns members of the marketing research staff to implement the project.

A *statistician* determines a sample group of consumers to be studied. A *senior analyst* or *project director* might design a questionnaire or a mail or telephone survey for field interviewers to use. *Coders* and *tabulators* synthesize the results, which are reviewed by a *research analyst*, who studies the results and makes recommendations based on the findings.

Advertising researchers specialize in studying the effects of advertising. They pretest commercials, test-market new products, and analyze the appropriateness of the various media (radio, television, newspapers, magazines, or direct mail) for a particular product or advertiser. Beginners in this field start by coding and tabulating data. They move on to interviewing and writing reports and may move up to jobs as research assistants as they gain experience.

Many opportunities for part-time work exist in marketing research. Coding, tabulating, interviewing, and making telephone surveys are jobs for which research organizations often hire people who can work odd hours or during peak workloads. High school and college students and homemakers will find this a good field for summer jobs or for weekend or evening work.

Related jobs are advertising account executive, advertising manager, advertising worker, mathematician, statistician, and psychologist.

Places of employment and working conditions

Most market researchers are employed by manufacturers, advertising agencies, and market research firms. The largest corporations are in Chicago and New York City, but job opportunities exist in almost every large city.

The usual workweek is 40 hours, but assignments for conducting interviews and surveys are likely to require evening and weekend work. Market researchers often work under pressure and may be called on to work overtime to meet deadlines. Although this is basically an office job, travel is often a necessary part of the package in the information-gathering stages. The travel may be local or far afield, depending on the scope and design of the research project.

Qualifications, education, and training

Assertiveness, analyzing skills, and communication skills are paramount.

High school courses should include English, mathematics, and public speaking. Summer or part-time jobs coding or taking surveys are useful experience.

A college degree is required for just about all of the full-time jobs in marketing research. A bachelor's degree in liberal arts, business administration, marketing, economics, or mathematics is necessary for most trainee positions. Courses in English, marketing, economics, statistics, psychology, sociology, and political science should be included. A knowledge of data processing is also important, as the use of computers for sales forecasting, distribution, and cost analysis is standard.

Advanced degrees are becoming requisite for jobs beyond the entry level and for promotion. Job applicants with a combination background—for example, a bachelor's degree in statistics and a master's degree in marketing or business administration—have a good chance of being hired at the management level right out of college. Industrial marketing firms prefer a bachelor's degree in a related field, such as engineering, plus a master's degree in a marketing-related field.

Potential and advancement

Job opportunities will be steady in this profession, with most opportunities created by replacement needs. People with advanced degrees in marketing and an understanding of statistics and marketing will be the most in demand.

Promotion is slower in this field than in most others requiring similar training; the pay scale for beginners, however, is better than that in many other fields. Once a marketing research worker attains the research assistant level, promotion is possible to junior analyst, and then to senior analyst or project director. Top jobs, such as marketing research director, are few and require many years of experience plus solid management skills.

Many experienced marketing researchers go into business for themselves, doing independent marketing surveys or acting as marketing consultants.

Income

Experienced analysts earn an average of about $48,330 a year. Those with the most experience and responsibility can earn $94,810 or more.

Additional sources of information

American Marketing Association
250 South Wacker Drive, Suite 200
Chicago, IL 60606

Marketing Research Association
1344 Silas Deane Highway, Suite 306
Rocky Hill, CT 06067-0230
www.mra-net.org

MATHEMATICIAN

The job

The work of mathematicians falls into two sometimes overlapping categories: applied and theoretical mathematics.

Theoretical, or pure, mathematicians develop new principles and seek new relationships among existing principles of mathematics. This basic knowledge is the foundation for much of the work in the second category, applied mathematics. In this area, mathematical theories are used to develop theories and techniques for solving practical problems in business, government, and the natural and social sciences. Mathematicians may work in the field of statistics as well as in actuarial jobs, computer programming, economics, or systems analysis.

Many mathematicians, usually theoretical mathematicians, work in colleges, where they teach or do research. Mathematicians serve in the private sector in the aerospace, communications, machinery, and electrical equipment industries. The Department of Defense and National Aeronautics and Space Administration employ most of those who work for the federal government.

Related jobs are economist, marketing researcher, statistician, and actuary.

Places of employment and working conditions

Mathematicians work in government agencies, private firms, and as faculty members at colleges and universities. Some mathematicians work alone, and some are members of research teams.

While those working for government agencies and private firms usually have structured work schedules, they may need to accommodate their schedules to deadlines, work overtime, and travel to seminars or conferences. College faculty have more flexible schedules, with their time devoted to teaching, research, consulting, and administrative responsibilities.

Qualifications, education, and training

Mathematicians need good reasoning ability and persistence in solving problems. In applied mathematics especially, they should be able to communicate effectively with nonmathematicians in the discussion and solution of practical problems.

A prospective mathematician should take as many mathematics courses as possible while still in high school and should obtain a bachelor's degree that includes courses in analytical geometry, calculus, differential equations, probability and statistics, mathematics analysis, and modern algebra.

Most positions in research or in university teaching require an advanced degree, frequently a Ph.D. Private industry also prefers candidates with advanced degrees. The federal government requires a bachelor's degree.

For work in applied mathematics, a background in a specialty field such as engineering, economics, or statistics is necessary. This can be accomplished by including a minor in one of these fields while in college. In modern industry, knowledge of computer programming is essential to solving complex problems.

Nearly 240 colleges and universities offer a master's-degree program in mathematics, and about 200 also offer a Ph.D. program. Candidates for graduate degrees in mathematics concentrate on a specific field such as algebra, geometry, or mathematical analysis and conduct research in addition to taking advanced courses.

Potential and advancement

There are nearly 34,000 mathematicians in the United States, and about 20,000 of those hold mathematics faculty positions in colleges and universities.

Employment of mathematicians is expected to decline through 2008, with the best opportunities for those with additional training in a related field such as statistics or computer science. Holders of a doctorate in applied mathematics will be in greater demand in industry than those who specialize in theoretical mathematics.

Mathematicians with a master's degree will face competition for research and teaching jobs, but there will be many opportunities in applied mathematics fields. Holders of a bachelor's degree with some experience in computer science will have good opportunities in computerized data processing activities. Those who fulfill the necessary requirements may become high school mathematics teachers.

Income

Average annual salaries for mathematicians start at $37,300 for those with a bachelor's degree, $42,000 for holders of a master's degree, and $58,900 for Ph.D.s, depending on the employer.

College and university teachers are paid at the same rate as other faculty members; salaries tend to be lower than in private industry or government.

Additional sources of information

American Mathematical Society
Department of Professional Programs and Services
P.O. Box 6248
Providence, RI 02940-6248
www.ams.org

Mathematical Association of America
1529 18th Street NW
Washington, DC 20036
www.maa.org

Society for Industrial and Applied Mathematics
3600 University City Science Center
Philadelphia, PA 19104-2688
www.siam.org/alterindex.htm

MECHANICAL ENGINEER

The job

The production, transmission, and use of power is the concern of mechanical engineers. They design and develop power-producing machines such as internal combustion engines and rocket engines and power-using machines such as refrigeration systems, printing presses, and steel-rolling mills.

The specific work of mechanical engineers varies greatly from industry to industry because of the wide range of possible applications of their skills and training; many specialties within the field have developed as a result. These include motor vehicles, energy conversion systems, heating, and machines for specialized industries, to name a few. Many mechanical engineers are involved in research and testing, while others work mainly in production and maintenance. Some use their training as a background for technical sales.

Nearly three-fifths of all mechanical engineers are employed in manufacturing, mainly in the electrical equipment, transportation equipment, primary and fabricated metals, and machinery industries. Others work for engineering consulting firms, government agencies, and educational institutions.

Places of employment and working conditions

Mechanical engineers work in all parts of the country, with the heaviest concentrations in industrialized areas.

Qualifications, education, and training

The ability to think analytically, a capacity for details, and the ability to work as part of a team are necessary. Good communication skills are also important.

Mathematics and the sciences must be emphasized in high school.

A bachelor's degree in engineering is the minimum requirement in this field. In a typical curriculum, the first two years are spent in the study of basic sciences such as physics and chemistry, mathematics, introductory engineering, and some liberal arts courses. The remaining years are usually devoted to specialized engineering courses.

Engineering programs can last from four to six years. Those that require five or six years to complete may award a master's degree or may provide a cooperative plan of study plus practical work experience in a nearby industry.

Because of rapid changes in technology, many engineers continue their education throughout their careers. A graduate degree is necessary for most teaching and research positions and for many management jobs. Some specialties such as nuclear engineering are taught only at the graduate level. Some persons obtain graduate degrees in business administration.

Engineering graduates usually work under the supervision of an experienced engineer or in a company training program until they become acquainted with the requirements of a particular company or industry.

All states require licensing of engineers whose work may affect life, health, or property or who offer their services to the public. Those who are licensed are called registered engineers. Requirements for licensing include graduation from an accredited engineering school, four years of experience, and passing a written examination.

Potential and advancement

Nationwide, there are about 220,000 mechanical engineers. The projected average demand for mechanical engineers—as a result of growth in the industrial machinery and machine tools field—means sufficient job opportunities in this field through 2008.

Income

Starting annual salaries in private industry average $43,300 for mechanical engineers with a bachelor's degree, $51,900 for those with a master's degree, and $64,300 for those with a Ph.D.

Experienced engineers average $53,290 a year in private industry.

Additional sources of information

Accreditation Board for Engineering and Technology
111 Market Place, Suite 1050
Baltimore, MD 21202-4012
www.abet.org

American Society of Mechanical Engineers
Three Park Avenue
New York, NY 10016
www.asme.org

Junior Engineering Technical Society
1420 King Street, Suite 405
Alexandria, VA 22314-2794
www.jets.org

National Society of Professional Engineers
1420 King Street
Alexandria, VA 22314-2794
www.nspe.org

Society of Women Engineers
120 Wall Street, 11th Floor
New York, NY 10005
www.swe.org

MEDICAL ASSISTANT

The job

Medical assistants perform administrative tasks and work with patients, helping doctors keep their practices running efficiently.

Medical assistants' duties vary from office to office and depend on the size of the medical practice. In smaller practices, they have a wider range of responsibilities, often performing both administrative and clinical tasks. In larger practices, they may specialize in a particular area.

Laws regarding the procedures that medical assistants are permitted to perform vary from state to state, but the more common clinical tasks they are allowed to perform include taking and recording medical histories and vital signs, explaining treatments to patients, preparing patients for examination, and assisting in examinations.

After an examination, medical assistants may collect laboratory specimens and perform basic laboratory tests, dispose of contaminated supplies, and sterilize instruments.

The administrative duties that medical assistants often perform include answering telephones, greeting patients, recording and filing medical records, filling out insurance forms, scheduling appointments, arranging for hospital admission and laboratory tests, and taking care of billing and bookkeeping.

Some medical assistants specialize in a certain branch of medicine such as podiatry or ophthalmology.

Places of employment and working conditions

Most medical assistants work in doctors' offices; some work in the offices of optometrists, podiatrists, and chiropractors. Others work in hospitals.

Medical assistants usually have a 40-hour workweek, which may include some weekend and evening hours.

Qualifications, education, and training

Medical assistants spend a large amount of time working with people, so they must be neat, pleasant, and courteous. They must be able to follow doctors' instructions closely and also listen to and understand patients' needs.

There are no specific education requirements for medical assistants, and some still receive their training on the job. However, formal programs in medical assisting are offered at the secondary and postsecondary levels in technical high schools, vocational schools, community and junior colleges, and universities. Most doctors now prefer to hire medical assistants with formal training.

Two agencies accredit medical assisting programs: the Commission on Accreditation of Allied Health Education Programs and the Accrediting Bureau of Health Education Schools. These programs usually include course work in biological sciences, medical terminology, typing, transcription, record keeping, accounting, insurance processing, and computer science.

There are no general licensing requirements for medical assistants, but some states require passing a test or completing a course for assistants who perform certain procedures such as taking x-rays, drawing blood, or giving injections.

Several associations certify or register medical assistants who meet their requirements. Employers often prefer to hire people who are certified and have experience.

Potential and advancement

There are about 252,000 medical assistants in the United States. Job opportunities should be good through 2008 due to the increasing demands for medical care.

Opportunities will be excellent for candidates with formal training, experience, or both. Those who are certified and have computer and word processing skills will have even greater advantages when seeking employment.

Medical assistants may advance by becoming office managers. They also may become consultants for medical office management or for the medical insurance industry. Some work for hospitals as ward clerks, medical record clerks, phlebotomists, and electrocardiogram technicians. Others get further education and become nurses or work in some field of medical technology.

Income

Earnings for medical assistants vary widely and depend on the individual's credentials and level of experience, the size and location of the employer, and the number of hours worked. Experienced medical assistants generally earn between $17,020 and $24,340 a year.

Additional sources of information

American Association of Medical Assistants
20 North Wacker Drive, Suite 1575
Chicago, IL 60606-2903
www.aama-ntl.org

Registered Medical Assistants of American Medical
  Technologists
710 Higgins Road
Park Ridge, IL 60068-5765
www.amt1.com

MEDICAL LABORATORY TECHNOLOGIST

The job

Medical laboratory work often appeals to people who would like a career in the medical field but who are not necessarily interested in direct care of patients. Technologists and other workers in medical laboratories are involved in the analysis of blood, tissue samples, and body fluids. They use precision instruments, equipment, chemicals, and other materials to detect and diagnose diseases. In some instances, such as blood testing, they also gather the specimens to be analyzed.

Medical laboratory technologists work under the direction of a pathologist (a physician who specializes in the causes and nature of disease) or another physician or scientist who specializes in clinical chemistry, microbiology, or other biological sciences.

Medical technologists, who have four years of training, usually perform a wide variety of tests in small laboratories; those in large laboratories usually specialize in a single area such as parasitology, blood banking, or hematology (study of blood cells). Some do research, develop laboratory techniques, or perform supervisory and administrative duties.

Medical laboratory technicians, who have two years of training, have much the same testing duties but do not have the same in-depth knowledge that technologists have. Technicians may also specialize in a particular field but are not usually involved in administrative work.

Medical laboratory assistants have about one year of formal training. They assist the technologist and technicians in some routine tests and are generally responsible for the care and sterilization of laboratory equipment, including glassware and instruments, and do some record keeping.

Most technologists, technicians, and laboratory assistants work in hospital laboratories. Others work in physicians' offices, independent laboratories, blood banks, public health agencies and clinics, pharmaceutical firms, and research institutions. The federal government employs them in the U.S. Public Health Service, the armed forces, and the Department of Veterans Affairs.

Places of employment and working conditions

Work in this field is available in all areas of the country, with the largest concentrations in major cities.

Medical laboratory personnel work a 40-hour week, with night and weekend shifts if they are employed in a hospital. Laboratories are usually clean and well lighted and contain a variety of testing equipment and materials. Although unpleasant odors are sometimes present and the work involves the processing of specimens of many kinds of diseased tissue, few hazards exist because of careful attention to safety and sterilization procedures.

Qualifications, education, and training

A strong interest in science and the medical field is essential. Manual dexterity, good eyesight, and normal color vision are likewise necessary. Aspirants must also show attention to detail, accuracy, the ability to work under pressure, and a sense of responsibility for their work.

High school students interested in this field should take courses in science and mathematics and should select a training program carefully.

Medical technologists must have a college degree with a major in medical technology or one of the life sciences. Technologists who perform complex tests must have at least an associate degree. Most technologists have a bachelor's degree. Some have a combination of work experience and specialized training.

Technicians may receive training in two-year educational programs in junior colleges, in two-year courses at four-year colleges and universities, in vocational and technical schools, or in the armed forces.

Medical laboratory assistants usually receive on-the-job training. Some hospitals—and junior colleges and vocational schools in conjunction with hospitals—also conduct one-year training programs, some of which are accredited by the Accrediting Bureau of Health Education Schools. A high school diploma or equivalency diploma is necessary.

Medical technologists may be certified by the Board of Registry of the American Society of Clinical Pathologists, American Medical Technologists, the National Certification Agency for Medical Laboratory Personnel, or the Credentialing Commission of the International Society of Clinical Laboratory Technology. These same organizations also certify technicians.

Some states require technologists and technicians to be licensed. This usually takes the form of a written examination. Other states often require registration.

Potential and advancement

There are about 313,000 persons employed as medical laboratory workers. Medical laboratory technologists will find an average number of job opportunities through 2008. Population growth and improvements in diagnostics will increase the amount of testing. However, simpler tests and better automation will limit the number of technologists required to support this new workload. Job opportunities will probably be slightly better for technicians and assistants because the increasing use of automated lab equipment will allow them to perform tests that previously required technologists. Technologists will be needed for supervisory and administrative positions, however, and will continue to be in demand in laboratories where their level of training is required by state regulations or employer preference.

Advancement depends on education and experience. Assistants can advance to the position of technician or technologist by completing the required education; technicians can advance to supervisory positions or complete the required education to become technologists. Advancement to administrative positions is usually limited to technologists.

Income

Salaries in this field vary with the employer and geographic location; the highest salaries are paid in the larger cities. Medical technologists earn between $24,970 and $39,810. The median salary is about $32,440.

Additional sources of information

Accrediting Bureau of Health Education Schools
803 West Broad Street, Suite 730
Falls Church, VA 22046
www.abhes.org

American Medical Technologists
710 Higgins Road
Park Ridge, IL 60068
www.amt1.com

American Society for Clinical Laboratory Science
7910 Woodmont Avenue, Suite 530
Bethesda, MD 20814

American Society of Clinical Pathologists
Board of Registry
P.O. Box 12277
Chicago, IL 60612
www.ascp.org/bor

International Society for Clinical Laboratory Technology
917 Locust Street, Suite 1100
St. Louis, MO 63101-1413

MEDICAL RECORD TECHNICIAN

The job

Medical record technicians are responsible for keeping an accurate, permanent file on patients treated by doctors and hospitals.

When patients are undergoing treatment, doctors and hospitals keep records of the patient's medical history, results of physical exams, x-ray and lab test reports, diagnosis and treatments, and doctors' and nurses' notes. Also included is information about patients' symptoms, the tests undergone, and the response to treatment.

Medical record technicians assemble, organize, and check the completeness and accuracy of these records. Usually, doctors and nurses record their information and observations on computer, and medical record technicians must retrieve the data.

After medical record technicians have gathered all of the information, they consult classification manuals and assign codes to the diagnoses and procedures included in the record. They then assign the patient to a diagnosis-related group (DRG), which determines the amount the hospital will be reimbursed if the patient is covered by Medicare or other insurance programs that use the DRG system.

The medical records that technicians keep provide vital clinical information that helps in treatment, research, and training of medical personnel. Medical records also are important for documentation in the case of legal actions and for insurance claims and Medicare reimbursement.

Medical record technicians sometimes analyze data and provide statistics that help hospital administrators and planners keep the hospital running efficiently.

Medical record technicians also sometimes collect and interpret medical records for law firms, insurance companies, government agencies, researchers, and patients.

Qualifications, education, and training

Medical record technicians who have earned the credential *accredited record technician* are generally preferred by employers. To become accredited, applicants must pass a written examination given by the American Health Information Management Association (AHIMA). The requirement for taking the test is the completion of a two-year associate-degree program accredited by the Commission on Accreditation of Allied Health Education Programs in collaboration with AHIMA.

Medical record technician programs include course work in biological sciences, medical terminology, medical record science, business management, governing laws, and basic computer data processing.

Potential and advancement

There are about 92,000 medical record technicians, and opportunities through 2008 should be excellent for candidates who have completed a formal training program primarily because of the importance of this function in managing health care costs.

The three major routes of advancement for medical record technicians are teaching, managing, and specializing. Experienced technicians who have a master's degree in a related field sometimes go into teaching. They can also advance into the management of a medical record department or into a specialty such as Medicare coding or tumor registry.

Income

Medical record technicians earn an annual median salary of $30,500 in the private sector and about $27,500 working for the federal government.

Additional source of information

American Health Information Management Association
233 North Michigan Avenue, Suite 2150
Chicago, IL 60601
www.ahima.org

MEDICAL SECRETARY

The job

Secretaries are the center of communication in an office. The duties they perform keep offices running efficiently. Medical secretaries are specialized secretaries who are employed by physicians or medical scientists.

Medical secretaries transcribe dictation, type letters, and help doctors or medical scientists prepare reports, speeches, and articles.

They also have responsibilities similar to those of other secretaries. They take shorthand, greet visitors, keep track of appointments, make travel arrangements, and manage the employer's paperwork.

Places of employment and working conditions

Medical secretaries are employed throughout the country in physicians' offices, hospitals, and health agencies.

Working conditions vary, but full-time medical secretaries usually work a 37- to 40-hour week.

Qualifications, education, and training

Medical secretaries must be accurate and neat. They must display discretion and initiative and have a good command of spelling, grammar, punctuation, and vocabulary. They need to know medical terms and be familiar with hospital or laboratory procedures. Strong computer skills are also required.

High school business courses are valuable and so are college preparatory courses because secretaries should have a good general background. Aspiring medical secretaries should take as many English courses as possible.

Secretarial training as part of a college education or at a private business school is preferred by many employers. Training for specialty areas such as medicine can take a year or two.

Well-trained and highly experienced secretaries may qualify for the designation *certified professional secretary* (CPS) by passing a series of examinations given by the Institute for Certifying Secretaries, a division of Professional Secretaries International. This mark of achievement in the secretarial field is recognized by many employers.

Potential and advancement

There are 219,000 medical secretaries in the country. The demand for well-qualified medical secretaries will continue to grow as the demand for medical services increases. Job opportunities should be good through 2008.

Opportunities for advancement depend on the acquisition of new or improved skills and on increasing knowledge of the medical field. Some medical secretaries may become administrative assistants or office managers.

Income

Salaries for medical secretaries vary greatly and depend on the individual's level of skill, experience, and responsibility; the area of the country; and the type of employer.

The average annual salary for medical secretaries is $22,390, with a range from $18,700 to $29,400. Salaries tend to be lowest in the South and higher in northern and western cities.

Additional source of information

Professional Secretaries International
1502 Northwest Ambassador Drive
P.O. Box 20404
Kansas City, MO 64195-0404

METALLURGICAL ENGINEER

The job

Metallurgical engineers develop methods to process and convert metals into usable forms. Other scientists who work in this field are called *metallurgists* or *materials scientists*, but the distinction between scientist and engineer in this field is so small as to be almost nonexistent.

There are three main branches of metallurgy: extractive or chemical, physical, and mechanical. *Extractive metallurgists* are engaged in the processes for extracting metals from ore, refining, and alloying. *Physical metallurgists* work with the nature, structure, and physical properties of metals and alloys to develop methods for converting them into final products. *Mechanical metallurgists* develop methods to work and shape metals. These include casting, forging, rolling, and drawing.

Most metallurgical engineers are employed by the metalworking industries— iron, steel, and nonferrous metals—where they are responsible for specifying, controlling, and testing the quality of the metals during manufacture. Others work in industries that manufacture machinery, electrical equipment, and aircraft and aircraft parts, as well as in mining. Some work in federal agencies such as the Bureau of Mines.

The development of new, lightweight metals for use in communications equipment, computers, and spacecraft is a growing field for metallurgical engineers, as are the processing and recycling of industrial waste and the processing of low-grade ores. Problems associated with the use of nuclear energy will also require the expertise of metallurgists and metallurgical engineers.

Places of employment and working conditions

The work settings of metallurgical engineers vary from laboratories to smelting and mining locations to factory production lines. Some of these operations are located in remote areas.

Qualifications, education, and training

The ability to think analytically, a capacity for details, and the ability to work as part of a team are necessary. Good communication skills are also important.

Mathematics and the sciences must be emphasized in high school.

A bachelor's degree in engineering is the minimum requirement in this field. In a typical curriculum, the first two years are spent in the study of basic sciences such as physics and chemistry, mathematics, introductory engineering, and some liberal arts courses. The remaining years are usually devoted to specialized engineering courses.

Engineering programs can last from four to six years. Those requiring five or six years to complete may award a master's degree or may provide a cooperative plan of study plus practical work experience in a nearby industry.

Because of rapid changes in technology, many engineers continue their education throughout their careers. A graduate degree is necessary for most teaching and research positions and for many management jobs. Some specialties are taught only at the graduate level. Some persons obtain graduate degrees in business administration.

Engineering graduates usually work under the supervision of an experienced engineer or in a company training program until they become acquainted with the requirements of a particular company or industry.

All states require licensing of engineers whose work may affect life, health, or property or who offer their services to the public. Those who are licensed are called registered engineers. Requirements for licensing include graduation from an accredited engineering school, four years of experience, and passing a written examination.

Potential and advancement

Slow growth is expected in this field through 2008, but research and testing services, along with engineering and architectural firms, should provide some openings as they design new materials for their industrial customers.

Income

Starting annual salaries in private industry average $43,100 for metallurgical engineers with a bachelor's degree and $49,900 for those with a master's degree.

Experienced engineers average $52,610 a year in private industry.

Additional sources of information

Accreditation Board for Engineering and Technology
111 Market Place, Suite 1050
Baltimore, MD 21202-4012
www.abet.org

ASM International
Student Outreach Program
Materials Park, OH 44073-0002
www.asm-intl.org

Junior Engineering Technical Society
1420 King Street, Suite 405
Alexandria, VA 22314-2794
www.jets.org

Minerals, Metals, and Materials Society
420 Commonwealth Drive
Warrendale, PA 15086-7514

National Society of Professional Engineers
1420 King Street
Alexandria, VA 22314-2794
www.nspe.org

Society of Women Engineers
120 Wall Street, 11th Floor
New York, NY 10005
www.swe.org

METEOROLOGIST

The job

The study of the atmosphere—its physical characteristics, motions, and processes—is the work of meteorologists. Although the best-known application of
this study is in weather forecasting, meteorologists are also engaged in research
and problem solving in the fields of air pollution, transportation, agriculture, and
industrial operations.

Physical meteorologists study the chemical and electrical properties of the
atmosphere as they affect the formation of clouds, rain, and snow. *Climatologists*
analyze past data on wind, rainfall, and temperature to determine weather patterns for a given area; this work is important in designing buildings and in planning effective land use. *Operational* or *synoptic meteorologists* study current

weather information, such as temperature, humidity, air pressure, and wind velocity, in order to make short- and long-range forecasts.

The largest single employer of civilian meteorologists is the National Oceanic and Atmospheric Administration, which employs about 2,600 meteorologists at stations in all parts of the United States.

Some meteorologists work for private industry, including airlines, weather consulting firms, manufacturers of meteorological instruments, radio and television stations, and the aerospace industry.

Colleges and universities employ meteorologists in teaching and research.

Related jobs are geologist, geophysicist, and oceanographer.

Places of employment and working conditions

Meteorologists work in all areas of the United States.

Because they continue around the clock, seven days a week, jobs in weather stations entail night and weekend shifts. Some stations are at remote locations and may require the meteorologist to work alone.

Qualifications, education, and training

Curiosity, analytical thinking, and attention to detail are necessary qualities for a meteorologist.

High school should include as many science, mathematics, and computer courses as possible.

A bachelor's degree with a major in meteorology or a related field is the minimum requirement for entry-level jobs. The federal government requires a bachelor's degree with 24 semester hours of meteorology, 6 hours of physics, 6 hours of analysis and prediction of weather systems, 2 hours of remote sensing, and course work in calculus, computer science, and physical science. Teaching positions, research, and many jobs in private industry require advanced degrees.

Potential and advancement

In the United States, there are about 8,400 civilian meteorologists as well as thousands of members of the armed forces who do forecasting and meteorological work. Although average growth is expected in this field through 2008, meteorologists will face competition for jobs. The National Weather Service recently completed extensive modernization of its equipment and has reduced hiring. Likewise, few new positions are expected in other areas of the federal government. However, some new jobs will be created in private industry as media, agricultural, and transportation firms begin to make greater use of private weather forecasting and meteorological services.

Meteorologists with advanced degrees and experience can achieve supervisory and administrative positions, or start their own weather consulting services.

Income

The federal government pays average starting salaries of $20,600 or $25,500 a year, depending on college grades, to meteorologists with a bachelor's degree. Rates are $25,500 or $31,200 for those with a master's and $37,700 to $45,200 for those with a Ph.D.

The average annual salary for experienced meteorologists employed by the federal government is $62,500.

Average entry-level salaries of those in the private sector are between $38,570 and $75,260, depending on responsibilities and experience.

Additional sources of information

American Geophysical Union
2000 Florida Avenue NW
Washington, DC 20009
www.agu.org

American Meteorological Society
45 Beacon Street
Boston, MA 02108
www.ametsoc.org/AMS

MINING ENGINEER

The job

Mining engineers frequently specialize in a specific mineral such as coal or copper. They find, extract, and prepare minerals for manufacturing use.

Some mining engineers work with geologists and metallurgical engineers to locate and appraise new ore deposits. Others design and supervise construction of open-pit and underground mines, including mine shafts and tunnels, or design methods for transporting minerals to processing plants.

Mining engineers engaged in the day-to-day operations of a mine are responsible for mine safety, ventilation, water supply, power and communication, and equipment maintenance. Direction of mineral processing operations, which requires separating the usable ore from dirt, rocks, and other materials, is also usually the responsibility of a mining engineer.

Some mining engineers specialize in the design and development of new mining equipment. An increasing number work on the reclamation of mined land and on air and water pollution problems related to mining.

Most mining engineers work in the mining industry. Others work for mining equipment manufacturers or as independent consultants. Federal and state agencies also employ mining engineers on regulatory bodies and as inspectors.

Places of employment and working conditions

Most mining engineers work at the location of the mine, usually near small communities in rural areas. Many find employment opportunities overseas.

The work can be hazardous because some time is usually spent underground.

Qualifications, education, and training

The ability to think analytically, a capacity for detail, and the ability to work as part of a team are necessary. Good communication skills are also important.

Mathematics and the sciences must be emphasized in high school.

A bachelor's degree in engineering is the minimum requirement in this field. In a typical curriculum, the first two years are spent in the study of basic sciences such as physics and chemistry, mathematics, introductory engineering, and some liberal arts courses. The remaining years are usually devoted to specialized engineering courses.

Engineering programs can last from four to six years. Those that require five or six years to complete may award a master's degree or may provide a cooperative plan of study plus practical work experience with a nearby industry.

Because of rapid changes in technology, many engineers continue their education throughout their careers. A graduate degree is necessary for most teaching and research positions and for many management jobs. Some persons obtain graduate degrees in business administration.

Engineering graduates usually work under the supervision of an experienced engineer or in a company training program until they become acquainted with the requirements of a particular company or industry.

All states require licensing of engineers whose work may affect life, health, or property or who offer their services to the public. Those who are licensed are called registered engineers. Requirements include graduation from an accredited engineering school, four years of experience, and passing a written examination.

Potential and advancement

There are about 4,400 mining engineers. Employment opportunities will not be good through 2008 because of the low demand for coal, metals, and other minerals. However, if these commodities should come into demand because of the lack of availability and high price of other energy sources, employment opportunities will improve. Other factors that may bring about job growth include technological advancements, enforcement of mine health and safety regulations, more efficient methods of mining and processing ores, and a demand for less widely used ores. Job opportunities may be better abroad than within the United States.

Income

Starting annual salaries in private industry average $39,600 for those with a bachelor's degree. Experienced mining engineers earn an average of $56,090.

Additional sources of information

Accreditation Board for Engineering and Technology
111 Market Place, Suite 1050
Baltimore, MD 21202-4012
www.abet.org

Junior Engineering Technical Society
1420 King Street, Suite 405
Alexandria, VA 22314-2794
www.jets.org

National Society of Professional Engineers
1420 King Street
Alexandria, VA 22314-2794
www.nspe.org

MINISTER (PROTESTANT)

The job

Protestant ministers lead their congregations in worship services and administer the rites of baptism and holy communion. They perform marriages, conduct funerals, visit people who are sick, and counsel members of the congregation who seek guidance. Ministers are also usually involved in community activities.

The exact services provided by ministers differ among denominations. The greatest number of ministers are affiliated with the five largest denominations: Baptist, United Methodist, Lutheran, Presbyterian, and Episcopal. Some serve small congregations, for which they provide all services; ministers of large congregations usually have one or more assistants who share duties.

Many ministers serve as chaplains in the armed forces, hospitals, prisons, or colleges and universities. Others teach in seminaries.

Some denominations are now allowing women to enter the ministry, but other denominations and some congregations continue to oppose this practice, so women interested in becoming ministers should seek the counsel of clergy in the denomination of their choice.

Places of employment and working conditions

Ministers work in communities of all sizes. Larger communities may support more than one congregation of a particular denomination. Working hours can be long and are often irregular. Some ministers lead more than one congregation, especially in rural areas, and may spend considerable time in travel.

Qualifications, education, and training

The most important quality for anyone considering the ministry as a calling is a deep religious faith. A minister must also be a model of moral and ethical conduct.

Educational requirements vary, depending on denomination. Some denominations have no formal educational requirements, but many stipulate at least a bachelor's. Often, the requirement is a doctor of ministry degree, which involves two or three years of study following college.

Potential and advancement

About 400,000 ministers serve Protestants in the United States. Limited growth is expected in this field through 2008 because of the limited growth of church membership and the high number of qualified candidates. Employment opportunities will vary among denominations and geographic regions. Most openings will occur to replace personnel who retire or leave the ministry. Those who are willing to work in rural areas or for small congregations will find the greatest number of openings.

Income

Earnings vary widely, depending on the size and location of the congregation. Some congregations base pay on the average pay in the community. Additional benefits, such as cars and housing, are often included.

Additional sources of information

Anyone interested in becoming a minister should seek the counsel of a minister within the denomination of his or her choice. Theological schools can provide information on admission requirements.

MODEL

The job

Models demonstrate and sell a wide variety of goods and services. They display clothes for local fashion shows as well as for high-fashion magazines, those working in television commercials sell everything from toothpaste to home appliances, and photographers and artists often employ models in the course of their projects. Models usually specialize in live or photographic work.

Photographic models are usually hired for an individual assignment. Most model clothes or cosmetics, but they also promote many other products. In addition to posing for still photography, models may appear in television commercials, especially if they have some acting ability or training.

Live modeling encompasses various specialty areas. *Fashion models* usually work before an audience, modeling the creations of a well-known designer at fashion shows. *Showroom* or *fitting models* work in the manufacturer's or distributor's display room, where they model the employer's products for prospective retail buyers and work with designers during the fitting stages of new designs.

Informal models work in local department stores and custom shops, at manufacturers' trade shows and exhibits to demonstrate products, and for artists and art schools.

Most models contract with a modeling agency to help ensure a continuous flow of assignments.

Places of employment and working conditions

Some modeling jobs are available in almost every community, but Chicago, Detroit, Los Angeles, and especially New York City provide the largest number of assignments. New York City's garment district has hundreds of clothing manufacturers, designers, and wholesalers who employ permanent models to display their products. These models must usually meet certain standard physical requirements because sample clothes must fit the person without alteration. For women, this means a height of 5 feet 7 inches to 5 feet 9½ inches and a weight of 110 to 122 pounds. Male models must be 6 feet tall and wear a size-40 suit. Specialty lines, such as teenage clothes or styles for mature women, may have other requirements.

Photographic models must be thinner than other models because the camera adds at least 10 pounds to a model's appearance.

Qualifications, education, and training

Distinctive and attractive physical appearance, good health, physical stamina, the ability to withstand the pace and pressure of the field, and competitiveness are all necessary for a successful model.

There are no educational requirements for a model, but any training in acting, dancing, art, or fashion design is valuable.

Modeling schools in many communities offer instruction in basics such as proper posture, hairstyling and makeup, and how to pose in front of a camera, but these schools do not provide job assignments. Some modeling agencies also provide training.

Potential and advancement

There are always many more applicants than jobs in this glamorous field. Because most assignments go to experienced professionals, aspiring models should get as much local experience as possible before trying for a job in the larger cities or agencies.

Modeling can be a stepping-stone to many other careers in the fashion world. Fashion magazines, cosmetic firms, and department stores often hire former models for a variety of positions. Some models go into acting.

Income

A few top models earn as much as $500,000 a year, but most earn considerably less.

Models who register with an agency pay the agency a commission for each new assignment they receive. Steadily employed models can expect to earn $42,800 or more a year.

Additional sources of information

Fashion Group
Nine Rockefeller Plaza, 17th Floor
New York, NY 10020

Federation of Apparel Manufacturers
450 Seventh Avenue
New York, NY 10001

MUSEUM CURATOR

The job

A museum curator is in charge of a museum or a museum department. The curator is responsible for planning exhibits; acquisition of material within budgetary limitations; development, care, and classification of collections; and laboratory research and field studies, including museum-sponsored expeditions.

There are thousands of museums of various sizes in the United States. They are maintained by the federal government, state and local governments, nonprofit corporations, colleges and universities, business groups and industries, and private individuals and societies.

Some curators are employed by historical museums. These museums may specialize in the artifacts and memorabilia of a particular period in history; a specific area, industry, or group of people; a single person, such as a president; a sport; or an item, such as toys. They vary from small, local museums to large, world-renowned institutions.

The largest in individual size are the natural history museums. Their collections are the most widely diversified, and research and field expeditions form a major part of their programs. They employ *anthropologists* (experts in the study of humanity and its domain through the ages), *botanists* (plant-life specialists), *geologists* (scientists who study the structure and materials of the earth), and *zoologists* (specialists in all phases of animal life). Natural history museums also regularly publish materials reflecting the results of their research and field studies.

Many museum curators work for art museums, which collect and exhibit art objects of all kinds, including paintings, prints, drawings, photographs, sculpture, ceramics, jewelry, textiles, woodwork, and carvings. Some major art museums have schools of art and design.

Curators employed by outdoor museums often oversee complete towns or villages such as Williamsburg, Virginia, or zoological parks or arboretums. A uniquely American idea, the trailside museum, incorporates bird, botanical, or geological walks with animal life. The Petrified Forest in Arizona is such a museum.

A related job is historian.

Places of employment and working conditions

Curator positions exist throughout the United States, but the majority are in the major cities that have the most museums—Boston, Chicago, Los Angeles, New York City, and Washington, D.C.

Working conditions vary greatly with the size and type of museum and the specialty of the curator. Some curators work closely with the public; others work alone and spend most of their time processing records; still others may install or restore exhibits and have to climb, stretch, and lift heavy objects.

Qualifications, education, and training

Patience, a logical mind, creative imagination, physical stamina, administrative ability, interpersonal and communication skills, and computer proficiency are necessary for a museum curator. A curator is also usually a specialist in a particular field, such as art, or in a specific discipline, such as anthropology.

In high school, a college preparatory course should be pursued. If the student is already interested in a specific area of museum work, the appropriate courses such as art, history, or science should be emphasized. The study of one or more languages also should begin in high school and continue in college. French, German, Spanish, Italian, Latin, or Greek are recommended.

College courses should be related to the student's field of interest. A bachelor's degree in history, art history, fine arts, anthropology, or one of the natural sciences is the usual first step. Some colleges and universities offer a bachelor's or master's degree in museum studies.

A master's degree, and in some cases a Ph.D., is necessary for most curator positions.

Many museums, colleges, and universities offer assistantships, fellowships, internships, apprenticeships, summer programs, and certification programs. These offerings are usually part of an undergraduate or graduate curriculum, but some are open to other experienced museum employees. Some, especially summer programs, are also open to high school students.

Potential and advancement

This is a hotly competitive job field, and thousands of new graduates apply each year for the few available openings. Those with a graduate degree and some part-time or summer experience have the best chance of being offered a job.

It takes years of training and experience to achieve the level of curator. One of the drawbacks of this field is the slowness with which advancement occurs, especially in older, established museums.

Income

Salaries in the federal government average between $40,400 and $59,200 per year.

Experienced curators working for the private sector average between $23,090 and $43,840 per year.

Additional source of information

American Association of Museums
1575 I Street NW, Suite 400
Washington, DC 20005
www.aam-us.org

MUSICIAN

The job

Professional musicians play in symphony orchestras, dance bands, rock groups, and jazz combos and accompany individual performances, musical comedies, and opera performances. Others teach in music conservatories and colleges and universities or give private lessons. Many musicians combine performing careers with teaching or with arranging and composing.

A few musicians specialize in library science for work in music libraries or study psychology for work in music therapy in hospitals. The armed forces also offer career opportunities for musicians.

Musicians put in many hours of practice and rehearsal in addition to performing. Many find that they are unable to support themselves by music alone and can pursue it only as a part-time career.

Places of employment and working conditions

Musicians work throughout the country, but the best opportunities are in large metropolitan areas and in the cities where entertainment and recording activities are concentrated—New York City, Chicago, Los Angeles, Nashville, Miami, and New Orleans.

Musicians normally work evenings and weekends and usually do a lot of traveling. The work is often unsteady, and performers do not usually work for one employer for any length of time.

Qualifications, education, and training

Necessary qualities for a professional musician, in addition to musical talent, are creative ability, poise and stage presence, self-discipline, and physical stamina.

Computer skills are valuable, as more and more musicians are composing and editing music with the help of computers.

Musicians usually start studying an instrument at an early age through private lessons. Those who perform popular music gain experience by participating in amateur programs, by forming small groups or bands, and by gradually obtaining work with better-known bands as they develop a reputation. Some expand their knowledge and understanding of music through classical training.

Classical musicians study privately, in music conservatories, or in colleges and universities that have strong classical music programs. Auditions are usually required for entrance into these schools or for private lessons with the most highly regarded teachers.

Music conservatories and colleges and universities offer bachelor's-degree programs that include liberal arts courses in addition to musical training. Many schools also offer a bachelor's-degree program in music education, which qualifies graduates for state certification, required for elementary and secondary teaching positions.

College teaching positions usually require advanced degrees, except in the case of uniquely talented musicians.

Potential and advancement

Nationwide, about 273,000 musicians work as performers, with many more employed as teachers. Opportunities in this field are expected to grow at an average rate through 2008. However, competition for jobs in this field is always keen, especially for positions that offer stable employment.

Income

Music teachers earn salaries comparable to salaries of other faculty in the same school.

Earnings of musicians vary widely and depend on geographic location as well as professional reputation. Many musicians work part-time or face periods of unemployment throughout the year. Successful independent musicians can earn more than salaried musicians or music teachers.

Annual salaries for orchestra members range from $21,000 to $95,000.

Median earnings for musicians and singers are $30,020 per year.

Additional sources of information

American Federation of Musicians of the United States and
    Canada
1501 Broadway, Suite 600
New York, NY 10036

American Music Conference
5140 Avenida Encinas
Carlsbad, CA 92008-4391

Music Educators National Conference
1806 Robert Fulton Drive
Reston, VA 22091

National Association of Schools of Music
11250 Roger Bacon Drive, Suite 21
Reston, VA 22091
www.arts-accredit.org

NEWSPAPER REPORTER

The job

Newspaper reporters gather the latest news and write about it. They research stories, interview people, attend public events, and do whatever else is necessary to give a complete report of a news item. When deadlines require it, reporters may phone in their information to be transcribed by a rewriter.

General assignment reporters handle all types of news stories; other reporters are assigned to a "beat," such as police stations, the courts, or sports. Reporters with specialized backgrounds may be assigned to write about and analyze the news in such fields as medicine, politics, labor, or education.

On small newspapers, reporters often take their own photographs, do some layout or editorial work, solicit subscriptions and advertising, and perform some general office duties.

Some reporters work for national news services, where they are usually assigned to a large city or to a particular specialty. *Stringers* work part-time for one or more employers and are paid according to how much of their work is published.

Beginning reporters usually work for small daily or weekly newspapers, where they function as general assignment reporters or copyeditors. As they gain experience, they cover more substantial news.

A related job is newspaper and magazine editor.

Places of employment and working conditions

Newspaper reporters work in communities of all sizes. Although the majority of newspapers are in medium-size towns, most reporters work in cities where each daily newspaper employs many reporters.

Reporters generally work a five-day, 35- to 40-hour week. On morning newspapers, the working hours are from late afternoon to midnight. Coverage of certain news events sometimes requires extended or irregular working hours, and a fast pace and constant deadline pressures are a part of every reporter's working life. Reporters can be placed in dangerous situations: covering crimes, political unrest, and natural disasters.

Qualifications, education, and training

Writing skills, curiosity, resourcefulness, an accurate memory, stamina, and the ability to work alone are essential.

High school should include as many English courses as possible, as well as keyboarding, social sciences, and experience on school publications. Knowledge of desktop publishing, computer graphics, and photography is also important. Summer or part-time jobs on local newspapers can provide valuable experience.

Most newspapers require a news reporter to have a bachelor's degree in either journalism or liberal arts; some require a master's degree. Small newspapers will usually accept less education if the applicant demonstrates exceptional ability or has at least junior college training in the basics of journalism. Larger papers prefer to hire reporters who have three to five years of experience.

Potential and advancement

About 67,000 persons work as newspaper reporters in the United States. Employment in the profession is expected to grow little through 2008, mainly because of mergers, reduced circulation, and increased costs. There will be heavy competition for positions with large city newspapers; the best opportunities for beginning reporters lie with small-town and suburban newspapers, radio and television stations, and on-line newspapers and magazines.

Reporters can advance to editorial or administrative positions or can move on to larger newspapers or press services. Some become columnists, correspondents, editors, or top executives. Others turn to public relations, writing for magazines, or preparing news copy for radio and television.

Income

The average salary for reporters and correspondents is $19,210 to $40,930 per year. Television reporters earn, on average, $33,200 to $55,000 per year.

Additional sources of information

Accrediting Council of Education in Journalism and Mass
    Communications
University of Kansas School of Journalism
Stauffer-Flint Hall
Lawrence, KS 66045
www.ukans.edu/~acejmc

Dow Jones Newspaper Fund
P.O. Box 300
Princeton, NJ 08543-0300
www.dowjones.com

Newspaper Guild
Research and Information Department
501 Third Street NW, Suite 250
Washington, DC 20001
www.newsguild.org

NURSE, LICENSED PRACTICAL

The job

Licensed practical nurses (LPNs) provide much of the bedside care for patients in hospitals, nursing homes, and extended-care facilities. They work under the direction of physicians and registered nurses and perform duties that require technical knowledge but not the professional education and training of a registered nurse. In some areas, they are called *licensed vocational nurses.*

LPNs take and record temperatures and blood pressures, change dressings, bathe patients, care for newborn infants, and perform certain special procedures. In states where they are allowed, LPNs also administer medicines and start intra-venous fluids.

Those who work in private homes provide daily nursing care and sometimes prepare meals for the patient. LPNs employed in physicians' offices or clinics may perform some clerical chores and schedule appointments.

Places of employment and working conditions

Licensed practical nurses work in all areas of the country, most of them in hos-pitals and nursing homes.

LPNs usually work a 40-hour week, but because patients require 24-hour care, they may work some nights, weekends, and holidays. Nurses spend most of their working hours on their feet and help patients move in bed, stand, or walk. They also must contend with the stress of working with sick patients and their families.

LPNs face many hazards and difficulties on their jobs. They often come into contact with caustic chemicals, radiation, and infectious diseases. They may also suffer from back injuries and muscle strains when moving patients. Moreover, the people under their charge may often be confused, angry, or depressed.

Qualifications, education, and training

Anyone interested in working as a licensed practical nurse should have a concern for people who are sick, be emotionally stable, and have physical stamina. The ability to follow orders and work under close supervision is also necessary.

A high school diploma is not always necessary for enrollment in a training program, although it is usually preferred. One-year, state-approved programs are offered by trade, technical, and vocational schools; high schools; junior colleges; local hospitals; health agencies; and private institutions. Some army training pro-grams are also state-approved.

Applicants for state licensing must complete a program in practical nursing that has been approved by the state board of nursing and must pass a written examination.

Potential and advancement

America has about 692,000 licensed practical nurses. The employment outlook is average through the next decade.

Career advancement is limited for people without formal education or additional training. Training programs in some hospitals help LPNs attend school part-time to complete the educational requirements necessary to become registered nurses.

Income

Annual salaries for LPNs average about $26,940.

Additional sources of information

Communications Department
National League for Nursing
61 Broadway
New York, NY 10006
www.nln.org

National Association for Practical Nurse Education and Service
1400 Spring Street, Suite 330
Silver Spring, MD 20910

National Federation of Licensed Practical Nurses
1418 Aversboro Road
Garner, NC 27529-4547

NURSE, REGISTERED

The job

Registered nurses (RNs) play a major role in health care. As part of a health care team, they administer medications and treatments as prescribed by a physician, provide skilled bedside nursing care for people who are sick or injured, and aid in the prevention of illness and promotion of good health.

Most nurses are employed in hospitals, where they are assigned to a specific unit, such as a postsurgery floor, the children's area (pediatrics), or the maternity section. Some specialize in operating-room work.

Doctors, dentists, and oral surgeons employ nurses in their offices to perform routine laboratory and administrative work in addition to nursing duties. *Industrial nurses* work in corporate and industrial settings and assist with health examinations, treat minor injuries of employees, and arrange for further medical care if it is necessary. They may also do some record keeping and process claims for medical insurance and workers' compensation.

Community health nurses work with patients in their homes, the schools, public health clinics, and other community settings. Nurses also teach in nursing schools and conduct continuing education courses for registered and licensed practical nurses.

Private-duty nurses are self-employed nurses who provide individual care in hospital or home for a patient who needs constant attention. This care may be required for just a short time or for extended periods.

Registered nurses who receive special advanced training may become *nurse practitioners*. They are permitted to perform some services, such as physical examinations, that have traditionally been handled by physicians. Nurse practitioners are an important part of the staff in many neighborhood health centers.

The federal government employs nurses in the Department of Veterans Affairs and the U.S. Public Health Service and as commissioned officers in the armed forces.

Most nurses are women, but men are entering the field in increasing numbers.

Places of employment and working conditions

Nurses are usually on their feet most of the day. Those who work in hospitals, in nursing homes, or as private-duty nurses must be prepared to work evenings, weekends, and holidays.

Nurses need physical and emotional strength to manage the stresses of their jobs. They face the dangers of infectious diseases and the hazards of working with radiation, chemicals, and gases. They also must be careful to avoid back injuries and muscle strain when moving patients.

Qualifications, education, and training

Nurses need the ability to follow orders precisely, use sound judgment in emergencies, and cope with human suffering. They must have physical and emotional stamina.

In high school, students should pursue a college preparation program with an emphasis on science.

There are three types of training for registered nurses. Many hospitals offer three-year diploma programs in their own nursing schools that combine classroom instruction and clinical experience within the hospital. Four-year bachelor's-degree programs are available at many colleges. Two-year associate-degree programs are offered by some junior and community colleges. These degree programs are combined with clinical practice in an affiliated hospital or health care facility.

A bachelor's degree is required for administrative or management positions in nursing; research, teaching, and clinical specializations usually require a master's degree.

Potential and advancement

There are about 2.1 million registered nurses in the United States, 60 percent of whom work in hospitals. Future employment opportunities should be excellent for some time due to above-average growth in this field. More jobs will be available in nursing homes and home health organizations than in traditional hospital settings.

Experienced hospital nurses can advance to head nurse or assistant director or director of nursing services. Many supervisory and management positions require a bachelor's degree, however.

Income

Registered nurses working in hospitals earn average annual salaries of about $40,690. The lowest 10 percent earn $29,480, while the top 10 percent earn $69,300 or more per year.

Additional sources of information

American Nurses' Association
600 Maryland Avenue SW
Washington, DC 20024-2571
www.nursingworld.org

Communications Department
National League for Nursing
61 Broadway
New York, NY 10006
www.nln.org

NURSERY WORKER

The job

Plant nurseries grow and sell trees, flowers, shrubs, and other plants. They may be wholesale or retail operations, garden centers, or mail-order businesses.

Nursery workers perform a variety of special tasks: plant propagation through seeds, cuttings, and root division; preparation of soil in outdoor growing areas; greenhouse management; weed, disease, and insect control; plant breeding; storage and packaging of plants; and business operations.

Nursery workers are also employed by other establishments that use large numbers of plants and trees requiring expert care and maintenance. These include parks and botanical gardens; large estates and institutions, such as schools; industrial and commercial facilities with extensive outdoor areas; and planned residential areas, such as retirement communities and public housing.

State and federal government agencies employ nursery workers in agricultural extension services, inspection and law enforcement, and developmental and administrative positions.

Some specially trained nursery workers are called *plant scientists*. They do research on specific plants or groups of plants, especially food-producing plants, to improve their yield or to find solutions to problems such as insect infestation. Plant scientists also develop new plants.

Related jobs are landscape architect, farmer, range manager, and biologist.

Qualifications, education, and training

Curiosity about and an affinity for growing things are essential for anyone in this field. Good health, average strength, manual dexterity, color perception, a sense of design, and patience are likewise important. Business management skills and sales ability are also valuable.

High school courses in science, social studies, mathematics, mechanical drawing, and art are good preparation for this field. Summer jobs at plant nurseries or with landscape contractors provide practical experience.

There are no specific educational requirements for nursery workers, and many acquire their skills through on-the-job training. Many employers, however, prefer some formal training for those who work as managers. Two-year courses in this field are available at junior and community colleges, four-year colleges, and technical and vocational schools.

Nursery workers who are in charge of grounds keeping for large companies usually need at least a bachelor's degree and in some cases need an advanced degree. Majors in the biological sciences, landscape architecture, urban planning, and environmental design are optimal.

Research work requires advanced study in a specialty field such as agronomy, entomology, chemistry, soil science, or biology.

Potential and advancement

This is a growing field of employment at all levels. Openings exist in small local nurseries, in large retail and wholesale companies, and in basic research. In the future, there is expected to be a greater demand for specialists in ornamental nursery stock, agricultural products, and insect and plant disease control.

For the most part, advancement depends on ambition and experience. Many persons start as laborers and then work their way up through jobs as landscape helpers, groundskeepers, greenhouse workers, tree trimmers, or other positions. Supervisory and management positions are available to those who acquire a broad range of experience and knowledge. Many managers advance by opening their own nursery businesses.

Income

Earnings vary widely and depend on the size and location of the business and the worker's education and experience.

Salaries vary from nursery workers who earn minimum wage to nursery managers who may earn more than $20 per hour.

Additional source of information

American Association of Nurserymen
1250 I Street NW, Suite 500
Washington, DC 20005

OCCUPATIONAL THERAPIST

The job

This fast-growing field offers personal satisfaction as well as financially reward-ing job opportunities. Occupational therapists work with physically and emo-tionally disabled people, helping some to return to normal functions and activities and others to make the fullest use of their talents.

Occupational therapists plan and direct educational, vocational, and recre-ational activities; evaluate capabilities and skills; and plan individual therapy pro-grams, often working as part of a medical team. Their clients are all ages and can range from a stroke victim relearning daily routines such as eating, dressing, and using a telephone to an accident victim learning to reuse impaired limbs before returning to work.

To restore mobility and dexterity to hands disabled by injury or disease, occu-pational therapists teach manual and creative skills through the use of crafts such as weaving, knitting, and leather working. They design games and activities es-pecially for children or make special equipment or splints to aid disabled patients.

Occupational therapists use computer games to help clients develop decision-making and problem-solving skills. They also help clients learn to move and communicate using computer-aided adaptive equipment.

Many part-time positions are available for occupational therapists; some occupational therapists work for more than one employer, traveling between job locations and clients.

In addition to hospital rehabilitation departments, other types of organizations that employ occupational therapists are rehabilitation centers and nursing homes, schools, mental health centers, schools and camps for children with disabilities, state health departments and home-care programs, Department of Veterans Affairs hospitals and clinics, psychiatric centers, and schools for people with learning and developmental disabilities.

Most occupational therapists are women, but the number of men entering the field has been increasing. Because there are many opportunities for part-time work, this is an attractive field for people with family responsibilities.

Related jobs are physical therapist and respiratory therapist.

Places of employment and working conditions

Occupational therapists usually work a 40-hour week, which may include weekends and evenings. Those who work for schools have regular school hours.

Therapists spend a lot of time on their feet, and they may be subject to back injuries and muscle strains from lifting and moving patients and equipment. Therapists who give home health care may spend hours a day commuting.

Qualifications, education, and training

Maturity, patience, imagination, manual skills, and the ability to instruct are important, as is a sympathetic but objective attitude toward illness and disability.

Anyone considering this career field should have high school science courses, especially biology and chemistry. Courses in health, social studies, and computer science along with training in crafts are also important. Volunteer work or a summer job in a health care facility can provide valuable exposure to this field.

A bachelor's degree in occupational therapy is required to practice in this field. All states, Puerto Rico, and the District of Columbia require a license. Eighty-eight colleges and universities offer bachelor's degrees in occupational therapy.

Some schools offer a shorter program leading to certification or to a master's degree in occupational therapy for students who have a bachelor's degree in another field.

Study includes physical, biological, and behavioral sciences as well as the application of occupational theory and skills. Students are also required to spend six months working in hospitals or health agencies to gain clinical experience.

Graduates of accredited programs take the certification examination of the American Occupational Therapy Certification Board to become registered occupational therapists.

Potential and advancement

There are about 73,000 occupational therapists in America. A large number are employed in hospitals. Employment in this field is expected to grow substantially as the population ages and as students with disabilities receive expanded services now mandated by federal law. Based on this forecast, job opportunities will be excellent on the whole throughout 2008.

Advancement in this field is usually to supervisory or administrative positions. More occupational therapists are expected to enter private practice, as laws now permit these providers to bill Medicare directly. Advanced education is necessary for those wishing to teach, do research, or advance to top administration levels.

Income

The median annual salary for occupational therapists is $48,230. Therapists in private practice usually earn more.

Additional source of information

American Occupational Therapy Association
P.O. Box 31220
4720 Montgomery Lane
Bethesda, MD 20824-1220
www.aota.org

OCEANOGRAPHER

The job

Using the principles and techniques of natural science, mathematics, and engineering, oceanographers study the movements, physical properties, and plant and animal life of the oceans. They make observations, conduct experiments, and collect specimens at sea that are later analyzed in laboratories. Their work contributes to improving weather forecasting, locating fishing, identifying petroleum and mineral resources, and improving national defense.

Most oceanographers specialize in one branch of the science. *Marine biologists* study plant and animal life in the ocean to determine the effects of pollution on marine life. Their work is also important in improving and controlling sport and commercial fishing. *Marine geologists* study underwater mountain ranges, rocks, and sediments of the oceans to locate regions where minerals, oil, and gas may be found. Other oceanographic specialists study the relationship between the sea and the atmosphere and the chemical composition of ocean water and sediments. Others with engineering or electronics training design and build instruments for oceanographic research, lay cables, and supervise underwater construction.

Many oceanographers work for colleges and universities. In addition to holding teaching positions, they take part in research projects sponsored by universities at sea and in facilities along U.S. coasts.

The U.S. Navy and the National Oceanic and Atmospheric Administration employ oceanographers. State fisheries employ a few. In addition, an increasing number of oceanographers are being hired by private industry, particularly in aquaculture, construction, oceanographic equipment manufacturing, and chemistry.

Related jobs are that of a chemist, geologist, geophysicist, life scientist, and meteorologist.

Places of employment and working conditions

Most oceanographers work in the states that border the ocean, such as California, Maryland, and Virginia.

Oceanographers engaged in research that requires sea voyages are often away from home for long periods, and they may have to live and work in cramped quarters.

Qualifications, education, and training

Anyone interested in this career field should have curiosity and the patience necessary to collect data and conduct research.

High school should include as many science and mathematics courses as possible. Computer science courses are useful because computer modeling is an increasingly important tool for oceanographers. Hobbies or summer jobs that involve boating or ocean fishing are helpful.

A bachelor's degree with a major in oceanography, chemistry, biology, earth or physical sciences, mathematics, or engineering is the first step for a would-be oceanographer and is usually sufficient for entry-level jobs such as research assistant.

Graduate training in oceanography or a basic science is required for most jobs in research and training and for all top-level positions; a Ph.D. is required for many. Graduate students usually spend part of their time at sea conducting experiments and learning the techniques of gathering oceanographic information.

Potential and advancement

This a relatively small field, but it is expected to experience average growth through 2008. The increased emphasis on environmental protection and the low number of recent graduates should create good job opportunities.

Oceanographers with advanced degrees and experience can move up to administrative or supervisory positions in research laboratories. They may also become directors of surveys or research programs.

Income

Oceanographers employed by colleges and universities receive the same salaries as those of other faculty members. In addition, they may earn extra income from consulting, lecturing, and writing.

The average yearly salary for experienced oceanographers working for the federal government is about $66,000.

Additional sources of information

American Society of Limnology and Oceanography
Virginia Institute of Marine Science
College of William and Mary
Route 1208
Gloucester Point, VA 23062

International Oceanographic Foundation
3979 Rickenbacker Causeway
Virginia Key
Miami, FL 33149

U.S. Civil Service Commission
Washington Area Office
1900 E Street NW
Washington, DC 20415

OFFICE MANAGER

The job

The title *office manager* brings to mind the secretary or clerk who has worked his or her way up in the office hierarchy to the top supervisory position. While this description is accurate to some degree, the field also includes office management positions that are much more complex and far-reaching.

In a small or medium-size company, an office manager hires, trains, evaluates, and manages staff. He or she supervises the day-to-day work of a clerical staff that might include accounting functions such as billing, maintenance of personnel records, payroll, and all other secretarial and clerical functions. The mail room, telephone switchboard, and duplicating and copier equipment also are part of the office manager's responsibilities. The size and makeup of the office staff depend on the company and its requirements.

In a large company, the office manager is responsible for a large and complex office staff, often at multiple locations. With one of many possible titles—*director of secretarial support systems, administrative manager, office administrator*—a manager at this level is involved in systems analysis and electronic data processing as well as office systems, procedures, and operations.

A rapidly growing specialty within this field is management of a centralized word processing facility within a company in which trained specialists, specific procedures, and the latest in automatic equipment are combined to meet the clerical needs of a variety of departments. The *word processing manager* coordinates the word processing services with the needs of the user departments and is responsible for staff levels and training, budgets, and design and implementation of word processing systems.

The number of clerical workers varies with the nature of the organization. The greatest concentrations of clerical workers and managers necessary to oversee their work are in public administration, insurance, finance, and banking. Other prominent employers are the wholesale and retail fields and manufacturing firms.

Related jobs are accountant, bank officer, civil service worker (federal, municipal, and state), computer programmer, industrial engineer, personnel manager, secretary, and systems analyst.

Places of employment and working conditions

Although the usual office workweek is 40 hours, office managers often put in extra hours. The responsibilities of planning and organization plus meetings with executives of user departments sometimes add many hours to the daily schedule. In organizations that work around the clock, the office manager may be required to work evenings, weekends, or holidays.

The entire clerical staff may work under considerable pressure at times to meet deadlines and handle busy seasons.

Qualifications, education, and training

A successful office manager must have a talent for organization, an analytical mind, and the ability to work with detail. Creativity, resourcefulness, flexibility, self-assurance, tact, and the ability to get along with people are also necessary. Good communication skills and computer skills are solid assets.

A high school student looking forward to a career in office management should include business courses as well as any courses necessary to enter college or a good business school. Work experience in an office in a part-time or summer job is valuable preparation.

A college degree is usually necessary for a person to achieve the top levels in this field. Small businesses that require a degree often prefer a bachelor's degree in accounting, while large companies often prefer a degree in business administration. Some colleges offer a major or minor in office management.

Business schools, trade and technical schools, community colleges, and university extension programs also offer a variety of programs in this field, some leading to a degree. In addition to courses in office management, the curriculum should include systems and procedures, data processing, accounting, and personnel management to provide diversified business training. Some two- and four-year degree programs offer electives in law or economics and other liberal arts courses to provide a well-rounded education.

Home-study programs are also available for office management. The diploma awarded by such programs does not carry the prestige of a college degree, but many people find these courses convenient for supplementary study in specific areas of business management.

Large corporations often have training programs in office management, but these programs are usually open only to college graduates.

Regardless of educational background, people in this field continue to study throughout their careers. New developments in office technology alone would require this. In addition to taking college courses, most office managers attend seminars and conferences sponsored by various professional societies as well as training sessions and workshops presented by office equipment manufacturers.

Potential and advancement

There are more than 1.6 million office managers in the country. Applicants likely will face keen competition for jobs through 2008. The best opportunities will be for those with a college degree and diversified business experience. While there will continue to be a place for the skilled clerical worker who advanced through the ranks, the growing complexity of the office communications and data processing functions of even small companies will require more comprehensive knowledge and training than is acquired by that route.

Office managers are already at the middle-management level. In companies in which the office administration function is a major component of the firm's service, office managers can advance to top-level executive positions.

Income

Salaries of office managers vary widely and depend on the size and location of the company, the size of the clerical staff, the responsibilities of the manager, and the complexity of the operation. The salary for a supervisor or manager averages $31,090 annually.

Additional sources of information

Administrative Management Society
4622 Street Road
Trevose, PA 19047

American Management Association
1601 Broadway, 10th Floor
New York, NY 10019-7420
www.amanet.org

Association of Information Systems Professionals
104 Wilmot Road, Suite 201
Deerfield, IL 60015

OFFICER, U.S. ARMED FORCES

The job

A career as an officer in the U.S. Army, Navy, Marines, or Coast Guard may be achieved through different methods: the Reserve Officers Training Corps (ROTC); the service academies; officer candidate schools, such as the National Guard State Officer Candidate School and the Uniformed Services University of Health Sciences; and other programs.

Places of employment and working conditions

Members of the U.S. armed forces serve throughout the world. Although some effort is made to allow choice of location at the time of enlistment, assignments are not always to the location of choice.

Officers who receive their training at one of the service academies as well as those who receive their training and college education through ROTC scholarships are obligated to serve on active duty for a stipulated period. Other officers serve various lengths of time on active duty.

Military service demands strong self-discipline and a willingness to accept odd hours, life in remote locations or in cramped quarters aboard ship, and the possible dangers of combat.

Qualifications, education, and training

Leadership qualities are important for anyone interested in a career as an officer. Applicants must be between 17 and 35 years of age, be U.S. citizens or immigrant aliens with permanent-resident status, have no felony record, and have a birth certificate. The service academies require a rigorous physical examination and have specific height, weight, eyesight, color vision, and hearing requirements. Those who are 17 must have the permission of a parent or guardian. Candidates up to the age of 35 are accepted in all branches except the air force. All candidates must enter the air force before their 28th birthday. Applicants must pass a written exam, the Armed Services Vocational Aptitude Battery. The academies also require cadets to remain unmarried until after graduation, and single parents usually are ineligible.

High school courses should include English, science, and mathematics. Extracurricular activities that develop leadership qualities are also valuable.

The federal service academies provide a four-year college education that leads to a bachelor of science degree.

ROTC programs are offered at participating colleges and universities; some scholarships are available. Participants take two to five hours of military instruction each week in addition to their regular classes. Information on ROTC programs may be obtained directly from participating colleges or from local recruiting offices of the various services.

Enlisted personnel in the various services may be appointed to officer candidate school through classification exams and interviews and grades received on specific aptitude tests and the Officer Candidate Test. Civilian applicants should apply at local recruiting offices, where they may take the appropriate examinations.

Applicants for West Point, Annapolis, and the Air Force Academy must be appointed by their congressperson. The Coast Guard Academy does not require applicants to be appointed; the Coast Guard recruits through an annual nationwide competition. The army, navy, and air force academies require the College Board Entrance Exam, while the Coast Guard requires the SAT or ACT. High school guidance counselors can usually provide up-to-date information on requirements at the service academies, or interested students may write to the academies directly.

Direct appointments are available for health care and legal professionals and those interested in joining the chaplain corps.

Commissioned officers can receive flight training in any branch of the armed forces. The army has a direct-enlistment option for warrant officer aviators.

Potential and advancement

The need for qualified officers in all of the services will provide career opportunities for applicants with a wide range of skills, and promotion to higher rank is possible for everyone. The number of active-duty personnel is expected to remain constant, and job opportunities should be good. As military jobs become more technical and complex, people with the best educational backgrounds will find the greatest opportunities.

Income

Depending on their pay grade, officers earn monthly starting salaries ranging between $1,640.40 and $1,968.90. They also receive free room and board (or a housing and subsistence allowance), medical and dental benefits, 30 days' paid vacation a year, a military clothing allowance, military supermarket and department store shopping privileges, and travel opportunities. They may receive retirement benefits after 20 years of service.

Additional sources of information

High school and college guidance counselors and local recruiting offices can provide information on careers in the armed forces. Information is also available at www.militarycareers.com.

OPERATING ENGINEER

The job

Operating engineers, also called *material moving equipment operators*, operate all kinds of construction equipment. They are usually classified by the type or capacity of the machines they operate.

Heavy equipment operators are highly skilled in the operation of complex machinery such as cranes. They must accurately judge distances and heights while operating the buttons, levers, and pedals that rotate the crane, raise and lower the boom and load line, and open and close attachments such as steel-toothed buckets or clamps for lifting materials. At times, operators work without being able to see the pickup or delivery point, relying on hand or flag signals from another worker. When constructing new buildings, they work far above the ground.

The operation of medium-size construction equipment requires fewer controls and is done at ground level. *Bulldozer operators*, for example, lift and lower the blade and move the bulldozer back and forth over the construction area. Trench excavators, paving machines, and other construction equipment are also in this category.

Lightweight equipment such as an air compressor is the simplest to operate. (An air compressor is a diesel engine that takes in air and forces it through a narrow hose. The resulting pressure is used to run special tools.) The operator makes sure the compressor has fuel and water, adjusts and maintains pressure levels, and makes minor repairs.

About 36 percent of all operating engineers work in manufacturing; a significant percentage work in construction.

Many operating engineers work for contractors in large-scale construction projects such as highways, dams, and airports. Others work for utility companies and business firms that do their own construction; state and local highway and public works departments; and factories and mines using power-driven machinery, hoists, and cranes. Very few operating engineers are self-employed.

The International Union of Operating Engineers is the bargaining unit for many workers in this field.

Places of employment and working conditions

Most operating engineers work outdoors. They usually work steadily during the warm months but have slow periods in cold months or in bad weather. Operation of medium-size equipment is physically tiring because of constant movement and the jolting and noise levels of the equipment. Equipment operators engaged in highway construction sometimes work in remote locations.

Qualifications, education, and training

Operating engineers need physical stamina, mechanical ability, excellent eyesight and eye-hand coordination, and manual dexterity.

Driver education and automobile mechanics courses in high school are helpful, and experience in operating a tractor or other farm equipment can provide a good background for this work.

Some private schools offer instruction in the operation of certain types of construction equipment, but anyone considering such a school should check with local construction employers for their opinion of the training received by the school's graduates. Not all schools produce suitably trained people.

Most employers prefer to hire high school graduates who have completed a formal apprenticeship program because they are more thoroughly trained and can operate a variety of equipment. Programs are usually sponsored and supervised by a joint union-management committee; the armed forces also provide apprenticeship programs. An apprenticeship consists of at least three years of on-the-job training plus 144 hours per year of related classroom instruction in hydraulics, engine operation and repair, cable splicing, welding, safety, and first aid.

Apprenticeship applicants usually need a high school or vocational school diploma. They must be at least 18 years old.

Apprentices initially work as helpers. They clean, grease, repair, and start engines. Within the first year, they usually begin to perform simple machine operations and progress to more complex operations, always under the supervision of an experienced operating engineer.

Potential and advancement

There are about 808,000 operating engineers in the country. Employment of operating engineers is not expected to grow much through 2008, but many opportunities will arise as experienced workers transfer to other careers or leave the labor force. Because this field is sensitive to cycles in the economy, employment of operating engineers may fluctuate from year to year. Increased automation, which is making operating engineers more efficient, is also expected to limit the number of job openings.

Income

Wage rates depend on the machine being operated. Average earnings for all operating engineers are about $23,360 to $30,510 per year. Pay scales are generally highest in metropolitan areas.

Additional sources of information

Associated General Contractors of America
1957 E Street NW
Washington, DC 20006

International Union of Operating Engineers
1125 17th Street NW
Washington, DC 20036

OPERATIONS RESEARCH ANALYST

The job

An organization or system can usually be operated in several ways, but the best way is not necessarily the most obvious one. Operations research specialists use their knowledge of engineering, mathematics, and economics to decide on the most efficient means to use all available resources to achieve maximum results.

This relatively new field is concerned with the design and operation of worker-machine systems. Using scientific methods of analysis, operations research analysts decide on the best allocation of resources within an organization or system. These resources include time, money, trained people, space, and raw materials.

In another application of operations research techniques, analysts might apply appropriate theories and methods to two possible research projects that are competing for funding. The analysis could produce information on which project would probably achieve the best results in the shortest time with the available money and other resources.

The applications of operations research are numerous. Originated during World War II to facilitate the allocation and tactical employment of available equipment, workers, and materials, operations research is now a standard and growing aspect of management in industry, marketing, capital development, financial planning, government, and exploration activities.

Some people in this field are engaged in teaching and research.

Related jobs are industrial engineer, systems analyst, and office manager.

Places of employment and working conditions

Most operations research analysts work in an office setting; some work in classrooms, outdoors, and in laboratories, factories, and hospitals. Deadline pressure and overtime are often part of the job.

Qualifications, education, and training

An analytical mind, resourcefulness, patience, good communication skills, and the ability to get along with people are necessary. Strong computer skills are also essential. Operations research analysts should be competent in database management and programming; they will also need to master a variety of software programs.

High school should include as much mathematics and science as possible.

A degree in engineering, mathematics, economics, or the physical sciences is an acceptable beginning for this field since there is no typical operations research program. However, graduate study is usually necessary. Continuing education is common, and many employers sponsor it.

Potential and advancement

Good job opportunities should exist through 2008 for those who pursue operations research as a primary career or as an adjunct to another area of specialization. Those with graduate degrees will have the easiest time finding jobs.

The potential for advancement in this field is excellent. Experienced analysts can rise to supervisory and management positions in all types of organizations. Because this field provides exposure to the full spectrum of operations within a company or an organization, it is becoming recognized as a major training ground for senior management and executive positions.

Many experienced operations research analysts become management consultants, opening their own companies or working for an established management consulting firm.

Income

On average, experienced operations research analysts within an organization earn from $50,000 to $72,090 a year. Government positions pay an average of $72,000 a year.

Additional source of information

Operations Research Society of America
1314 Guilford Avenue
Baltimore, MD 21202

OPHTHALMOLOGIST

The job

Ophthalmologists are also called *eye physicians-surgeons*. They are qualified physicians and osteopathic physicians who have completed additional specialized training in the treatment of eye diseases and disorders. They treat a full range of eye problems—including vision deficiencies, injuries, infections, and other disorders—with medicines, therapy, corrective lenses, or surgery. Their job is distinct from that of optometrists and opticians, who are not physicians and treat only vision problems.

Most ophthalmologists are in private practice. Others are employed by hospitals and clinics, medical schools and research foundations, federal and state agencies, and the armed forces.

Related jobs are optometrist, dispensing optician, physician, and osteopathic physician.

Places of employment and working conditions

Ophthalmologists work in all areas of the country. Those who are osteopathic physicians are concentrated in the areas that have osteopathic hospital facilities. The workweek for ophthalmologists is from 35 to 50 hours. Those involved in general patient care are always on call for emergencies.

Qualifications, education, and training

Information on the training and licensing requirements for the jobs of **physician** and **osteopathic physician** is contained in the appropriate descriptions elsewhere in this book.

An additional three to five years of residency in an accredited ophthalmology program must be completed by doctors who wish to specialize in this field. Candidates for the specialty must then pass the certification examination of the American Board of Medical Specialists or the American Osteopathic Association.

Potential and advancement

The demand for ophthalmologists will continue to rise as the population grows. Greater interest in eye care, the growing number of senior citizens, and the increase in health insurance plans will add to the need for qualified practitioners of this medical specialty.

Income

Ophthalmologists who start a private practice face a few lean years until the practice is established. In addition, a sizable investment in specialized equipment is necessary. Earnings during this early period may barely meet expenses.

As a practice develops, earnings usually increase substantially. Average annual earnings for all ophthalmologists are in the $164,000 range. In general, ophthalmologists in private practice earn more than those in salaried positions.

Additional sources of information

American Academy of Ophthalmology
655 Beach Street
P.O. Box 7424
San Francisco, CA 94109

American Medical Association
515 North State Street
Chicago, IL 60610
www.ama-assn.org

OPTICIAN, DISPENSING

The job

More than half the people in the United States use some form of corrective lenses (eyeglasses or contact lenses). These corrective lenses are prepared and fitted by dispensing opticians, also called *ophthalmic dispensers*. Working with the prescription received from an ophthalmologist (eye physician) or optometrist, the dispensing optician provides the customer with appropriate eyeglasses. He or she measures the customer's face, aids in the selection of the appropriate frames, directs the work of ophthalmic laboratory technicians who grind the lenses, and fits the completed eyeglasses.

In many states, dispensing opticians also fit contact lenses, which requires even more skill, care, and patience than the preparation and fitting of eyeglasses. Opticians measure the corneas of the customer's eyes and, following the ophthalmologist's or optometrist's prescription, prepare specifications for the contact lens manufacturer. The optician also instructs customers on how to insert, remove, and care for their contact lenses and provides follow-up attention during the first few weeks of wear.

Some dispensing opticians specialize in the fitting of artificial eyes and cosmetic shells to cover blemished eyes. Some also do their own lens grinding.

Most dispensing opticians work for retail optical shops or other retail stores with optical departments. Ophthalmologists and optometrists who sell glasses directly to patients also employ dispensing opticians, as do hospitals and eye clinics. Some dispensing opticians operate their own retail shops and sell other optical goods such as binoculars, magnifying glasses, and sunglasses.

Places of employment and working conditions

Dispensing opticians are located throughout the United States, with most employed in large cities and in the more populous states. Working conditions are usually quiet and clean, with a workweek of five or six days. Dispensing opticians who own their own businesses usually work longer hours than those employed by retail shops or by ophthalmologists and optometrists. Those who work in retail shops may be required to work evenings or weekends.

Qualifications, education, and training

The ability to do precision work is essential for anyone planning a career as a dispensing optician. Patience, tact, and interpersonal skills are other valuable assets.

Applicants for entry-level jobs need a high school diploma with courses in the basic sciences. Courses in physics, algebra, geometry, and mechanical drawing are especially valuable.

Most opticians acquire their skills through on-the-job training. A small number learn their trade in the armed forces. In addition, many large manufacturers of contact lenses offer nondegree courses in lens fitting.

Twenty-five accredited programs offer a two-year full-time course in optical fabricating and dispensing that leads to an associate degree. Students learn optical mathematics, optical physics, and the use of precision measuring instruments. Some shorter programs last one year or less.

Apprenticeship programs lasting from two to five years are also available. In these programs, students study optometric technical subjects as well as basic office management and sales, and work directly with patients in the fitting of eyeglasses and contact lenses.

Twenty-one states require that dispensing opticians be licensed. Specific requirements vary but generally include minimum standards of education and training, along with a written or practical examination. Some states require graduates to have up to one year's experience before taking the exam.

Potential and advancement

About 71,000 persons work as dispensing opticians nationwide. Employment opportunities in this field are expected to expand steadily as the population rises. Increased health insurance coverage, Medicare services, and state programs to provide eye care to low-income families—along with current fashion trends, which encourage sales of more than one pair of glasses to individual buyers—will add to the demand for dispensing opticians.

However, because the industry is small and sensitive to fluctuations in the economy, the actual number of job openings will be modest compared with other fields.

Many dispensing opticians go into business for themselves. Others advance to positions in the management of retail optical stores or become sales representatives for wholesalers or manufacturers of eyeglasses or contact lenses.

Income

Earnings for dispensing opticians vary a great deal. Highest earnings are in states that require licensure. Experienced opticians average $28,560 per year, and those with managerial responsibilities average $37,080.

Additional sources of information

National Academy of Opticianry
8401 Corporate Drive, Suite 605
Landover, MD 20785
www.nao.org

Opticians Association of America
10341 Democracy Lane
Fairfax, VA 22030-2521
www.opticians.org

OPTOMETRIST

The job

More than half of the U.S. population wears eyeglasses or contact lenses. Before obtaining lenses, people need an eye examination and a prescription to obtain the correct lenses for their particular eye problem. Optometrists (doctors of optometry) provide the bulk of this care.

In addition to treating vision problems, optometrists check for disease. When evidence of disease is found, the optometrist refers the patient to the appropriate medical practitioner. Optometrists also test depth and color perception and the ability to focus and coordinate the eyes. They may prescribe corrective eye exercises or other treatments that do not require surgery. Optometrists can utilize medications for diagnosis, and in most states they can also treat eye diseases with drugs.

Some optometrists specialize in treating children or seniors or work only with people who are partially sighted and who must wear microscopic or telescopic lenses. Industrial eye-safety programs also are an optometric specialty. A few optometrists are engaged in teaching and research.

Although most optometrists are in private practice, many others are in partnerships or in group practice with other optometrists or with other physicians as part of a health care team. Some work in retail vision chain stores. Many combine private, group, or partnership practice with work in specialized hospitals and eye clinics.

Some optometrists serve as commissioned officers in the armed forces. Others are consultants to engineers specializing in safety or lighting; to educators in remedial reading; and to health advisory committees of federal, state, and local governments.

Places of employment and working conditions

Although most optometrists work in metropolitan areas of larger cities, opportunities exist in towns and cities of all sizes.

Most self-employed optometrists can set their own work schedules, but they often work longer than 40 hours a week. Weekend or evening hours may be set up to accommodate patients. Because the work is not physically strenuous, optometrists can practice past the normal retirement age.

Qualifications, education, and training

Because two-thirds of all optometrists are self-employed, anyone planning on a career in this field needs business ability and self-discipline in addition to interpersonal skills.

High school preparation should emphasize science, and business courses are also helpful.

The doctor of optometry degree is awarded after successful completion of at least seven years of college. Preoptometrical study should include English, mathematics, physics, chemistry, and biology or zoology. Some schools also require psychology, social studies, literature, philosophy, and foreign languages.

Admission to optometry schools is highly competitive. Because the number of qualified applicants typically exceeds the available places, applicants need superior grades in preoptometric courses to increase their chances of acceptance by one of the 17 schools and colleges of optometry approved by the Council on Optometric Education of the American Optometric Association.

All states and the District of Columbia require optometrists to be licensed. Candidates must pass a written and clinical state board examination after graduating from an accredited school.

Optometrists who wish to advance in a specialized field of optometry may study for a master's or Ph.D. degree in visual science, physiological optics, neurophysiology, public health, health administration, health information and communication, or health education. Career officers in the armed forces also have an opportunity to work toward advanced degrees and to do research.

Potential and advancement

There are about 38,000 practicing optometrists nationwide, many of them in private practice. Employment opportunities are expected to grow steadily through 2008. Expanded coverage of optometric services by health insurers, greater recognition of the importance of good vision, and the growing population—especially older people, who are most likely to need eyeglasses—should bolster demand for providers.

Income

Incomes for optometrists vary greatly with location, specialization, and factors such as private or group practice. New optometry graduates average $55,000 in their first year.

Experienced optometrists average between $43,750 and $93,700 a year. Those in salaried positions earn more initially, but private practices are more lucrative in the long run.

Additional source of information

American Optometric Association
Educational Services
243 North Lindbergh Boulevard
St. Louis, MO 63141-7881
www.aoanet.org

OSTEOPATHIC PHYSICIAN

The job

The dictionary defines *osteopathy* as "a system of medical practice based on the theory that diseases are due chiefly to a loss of structural integrity in the tissues and that this integrity can be restored by manipulation of the parts, supported by the use of medicines, surgery, proper diet, and other therapy."

Most osteopathic physicians are family doctors engaged in general practice. They see patients at the office or make house calls and treat patients in osteopathic and other private and public hospitals. Some osteopathic physicians specialize in such fields as internal medicine, neurology, psychiatry, ophthalmology, pediatrics, anesthesiology, physical medicine and rehabilitation, dermatology, obstetrics and gynecology, pathology, proctology, radiology, and surgery.

The majority of osteopathic physicians are in private practice, although a few hold salaried positions in private industry or government agencies. Others hold full-time positions with osteopathic hospitals and colleges, where they are engaged in teaching, research, and writing.

Places of employment and working conditions

Most osteopathic physicians practice in states that have osteopathic hospital facilities; more than half of these facilities are in Florida, Michigan, Pennsylvania,

New Jersey, Ohio, Texas, and Missouri. Most general practitioners are located in smaller towns and cities; specialists are usually located in larger cities.

Qualifications, education, and training

Anyone interested in becoming an osteopathic physician should have emotional stability, patience, tact, and interpersonal skills.

The education requirements for the doctor of osteopathy (D.O.) degree include a minimum of three years of college (although almost all applicants have a bachelor's degree) plus a three- to four-year professional program. The education and training of an osteopathic physician is expensive due primarily to the length of time involved. Federal and private funds are available for loans, and federal scholarships are available to those who qualify and agree to a minimum of two years of service for the federal government after completion of training.

Undergraduate study must include courses in chemistry, physics, biology, and English, with high grades an important factor in acceptance into professional programs. In addition to superior grades, schools require a good score on the Medical College Admission Test and letters of recommendation. One important qualification is the applicant's desire to study osteopathy rather than some other field of medicine.

During the first half of the professional program, the student studies basic sciences such as anatomy, physiology, and pathology as well as the principles of osteopathy. The second half of the program consists primarily of clinical experience. After graduation, a 12-month internship is usually completed at one of the osteopathic hospitals approved for internship or residency by the American Osteopathic Association. Those who intend to specialize must complete additional training of up to seven years.

All practicing osteopathic physicians must be licensed. State licensing requirements vary, but all states require graduation from an approved school of osteopathic medicine and a passing grade on a state board examination. Most states require internship at an approved hospital.

A Ph.D. may be required for some teaching and research positions.

Potential and advancement

Population growth and an increase in the number of persons covered by medical insurance will contribute to a rise in demand for osteopathic physicians. Ongoing concern about health care costs will mean greater demand for general practitioners than for specialists. The greatest demand will continue to be in states where osteopathic medicine is well known and accepted as a method of treatment.

Opportunities for new practitioners are best in rural areas (many localities lack medical practitioners of any kind), small towns, and suburbs of large cities. The availability of osteopathic hospital facilities should be considered when one is selecting a location in which to practice.

New physicians will be more likely to accept salaried jobs with medical clinics, group practices, and health care networks as opposed to entering solo practice.

Income

As is usually the case in any field in which setting up an individual practice is the norm, earnings in the first few years tend to be low. Income generally rises substantially once the practice becomes established and, in the case of osteopathic physicians, is high in comparison with other professionals. Geographic location and the income level of the community also affect the level of income. The average annual income of general practitioners is $132,000.

Additional sources of information

American Osteopathic Association
Department of Public Relations
142 East Ontario Street
Chicago, IL 60611
www.aoa-net.org

American Association of Colleges of Osteopathic Medicine
5550 Friendship Boulevard, Suite 310
Chevy Chase, MD 20815-7321
www.aacom.org

PARALEGAL

The job

Lawyers often face a tremendous workload; every legal specialty requires extensive research, drafting and filing of documents, and preparation of reports. Many lawyers hire paralegals, or legal assistants, to help them accomplish these tasks.

Paralegals perform many of the same duties as lawyers, but they are prohibited from actually practicing law—accepting clients, setting legal fees, giving legal advice, or presenting a case in court. Paralegals work under the supervision of lawyers because lawyers are ultimately responsible for their work.

Paralegals' responsibilities depend on the type and size of employer. Paralegals working for litigators assist in preparing a case for trial. They may conduct interviews and investigations to determine the facts of a case. They also may research laws, judicial decisions, and any other material that could be relevant to the case. They then must prepare reports of their findings so that the lawyer can determine the best strategy for the case. If a lawsuit is filed, the paralegal prepares necessary documents and files them with the court, helps formulate legal arguments, and assists the lawyer during the trial.

Paralegals working for lawyers in other specialties, such as corporation law, patent law, and tax law, often draw up documents and prepare tax returns.

Many major corporations employ full-time attorneys to handle their legal affairs. Paralegals assist them in tasks such as preparing financial reports, employee contracts, and employee benefit plans.

Other employers of paralegals are government agencies and community legal service projects.

Paralegals working in large law firms frequently specialize in some area of the law. The duties of paralegals in small or medium-size law firms often vary from day to day.

Places of employment and working conditions

Most paralegals work for private law firms. Another large employer is the federal government. Some also work for state and local governments. A small number of paralegals work for corporations such as banks, real estate companies, and insurance companies.

Paralegals working for large law firms often work long hours and are under pressure to meet deadlines. Those working for corporations and the government usually work about 40 hours a week.

Entry-level paralegals may become frustrated with their jobs because of the routine tasks they are assigned. However, as paralegals gain experience, they are often given more responsible, challenging tasks.

Qualifications, education, and training

Paralegals must be able to think logically and communicate effectively in speaking and writing. They must have good research skills and understand legal terminology.

There are no formal educational requirements, but most employers prefer to hire paralegals with training from a four-year college, law school, community or junior college, business school, or proprietary school.

Most formal paralegal programs take two years to complete, but some bachelor's-degree programs last four years. Another type of program can be completed in a few months if the student already has a bachelor's degree.

The course work in paralegal programs includes subjects such as law and legal research, specialized areas of the law, and legal applications for computers. Some programs offer internships that provide valuable practical experience.

Some employers prefer to provide on-the-job training for experienced legal secretaries or for workers with college education but no legal experience.

The National Association of Legal Assistants offers voluntary certification to paralegals who meet certain requirements of education and experience. Paralegals who meet these requirements then take a two-day examination; if they pass it, they earn the title *certified legal assistant* (CLA). Voluntary certification is also available through the National Federation of Paralegal Associations, leading to the title registered paralegal (RP).

Potential and advancement

There are about 136,000 paralegals in the U.S. workforce. Much growth is expected in this field through 2008, but the number of people entering the field is also expected to increase significantly; as a result, there will be keen competition for jobs.

The largest employers will be private law firms, but there will be more opportunities in many types of companies as they recognize that paralegals can perform many of the same functions as lawyers at less pay.

As paralegals gain experience, they advance by being given more responsible, challenging, and interesting tasks. In firms with large staffs, some paralegals become managers or supervisors.

Income

Salaries for paralegals depend on the level of their education and experience, the type and size of employer, and the geographic location of the job.

Paralegals earn an average annual salary of about $34,000. Beginning paralegals start at an average of $30,000 a year.

Many paralegals also receive annual bonuses.

The average annual salary for paralegals employed by the federal government is $43,900.

Additional sources of information

American Association for Paralegal Education
P.O. Box 40244
Overland Park, KS 66204
www.aafpe.org

National Association of Legal Assistants
1516 South Boston Street, Suite 200
Tulsa, OK 74119
www.nala.org

National Paralegal Association
P.O. Box 406
Solebury, PA 18963

PAROLE OFFICER

The job

An offender who has completed a sentence in a prison or jail is usually assigned a parole officer upon release. The ex-offender is required to report to the parole officer at specific time intervals, and the parole officer, in turn, provides counseling and assistance during the transition from prison to community life.

The parole officer helps the ex-offender find a job or secure job training; arranges for welfare or other public assistance for the family, if necessary; and provides support and a helping hand in any way possible to aid the parolee in his or her return to society. The parole officer's main concern is helping the parolee go straight instead of resuming criminal behavior.

Probation officers deal with juvenile delinquents and first offenders, who are often released by the court, subject to proper supervision, instead of being sentenced to jail or prison. A probation officer may also be involved in the presentencing investigation of a defendant's family, background, and education and any problems contributing to the defendant's offense.

Parole and probation officers are usually employed by state or municipal governments. In the course of their work, they interact with teachers, chaplains, social workers, rehabilitation counselors, local employers, and community organizations. Some parole and probation officers come from the ranks of police officers.

Among the most important ingredients of the work of a probation officer is the rapport the officer is able to establish with a juvenile offender. The opportunity to discuss problems with an understanding adult can result in the juvenile's being put back on the right track. At the same time, the probation officer must be objective enough not to be deceived by lies or false promises of better behavior.

Related jobs are police officer (municipal and state), social worker, corrections officer, and rehabilitation counselor.

Places of employment and working conditions

Emotional wear and tear is a factor in the work of parole and probation officers. The frustration of seeing a parolee or juvenile return to a life of crime in spite of great effort is part of every officer's experience.

In many jobs, the caseload itself can be a hindrance to effective work. Instead of carrying the recommended 30 to 50 cases, many parole and probation officers must keep track of up to 100 assigned cases. This makes it virtually impossible to give each person the attention and help that is usually necessary.

Qualifications, education, and training

Personal characteristics of understanding, objectivity, good judgment, and patience are necessary. Good communication skills and the ability to motivate people are also important.

High school courses should include the social sciences, English, and history.

People who work in this field need a bachelor's degree in sociology, psychology, criminology, or law. Those who start out as police officers usually acquire additional training in these fields through college courses. Many employers also require one or two years of experience in a correctional institution or another social agency or a master's degree in sociology or psychology.

Potential and advancement

Worker shortages in all areas of law enforcement will increase as the population grows. The demand for qualified parole and probation officers will be especially great in large metropolitan areas.

Parole and probation officers are not usually promoted to other positions, but they advance in salary as they gain experience. Some officers advance by acquiring additional education that qualifies them for positions in other areas of law enforcement.

Income

Probation and parole officers earn about $32,100 a year.

Additional sources of information

American Correctional Association
8025 Laurel Lakes Court
Laurel, MD 20707-5075

National Council on Crime and Delinquency
685 Market Street, Suite 620
San Francisco, CA 94105

PERSONNEL MANAGER

The job

Personnel managers conduct and supervise the employment functions of a company. These include recruiting, hiring, and training employees; developing wage and salary scales; administering benefit programs; complying with government labor regulations; and other responsibilities that affect the company's employees.

In a small company, a personnel manager performs all these functions, usually assisted by one or two workers who help with interviewing and perform clerical duties. In a large company, the personnel manager supervises a staff of trained personnel workers that includes some or all of the following specialists.

A *personnel recruiter* searches for qualified job applicants through advertisements and employment agencies. A recruiter may also travel to college campuses to talk to students who are about to graduate. *Employment interviewers* screen job applicants, sometimes administer and interpret tests, and may make some final hiring decisions.

Job analysts collect and analyze detailed information on each job within a company to prepare a description of each position. These descriptions include the duties of a particular job and the skills and training necessary to perform the job. Position descriptions are used by *salary and wage administrators* when they develop or revise pay scales for a company. They also use information gathered in surveys of wages paid by other local employers or by other companies within the same industry. Wage and salary administrators also work within government regulations, such as minimum wage laws.

Training specialists may supervise or conduct orientation sessions for new employees, prepare training materials and manuals, and administer in-house training programs for employees who want to upgrade existing skills or gain promotion.

In some companies, a training specialist may be responsible for apprenticeship-to-management training programs.

An *employee benefits supervisor* provides information and counseling to employees regarding the various benefits offered by a company. The supervisor is also in charge of the administration of these programs, which may include health, life, and disability insurance and pension plans. Other employee services such as cafeterias, newsletters, and recreational facilities may also be part of the package.

Some companies employ a special personnel worker to manage all matters pertaining to the government's equal employment opportunity regulations and the company's affirmative action programs.

Personnel workers in federal, state, and local government agencies have the added duties of devising, administering, and scoring the competitive civil service examinations that are administered to all applicants for public employment. Others oversee compliance with state and federal labor laws, health and safety regulations, and equal employment opportunity programs.

Personnel specialists also work for private employment agencies, executive search organizations, and agencies that place temporary office workers. A few work as self-employed management consultants, and others teach at the college and university level.

Related jobs are employment counselor and labor relations specialist.

Job opportunities for personnel specialists and personnel managers exist throughout the country, with the largest concentrations in highly industrialized areas.

Qualifications, education, and training

Integrity and fairmindedness are important qualifications for people interested in personnel work because they are often called on to act as the liaison between the company and its employees in the day-to-day administration of company policies. Personnel professionals must be able to work with people of many educational levels and must have excellent written and oral communication skills.

In high school, a college preparatory course should emphasize English, social studies, and computer skills.

Some personnel workers enter the field as clerical employees in a personnel office and gain experience and expertise in one or more specialty areas over time. In some small and medium-size companies, they may advance to personnel manager positions on the basis of experience alone, but most employers require a college education even for entry-level jobs in personnel.

People in personnel work come from a variety of college majors. Some employers prefer a well-rounded liberal arts background; others want a business administration degree. A few insist on a degree in personnel administration or in industrial or labor relations. Government agencies prefer applicants who have majored in personnel administration, political science, or public administration. Any courses in the social sciences, the behavioral sciences, and economics are valuable.

Graduate study in industrial or labor relations is necessary for some top-level jobs in personnel work. Some teachers and consultants in this field have a Ph.D.

Potential and advancement

About 597,000 people nationwide are employed in the overlapping fields of personnel and labor relations. These fields are expected to grow quickly, with the largest growth in the private sector as employers try to provide better training and employee relations programs for the growing workforce. Recent rulings on issues such as equal employment opportunity and family leave will increase demand for experts in these areas.

Income

Experienced personnel managers earn annual salaries of between $35,400 and $73,830. Starting salaries average $29,800 for those with a bachelor's degree.

Additional sources of information

American Society for Training and Development
1640 King Street, Box 1443
Alexandria, VA 22313
www.astd.org

International Personnel Management Association
1617 Duke Street
Alexandria, VA 22314

Society for Human Resource Management
606 North Washington Street
Alexandria, VA 22314

PETROLEUM ENGINEER

The job

Petroleum engineers are responsible for exploring and drilling for oil and gas and for efficient production from the site. Some concentrate on research and development into methods to increase the proportion of oil recovered from each reservoir.

Most petroleum engineers are employed by the major oil companies and by the hundreds of small, independent oil exploration and production firms. Drilling equipment manufacturers and suppliers also employ petroleum engineers. In addition, engineering consulting firms and independent consulting engineers use their services, and federal and state agencies employ petroleum engineers on regulatory boards and as inspectors.

Banks and other financial institutions sometimes employ petroleum engineers to provide information on the economic value of oil and gas properties.

Places of employment and working conditions

Most petroleum engineers work in California, Louisiana, Oklahoma, and Texas. Many work overseas for U.S. companies and foreign governments.

This can be dirty work and is sometimes dangerous. Assignments to offshore oil rigs or remote foreign locations can make family life difficult.

Qualifications, education, and training

The ability to think analytically, a capacity for details, and the ability to work as part of a team are necessary. Good communication skills are also important.

Mathematics and the sciences must be emphasized in high school.

A bachelor's degree in engineering is the minimum requirement in this field. In a typical curriculum, the first two years are spent in the study of basic sciences such as physics and chemistry, mathematics, introductory engineering, and some liberal arts courses. The remaining years are usually devoted to specialized engineering courses.

Engineering programs can last from four to six years. Those requiring five or six years to complete may award a master's degree or may provide a cooperative plan of study plus practical work experience with a nearby industry.

Because of rapid changes in technology, many engineers continue their education throughout their careers. A graduate degree is necessary for most teaching and research positions and for many management jobs.

Engineering graduates usually work under the supervision of an experienced engineer or in a company training program until they become acquainted with the requirements of a particular company or industry.

All states require licensing of engineers whose work may affect life, health, or property or who offer their services to the public. Those who are licensed are called registered engineers. Requirements for licensing include graduation from an accredited engineering school, four years of experience, and passing a written examination.

Potential and advancement

Employment in this field is expected to decline through 2008. However, the small number of graduates should be in balance with the number of job openings.

Income

Salaries for experienced engineers average $57,160 to $85,460 per year in private industry. Those in the federal government earn an average of $67,100.

Additional sources of information

Accreditation Board for Engineering and Technology
111 Market Place, Suite 1050
Baltimore, MD 21202-4012
www.abet.org

Junior Engineering Technical Society
1420 King Street, Suite 405
Alexandria, VA 22314-2794
www.jets.org

National Society of Professional Engineers
1420 King Street
Alexandria, VA 22314-2794
www.nspe.org

Society of Petroleum Engineers
P.O. Box 833836
Richardson, TX 75080
www.spe.org

Society of Women Engineers
120 Wall Street, 11th Floor
New York, NY 10005
www.swe.org

PHARMACIST

The job

Pharmacists dispense drugs and medicines prescribed by physicians and dentists, advise on the use and proper dosage of prescription and nonprescription medicines, and work in research and marketing positions. Many pharmacists own their own businesses.

The majority of pharmacists work in community pharmacies (drugstores). These range from one-person operations to large retail establishments employing a staff of pharmacists.

Hospitals and clinics employ pharmacists to dispense drugs and medication to patients, advise the medical staff on the selection and effects of drugs, buy medical supplies, and prepare sterile solutions. In some hospitals, they also teach nursing classes.

Pharmaceutical manufacturers employ pharmacists in research and development and in sales positions. Drug wholesalers also employ them as sales and technical representatives.

The federal government employs pharmacists in hospitals and clinics of the Department of Veterans Affairs and the U.S. Public Health Service; in the Department of Defense; in the Food and Drug Administration; in the Department of Health, Education and Welfare; and in the Drug Enforcement Administration. State and local health agencies also employ pharmacists.

Many community and hospital pharmacists also do consulting work for nursing homes and other health facilities that do not employ a full-time pharmacist.

Places of employment and working conditions

Just about every community has a drugstore employing at least one pharmacist. Most job opportunities, however, are in larger cities and densely populated metropolitan areas.

Pharmacists average about a 40-hour workweek; those who are self-employed average an additional 10 hours a week. Pharmacists in community pharmacies work longer hours—including evenings and weekends—than those employed by hospitals and other health care institutions, pharmaceutical manufacturers, and drug wholesalers. Since some community and hospital pharmacies are open around the clock, in-house pharmacists may have to work nights, weekends, and holidays.

Qualifications, education, and training

Prospective pharmacists need an interest in medicine as well as orderliness and accuracy, business ability, honesty, and integrity.

Biology and chemistry courses, along with some business courses, should be taken in high school.

At least five years of study beyond high school is necessary to earn a degree in pharmacy. A few colleges admit pharmacy students immediately following high school, but most require one or two years of prepharmacy college study in mathematics, basic sciences, humanities, and social sciences.

Colleges of pharmacy are accredited by the American Council on Pharmaceutical Education. Most of these schools award a bachelor of science (B.S.) degree upon completion of the required course of study. Some schools also offer an advanced-degree program leading to a doctor of pharmacy (Pharm.D.) degree. A few schools offer only the Pharm.D. degree.

A Pharm.D. degree or a master's or Ph.D. in pharmacy or a related field is usually required for research, teaching, and administrative positions.

Pharmacists are required to obtain a license to practice. An applicant must usually have graduated from an accredited pharmacy college, passed a state board examination, and had a specified amount of practical experience or internship. Many pharmacists are licensed to practice in more than one state, and most states will grant a license without examination to a qualified pharmacist licensed by another state.

Potential and advancement

Nationwide, about 185,000 people work as pharmacists. Slower-than-average growth is expected in the field, despite increased pharmaceutical needs as the population ages. Automation of drug dispensing, increased use of pharmacy technicians, mail-order drugs, and managed care are reducing the number of jobs.

Many pharmacists in salaried positions advance by opening their own community pharmacies. Those employed by chain drugstores may advance to management positions or executive-level jobs within the company. A hospital pharmacist may advance to director of pharmacy service or to other administrative positions.

Pharmacists employed by the pharmaceutical industry have the widest latitude of advancement possibilities because they can pursue management, sales, research, quality control, advertising, production, or packaging. There will be fewer job opportunities, however, with manufacturers than in other areas of pharmacy.

Income

Pharmacists working in chain drugstores earn an average of $63,400 a year, hospital pharmacists average $62,600 a year, and those employed by the federal government average $61,700.

Additional sources of information

American Association of Colleges of Pharmacy
1426 Prince Street
Alexandria, VA 22314
www.aacp.org

American Society of Hospital Pharmacists
7272 Wisconsin Avenue
Bethesda, MD 20814

National Association of Boards of Pharmacy
700 Busse Highway
Park Ridge, IL 60068

PHOTOGRAPHER

The job

A photographer takes pictures as an artistic or commercial occupation. Some specialize in portrait photography; others work as photojournalists or industrial photographers. Photographers with knowledge in a particular field may specialize in scientific, medical, or engineering photography. In addition, the ranks of artists who adopt photography as an art form have undergone a surge in recent years.

Portrait photographers take pictures of individuals and groups in studios, at weddings, and at other types of gatherings. Many portrait photographers own their own studios and often begin their careers working part-time. These members of the profession need firm business skills to succeed in their own ventures. They must also have a knack for getting subjects to relax.

Commercial photographers, many of whom work in advertising, photograph everything from livestock to buildings to manufactured articles. They must be familiar with many photographic techniques.

Industrial photographers work in industry and shoot everything from people photos for the company newspaper or stockholders' report to glossies of products or manufacturing processes. Those who specialize in fields such as science or medicine may use special equipment and techniques such as infrared photography, x-rays, or time-lapse photography.

Photojournalists are newspaper and magazine photographers, who must have a "nose for news" in addition to photographic skills. Those who work for nationwide publications or prestigious newspapers are among the highest-paid photographers.

Other specialists include *educational photographers*, who prepare slides, filmstrips, and movies for classroom use; *photomicrographers*, who work with microscopes; and *photogrammetrists*, who specialize in the use of aerial photographs for surveying.

Most photographers work in portrait or commercial studios. The next largest group is photojournalists. Government agencies and industrial firms employ a significant number, and a few photographers teach in colleges and universities. More than half of all photographers are self-employed.

Places of employment and working conditions

Photographers work in all areas of the United States.

Those employed in salaried jobs usually work a 35- to 40-hour, five-day week. Those in business for themselves work longer hours. Press photographers usually have to work some evening and weekend hours to cover news assignments. Free-lance, press, and commercial photographers do a considerable amount of traveling.

Qualifications, education, and training

Good eyesight and color vision, artistic ability, and manual dexterity are neces-sary for a photographer. Patience, accuracy, and an aptitude for detail work are also important.

Technical training is the best preparation and is usually necessary for indus-trial, medical, or scientific work. Photographic training is available in four-year colleges, universities, junior colleges, and art schools. The armed forces also train many photographers. Two-year training courses sometimes offer an associate degree in photography. Some colleges offer a bachelor's degree in photography, and a few offer a master's degree in specialized areas such as photojournalism. Art schools provide useful training in design and composition but do not usually offer technical training in photography.

A background in a particular science, medical, or engineering field is neces-sary for many specialty areas of photography. Some employers may require a bach-elor's degree in a particular field in addition to photographic skills and experience. News photographers may be expected to have a background in journalism.

Computers are increasingly used by photographers. Self-employed photogra-phers find them useful for bookkeeping. Computers are also used to scan photos and convert them to digital form. These digital images can be manipulated to achieve a desired effect or stored, like music, on compact discs to create an elec-tronic portfolio. As image quality improves and costs go down, this technique will become more commonplace.

Potential and advancement

The field is expected to grow slowly over the next decade as the demand for photojournalists lessens. Portrait photographers should find opportunities, as will those who can produce digital images for the Internet. Competition for jobs is likely to be keen, given the popularity of the field.

Advancement usually depends on experience. Some industrial and scientific photographers may be promoted to supervisory positions; magazine and news pho-tographers may eventually become photography editors or heads of graphic arts departments. Self-employed photographers advance as they build a reputation and receive more lucrative assignments. Photographers in salaried positions may open their own studios or do freelance work.

Income

Photographers who are experienced earn an average salary between $30,820 and $43,860 a year.

Self-employed and freelance photographers sometimes earn more than salaried photographers; they often do not. Their earnings are affected by the number of hours they devote to the business, the type of clientele, the quality of their work, and their marketing ability.

Additional source of information

Professional Photographers of America
229 Peachtree Street NE, Suite 2200
Atlanta, GA 30303

PHOTOGRAPHIC LABORATORY TECHNICIAN

The job

The development of film, preparation of prints and slides, enlarging and retouching of photographs, and other film-processing chores are performed by photographic laboratory technicians. They service both the amateur photographer (in labs that mass-process film) and the professional photographer (in independent labs or for individual studios).

All-around *precision photographic process workers* can perform all tasks necessary to develop and print film, including enlarging and retouching. They can process black and white negative, color negative, or color positive work. Because color work is more difficult than black-and-white, some highly skilled technicians specialize as *color technicians.*

Technicians who work in photography studios often function as assistants to the photographer, setting up lights and cameras. Many future photographers begin this way, dividing their time between processing film and learning photography.

In some labs, technicians may be assisted by helpers or assistants who specialize in just one process such as developing or retouching. In large photo labs with automatic film-processing equipment, *darkroom technicians* supervise semi-skilled workers who handle many individual tasks such as film numbering, chemical mixing, or slide mounting.

Places of employment and working conditions

Photographic laboratory technicians are employed in all parts of the country, with most job opportunities in large cities.

Photographic laboratory technicians usually work a 40-hour week. In labs that process film for amateur photographers, the summer months and several weeks after the Christmas season require considerable amounts of overtime. Jobs in this field are not physically strenuous, but many of the semiskilled jobs are repetitious and fast paced; some of the processes can cause eye fatigue.

Qualifications, education, and training

Good eyesight and color vision are necessary, as is manual dexterity.

A high school diploma is not always necessary but can provide a good background. Chemistry and mathematics courses are valuable, and any courses, part-time jobs, and amateur photography and film-processing work are helpful. Computer skills are valuable because more and more commercial photographic processing is being done on computers rather than in traditional darkrooms.

Most *photographic process technicians* acquire their skills through on-the-job training, which takes about three years. Others attend trade or technical schools or receive their training in the armed forces.

A few junior and community colleges offer a two-year course in photographic technology leading to an associate degree. College-level training is helpful in attaining supervisory and management positions.

Potential and advancement

There are about 63,000 people across America employed in some phase of photographic laboratory work. This job field is expected to decline through 2008 as digital photography becomes more affordable and more popular.

Income

Earnings for photographic process technicians vary according to the worker's level of skill, experience, and geographic location. Median earnings for full-time workers are about $10.39 per hour.

Additional source of information

Photo Marketing Association International
3000 Picture Place
Jackson, MI 49201

PHYSICAL THERAPIST

The job

At some point in their treatment, accident and stroke victims, children with disabilities, and older persons with physical impairments are usually referred by their doctors to a physical therapist. The therapist will design and carry out a program of testing, exercise, massage, or other therapeutic treatment to increase strength, restore the range of motion, relieve pain, and improve the condition of muscles and skin.

Physical therapists provide direct patient care and usually do an independent evaluation of the patient's needs. However, the therapist works in close cooperation with the physician and any other specialists involved in the care of the patient, such as vocational therapists, psychologists, and social workers. In large hospitals and nursing homes, physical therapists may carry out a program designed by the director or assistant director of the physical therapy department rather than develop the program themselves. Some physical therapists specialize in one category of patient such as children or seniors or one type of condition such as arthritis, amputation, or paralysis.

Most physical therapists work in hospitals. Nursing homes employ a growing number and also use the services of self-employed therapists. Rehabilitation centers, schools for children with disabilities, public health agencies, physicians' offices, and the armed forces are other employers. Some therapists work with patients in their own homes or provide instructions to the patient and the patient's family on how to continue therapy at home.

Because this field has many opportunities for part-time practitioners, it appeals to people with family responsibilities.

Places of employment and working conditions

Physical therapists are employed throughout the country, with the largest number working in cities having large hospitals or medical centers.

Physical therapy, unlike many other medical procedures, does not have to be provided on a 24-hour basis, so most therapists work a 40-hour week. In the case of self-employed and part-time therapists, some evening and weekend work may be required.

The job can be physically demanding because therapists must lift and reposition patients and move heavy equipment.

Qualifications, education, and training

Patience, tact, emotional stability, and skill in working with people are important for anyone interested in this field. Manual dexterity and physical stamina are also needed.

High school students considering this field should take courses in health, biology, social science, mathematics, and physical education. Part-time or volunteer work in the physical therapy department of a hospital can provide a close look at the work for anyone trying to decide on a career in physical therapy. Competition for admission to physical therapy programs is intense, so good grades are essential.

There are two types of programs for physical therapy training: a four-year bachelor's degree in physical therapy or a master's-degree program. The master's program is designed for people who have a bachelor's degree in a related field and want to become physical therapists. A master's degree is also useful for pursuing administrative, research, or teaching positions.

Physical therapists must be licensed. A degree or certificate from an accredited program and a passing grade on a state board examination are required for obtaining a license.

Potential and advancement

There are about 120,000 licensed physical therapists in the United States. Employment in the field is expected to expand rapidly as the demand grows for more rehabilitative facilities for accident victims, senior citizens, and children with disabilities. Opportunities for part-time work will also continue to grow.

Advancement in this field depends on experience and education level, especially for teaching, research, and administrative positions.

Income

Physical therapists earn about $56,600 a year. Earnings of therapists in private practice tend to exceed those of salaried workers.

Additional source of information

American Physical Therapy Association
1111 North Fairfax Street
Alexandria, VA 22314-1488
www.apta.org

PHYSICIAN

The job

Physicians diagnose diseases, treat illnesses and injuries, and are involved in research, rehabilitation, and preventive medicine.

Most physicians specialize in a particular field, such as internal medicine, general surgery, psychiatry, or pediatrics. The fastest-growing specialty is family practice, which emphasizes general medicine.

Most new physicians open their own offices or join associate or group practices. Those who enter the armed forces start with the rank of captain in the army or air force or the rank of lieutenant in the navy. Other federal positions are in the Department of Veterans Affairs, the U.S. Public Health Service, and the Department of Health and Human Services.

Places of employment and working conditions

Just about every community has at least one physician.

The northeastern states have the highest ratios of physicians to population; the southern states have the lowest. Physicians tend to locate in urban areas close to hospital facilities and educational centers; rural areas are often underserved.

Many physicians have long and irregular working hours. Specialists generally work fewer hours than general practitioners. Physicians have the option of curtailing their practices as they grow older, thus being able to work at a reduced pace past the normal retirement age.

Qualifications, education, and training

Anyone interested in this field must have a strong desire to serve people who are sick and injured. It requires emotional stability, the ability to make quick decisions in an emergency, and the capacity to relate well to people. The study of medicine is long and expensive and requires a commitment to intense, vigorous training.

High school should include as much mathematics and science as possible, and grades should average B or above.

Most medical school applicants have a bachelor's degree, although medical schools will accept three years of premedical college study. Competition for entrance into medical school is fierce. Premedical college grades of B or better are usually necessary along with a high grade on the Medical College Admission Test. Other relevant factors are the applicant's character, personality, and leadership qualities; letters of recommendation; and, in state-supported medical schools, area of residence.

It usually takes four years to complete medical school; students with outstanding ability sometimes complete it in three. A few schools have programs that allow completion of premedical and medical studies in a total of six years.

The first half of medical school is spent in classrooms and laboratories studying medical sciences. The remaining time is spent in clinical work under the supervision of experienced physicians. At completion of medical school, students are awarded a doctor of medicine (M.D.) degree.

After graduation, a three-year hospital residency is usually completed. Those seeking certification in a specialty spend up to seven years in advanced residency training; this may be followed by two or more years of practice in the specialty before the required specialty board examination is taken.

Physicians who intend to teach or do research must earn a master's or Ph.D. degree in a field such as biochemistry or microbiology.

All physicians must be licensed to practice medicine. Requirements usually include graduation from an accredited medical school, completion of a residency program, and a passing grade on a licensing examination—usually the National Board of Medical Examiners (NBME) test. Applicants who have not taken the NBME test must sit for the Federation Licensing Examination, which is accepted by all jurisdictions. Physicians licensed in one state can obtain a license in most other states without further examination.

Graduates of foreign medical schools must pass an examination given by the Educational Commission for Foreign Medical Graduates before they are allowed to serve a residency in the United States.

Potential and advancement

There are about 577,000 professionally active physicians in the United States. Employment opportunities should be good through 2008 due to the growing demands for health care. In addition, the number of medical students has leveled off and is expected to decline in coming years, reducing the competition for jobs. Opportunities will continue to be greatest for physicians who wish to establish practices in areas of the country that have traditionally lacked sufficient medical services, such as rural and inner-city areas. Primary-care practitioners, such as family physicians, pediatricians, and internal medicine specialists, will continue to be most in demand.

Income

Physicians have the highest average annual earnings of any occupational or professional group—between $120,000 and $250,000.

New physicians setting up their own practices usually have a few lean years in the beginning, but once a practice is established, earnings rise rapidly. Physicians in a private practice usually earn more than those in salaried positions, and specialists earn considerably more than general practitioners.

Because practitioners in metropolitan areas have much better incomes than those in rural areas, some rural communities offer a guaranteed annual income to a physician who is willing to practice in that locale.

Additional sources of information

American Medical Association
515 North State Street
Chicago, IL 60610
www.ama-assn.org

Association of American Medical Colleges
Section for Student Services
2450 N Street NW
Washington, DC 20037-1131
www.aamc.org

PHYSICIAN ASSISTANT

The job

Physician assistants, or PAs, relieve primary-care physicians of some of their duties. They are trained to perform such medical procedures as taking medical histories, performing physical examinations, making preliminary diagnoses, prescribing treatments, and suggesting medications and drug therapies. In some states, PAs are permitted to prescribe medication.

PAs also treat minor medical problems such as cuts and burns. They provide pre- and postoperative care and sometimes assist in surgery.

PAs work in several medical specialties, including family practice, internal medicine, general and thoracic surgery, emergency medicine, and pediatrics.

Places of employment and working conditions

PAs work in physicians' offices, hospitals, and clinics. Some work in inner-city or rural clinics that are served by a physician once or twice a week. The rest of the week, the PA independently provides health care services after consulting with the supervising physician by telephone.

PAs' schedules depend on the work setting. Usually, they share the same work hours as the supervising physician. If the employer provides 24-hour medical care, they may be required to work nights, weekends, and holidays. Some PAs are required to be on call.

Qualifications, education, and training

PAs should enjoy working with people. Leadership skills, confidence, and emotional stability are also important qualities.

Almost all states require that PAs complete an accredited formal education program. There are currently 116 educational programs for physician assistants. Most offer a bachelor's degree; others offer a certificate, an associate degree, or a master's degree.

Admission requirements for many programs include two years of college and work experience in the health field. Many applicants already have a bachelor's or master's degree and experience in another health care field, such as nursing.

PA programs are usually two years long. They are offered by medical schools, schools of allied health, and four-year colleges; a few are sponsored by community colleges or hospitals. Course work includes classroom instruction and supervised experience in clinical practice.

Most states have laws concerning the qualifications or practice of PAs and require them to pass a certifying exam given only to graduates of accredited programs. Continuing medical education and periodic recertification exams are required to maintain certification. PAs may also need additional education to pursue a specialty, such as surgery.

Potential and advancement

There are about 66,000 physician assistants in the country. There should be good opportunities for physician assistants through 2008. The health services industry is expected to expand greatly, and PAs will be in demand to relieve doctors of some of their more routine tasks and assist them in more complex medical and surgical procedures.

PAs sometimes advance by taking additional training that allows them to work in a specialty area such as surgery or emergency medicine. Others earn higher salaries and are given more responsibility as they gain experience and increase their knowledge. PAs, though, are always supervised by doctors.

Income

The average starting salary for physician assistants is about $54,000 a year. Experienced physician assistants earn an average annual salary of about $62,200.

Additional sources of information

American Academy of Physician Assistants
950 North Washington Street
Alexandria, VA 22314-1552
www.aapa.org

American Medical Association
515 North State Street
Chicago, IL 60610
www.ama-assn.org

PHYSICIST

The job

Physicists develop theories that describe the fundamental forces and laws of nature. Most physicists work in research and development. Their work in recent years has contributed to progress in such fields as nuclear energy, electronics, communications, aerospace, and medical instrumentation.

Physicists usually specialize in one branch of the science: elementary particle physics; nuclear physics; atomic, electron, and molecular physics; physics of condensed matter; optics; acoustics; plasma physics; or the physics of fluids.

Many physicists teach or do research in colleges and universities. Private industry employs physicists mainly in companies manufacturing chemicals, electrical equipment, aircraft, and missiles. About 20 percent of all physicists work for the federal government, most of them in the Departments of Defense and Commerce and in the National Aeronautics and Space Administration.

Places of employment and working conditions

Physicists are employed in all parts of the country, with the heaviest concentrations in industrial areas and areas with large college enrollments.

Physicists usually work in offices and laboratories. They have regular working hours.

Qualifications, education, and training

Physicists must have an inquisitive mind, imagination, the ability to think in abstract terms, and mathematical aptitude.

High school courses in science, mathematics, and computer technology are necessary preparation.

A career in physics almost always requires a Ph.D. A bachelor's degree in physics or mathematics is usually the first step, followed by a master's degree. Some graduate students are able to work as research assistants while they study for a master's degree and may be hired as instructors while completing the Ph.D. requirements. A bachelor's or master's degree is sufficient for some technician and research jobs in private industry and for nonresearch positions in the federal government.

Potential and advancement

Job opportunities are expected to be flat through 2008. Cuts in the federal budget, reduced grant money, and curtailment of private and government research programs will reduce demand for physicists.

Physicists advance to more complex tasks as they gain experience and may move up to positions as project leaders or research directors; some advance to top management jobs. Physicists who develop new products often form their own companies.

Income

Annual salaries for physicists with a Ph.D. average $70,000; those with a master's, $57,000; and those with a bachelor's, $54,000. Physicists working for the federal government earn an average of $79,400.

Additional sources of information

American Institute of Physics
Career Planning and Placement
One Physics Ellipse
College Park, MD 20740-3843
www.aip.org

American Physical Society
Education Department
One Physics Ellipse
College Park, MD 20740-3844
www.aps.org

PLUMBER AND PIPE FITTER

The job

Plumbing and pipe fitting is usually considered a single trade, with workers specializing in one or the other component. Plumbers install, repair, and maintain water, gas, and waste-disposal systems in homes, schools, factories, and other buildings; pipe fitters install high- and low-pressure pipes that carry hot water, steam, and other liquids and gases used in industrial processes. They also install automatic controls used to regulate electrical, heating, and cooling systems.

Plumbers and pipe fitters work from blueprints and use a variety of hand and power tools. They glue, solder, or weld pipe connections to prevent leaks and may have to drill holes in ceilings, floors, or walls or hang steel supports from ceilings to position pipes properly.

Most plumbers and pipe fitters work for contractors engaged in new construction. A substantial number of plumbers are self-employed or work for contractors who do repair, alteration, and remodeling work in homes and other buildings. Others are employed by government agencies and public utilities, do maintenance work in industrial and commercial buildings, or work in construction of ships and aircraft. Many pipe fitters are employed as maintenance personnel in the petroleum, chemical, and food-processing industries.

Places of employment and working conditions

Plumbers and pipe fitters work throughout the country in communities of all sizes. The largest concentrations are in heavily industrialized areas, especially those with petroleum, chemical, or food-processing plants.

Plumbers and pipe fitters often work in cramped or uncomfortable positions and must stand for long periods. They are subject to cuts and burns and risk falls from ladders.

Many plumbers and pipe fitters belong to the United Association of Journeymen and Apprentices of the Plumbing and Pipe Fitting Industry of the United States and Canada. Those who are contractors usually belong to the National Association of Plumbing-Heating-Cooling Contractors.

Qualifications, education, and training

Mechanical aptitude and physical stamina are necessary for this job field.

A high school diploma is required. Vocational or technical school training is usually preferred, and courses in chemistry, general mathematics, mechanical drawing, physics, and shop are useful.

Apprenticeship to experienced workers is considered the best way to learn all aspects of the trade. Apprenticeship programs are usually sponsored by local union-management committees and last four to five years. Applicants must be at least 18 years old and in good physical condition. Those accepted receive four years of on-the-job training and spend about 144 hours each year in related classroom instruction.

Armed forces training in this field is another respected way to begin this career. Those who train in the armed forces are usually given credit for their experience when entering civilian apprenticeship programs.

Most communities mandate that plumbers and pipe fitters be licensed. This requires a passing grade on an examination covering knowledge of the trade and of local building and plumbing codes.

Potential and advancement

In the United States, there are 426,000 plumbers and pipe fitters. Job opportunities in this field are expected to be good through 2008. Although the field is expected to grow more slowly than other occupations, the number of qualified workers is also growing slowly.

Plumbers and pipe fitters can advance to supervisory positions. Many prefer to advance by going into business for themselves.

Income

Plumbers and pipe fitters have median hourly earnings of $16.67. Most earn between $12.81 and $22.18 an hour.

Apprentices begin at about 50 percent of the wage rate paid to experienced plumbers and pipe fitters and earn more as they acquire skills.

Additional sources of information

National Association of Plumbing-Heating-Cooling
   Contractors
P.O. Box 6808
Falls Church, VA 22040

National Fire Sprinkler Association
P.O. Box 1000
Patterson, NY 12563

United Association of Journeymen and Apprentices of the
   Plumbing and Pipe Fitting Industry of the United States and
   Canada.
P.O. Box 37800
Washington, DC 20013

PODIATRIST

The job

The diagnosis and treatment of diseases and deformities of the feet is the special field of podiatrists. They treat corns, bunions, calluses, ingrown toenails, skin and nail diseases, deformed toes, and arch disabilities. If a person's feet show symptoms of medical disorders that affect other parts of the body (such as arthritis or diabetes), the podiatrist will refer the patient to a medical doctor while continuing to treat the patient's foot problem.

In the course of diagnosis, podiatrists may take x-rays and perform blood tests or other pathological tests. They perform surgery; fit corrective devices; and prescribe drugs, physical therapy, and proper shoes.

Most podiatrists provide all types of foot care, but some specialize in foot surgery, orthopedics (bone, muscle, and joint disorders), children's foot ailments, or foot problems of geriatric patients.

Some podiatrists purchase established practices or spend their early years in a salaried position while gaining experience and earning the money to set up their own practices. Podiatrists in full-time salaried positions usually work in hospitals, in podiatric medical colleges, or for other podiatrists. Public health departments and the Department of Veterans Affairs also employ full- and part-time podiatrists, and some podiatrists serve as commissioned officers in the armed forces.

Places of employment and working conditions

Podiatrists work in all sections of the country but are more numerous in or near one of the seven states that have colleges of podiatric medicine.

Most podiatrists are in private practice, work about 40 hours a week, and set their own schedules. They also spend some hours handling the administration and paperwork of their offices. Podiatrists who work for hospitals or health maintenance organizations may be required to work nights or weekends. This is not physically strenuous work, a fact that allows practitioners in private practice to work past normal retirement age.

Qualifications, education, and training

Anyone interested in a career as a podiatrist should have specific aptitude, manual dexterity, and an ability to work well with people.

High school courses in mathematics and science are important preparation.

The degree of doctor of podiatric medicine (D.P.M.) is available after successful completion of at least three years of college and four years of a school of podiatric medicine. Competition for entry in these schools is strong, and although three years of college is the minimum requirement, most successful applicants have a bachelor's degree and an overall grade point average of B or better. College study must include courses in English, chemistry, biology or zoology, physics, and mathematics. All schools of podiatric medicine also require applicants to take the Medical College Admission Test (MCAT).

The first two years in podiatry school are spent in classroom and laboratory study of anatomy, bacteriology, chemistry, pathology, physiology, pharmacology, and other basic sciences. In the final two years, students obtain clinical experience. Additional study and experience are necessary for practice in a specialty.

All podiatrists must be licensed. Requirements include graduation from an accredited college of podiatric medicine and passing grades on written and oral state board proficiency examinations. Many states also require a residency in a hospital or clinic. A majority of states grant licenses without examination to podiatrists licensed by another state.

Potential and advancement

There are about 14,000 practicing podiatrists in the United States, most of them located in large cities. Employment in this profession is expected to grow at an average rate through 2008.

Increasing population, especially the growing number of older people who need foot care and who are covered by Medicare, will contribute to the demand for podiatrists.

New graduates can expect some competition for salaried positions, especially in the areas surrounding colleges of podiatric medicine. Establishing a private practice will also be more difficult in these locations.

Income

Most newly licensed podiatrists set up their own practices and, as in most new practices, earn much less in the early years than they will after becoming established. The average yearly income of podiatrists is about $116,000 for those in private practice and $79,530 for those in salaried positions.

Additional sources of information

American Association of Colleges of Podiatric Medicine
1350 Piccard Drive, Suite 322
Rockville, MD 20850-4307
www.aacpm.org

American Podiatric Medical Association
9312 Old Georgetown Road
Bethesda, MD 20814-1612
www.apma.org

POLICE OFFICER, MUNICIPAL

The job

The duties of a police officer may include law enforcement, crowd and traffic control, criminal investigations, communications, and specialties such as handwriting and fingerprint identification or chemical and microscopic analysis. All police officers are trained in first aid.

In a small community, police officers perform a wide variety of duties, while those in a large city may be assigned to one type, such as traffic, canine patrol, accident prevention, or mounted and motorcycle patrols. Law enforcement is complex, and each police force is tailored to meet the particular problems of its community. A city of any size that has heavy traffic congestion will need more police assigned to accident prevention and traffic control; a city with a high juvenile crime rate will use more officers in criminal investigation and youth aid services.

New police officers usually begin a patrol duty with an experienced officer to become thoroughly familiar with the city and its law enforcement requirements. This probationary period can last from a few months to three years.

All police officers report to police headquarters at regular intervals by radio or telephone or through police call boxes. They also prepare written reports about their activities and may be called on to testify in court on cases they handle.

Detectives are plain-clothes police officers whose primary activity is to carry out investigative procedures. They are often assigned to a specific case, such as a murder investigation, or a particular type of case, such as illegal drugs. Detectives gather information and evidence to be used by police and prosecuting attorneys.

Places of employment and working conditions

Police officers work throughout the country in communities of all sizes.

The usual workweek of a police officer is 40 hours, including shift work and weekend and evening hours. Payment for extra hours worked on some police forces takes the form of extra time off. Officers must often work outdoors in all kinds of weather and are subject to call at any time.

Police officers face the constant threat of injury or death in their work. The injury rate for police officers is higher than in many other occupations.

Qualifications, education, and training

A police officer should be honest, have a sense of responsibility and sound judgment, and enjoy working with people and serving the public. Good health and physical stamina are also necessary.

High school courses should include English, U.S. history, and civics and government. Physical education and sports are helpful in developing stamina and agility.

In some large cities, high school graduates who are still in their teens may be hired as police cadets or trainees. They function as paid civilian employees and do clerical work while they attend training classes. If they have all the necessary qualifications, they may be appointed to the police force when they reach the qualifying age.

Local civil service regulations govern the appointment of police officers in most communities. Candidates must be at least 21 years old, be U.S. citizens, meet certain height and weight standards, and pass a rigorous physical examination. Character traits and backgrounds are investigated, and a personality test is sometimes administered. Most applicants must pass lie detector exams and drug tests. Applicants are usually interviewed by a senior police officer and, in some police departments, by a psychiatrist or psychologist.

An applicant's eligibility for appointment depends on his or her performance on a competitive examination, and on education and experience.

Most police departments require a high school education; a few cities require some college training. More and more police departments are encouraging their officers to continue their education and to study subjects such as sociology, psychology, law enforcement, criminal justice, and foreign languages. These courses are available in junior and community colleges as well as four-year colleges and universities.

New police officers go through a training period. In small communities, this may consist of working with experienced officers. Large cities have more formal training programs at police academies that last from 12 to 14 weeks. Officers receive classroom instruction in constitutional law and civil rights, state and local ordinances, accident investigation, patrol, and traffic control. They learn to use a gun, defend themselves from attack, administer first aid, and respond to emergencies.

Experienced police officers improve their performance, keep up-to-date, and prepare for advancement by taking various training courses at police department academies and colleges. They study crowd-control techniques, civil defense, the latest legal developments that affect police work, and advances in law enforcement equipment.

Potential and advancement

There are about 764,000 full-time police officers working in communities throughout the United States. All police departments are funded by local governments, and because police protection is considered essential, law enforcement expenses usually have a high priority in municipal budgets. As the population grows, the demand for police officers will also grow. Competition for jobs will remain, however, and applicants with some college training in law enforcement will have the best opportunities.

Advancement in police work depends on length of service, job performance, and written examinations. In some large departments, promotion may also allow a police officer to specialize in one type of duty, such as communications, traffic control, or working with juveniles.

Income

Police officers and detectives receive average annual salaries between $37,710 and $48,700. Many earn substantially more because of overtime pay.

Police officers are usually covered by liberal plans that allow them to retire after 20 or 25 years of service at half pay. Most police departments furnish revolvers, nightsticks, handcuffs, and other equipment and provide an allowance for uniforms.

Additional sources of information

Information is available from your local police departments and civil service commissions.

POLICE OFFICER, STATE

The job

State police officers, sometimes called *state troopers*, patrol the highways throughout the United States. They enforce traffic laws, issue traffic tickets to motorists who violate those laws, provide information to travelers, control traffic and summon emergency equipment at the scene of an accident or other emergency, sometimes check the weight of commercial vehicles, and conduct driver examinations.

In areas that do not have a local police force, state police officers may investigate crime. They also help city and county police forces to catch lawbreakers and control civil disturbances.

Some officers are assigned to training positions in state police schools or to specializations such as fingerprint classification or chemical and microscopic analysis of criminal evidence. A few have administrative duties.

Places of employment and working conditions

State police officers often work irregular hours because police protection is provided 24 hours a day. Sometimes they must work weekends and holidays.

State police officers spend most of their time driving in all kinds of weather. They may be involved in dangerous situations and have to risk their lives in the line of duty.

Qualifications, education, and training

Honesty, a sense of responsibility, and a desire to serve the public are important. Physical strength and agility are necessary, and height, weight, and eyesight standards must be met.

High school courses in English, government or civics, U.S. history, and physics are helpful. Physical education and sports develop stamina and agility. Driver education courses and military police training are also valuable.

State civil service regulations govern the appointment of state police officers. Applicants must be U.S. citizens at least 21 years old and must usually have a high school education. Applicants must pass a competitive written examination, a rigorous physical examination, and a character and background investigation.

Recruits enter a formal training program that lasts for several months. They study state laws and jurisdictions, patrol, traffic control, and accident investigation. They learn to use firearms, defend themselves from attack, handle an automobile at high speeds, and give first aid.

State police recruits serve a probationary period ranging from six months to three years. After gaining sufficient experience, some officers take advanced training in police science, administration, law enforcement, criminology, or psychology. Courses in these subjects are offered by junior colleges, four-year colleges and universities, and special police training institutions, including the National Academy of the Federal Bureau of Investigation.

Some states hire high school graduates who are still in their teens to serve as cadets. They study police work and perform nonenforcement duties such as clerical work. If they qualify, they may be appointed to the state police force when they reach 21.

Potential and advancement

Job opportunities should be good as concern about the rising crime rate continues. However, this career is attractive to many people, and competition for positions is expected to remain strong.

Promotion depends on the amount of time spent in a specific rank and the individual's standing on competitive examinations.

Income

Base salaries for state police officers are about $37,130 to $48,700. Actual earnings may be greater, as most officers are paid a significant amount of overtime.

Additional sources of information

State civil service commissions or state police headquarters, usually located in each state capital, can provide information to anyone interested in a career as a state police officer.

PRIEST (ROMAN CATHOLIC)

The job

Roman Catholic priests provide spiritual guidance, perform and administer rites and sacraments, and oversee the education of Catholics in the United States.

There are two main classifications of priests. *Diocesan priests*, also called *secular priests*, generally are assigned to a parish by the bishop of the diocese. They work as individuals to provide complete pastoral services for their congregations and are involved in the elementary and secondary schools of the parish and diocese.

Religious priests are part of a religious order such as the Jesuits or Franciscans. They perform specialized duty such as teaching or missionary work, which is assigned to them by their superiors in the order. Those involved in education usually work at the high school, college, or university level.

Places of employment and working conditions

There are Catholic priests in nearly every city and town and in many rural areas. The highest concentrations are in metropolitan areas where large Catholic parishes and educational institutions are located.

Working conditions for priests vary greatly. Those assigned to parishes usually work long and irregular hours. Priests are not permitted to marry, and the absence of a family life is a hardship for some priests.

Qualifications, education, and training

As with all members of the clergy, whatever denomination, a deep religious commitment and a desire to serve others are the most important qualifications for a priest. He must also be a model of moral and ethical conduct.

For young men who decide early in life to become priests, high school seminaries provide a college preparatory program.

Preparation for the priesthood requires eight years of study beyond high school. Seminary colleges provide a liberal arts program stressing philosophy and religion, behavioral sciences, history, and the natural sciences. Four or more additional years are spent in the study of the rites and teachings of the Catholic Church and in fieldwork.

Women are not eligible to enter the priesthood.

Potential and advancement

There are about 47,000 priests in the United States. The need for priests is expected to rise along with the growth in population, but the number of ordained priests has traditionally been insufficient to meet the needs of the Church and will probably continue to lag.

Newly ordained diocesan priests usually start out as assistants to pastors of established parishes. As they gain experience, they may advance to posts in larger parishes or be assigned to parishes of their own. Some priests advance to administrative positions within the diocese.

Newly ordained religious priests begin work immediately in the specialty for which they are trained. They may advance to administrative positions within the religious order or in the institutions where they work.

The Church encourages continuing education for ordained priests. Some priests pursue postgraduate work at U.S. universities or abroad, usually in Rome.

Income

The salaries of diocesan priests vary from diocese to diocese and average $12,936 to $15,483 a year. Priests assigned to a parish live in the parish rectory, where all living expenses are paid by the parish; a car allowance is usually provided. Some dioceses also provide group insurance and retirement benefits. When such benefits are included, the total value of compensation is usually about $30,713 a year.

Priests engaged in other than parish work are usually paid at least a partial salary by the institution that employs them. Housing is sometimes also provided.

Religious priests take a vow of poverty and are supported by their religious orders.

Additional sources of information

A man interested in entering the priesthood should seek the guidance of his parish priest or contact the diocesan director of vocations.

PRINTING PRESS OPERATOR

The job

The preparation, care, and operation of printing presses are the responsibilities of printing press operators. In a small commercial shop, an operator may run simple equipment and learn through on-the-job training; the operator on a giant newspaper or magazine press is a highly trained and experienced worker with several assistants.

The press operator sets up and adjusts the press, inserts type setups or plates and locks them into place, adjusts ink flow, and loads paper—by hand on a small press, with mechanical assistance on a large one. When printing is complete, the press operator or an assistant cleans the press and may oil it and make minor repairs.

Press operators are usually designated according to the type of press they operate: letterpress, gravure, or offset. Offset press operators are further designated as sheet-fed or web-press operators. (Web-fed presses use paper in giant rolls instead of single sheets.) Companies that switch from sheet-fed to web-fed presses must retrain the entire press crew because the two types of presses are very different. Web-fed presses are larger, operate at faster speeds, and require greater physical effort, monitoring of more variables, and faster decisions than sheet-fed presses.

Many plants have recently computerized their press operations, which saves time. Soon most plants will be converted, allowing printing press operators to monitor the printing process electronically—by pushing buttons.

Places of employment and working conditions

Printing press operators work throughout the country, but employment is greatest in large cities.

Most printing press operators work for commercial printing shops and newspaper plants. The remainder work for businesses, manufacturers, and other organizations that have in-house printing facilities. This includes many federal, state, and local government agencies.

Pressrooms are noisy, and press operators are subject to the hazards that go with working around machinery. Many printing companies have two or three shifts, and press operators may be required to do a certain amount of shift work; press operators who work for morning newspapers almost always work night shifts. Press operators often stand for long periods, and some presses require lifting of heavy plates and paper.

Qualifications, education, and training

Mechanical aptitude is important for a press operator. Physical strength is needed for some jobs.

High school courses in chemistry and physics are helpful. Printing shop classes can provide valuable experience.

Although some printing press operators acquire their skills through on-the-job training, most operators complete a formal apprenticeship program offered by a technical or trade school or a junior college. Most postsecondary school programs last one to two years.

An apprenticeship lasts from two to five years, depending on the press being learned. In addition to receiving on-the-job instruction, the apprentice must complete related classroom or correspondence-course work.

Recent technological changes mean that press operators will need specific computer skills. Those already in the field will need to retrain as equipment becomes computerized.

Potential and advancement

America has about 253,000 printing press operators, and the field is expected to grow more slowly than the average for all occupations through 2008. Although demand for books, magazines, and printed advertising will increase, computerization will drastically reduce the number of printing press operators.

Advancement usually takes the form of learning to operate a more complex press. In large shops, some press operators move up to supervisory positions.

Income

Earnings for printing press operators depend on the type of press on which they work, the area of the country in which they live, and whether or not they belong to a union. Hourly wages range from $9.08 to $14.91.

Additional sources of information

Graphic Arts Education and Research Foundation
1899 Preston White Drive
Reston, VA 20191
www.npes.org

Graphic Communications International Union
1900 L Street NW
Washington, DC 20036
www.gciu.org

Printing Industries of America
100 Daingerfield Road
Arlington, VA 22314
www.gain.org

PRODUCER/DIRECTOR OF
RADIO, TELEVISION, MOVIES, AND THEATER

The job

The jobs of producer and director are often combined in actual practice, but for clarity, this job description treats them as separate positions.

The *producer* is the business head of a production. Anyone with a script and a bankroll can be a producer, it has been said, but the successful ones have much more than that. They have taste and discrimination and the ability to raise money from backers.

A producer must be able to estimate production and operating costs, obtain or provide financing, hire a staff and performers, arrange for rehearsal facilities, and manage all other production details. In the theater and movies, producers take an enormous financial risk; radio and television are more stable fields. On any project, the producer is the boss because he or she controls the purse strings.

The *director* is the unifying force that brings together the diverse talents involved in a production. To some, the director is the most important element. A well-known director can attract top stars and backers to a production on the strength of his or her reputation. A good director is said to be part psychologist and part disciplinarian in the handling of the creative, temperamental, and strong-willed people who make up a production. He or she must have a working knowledge of costume, lighting, and design as well as acting. Most directors have at least some firsthand experience as actors. The director's ability to bring out the best in the performers, along with his or her interpretation of the script as a whole, usually means the difference between success or failure for a production.

In television and radio, the director's duties are a little different. The selection and scheduling of programs are also part of the director's organizational and administrative functions because many programs come prepackaged and ready for airing.

In the theater, touring shows employ an *advance director*. Because many shows send only the stars and a few other principal players on tour, remaining roles in the cast are filled by local actors. The advance director arrives ahead of time to select and rehearse the local cast and have the production ready when the stars arrive. This is not a very creative type of directing because all decisions have been made and the director must prepare the cast to duplicate the performances being given in other cities on the tour.

An important position in any production is that of *stage manager* (*floor manager* in radio and television), who is, in effect, the "executive in charge of operations." The stage manager sees that everyone gets on stage at the right moment and that lighting crews and stagehands operate on cue. The stage manager assigns dressing rooms, handles emergencies of all types, and is sometimes the understudy for one or more roles in a production. Many stage managers start out as actors and, although stage managing is a demanding specialty in its own right, go on to become directors or producers.

Places of employment and working conditions

There are opportunities for producers and directors in large cities throughout the country, but most are concentrated in Boston, Chicago, Houston, Los Angeles, New York City, Philadelphia, and San Francisco—the prime locations of the movie, television, and theater industries.

As with all aspects of the entertainment field, work is not steady. For a producer or a director, the pressures of assembling a new production are enormous. When the production is not a success, the financial and emotional costs can be staggering.

Qualifications, education, and training

A producer has to have business and administrative ability as well as a grasp of what the public wants in the way of entertainment. A director must have artistic talent and good judgment, emotional and physical stamina, a thorough knowledge of techniques and devices, patience, and assertiveness.

There are no educational requirements for either of these positions. In the case of the director, talent is the most important factor, combined with experience gathered through years of practice. Many of today's directors, however, received their basic training at a top drama school or college. Many colleges offer programs in dramatic arts that include course work in directing, production, costume, and other related fields, as well as radio and television courses. One big advantage of formal training is the opportunity it provides for an aspiring director to work in college productions.

Producers with an educational background that combines the arts and business administration skills have an advantage in the modern entertainment field.

Potential and advancement

Many opportunities exist outside the high-profile jobs at the top of the entertainment field. Community theaters, summer stock, touring shows, industrial shows, and commercial production companies all require producers and directors. Teaching positions are available at colleges, drama schools, and some secondary schools (many require teacher certification). The trend is toward a solid educational background combined with experience.

Although the field should experience average growth through 2008—fueled by the growth of cable television, home movie rentals, and television syndication—competition for jobs is intense because of the large number of interested job candidates.

All experience is valuable in this field; nothing is irrelevant. Getting a job in almost any capacity of performing or production is important for the beginner. From there, advancement comes through hard work, talent, and being noticed by the right people. A prop manager can work up to stage manager; an experienced actor can branch out into directing. Whatever the job, advancement to better companies, exposure on bigger radio or television stations, and working with well-known stars are the marks of progress.

Income

Producers' earnings vary greatly. In movies and the theater, earnings depend on the success or failure of individual productions. Television and radio are the most stable and dependable fields.

Directors also have sporadic earnings. Those working on Broadway earn the most—$100,000 plus royalties. Those in summer stock, community theaters, and touring shows have a wide range of earnings, depending on size and caliber of the productions—on average, $2,500 to $8,000 for a three- to four-week run of a production.

Radio and television provide full-time salaried positions for directors. Earnings depend on the station's size, with major networks paying the highest salaries.

Producers usually receive a percentage of the show's earnings; some get a set fee.

Additional source of information

Alliance of Motion Picture and Television Producers
15503 Ventura Boulevard
Encino, CA 91436-3140

Producers Guild of America
400 South Beverly Drive
Beverly Hills, CA 90212

PRODUCTION MANAGER, INDUSTRIAL

The job

Production managers coordinate the activities of production departments of manufacturing firms. They are part of middle management, just below corporate, or top-level management, which sets long-range goals and policies.

Production managers carry out the plans of top management by planning and organizing the actual production of company products. They work closely with industrial designers, purchasing managers, labor relations specialists, industrial traffic managers, and production supervisors. Their responsibilities include materials control (the flow of materials and parts into the plant), production control (efficient production processes), and quality control (testing of finished products).

Places of employment and working conditions

Production managers work throughout the country, with the largest concentrations in heavily industrialized areas.

Hours for production managers are often long and irregular. In addition to their specific duties, they spend considerable time on paperwork and in meetings and are expected to be available at all times to manage problems and emergencies.

Many production managers are required to travel frequently.

Qualifications, education, and training

Strong leadership qualities and communication skills are necessary, as is the ability to work well under pressure.

High school should include mathematics and science courses. A college degree is necessary for almost all jobs at this level. In some small companies, production supervisors or technical workers may occasionally rise through the ranks to production manager, but they usually acquire some college training along the way.

Some companies will hire liberal arts graduates as production managers, but most employers prefer a bachelor's degree or higher in engineering, marketing, or business administration. A very effective combination is a bachelor's degree in engineering and a master's degree in business administration.

Some companies have management training programs for new graduates. As a trainee, the employee spends several years, usually in a variety of departments, gathering experience.

Potential and advancement

Demand for production managers is projected to decline slightly through 2008. Many qualified candidates aspire to these jobs, so competition will be substantial. Best opportunities will be for college graduates who have accumulated experience in a variety of industrial production areas.

Because this is already a high management post, it takes outstanding performance to be promoted to the corporate level; only a very few get to be vice president of manufacturing. Most production managers advance by moving to a larger company where the responsibilities are greater and more complex.

Income

Salaries vary greatly from industry to industry and also depend on the size of the plant. Most production managers earn between $41,300 and $79,830 a year and receive bonuses based on performance.

Additional source of information

American Management Association
1601 Broadway, 10th Floor
New York, NY 10019-7420
www.amanet.org

PSYCHIATRIST

The job

A psychiatrist is a medical doctor (physician) who specializes in the problems of mental illness. Because a psychiatrist is also a physician, he or she is licensed to use a wider variety of treatments—including drugs, hospitalization, and somatic (shock) therapy—than others who treat people with mental illness.

Psychiatrists may specialize as to psychiatric technique and to age or type of patients treated.

Most psychiatrists are *psychotherapists* who treat individual patients directly. They sometimes see patients in groups or in a family setting.

Psychotherapy is a technique of verbal therapy that may be supplemented with other treatments such as medication. Some psychiatrists are *psychoanalysts*, who specialize in a technique of individual therapy based on the work of Sigmund Freud. Psychiatrists who practice this specialty must themselves undergo psychoanalysis in the course of their training. *Child psychiatrists* specialize in the treatment of children.

Some psychiatrists work exclusively in research, studying such aspects as the effect of drugs on the brain or the basic sciences of human behavior. Others teach at the college and university level. Research and teaching psychiatrists, however, usually combine their work with a certain amount of direct patient care.

In addition to operating in private practice, psychiatrists work in clinics, general hospitals, and private and public psychiatric hospitals. The federal government employs psychiatrists in the Department of Veterans Affairs and the U.S. Public Health Service.

Related jobs are psychologist and rehabilitation counselor.

Places of employment and working conditions

Psychiatrists work in all parts of the country, almost always in large metropolitan areas or near universities and medical schools.

This field can be emotionally wearing on the practitioner. The shortage of psychiatrists combined with the increasing demand for psychiatric services means that many practitioners are overworked and often cannot devote as much time as they would like to each patient.

The expense and time involved in securing an education for this field deter some people from pursuing it as a career.

Qualifications, education, and training

More than in any other field, the personality of the individual determines effectiveness. Emotional stability, patience, the ability to empathize with people, and a manner that encourages trust and confidence are absolutely necessary. The psychiatrist must be inquisitive, analytical, and flexible in the treatment of patients and must be acutely aware of his or her own limitations and biases.

A high school student interested in this field should take a college preparatory course that emphasizes science.

After high school, the training of a psychiatrist takes from 12 to 14 years. (Educational requirements for a **physician** are detailed under that job description.)

Upon receiving an M.D. degree and completing a one-year medical internship in a hospital approved by the American Medical Association (AMA), a prospective psychiatrist begins a three- to four-year psychiatric specialty program. This program must take place in a hospital approved for this purpose by the AMA and the American Psychiatric Association.

Training is carried on during a residency program that requires study, research, and clinical practice under the supervision of staff psychiatrists. After completion of the program and two years of experience, a psychiatrist is eligible to take the psychiatry examination of the American Board of Neurology and Psychiatry. Successful applicants then receive a diploma from this specialty board and are considered to be fully qualified psychiatrists.

At this point, a psychiatrist who wishes to specialize in child psychiatry must complete an additional two years of training, usually in a children's psychiatric hospital or clinic. A diploma in child psychiatry is then awarded after successful completion of the required examination.

Psychiatrists must also fulfill state licensing requirements before starting the residency period. Licensing requirements also are explained in the job description for **physician**.

Potential and advancement

Job opportunities are good for psychiatrists through 2008. Although there is currently an oversupply in certain regions of the United States, some forecasters predict a shortage in key areas of treatment, such as child psychiatry.

Psychiatrists may advance by building their practices. Some become experts in a particular branch of psychiatry. Those employed in psychiatric hospitals may advance to administrative positions, and those who teach in colleges and universities may advance through the academic ranks to become full professors.

Income

During training, psychiatric residents receive a salary and are often provided with living quarters; their average annual earnings usually are between $34,100 and $42,100.

Experienced psychiatrists' earnings are similar to earnings of other physicians. The average yearly salary is about $130,000, with some who work in private practice earning more.

Additional sources of information

American Medical Association
515 North State Street
Chicago, IL 60610
www.ama-assn.org

American Psychiatric Association
1400 K Street NW
Washington, DC 20005

PSYCHOLOGIST

The job

Psychologists study the behavior of individuals and groups to understand and explain their actions. Psychologists gather information through interviews and tests, studying personal histories, and conducting controlled experiments.

Psychologists may specialize in a wide variety of areas. *Experimental psychologists* study behavior processes by working with human beings as well as rats, monkeys, and pigeons. Their research includes motivation, learning and retention, sensory and perceptual processes, and genetic and neurological factors in human behavior. *Developmental psychologists* study the patterns and causes of behavior change in various age-groups. *Personality psychologists* study human nature, individual differences, and the ways in which these differences develop.

Social psychologists examine people's interactions with others and with the social environment. Their studies include group behavior, leadership, and dependency relationships. *Environmental psychologists* study the influence of environments on people; *physiological psychologists* study the relationship of behavior to the biological functions of the body.

Psychologists often combine several of these or other specialty areas in their work. They further specialize in the setting in which they apply their knowledge.

Clinical psychologists work in mental hospitals or clinics or maintain their own practices. They provide individual, family, and group psychotherapy programs. *Counseling psychologists* help people with problems of daily life—personal, social, educational, or vocational. *Educational psychologists* apply their expertise to concerns related to the education process, while *school psychologists* work with students and diagnose problems in behavior within the classroom, help in adjustment to school, and treat learning and social disorders.

Others work as *industrial and organizational psychologists* (personnel work), *engineering psychologists* (human-machine systems), and *consumer psychologists* (determining what motivates consumers).

Many psychologists work in colleges and universities as teachers, researchers, administrators, or counselors. Most of the rest work in hospitals, clinics, rehabilitation centers, and other health facilities. The remainder work in federal, state, and local government agencies; correctional institutions; research firms; or private practice.

Related jobs are psychiatrist, rehabilitation counselor, guidance counselor, marriage counselor, and social worker.

Places of employment and working conditions

Psychologists work in communities of all sizes. The largest concentrations are in areas with colleges and universities.

Working hours for psychologists are flexible in general. Their specialties, however, determine their schedules. Clinical and counseling psychologists, for example, often work in the evening to accommodate the work and school schedules of their patients.

Qualifications, education, and training

Sensitivity to others and an interest in people are important, as are emotional stability, patience, and tact. Research requires aptitude for detail, accuracy, and strong communication skills.

High school preparation should emphasize science and social science skills.

A bachelor's degree in psychology or a related field such as social work or education is only a first step because a Ph.D. is the minimum requirement for employment as a psychologist. Job seekers with only a bachelor's degree will be limited to positions as research or administrative assistants in mental health centers, vocational rehabilitation offices and correctional programs, government, or business. Some may work as secondary school teachers if they complete state certification requirements. Others accept entry-level positions with the federal government.

Stiff competition for admission into graduate psychology programs means that only the most highly qualified applicants are accepted. College grades of B or higher are necessary.

Two years of graduate study usually is necessary to earn a master's degree in psychology. Those with a master's degree qualify to work under the supervision of a psychologist to collect and analyze data and administer and interpret some kinds of psychological tests. They may also qualify for certain counseling positions such as school psychologist.

Three to five years of additional graduate work is required to earn a Ph.D. in psychology. Clinical and counseling psychologists need still another year or more of internship or other supervised experience.

A dissertation based on original research that contributes to psychological knowledge is required of Ph.D. candidates. Another degree in this field is the Psy.D. (doctor of psychology). Acquisition of this degree is based on practical work and examinations rather than a dissertation.

State licensing and certification requirements vary but usually stipulate a Ph.D. or Psy.D., one to two years of professional experience, and a written examination. Some states require continuing education for license renewal.

Potential and advancement

There are about 166,000 people working as psychologists in the United States. Employment in this field is expected to grow at an average rate; as noted, opportunities will be best for holders of doctoral degrees. Aspirants without advanced degrees will face much greater competition for job openings.

Knowledge of quantitative research methods and computer science is a distinct advantage in this field.

Income

The median salary for psychologists is $48,050.

Additional source of information

American Psychological Association
Research Office and Education in Psychology and
   Accreditation Offices
750 First Street NE
Washington, DC 20002
www.apa.org

PUBLIC RELATIONS WORKER

The job

Building, maintaining, and promoting the reputation and image of an organization or a public figure constitutes the work of public relations specialists. They use their skills in sales promotion, political campaigns, and many other fields.

A large corporation employs public relations workers to present the company in a favorable light to its various audiences—customers, employees, stockholders, and the community where the company is located. A college or university uses its public relations staff to present an image that will attract students. A government agency explains its work to the public by means of public relations specialists.

Public relations workers also have the opposite duty—to keep their employers aware of the attitudes of their various publics. For example, a public relations specialist for a manufacturing firm located in a city neighborhood might report that nearby residents blame the company for parking and traffic problems in the area. Resulting company efforts to provide more employee parking facilities or to reschedule deliveries and shipments to off-peak traffic hours would then be well publicized to improve the relations between the company and its nearby public.

In small businesses, one person may handle all public relation functions, including writing press releases and speeches for company officials, placing information with various news outlets, representing the employer at public functions, and arranging public appearances for executives. On a large public relations staff, a *public relations manager* would be assisted by several specialists, each responsible for a single phase of publicity. In some companies, public relations functions are combined with advertising or sales promotion.

Many public relations specialists work for consulting firms that provide services for clients on a fee basis. Others work for nonprofit organizations, advertising agencies, and political candidates. Those who work for government agencies are often called *public information specialists.*

Related jobs are advertising account executive, advertising manager, advertising worker, and newspaper reporter.

Places of employment and working conditions

Public relations specialists are found in organizations of all kinds and in all areas of the country. Public relations consulting firms, however, are concentrated in large metropolitan areas. More than half are located in New York City, Los Angeles, Chicago, and Washington, D.C.

The usual workweek in this profession is 35 to 40 hours, but attendance at meetings and community affairs can often mean overtime or evening hours. In some assignments, a public relations specialist may be on call at all times or may be required to travel for extended periods while accompanying a client such as a political candidate or other public figures.

Qualifications, education, and training

Self-confidence, enthusiasm, assertiveness, an outgoing personality, and imagination are necessary characteristics for success in public relations. The ability to motivate people, an understanding of human psychology, and outstanding communication skills are also necessary.

High school courses should emphasize English—especially writing skills. Any courses or extracurricular activities in public speaking or writing for school newspapers are valuable, as are summer or part-time jobs for radio or television stations or newspapers.

A college degree in journalism, communications, or public relations is the usual preparation for this line of work. Some employers prefer a degree in a field related to the firm's business—science, engineering, or finance, for example—plus course work or experience in public relations or communications. Other firms seek out college graduates who have work experience in a particular arm of the news media, which is how many writers, editors, and newspaper reporters enter public relations.

The Public Relations Society of America accredits public relations specialists who have worked in the field for at least five years. Applicants for this professional designation must pass a comprehensive six-hour examination that includes five hours of written and one hour of oral examination.

Job applicants in this field at all levels of experience are expected to present a portfolio of public relations projects on which they have worked.

Potential and advancement

About 122,000 people throughout the country work in public relations. Because this is a glamorous and popular field, competition for jobs is stiff. Over the long run, job opportunities are expected to increase substantially, but general economic conditions can cause temporary slow periods when companies delay expansion or cut public relations budgets. Job applicants with solid academic backgrounds plus some media experience will have the best job opportunities.

Advancement usually takes the form of responsibility for more demanding and creative assignments or transferring to a larger company. Experienced public relations specialists often start their own consulting firms.

Income

Public relations workers earn average annual salaries of between $34,500 and $46,300.

Experienced public relations specialists earn the highest salaries in large organizations with extensive public relations programs. The median annual salary in the federal government is $56,700.

Additional sources of information

PR Reporter
P.O. Box 600
Exeter, NH 03833

Public Relations Society of America
33 Irving Place
New York, NY 10003-2376
www.prsa.org

PURCHASING AGENT

The job

Purchasing agents buy the raw materials, products, and services that a company needs for its operation. They coordinate their buying schedules with company production schedules so that company funds will not be tied up unnecessarily in materials ordered too soon or in too large a quantity.

In small companies, a *purchasing manager*, assisted by a few purchasing agents and expediters, handles all aspects of buying. Large companies employ many purchasing agents, with each specializing in one item or in a group of related items.

Beginners in this field function as junior purchasing agents, ordering standard and catalog items until they gain enough experience to perform more difficult assignments.

About one-half of all purchasing agents work in wholesale trade or manufacturing industries. Others are employed by government agencies, construction companies, hospitals, and schools.

Related jobs are retail buyer, traffic manager, and production manager.

Places of employment and working conditions

Purchasing agents work in all sections of the country but are concentrated in heavily industrialized areas.

They usually work a standard 40-hour week but may have longer hours during peak production periods if they work in a seasonal industry.

Qualifications, education, and training

A purchasing agent must be able to analyze numbers and technical data to make responsible buying decisions, have a good memory for details, and be able to work independently.

High school should include mathematics and science; business and computer science courses are also helpful.

Small companies sometimes promote clerical workers or technicians into purchasing jobs or hire graduates of two-year colleges. Most companies, however, require at least a bachelor's degree in liberal arts or business administration with course work in purchasing, accounting, economics, and statistics. Companies that produce complex products such as chemicals or machinery may prefer a degree in science or engineering along with an advanced degree in business administration.

Regardless of educational background, beginners usually undergo an initial training period to learn the company's operating and purchasing requirements and procedures. Successful purchasing agents keep up with developments in their respective fields through participation in seminars offered by professional societies and by taking courses at local colleges and universities.

In private industry, the recognized marks of experience and professional competence are the designation certified purchasing manager (CPM) conferred by the National Association of Purchasing Management and the designation certified purchasing professional (CPP) or certified purchasing executive (CPE) conferred by the American Purchasing Society. In government agencies, the designation is certified public purchasing officer (CPPO), which is conferred by the National Institute of Governmental Purchasing. Education and experience standards as well as a series of examinations are conditions of certification.

Potential and advancement

Employment opportunities in this field will grow more slowly than average through 2008, with most job openings created by replacement needs. Computerization of inventory and purchasing tasks, along with a trend toward longer contracts with fewer suppliers, will reduce demand. The Federal Acquisition Streamlining Act of 1994 requires that many purchases be made electronically.

Purchasing agents can advance to purchasing manager and to executive positions such as director of purchasing or materials management. Some advance by moving to larger companies with more complex purchasing requirements.

Income

Purchasing agents earn median annual salaries of $41,830. Most earn between $29,930 and $63,520.

The average annual salary for purchasing agents in the federal government is $47,200.

Additional sources of information

National Association of Purchasing Management
Customer Service
2055 East Centennial Circle
P.O. Box 22160
Tempe, AZ 85285-2169
www.napm.org

National Institute of Governmental Purchasing
151 Spring Street
Herndon, VA 20170
www.nigp.org

RABBI

The job

Rabbis are the spiritual leaders of their congregations and teachers and interpreters of Jewish law and tradition. They conduct religious services, preside at
weddings and funerals, and provide counseling. There are four main types of congregations: Orthodox, Conservative, Reform, and Reconstructionist. Customs
and rituals may vary among them, but all congregations preserve the substance
of Jewish religious worship.

Rabbis also serve as chaplains in the armed forces, work in the many Jewish
social service agencies, and teach in colleges and universities.

Newly ordained rabbis usually begin as leaders of small congregations, assistants to experienced rabbis, or directors of Hillel Foundations on college campuses.

Places of employment and working conditions

Rabbis serve Jewish congregations in communities throughout the country. States
with large Jewish populations have the highest concentrations of rabbis—New

York, California, Pennsylvania, New Jersey, Illinois, Massachusetts, Florida, and Maryland, as well as Washington, D.C.

Depending on the size of the congregation and the number of assistants a rabbi has, working hours can be long and are often irregular.

Qualifications, education, and training

As is true of all clergy, rabbis must have a deep religious faith and a desire to serve people. Their ethical and moral conduct must be of the highest order.

Educational requirements depend on the branch of Judaism. College is required by most branches as preparation before entering a seminary. The seminary training usually lasts five years and includes the study of the Bible and Talmud, Jewish history, pastoral psychology, and public speaking.

Potential and advancement

There are about 5,025 rabbis serving Jews in the United States. Approximately 1,800 are Orthodox; 1,175, Conservative; 1,800, Reform; and 250, Reconstructionist.

There will be good opportunities for rabbis in all branches of the religion; opportunities will generally be best in nonurban areas, especially in smaller communities in the South, Midwest, and Northwest.

Income

Average annual earnings for rabbis range from $50,000 to $100,000.

Additional sources of information

Anyone considering this vocation should discuss his or her plans with a practicing rabbi. Information is also available from the following organizations:

Hebrew Union College—Jewish Institute of Religion (Reform)
One West Fourth Street
New York, NY 10012
www.huc.edu

Jewish Theological Seminary of America (Conservative)
3080 Broadway
New York, NY 10027
www.jtsa.edu

Rabbinical Council of America (Orthodox)
305 Seventh Avenue
New York, NY 10001
www.rabbis.org

Reconstructionist Rabbinical College
1299 Church Road
Wyncote, PA 19095
www.rrc.edu

RADIO/TELEVISION ANNOUNCER

The job

Radio announcers act as disc jockeys and present news reports, commercials, and other types of material. They may work from prepared scripts or deliver ad-lib commentary. In small stations, they may also operate the control board, write commercial and news copy, and sell radio advertising time.

Television announcers and radio announcers at large radio stations usually specialize in a particular field such as sports or news. They use written scripts and may do their own research and writing in some instances.

Some announcers work on a freelance basis, selling their services for individual assignments to networks, advertising agencies, and independent producers.

Places of employment and working conditions

Radio announcers are employed throughout the country in radio stations of all sizes. Television announcers do not have such a wide distribution and are concentrated in large metropolitan areas, where most television studios operate.

Announcers often work irregular hours such as during early-morning commuting time or late at night. At small stations, announcers often put in up to 12 hours a week in overtime. Because many stations operate 24 hours a day, seven days a week, announcers do their share of evening, weekend, and holiday duty.

Qualifications, education, and training

A pleasant speaking voice, a good command of language, a dramatic flair, and an interest in sports, music, and current events are necessary in this field.

High school courses should include writing, public speaking, and language arts. Extracurricular involvement in acting, sports, and music is helpful.

A college liberal arts background is excellent for a radio or television announcer. Some colleges and universities offer courses in the broadcasting field, and students may also gain valuable experience by working on the campus radio station.

Several private broadcasting schools offer training in announcing, but these should be screened with local broadcasters and Better Business Bureaus before enrolling.

Announcers who operate transmitters need to obtain a special permit from the Federal Communications Commission.

Potential and advancement

There are about 60,000 announcers employed by radio and television broadcasting stations in America. The popularity of this field combined with its relatively small size means stiff competition for jobs. The best opportunities for beginners exist in small radio stations; television stations usually hire only experienced announcers.

Announcers usually work in several stations over the course of their careers. As they gain experience, announcers advance by moving to larger stations, to stations in larger cities, or to network jobs. Others advance by getting their own programs or by developing a specialty such as sportscasting or news reporting.

Income

Salaries in broadcasting vary widely but are generally low, except for positions at major stations in large markets.

Announcers earn between $8.62 and $21.28 per hour.

Additional source of information

Broadcasting Education Association
1771 N Street NW
Washington, DC 20036

National Association of Broadcasters
1771 N Street NW
Washington, DC 20036
http:nab.org

RADIOLOGIC (X-RAY) TECHNOLOGIST

The job

In the medical field, x-ray pictures (radiographs) are taken by radiologic technologists who operate x-ray equipment. They usually work under the supervision of a radiologist—a physician who specializes in the use and interpretation of x-rays.

There are three specialties within the field of radiologic technology; a radiologic technologist works in all three areas.

The most familiar specialty is the use of x-ray pictures to study and diagnose injury or disease of the human body. In this specialty, the technologist positions the patient and exposes and develops the film. During fluoroscopic examinations (watching the internal movements of the body organs on a screen or monitor), the technologist prepares solutions and assists the physician.

The second specialty area is nuclear medicine technology—the application of radioactive material to aid in the diagnosis and treatment of illness or injury. Working under the direct supervision of a radiologist, the technologist prepares solutions containing radioactive materials that will be absorbed by the patient's internal organs and show up on special cameras or scanners. These materials trace the course of a disease or injury by showing the difference between healthy and diseased or damaged tissue.

Radiation therapy—the use of radiation-producing machines to provide therapeutic treatment—is the third specialty. Here, the technologist works under the direct supervision of a radiologist, applying the prescribed amount of radiation for a specified length of time.

During all these procedures, the technologist is responsible for the safety and comfort of the patient and must keep accurate and complete records of all treatments. Technologists also schedule appointments and file x-rays and the radiologist's evaluations.

About three-fifths of all radiologic technologists work in hospitals. The remainder work in medical laboratories, physicians' and dentists' offices, federal and state health agencies, and public school systems.

Places of employment and working conditions

Radiologic technologists are found in all parts of the country in towns and cities of all sizes. The largest concentrations are in cities with major medical centers and hospitals.

Full-time technologists usually work a 40-hour week. Those employed in hospitals that provide 24-hour emergency coverage have some shift work or may be on call. There are potential radiation hazards in this field, but careful attention to safety procedures and the use of protective clothing and shielding devices negate the risks.

Qualifications, education, and training

Anyone considering this career should be in good health, emotionally stable, and able to work effectively with people who are injured or ill. The job also demands patience and attention to detail.

A high school diploma or its equivalent is required for acceptance into an x-ray technology program. Programs approved by the Committee on Allied Health Education and Accreditation are offered by many hospitals, medical schools affiliated with hospitals, colleges and universities, and vocational and technical schools as well as the armed forces. The programs vary in length from one to four years; a bachelor's degree in radiologic technology is awarded after completion of the four-year course.

These training programs include courses in anatomy, physiology, patient care procedures, physics, radiation protection, film processing, medical terminology and ethics, radiographic positioning and exposure, and department administration.

Although registration with the American Registry of Radiologic Technologists (ARRT) is not required for work in this field, it is an asset in obtaining highly skilled and specialized positions. Thirty-five states require radiologic technologists to be licensed.

Potential and advancement

There are about 162,000 radiologic technologists in the United States at the present time. Employment in this field is expected to expand at an average pace through 2008. As outpatient care becomes more popular, an increasing number of jobs will be found at clinics and diagnostic imaging centers.

In large x-ray departments, technologists can advance to supervisory positions or qualify as instructors in x-ray techniques. There is more opportunity for promotion for those having a bachelor's degree.

Income

Technologists average about $32,880 in annual salary.

Sick leave, vacation, insurance, and other benefits are usually comparable to that of other employees in the same institution.

Additional source of information

American Society of Radiologic Technologists
15000 Central Avenue SE
Albuquerque, NM 87123-3917

RANGE MANAGER

The job

Range managers are specialists in grazing management. They plan the optimum combination of animals, size of herds, and conservation of vegetation and soil for maximum production without destroying the ecology of an area. Their work also involves timber production, outdoor recreation, erosion control, and fire prevention.

Most range managers work for the federal government in the Forest Service, the Soil Conservation Service, and the Bureau of Land Management. State governments employ range managers in fish and game agencies, land agencies, and extension services.

Private firms that employ range managers include coal and oil companies and large livestock ranches. United Nations agencies and foreign governments also employ American range managers.

Places of employment and working conditions

Most range managers work in the West and in Alaska.

Outdoor work is usual for range managers, and locations are often remote. They sometimes spend long periods away from home.

Qualifications, education, and training

Good physical condition, an affinity for the outdoors, and scientific interest are necessary. Communication skills are also important.

High school should include as many science courses as possible.

A bachelor's degree is the minimum requirement for becoming a range manager. Thirty-five colleges and universities offer degree programs in range management or range science; others offer some course work in this field. A degree in a related field such as forestry or agronomy is accepted by some employers. Studies include biology; chemistry; physics; mathematics; plant, animal, and soil sciences; and ecology. Electives in economics, computer science, forestry, wildlife, and recreation are desirable.

Graduate degrees in range management are usually necessary for teaching and research positions.

Potential and advancement

Although there likely will be slow growth in this field because of government cuts, job opportunities should be more plentiful than in the past because of numerous retirements and openings in the Natural Resource Conservation Service.

Income

Salaries average from $34,150 to $51,550, depending on education and experience. Experienced range managers may earn up to $75,330 a year.

Additional sources of information

Bureau of Land Management
Denver Service Center
Federal Center Building 50
Denver, CO 80255

Society for Range Management
445 Union Boulevard, Suite 230
Lakewood, CO 80228-1259
www.srm.org

REAL ESTATE AGENT/BROKER

The job

The sale and rental of residential and commercial properties are the domain of real estate agents and brokers. If they belong to the National Association of Realtors, brokers are called Realtors; agents are Realtor-associates. They also appraise, manage, or develop property. Some combine a real estate business with an insurance agency or a law practice.

Brokers are independent business owners who are responsible for all business matters relating to the firm's function. Some brokers operate a one-person firm, doing all the selling themselves.

Many real estate brokers employ *real estate salespeople*, or *agents*, to show and sell properties. Most real estate businesses sell private homes and other residential property. Some specialize in commercial or industrial property, or farms and undeveloped land.

Before a property can pass from the seller to the buyer, a title search must be made to prove that there is no doubt regarding the seller's right to sell the property. This abstract of title is performed by an *abstractor* or abstract company. The abstract is a condensed history of the property that includes the current ownership, chain of title (ownership), a description of the property, and, in chronological order, all transactions that affect the property. These include liens, mortgages, encumbrances, tax assessments, and other liabilities. Abstractors work for real estate firms, title insurance companies, and abstracting companies or may be self-employed.

Agents obtain listings (properties to sell) by signing an agreement with the seller that gives the agent and the real estate firm the right to represent the seller in disposing of the property. It is the agent's responsibility to locate a buyer by advertising the property and showing it to interested people. If the buyer requests it, the real estate agent may help the buyer obtain mortgage funds. In cases in which the seller's asking price is higher than what the buyer is willing to pay, the agent often acts as a negotiator to bring the sale to a successful conclusion. Agents also are present at closing when the property actually changes hands.

A successful real estate agent must be current with all local information relative to the type of property sold. An agent selling houses must know local tax and utility rates and the availability of schools, shopping facilities, and public transportation. A commercial or industrial property agent must be able to provide information on taxes, marketing facilities, local zoning regulations, the available labor market, and nearby railroad and highway facilities.

Most real estate salespeople are employed in relatively small businesses. Some large real estate firms employ several hundred agents in many branch offices, but 5 to 10 persons is the usual number employed by a single real estate business. Many agents sell real estate on a part-time basis.

A related job is real estate appraiser.

Places of employment and working conditions

Real estate agents and brokers work throughout the country in communities of all sizes.

The working hours of real estate agents and brokers are irregular, and evening and weekend hours are the norm. Both agents and brokers spend a large percentage of their time on the phone obtaining listings and are also responsible for the paperwork on the sales they manage.

Qualifications, education, and training

A pleasant personality, neat appearance, and tact are necessary qualities for a successful real estate agent. Sales ability along with a good memory for names and faces is also important.

Some real estate brokers prefer to hire college graduates with a degree in real estate or business, but most will hire high school graduates with sales ability.

All states and the District of Columbia require agents and brokers to be licensed.

A college degree is not necessary to obtain a license, but most states require 30 to 90 hours of classroom instruction. Local colleges, adult education programs, and correspondence schools offer the courses necessary to obtain a license, and many prospective real estate agents hold down a full-time job while studying for the career. Many brokers hire real estate students as office assistants or rent collectors while they are preparing for the state licensing exam, but others hire only those who have already obtained a license.

Some colleges and universities offer an associate or bachelor's degree with a major in real estate; several offer advanced education courses to agents and brokers.

To complete the licensing requirements, a prospective agent must be at least 18 years old, be a high school graduate, and pass a written test on real estate transactions and state laws regarding the sale of real estate.

Candidates for a broker's license must complete 60 to 90 hours of formal training, have a specified amount (usually one to three years) of real estate selling experience, and pass a more comprehensive exam. Some states waive the experience requirements if the candidate has a bachelor's degree in real estate.

Potential and advancement

There are about 347,000 licensed real estate agents and brokers in the United States. The employment outlook is good, and beginners will find it relatively easy to find a job. However, anyone entering real estate should be aware that it is difficult to earn enough to be self-supporting when working on commission.

In large real estate firms, experienced agents can advance to sales manager or general manager. Experienced sales workers often obtain a broker's license and go into business for themselves. Others go into property management or appraising. Many successful agents prefer to continue selling because the financial awards are attractive.

Income

When property is sold, the seller pays a percentage to the broker. The agent who sells the property receives part of that fee, usually about 50 percent, as a commission.

Earnings vary, but the annual average is about $28,020 for real estate agents and $45,640 for brokers.

Some real estate brokers provide their sales workers with benefits such as life and health insurance.

Additional source of information

National Association of Realtors
430 North Michigan Avenue
Chicago, IL 60611

REAL ESTATE APPRAISER

The job

A real estate appraiser studies and evaluates information about a property and estimates its market value. A written appraisal is then prepared to document the findings and conclusions.

An appraiser is usually required whenever a property is sold, insured, or assessed for taxation. Mortgage lenders require an appraisal for all standard transactions, as do federal, state, and local governments when acquiring property for public use. Insurance companies require an appraisal when determining the proper amount of insurance on a property.

An appraiser must be familiar with public records and their locations, be able to read blueprints and mechanical drawings, recognize good and bad construction materials, and be up-to-date on building zoning laws and government regulations. Appraisers usually specialize in one type of property, such as farms, single-family dwellings, industrial sites, or apartment houses.

Appraisers often enter the profession from other jobs in real estate sales or management, but more and more are entering appraisal directly. Those with a college education have the greatest chance of success. Beginners in appraisal usually start as appraisal assistants or trainees.

Opportunities for beginners exist in local assessors' offices and in federal, state, and city departments. Local independent appraisers also offer part-time and full-time work to beginners and college students studying real estate appraisal.

A related job is real estate agent/broker.

Places of employment and working conditions

Appraisers work in all areas of the country in towns and cities of all sizes wherever property is bought, insured, or taxed.

Much of an appraiser's time is spent away from the office inspecting properties and researching records. Independent appraisers set their own working hours but frequently work evenings and weekends to meet client deadlines. Appraisers who work in salaried positions usually have more regular working hours.

Appraisers spend varying amounts of time in travel if they evaluate property in other areas or in other countries. These appraisers are usually involved with industrial and commercial property or property for investment.

Qualifications, education, and training

An appraiser must have the highest standards of personal integrity and honesty and should possess good communication skills, both written and oral. An appraiser also needs good health and stamina because this is a physically demanding job.

Many private firms, financial institutions, and government agencies will hire only appraisers who have a college degree. Many colleges and universities offer programs in real estate and in real estate appraising. Other relevant courses are economics, finance, business administration, architecture, law, and engineering.

Appraisers may obtain professional recognition by working toward designations awarded by the American Institute of Real Estate Appraisers, the Society of Real Estate Appraisers, and the American Society of Appraisers.

Federal law requires that real estate appraisers be licensed or certified by the state. State licensing requirements must meet federal standards, but they are permitted to be more stringent than federal standards. Work experience and a passing score on a written examination are needed for certification.

Potential and advancement

High turnover will create good job opportunities, and average growth is expected in the field through 2008. Real estate appraising is affected by the swings in the economy. During times when the economy is weak, the earnings of appraisers decline, and many are forced to leave the occupation.

Income

Beginning real estate appraisers often work on a freelance basis and are paid by the job. They earn about $45,640 a year. More experienced appraisers earn between $49,000 and $80,070 a year.

Additional sources of information

Contact your state real estate commission for specific requirements in your area. Information is also available from:

Appraisal Institute
875 North Michigan Avenue, Suite 2400
Chicago, IL 60611

National Association of Realtors
430 North Michigan Avenue
Chicago, IL 60611

RECREATION WORKER

The job

Physical fitness has become important in today's culture, and people have more leisure time to devote to exercise and sports. There is thus a wide variety of opportunities and work settings for recreation workers—those who coordinate physical activity and sports programs that meet these needs.

Organized recreation programs are operated in a wide variety of settings: schools, churches, synagogues, nursing homes, corporations, playgrounds, health clubs, and primitive wilderness areas. In each of these settings, recreational workers organize and oversee programs that meet the needs of the people they serve. Types of activities that recreation workers plan include arts, crafts, fitness, and sports.

Some recreation workers plan activities for vacationers at theme parks and tourist attractions. Others are employed by companies to develop programs for their employees, such as bowling and softball leagues and structured fitness and exercise activities. Recreation workers are also employed at camps, where they teach sports such as swimming, hiking, and horseback riding. Instructing, coaching, and maintaining recreation centers are recreation workers' primary responsibilities.

Places of employment and working conditions

The majority of jobs for recreation workers are in urban areas, where most people live. Jobs in camping are usually found in heavily populated areas.

The average workweek is 35 to 40 hours. Recreation workers often have irregular hours, including nights and weekends. Much of recreation workers' time is spent outdoors, sometimes in poor weather conditions. The duties can be tiring, and workers are subject to injuries.

Qualifications, education, and training

Recreation workers must be enthusiastic, able to motivate people, and sensitive to people's needs.

Education requirements vary according to the type of job. Part-time summer jobs usually require only a high school diploma, while supervisory or administrative jobs may require a bachelor's or graduate degree.

Junior and community colleges offer associate degrees in parks and recreation, and 93 colleges and universities offer bachelor's-degree programs accredited by the National Recreation and Park Association (NRPA). The NRPA also offers certification as a mark of professional achievement.

Potential and advancement

There are about 241,000 recreation workers, and many more who work only during the summer. This field is expected to grow at an average rate through 2008 as more people become interested in fitness and health and have the money to purchase recreational services. Also, there is a growing demand for recreational services for senior citizens and people with disabilities. Competition for jobs will continue, however, because the number of job seekers is expected to exceed the number of openings.

The best opportunities will be in the commercial recreation industry and in social services. Because of budget cuts, there will be fewer opportunities in local governments. There is intense competition for full-time positions. Temporary seasonal jobs will offer the best opportunities.

To advance to supervisory or administrative positions, recreational workers should have experience and formal training in recreation as well as college courses in business management, personnel management, and accounting.

Income

Recreation workers employed full-time earn a median hourly wage of about $7.93. Most earn between $6.14 and $10.65. Those in supervisory positions may earn considerably more.

Additional sources of information

American Association for Leisure and Recreation
1900 Association Drive
Reston, VA 22091

National Recreation and Park Association
Division of Professional Services
22377 Belmont Ridge Road
Ashburn, VA 20148-4501
www.nrpa.org

YMCA National Office
101 North Wacker Drive
Chicago, IL 60606

REHABILITATION COUNSELOR

The job

Rehabilitation counselors work with people who have mental, physical, or emotional disabilities to help them become self-sufficient and productive. Many counselors specialize in one type of disability, such as mental illness or blindness.

In the course of designing an individual rehabilitation program, the counselor may consult doctors, teachers, and family members to determine the client's abilities and the exact nature of the disability. He or she, of course, also works closely with the client. Many counselors discuss training and career options with clients, arrange specialized training and specific job-related training, and provide encouragement and emotional support.

An important part of a counselor's work is identifying potential employers of people with disabilities. Many counselors keep in touch with members of the local business community and advocate for jobs for disabled workers. Once a person is placed in a job, the rehabilitation counselor tracks the daily progress of the employee and also confers with the employer about the employee's job performance and progress.

The amount of time spent with an individual client depends on the severity of the person's problems and the size of the counselor's caseload. Counselors in private organizations can usually spend more time with their clients than those who work for state and local agencies. Less experienced counselors and counselors who work with severely disabled people usually manage the fewest cases at one time.

Most rehabilitation counselors are employed by state or local rehabilitation agencies. Others work in hospitals or sheltered workshops or are employed by insurance companies and labor unions. The Department of Veterans Affairs employs psychologists who act as rehabilitation counselors.

Related jobs are employment counselor, psychologist, and social worker.

Places of employment and working conditions

Rehabilitation counselors work throughout the country, with the largest concentrations in metropolitan areas.

A 40-hour workweek is usual, but attendance at community meetings sometimes requires extra hours. A counselor's working hours are not all spent in the office; the job often includes trips to prospective employers, training agencies, and clients' homes.

The work of a counselor can be emotionally exhausting and sometimes discouraging.

Qualifications, education, and training

Anyone considering this field should have emotional stability as well as the capacity to accept responsibility, work independently, and motivate and guide other people. Patience is also a necessary characteristic of a rehabilitation counselor because progress often comes slowly over a long period.

High school courses in the social sciences should be part of a college preparatory course.

A bachelor's degree with a major in education, psychology, guidance, or sociology is the minimum requirement. This background is sufficient for only a few entry-level jobs.

Advanced degrees in psychology, vocational counseling, or rehabilitation counseling are necessary for almost all jobs in this field.

Most rehabilitation counselors work for state and local government agencies and are required to pass the appropriate civil service examinations before appointment to a position. Many private organizations require counselors to be certified; this is achieved by graduating from an accredited program, completing an internship, and passing the examination administered by the Commission on Rehabilitation Counselor Certification. To remain certified, rehabilitation counselors must retake the exam or complete 100 hours of continuing education every five years.

Potential and advancement

Employment opportunities are expected to be good, but because most job openings are in state and local agencies, the exact employment picture will depend to a great extent on government funding for such services.

Experienced rehabilitation counselors can advance to supervisory and administrative jobs.

Income

Rehabilitation counselors have median earnings of $38,650 per year. Most have annual salaries between $28,400 and $49,960.

Additional sources of information

American Counseling Association
5999 Stevenson Avenue
Alexandria, VA 22304-3300
www.counseling.org

National Rehabilitation Counseling Association
1910 Association Drive
Reston, VA 22091

RESPIRATORY THERAPIST

The job

Respiratory therapists provide treatment for patients with cardiorespiratory problems. Their role is important, and the responsibilities are great.

The therapists' work includes giving relief to chronic asthma and emphysema sufferers; emergency care in cases of heart failure, stroke, drowning, and shock; and treatment of acute respiratory symptoms in cases of head injuries, poisoning, and drug abuse. They must respond swiftly and start treatment quickly because brain damage may occur if a patient stops breathing for three to five minutes, and lack of oxygen for more than nine minutes almost invariably results in death.

In addition to respiratory therapists, the field includes *respiratory technicians* and *respiratory assistants*.

Therapists and technicians perform essentially the same duties, with therapists having greater responsibility for supervision and instruction.

Assistants have little contact with patients; their duties are usually limited to cleaning, sterilizing, and storing the respiratory equipment used by therapists and technicians.

Respiratory therapists and technicians work as part of a health care team, following doctors' or nurses' instructions. They use special equipment and techniques—respirators, positive-pressure breathing machines, and cardiopulmonary resuscitation—to treat patients. They are also responsible for keeping records of materials costs and charges to patients and for maintaining equipment and making minor repairs as needed. All respiratory therapy workers are trained to observe strict safety precautions in the use and testing of respiratory equipment to minimize the danger of fire.

Most respiratory therapists, technicians, and assistants work in hospitals in respiratory, anesthesiology, or pulmonary medicine departments. Others work for nursing homes, ambulance services, and oxygen equipment rental companies.

Places of employment and working conditions

Respiratory therapy workers are employed in hospitals throughout the country in communities of all sizes. The largest number of job opportunities are in large metropolitan areas that support several hospitals or medical centers.

Respiratory therapy workers usually work a 40-hour week and may be required to work evenings, nights, or weekends. Respiratory therapists spend much of their working time on their feet and experience considerable stress. They must be careful when working with gases, and they run the risk of catching an infectious disease.

Qualifications, education, and training

Anyone interested in entering this field should enjoy working with people and have a patient and understanding manner. The ability to follow instructions and work as a member of a team is also important. Manual dexterity and some mechanical ability are necessary in the operation and maintenance of the sometimes complicated equipment.

High school students interested in this field should take courses in health, biology, mathematics, physics, and bookkeeping.

Formal training in respiratory therapy is necessary for entering the field. About 327 institutions offer programs approved by the Commission on Accreditation of Allied Health Education Programs. All these programs require a high school diploma. Courses vary from two to four years and include both classroom and clinical work. Students study anatomy and physiology, chemistry, physics, microbiology, and mathematics. A bachelor's degree is awarded to those completing a four-year program, with an associate degree awarded from some of the shorter programs.

Programs lasting one or two years are also available for those with a bachelor's degree in another field who have taken required science course work. The American Medical Association accredits these programs.

Some respiratory therapists are registered respiratory therapists (RRTs). They obtain this designation by completing an examination of the National Board for Respiratory Care and meeting education and experience requirements.

Respiratory technicians can receive certification as a certified respiratory therapist (CRT) by passing a written examination. All respiratory technicians are certified as CRTs. More than 40 states currently license respiratory therapists.

Potential and advancement

There are currently about 86,000 respiratory therapists nationwide. The field is growing rapidly. Growth of health care services in general and the expanding use of respiratory therapy and equipment by hospitals, ambulance services, and nursing homes bolster job opportunities in this area, as more respiratory specialists are hired to release nurses and other personnel from respiratory therapy duties.

Advancement in this field depends on experience and education. Respiratory assistants can advance to the technician or therapist level by completing the required courses; technicians can advance by achieving certification or completing education and testing requirements for the therapist level.

Respiratory therapists can be promoted to assistant chief or chief therapist. With graduate study, they can qualify for teaching positions.

Income

The average annual salary for respiratory therapists is about $34,830.

Additional sources of information

American Association for Respiratory Care
11030 Ables Lane
Dallas, TX 75229-4593
www.aarc.org

National Board for Respiratory Care
8310 Nieman Road
Lenexa, KS 66214-1579
www.nbrc.org

RETAIL BUYER

The job

Every item carried in every store has been selected by a retail buyer. The owner of a small retail business functions as a retail buyer when ordering the store's merchandise, but large retail stores or chains employ professionally trained buyers to make decisions and purchases involving thousands, and sometimes millions, of dollars. The difference between a retail buyer and a purchasing agent is in the ultimate use of what they buy. The buyer purchases goods for resale; the purchasing agent buys material to be used by his or her firm.

This is an exciting, fast-paced, often nerve-racking job. The buyer must order merchandise that will satisfy the store's customers, sell at a profit, and move onto and off of the store's shelves within a reasonable time—with clothing and certain other items, this means seasonally. Buyers must be familiar with manufacturers and distributors, be attuned to fashion trends and local customer preferences, and work within the budget allotted for a particular store or department. They must be able to stock the basics as well as take advantage of unexpected good buys or a market for fad items.

Buyers work closely with sales staffs to keep up with customer likes and dislikes, and they study and analyze past store sales records and market research reports. They must be aware of the merchandise and prices of competitors and keep track of economic conditions in the areas where their customers live.

Some buyers are assisted by junior buyers, who handle routine chores such as verifying shipments. Junior buyers may also be involved in sales and often take part in store training programs.

Merchandise managers coordinate all the buying and selling activities of a large store or chain. The merchandise manager decides what merchandise to stock, devises the budget, and assigns different buyers to purchase certain items or lines of goods. Merchandising managers are also involved in sales promotion.

Places of employment and working conditions

About half of all buyers and merchandise managers work for retail and wholesale trade establishments. Although buyers are employed in all parts of the country, most job opportunities are in cities and large metropolitan areas such as New York City, Chicago, and Dallas.

Buyers often work more than 40 hours a week. Depending on the store's location and the type of merchandise being purchased, a buyer might travel as little as four or five days a month or might spend a much larger percentage of his or her working time in travel. While some buying trips are glamorous—to Paris, for example, for a showing of ladies' fashions—most are routine but fast paced.

Qualifications, education, and training

Anyone pursuing this field must be able to stand the pace and the pressure. A prospective buyer must be a good planner and able to make decisions, have good leadership and communication skills, and be assertive.

Many buyers have worked their way up the ladder from sales or stockroom positions. Others attend junior and four-year colleges that offer degree programs in marketing and purchasing. Many trade schools offer courses in fashion merchandising.

More and more employers are requiring college training, especially those who include buyers in their management or executive training programs. Most employers will accept applications from almost any field of college study and consider courses or experience in merchandising, fashion, sales, or business a plus.

The formal training programs in retail stores usually last several years and include classroom instruction combined with rotating assignments to various jobs and departments. The buyer trainee's first job will probably be as assistant or junior buyer.

Potential and advancement

There are about 547,000 buyers and merchandise managers working for retail firms. Job opportunities in this field will likely grow slowly through the next decade, with most openings occurring to replace employees who leave the field.

Increasing use of computers for inventory control and reordering merchandise will limit employment growth in the coming years.

This is a popular career field, and competition for available openings will be the norm. College graduates with courses or experience in relevant areas will have the best odds of securing choice positions.

It takes years of experience as a buyer to advance to the position of merchandise manager. A few experienced buyers and merchandise managers can also advance to top executive positions in store or chain management, but these positions are limited by the size and growth of the company.

Income

Salaries depend on the product line purchased, sales volume of the store, and seniority. Discount department stores, mass-merchandising firms, and large department store chains offer the highest salaries. Most buyers earn between $29,930 and $63,520 a year.

Buyers often earn large bonuses for exceptional performance and are included in store incentive plans such as profit sharing and stock options.

Additional source of information

National Retail Federation
325 Seventh Street NW, Suite 1100
Washington, DC 20004-2802
www.nrf.com

RETAIL SALES WORKER

The job

Whether they sell computers, food, furniture, or clothing, retail sales workers' main objective is to persuade the customer to purchase their merchandise. They accomplish this by showing how the product works, how it is made, and the variety of options available. Retail sales workers who sell complex products such as computers and software must have special skills and knowledge so that they can answer customers' questions in a clear, helpful manner.

Retail sales workers also make out sales checks; receive payment by cash, check, or charge; and give change and receipts. They are often responsible for the contents of a cash register and, depending on when they are scheduled to work, may have to count the money in the cash drawer and separate it from charge slips, coupons, and exchange vouchers. They may also have to deposit the money with the cash office.

Retail sales workers must know store procedures on returns and exchanges and must understand the store's security practices.

Some retail stores offer customer services such as gift wrapping, which sales workers also perform. During slow periods, retail sales workers may have to stock shelves or racks, arrange displays, take inventory, or price items.

Places of employment and working conditions

Every town and city has retail stores; jobs are distributed in much the same way as the population.

Most retail sales jobs are part-time positions, and employees often are scheduled to work during the evening and on weekends. During the Christmas season, hours are usually longer and vacation time is restricted.

Qualifications, education, and training

Retail sales workers must be friendly and courteous, have a neat appearance, communicate well, and enjoy working with people.

There are no formal educational requirements for retail sales. In small stores, an experienced worker or the manager or owner trains new employees in the store's procedures. Large stores often have formal training programs for beginners. Trainees are taught how to perform cash, check, and credit transactions as well as procedures for returns and special orders.

Some workers may be given specialized training for selling certain types of products. For example, workers selling appliances may receive instruction on the types of products available and the differences among them.

Potential and advancement

There are currently nearly 4.6 million retail sales workers in America, and employment opportunities are expected to be good through 2008. There traditionally is high turnover in this field, and retail sales are expected to grow.

Adverse economic conditions slow sales and reduce the demand for sales staff. However, because the turnover rate is so high, layoffs are unlikely.

As employees gain experience and achieve sales success, they are often moved into positions with higher potential for earnings. Even though a college education is becoming increasingly important for obtaining managerial or administrative positions, capable workers without a college degree are still often promoted to these jobs. In small stores, promotion opportunities are limited.

Income

Earnings for retail sales workers vary widely and depend in large part on the type of product they sell. Beginners are usually paid minimum wage.

Some sales workers are paid salary plus commission, and others are paid either by salary or by commission.

Average earnings for sales workers range from $6.18 to $9.84 an hour.

Additional source of information

National Retail Federation
325 Seventh Street NW, Suite 1100
Washington, DC 20004-2802
www.nrf.com

RETAIL STORE MANAGER

The job

The manager of a retail store, whether the store is large or small, has one goal: to operate the store at a profit. To this end, the manager applies years of accumulated training and experience.

Retailing is one of few remaining fields in which talented and hardworking people can advance all the way to the top regardless of education. Several career paths are possible, including sales work, merchandise and fashion buying, advertising, accounting, and personnel relations. Those who reach the level of store manager usually have experience in several of these areas.

Four major tasks are involved in conducting the business of a retail store: merchandising (buying and selling), store operations (staffing, shipping, and receiving), accounting, and advertising. In a small store, the manager performs all of these functions. The manager of a large store might handle one or two of these areas personally and assign assistant managers to supervise the others. In some stores, the manager provides overall supervision and policy making while employing four or more division heads to oversee specific functions. In chain stores, centralized buying and accounting relieves individual store managers of these two responsibilities.

Related jobs are retail buyer, purchasing agent, wholesaler, advertising manager, and personnel manager.

Places of employment and working conditions

This is a highly competitive field, and the store manager is under constant pressure to increase the sales volume. Many managers work 50 or more hours a week.

Managers employed by chain stores may be required to move frequently, especially during their early years with the company.

Qualifications, education, and training

Good judgment, tact, administrative ability, a feeling for what the public wants to buy, good communication skills, and the ability to interact effectively with all types of people are necessary for a store manager.

High school should include mathematics, English, and social sciences; distributive education (retail, production, and marketing training) programs, where available, provide an excellent background. Part-time or summer jobs in retail stores are good experience. Retail store managers should be computer literate because cash registers and inventory control systems are computerized.

Education requirements in this field vary greatly. Some large stores and many chain stores will accept high school graduates into their management training programs. Many large employers require a college degree in liberal arts, marketing, accounting, or business administration. Top positions in some stores require a master's degree in business administration.

Potential and advancement

Slower-than-average growth is expected for retail store managers through 2008. Positions in large independent stores will be the most competitive; entry-level jobs in retailing will be more plentiful.

Regardless of educational background and career path within retailing, advancement to the top positions requires years of experience and a record of success at each level. Sales volume figures are the deciding factor in the store manager's career. Increased sales can mean promotion to field manager or transfer to a more desirable store in a chain operation, or the opportunity to work for a larger independent store.

Income

Most store managers earn from $21,850 to $42,640 a year. Many also receive bonuses or participate in profit-sharing plans, based on store sales volume.

Additional source of information

National Retail Merchants Association
100 West 31st Street
New York, NY 10001

S

SAFETY ENGINEER

The job

The specific duties of safety engineers (also called *occupational safety and health specialists*) depend on where they work. In general, they are responsible for the safe operation of the employer's facilities and for the physical safety of the employees. They inspect, advise, and train.

In a large manufacturing plant, a safety engineer might develop a comprehensive safety program covering thousands of employees. This would include making a detailed analysis of each job, identifying potential hazards, investigating accidents to determine causes, designing and installing safety equipment, establishing safety training programs, and supervising employee safety committees.

In a trucking company, a safety engineer inspects heavy rigs such as trucks and trailers; checks out drivers for safe driving practices; and studies schedules, routes, loads, and speeds to determine their influence on accidents. In a mining company, a safety engineer inspects underground or open-pit areas for compliance with state and federal laws, designs protective equipment and safety devices and programs, and leads rescue activities in emergency situations.

Safety engineers are also concerned with product safety. They work with design engineers to develop products that meet safety standards and monitor manufacturing processes to ensure the safety of the finished product.

Other occupational safety and health specialists work as *fire protection engineers* to safeguard life and property from fire, explosion, and related hazards. Some specialists research the cause of fires and the flammability of building materials. Others identify hazards and develop protective measures and training programs. They work for fire equipment manufacturers, insurance rating bureaus, and consulting firms. Some are specialists in sprinkler or fire-detection systems.

Industrial hygienists detect and remedy industrial problems that affect the health of workers. They monitor noise levels, dust, vapors, and radioactivity levels. Some work in laboratories and study the effects of various industrial substances on humans and on air and water. They work with government regulatory agencies, environmental groups, and labor organizations as well as plant management.

Loss control consultants and *occupational health consultants* work for property-liability insurance companies. The services they provide include inspecting the premises for safety violations and giving advice, designing safety training programs, and designing health and medical programs. They also work with the insurance company's underwriters to assess risks and develop premium schedules.

Related jobs are claim representative, engineering and science technician, environmentalist, firefighter, industrial designer, and underwriter.

Places of employment and working conditions

Safety engineers and other occupational and health specialists work throughout the country, with the largest concentrations in heavily industrialized areas.

These jobs are usually active and often entail climbing and other strenuous activities in the course of inspections or emergency situations. Substantial travel is involved for some workers, especially consultants for insurance companies.

Qualifications, education, and training

Safety engineers and other safety and health specialists must have good communication skills and be able to motivate others. They should get along well with people and be able to interact effectively with constituents at all levels—from company president to production line worker. They should be assertive and have sound judgment. Good physical condition is also important.

A college preparatory course should be taken in high school, with emphasis on mathematics and science.

Graduates of two-year colleges are sometimes hired to work as technicians in this field, but most employers require at least a bachelor's degree in science or engineering. Some prefer a more specialized degree in a field such as industrial safety, safety management, or fire protection engineering or graduate work in industrial hygiene, safety engineering, or occupational safety and health engineering.

Technological advancements make continuing education a necessity in this line of work. Many insurance companies offer training seminars and correspondence courses; the Occupational Safety and Health Administration conducts courses in occupational injury investigation and radiological health hazards.

After having successfully completed examinations and the required years of experience, specialists in occupational health and safety may achieve certification from their respective professional societies. These designations include certified safety professional; certified industrial hygienist; and member, Society of Fire Protection Engineers.

Potential and advancement

Employment of occupational safety and health specialists is expected to grow at an average rate through 2008. Most job openings will occur in manufacturing and industrial firms.

In large companies, advancement to top-level management is possible for experienced occupational safety and health specialists.

Income

Beginning salaries average about $31,200 a year. Experienced workers earn about $48,670; corporate-level executives earn $72,280 or more.

Additional sources of information

American Industrial Hygiene Association
2700 Prosperity Avenue, Suite 250
Fairfax, VA 22031

American Society of Safety Engineers
1800 East Oakton Street
Des Plaines, IL 60018

Society of Fire Protection Engineers
1 Liberty Square
Boston, MA 02109

SALES MANAGER

The job

The title of *sales manager* means different things in different companies. In general, a sales manager is responsible for supervising a firm's sales staff.

Depending on the company's size and management structure and the level of responsibility of the sales manager, this could mean only the day-to-day coordination of the activities of sales workers, branch managers, and participants in sales training programs, or it could mean a corporate-level position that entails setting company marketing policy and sales goals. The sales manager may be responsible for a staff of five salespeople or for a marketing department employing hundreds.

Readers should refer to the separate job descriptions for sales positions that appear throughout this book: see **advertising salesperson, insurance agent and broker, manufacturer's sales representative, office manager, pharmacist, purchasing agent, real estate agent/broker, securities sales worker, travel agent,** and **wholesaler.**

SCHOOL ADMINISTRATOR

The job

School administrators have the responsibility of running the various schools and school systems in the United States. Their duties depend on whether they work at the state or local level, whether they work in a public or parochial school system or private school, and their areas of responsibility.

At the state level, a *superintendent of schools* or *director of education* oversees the functioning of the public school system and state colleges. The superintendent is responsible for setting and enforcing minimum standards for schools and teachers, administering teacher certification programs, and administering whatever state and federal funds are provided for education.

At the local level, a superintendent of schools is appointed by a local public school board or by a parochial school system to administer an individual school system. The system may consist of just a few schools or many schools. The superintendent hires and supervises all personnel; prepares the school budget; is responsible for physical maintenance of buildings and equipment; makes projections for future needs; and oversees curriculum and textbook decisions, purchasing, public transportation, and many other details. The superintendent's job is often a thankless one—with the local school board and citizens trying to keep taxes down and teachers trying to provide the best education possible for the students. It is the superintendent, working to appease both groups, who usually gets the blame for everything.

The superintendent is usually assisted by various other administrators. *Special-subject supervisors* coordinate the activities and curriculum of a specific subject area throughout all the schools in the system. The most common special areas are music, art, remedial reading, physical education, libraries, and business or technical education. *Special-education supervisors* plan and supervise the instruction of students with disabilities and, in school systems that provide them, programs for gifted students as well.

A *curriculum director* evaluates the subjects and activities included in the curricula of the schools within the system and makes recommendations to teachers and other administrators.

Within an individual school, the *principal* is responsible for the day-to-day operation of the school. The principal must operate within a budget, be both an educator and a business manager, develop and maintain a good working relationship with teachers and students, ensure discipline, and oversee building maintenance.

In a private school, the principal is often called a *headmaster* or *headmistress*. If the school also provides residence facilities for its students, the headmaster or headmistress has additional responsibilities besides those of a school principal. Living quarters, food, laundry, recreation facilities, and "substitute-parent" functions would then be part of his or her duties as well.

Places of employment and working conditions

School administrators operate under constant pressure, especially at the highest levels. Frustration is often part of the job, and administrators must face the fact that they are often resented by the very people they work to serve.

Hours for most administrators are long and irregular. Evening meetings and civic functions often push the total up to 50 or 60 hours or more a week.

Qualifications, education, and training

An interest in the development of children, the ability to get along with people, communication and business skills, patience, tact, and sound judgment are necessary.

The first step in this career field is a degree in teaching or education. (See the job descriptions for **teacher** elsewhere in this book for educational requirements at the elementary, secondary, and college levels.)

Graduate study in educational administration is necessary for most administrative positions. A master's degree is the minimum requirement; top-level positions in large schools or school systems usually require a Ph.D. or an Ed.D. Administrators in the public school system must have a state teaching certificate.

Potential and advancement

There are about 447,000 school administrators in the United States at the present time. Employment will grow at an average rate, according to forecasts, but there will be stiff competition for all jobs. Those persons who combine the appropriate educational credentials with wide experience will have the best chance of being offered the choice jobs at all levels.

Advancement in this field may be from teacher up through the ranks in a single school system or may take the form of moving to a larger school system. Administrators in middle-level positions in large systems often advance by accepting top-level positions in smaller school systems or private schools.

Income

Earnings vary widely, depending mainly on the size and location of the school system, the position's level of responsibility, and the administrator's level of experience.

Most public school principals earn annual salaries of $64,653 to $74,380.

Additional sources of information

American Association of School Administrators
1801 North Moore Street
Arlington, VA 22209
www.aasa.org

National Education Association
1201 16th Street NW
Washington, DC 20036

SECRET SERVICE AGENT

The job

The U.S. Secret Service is part of the Department of the Treasury and employs special agents and uniformed officers.

Special agents have both protective and investigative responsibilities. Their primary responsibility is the protection of the president of the United States. They also protect the vice president, the president-elect and vice president-elect, a former president and his wife, the widow of a former president until her death or remarriage, minor children of a former president until age 16, major presidential and vice presidential candidates, and visiting heads of foreign states or foreign governments.

Special agents also work to suppress counterfeiting of U.S. currency and securities and investigate and arrest people involved in forging and cashing government checks, bonds, and securities. All special agents must qualify for both protective and investigative assignments.

The Secret Service Uniformed Division employs *uniformed officers* to provide protection for the president and his immediate family while they are in residence at the White House. The duties of these officers, previously called the White House Police, have been expanded to include protection of the vice president and his immediate family, the White House and grounds, the official residence of the vice president in Washington, D.C., buildings in which presidential offices are located, and foreign diplomatic missions located in the metropolitan Washington, D.C., area or such other areas of U.S. territories and possessions as the president may direct.

Uniformed officers carry out their responsibilities through foot and vehicular patrols, fixed posts, and canine teams.

Treasury security force officers are also a part of the Secret Service Uniformed Division. They are responsible for security at the main treasury building and the treasury annex and at the office of the secretary of the treasury. They have investigative and special arrest powers in connection with laws violated within the treasury building, including forgery and fraudulent negotiation or redemption of government checks, bonds, and securities.

Related jobs are FBI special agent, CIA worker, and police officer.

Places of employment and working conditions

Special agents may be employed at Secret Service headquarters in Washington, D.C., or at one of more than 100 field offices and residential agencies throughout the United States. Uniformed officers and treasury security force officers work in Washington, D.C.

Special agents must be willing to work wherever they are assigned and are subject to frequent reassignment. Because the protective responsibilities of the Secret Service go on around the clock, all agents and officers perform some shift work.

Qualifications, education, and training

Each of these three Secret Service jobs has separate physical and educational requirements. All, however, require a comprehensive background investigation and top-secret security clearance.

Applicants for special agent appointments must be less than 37 years of age at the time of entrance to duty unless they have federal law enforcement experience. They must be in excellent physical condition; pass a rigorous medical examination; have weight in proportion to height; and have distance vision, uncorrected, of 20/20 in one eye and no less than 20/30 in the other.

Applicants must have a bachelor's degree in any major field of study or three years of relevant work experience. A passing grade on the Treasury Enforcement Agent Examination, administered by area offices of the U.S. Civil Service Commission, is a prerequisite for consideration. Applicants who pass the agent examination and are appointed may have to wait an extended period for a vacancy to occur; it is usually during this period that background investigations are completed.

Once active duty begins, special agents receive eight weeks of general investigative training at the Federal Law Enforcement Training Center in Glynco,

Georgia, and specialized training with their particular agencies for another 17 weeks. They study protective techniques, criminal law, investigative procedures and devices, document and handwriting examination and analysis, first aid, use of firearms, and arrest techniques. They also receive on-the-job training. Advanced in-service training programs continue throughout an agent's career.

Potential and advancement

From time to time, the service may actively recruit for a specific job category, but for the most part, job opportunities are limited. The extremely high public interest in this work means that only the most qualified applicants are considered for appointment. Even after acceptance, special agents must wait until a vacancy occurs before they begin active service.

Promotion depends on performance and the needs of the Secret Service.

Income

Depending on their experience, special agents start at about $34,400 to $43,000, including overtime pay; experienced agents earn an average of $67,300. Supervisory agents start at $63,600.

Additional sources of information

The nearest area office of the U.S. Civil Service Commission can supply information on examination schedules. To contact the Secret Service directly:

United States Secret Service
Personnel Division
1800 G Street NW
Washington, DC 20223
www.ustreas.gov/usss

SECRETARY

The job

A secretary is the center of communication activities in a firm or department. The secretary transmits information from the employer to other members of the staff and to other organizations. Most secretaries type, take shorthand, greet visitors, keep track of the employer's appointments, make travel arrangements, and generally relieve the employer of excess paperwork.

Executive secretaries work for the top executives in an organization. Jobs at this level require top-notch skills and usually some college education. *Social secretaries* arrange social functions, answer personal correspondence, and keep the employer informed about all social activities. Public figures such as politicians, elected officials, celebrities, and others with a busy social life usually employ social secretaries.

Some secretaries have training in specialized areas. *Medical secretaries* study medical terminology to prepare case histories and medical reports. *Legal secretaries* are trained to do some legal research and to help prepare briefs; they are familiar with legal terminology and the format of legal papers. *Technical secretaries* assist engineers and scientists in drafting reports and research proposals. They are acquainted with scientific and mathematical terms and are trained in the use of the technical vocabulary and symbols applicable to these fields.

Stenographers take dictation and then transcribe their notes on a computer or word processor. They do not perform the wide range of duties that a secretary does, although in some offices, stenographers perform routine chores such as filing, answering the phone, or operating office machines. Stenographers may also specialize in medical, legal, or technical work; some specialize in a foreign language. *Public stenographers* serve traveling businesspeople or others who have only occasional need for stenographic services. They are usually located in large hotels and busy downtown areas of cities.

Shorthand reporters are specialized stenographers who record all statements made during a proceeding. They record the sessions of state legislatures, the Congress of the United States, meetings and conventions, and out-of-court testimony for attorneys. Their transcription then becomes the official record of the proceeding. Many shorthand reporters work as *court reporters*, who take down all statements made during legal proceedings in courts of law.

Places of employment and working conditions

Secretaries and stenographers are employed throughout the country. About half are employed by educational, health, legal, and business firms and other types of companies in the service sector.

Working conditions vary, but full-time secretaries and stenographers usually work a 37- to 40-hour week. Shorthand reporters may work irregular hours and may have to sit for long periods while recording an event.

Qualifications, education, and training

The work product of secretaries and stenographers must be accurate and neat. They must display discretion and initiative and have a good command of spelling, grammar, punctuation, and vocabulary. Shorthand reporters must have good hearing and be able to concentrate amid distractions; strong computer skills are increasingly important.

High school business and college preparatory courses are valuable because secretaries and stenographers should have a good general background. Either type of high school preparation should include as many English courses as possible.

Secretarial training as part of a college education or at a private business school is preferred by many employers. Training can vary from a few months for basic instruction in shorthand and typing to a year or two for some of the specialty areas, such as medicine or law. Shorthand reporters usually complete a two-year program in a shorthand reporting school.

Well-trained and highly experienced secretaries may qualify for the designation certified professional secretary (CPS) by passing a series of examinations given by Professional Secretaries International. This mark of achievement in the secretarial field is recognized by many employers.

Potential and advancement

There are more than 3.2 million people employed in this field nationwide.

The demand for qualified secretaries likely will remain constant, but the outlook varies by field. Stenographers will not be as much in demand in the future, as a result of the increased use of dictation machines and word processing centers. Medical and legal secretaries are expected to be in much greater demand than others.

The large size of this field, along with a moderate turnover rate, should create enough openings to accommodate most job seekers.

Opportunities for advancement depend on the acquisition of new or improved skills and on increasing knowledge of the employer's business or industry. Some private firms and government agencies have their own training facilities to help employees upgrade their skills.

Executive secretaries are sometimes promoted to management positions in recognition of their extensive knowledge of the employer's operation.

Income

Salaries for secretaries vary greatly and depend on the employee's level of skill, experience, and responsibility; the area of the country; and the type of industry.

The average annual salary for secretaries is $25,500, with a range from $18,770 to $29,400. Secretaries working in the West and Midwest earn higher salaries in general than those working in the Northeast and the South. Also, secretaries in the transportation, legal, and public utilities industries tend to earn the highest salaries, while secretaries in retail trade, finance, real estate, and insurance tend to earn the lowest.

Additional sources of information

National Court Reporters Association
8224 Old Courthouse Road
Vienna, VA 22182

Professional Secretaries International
10502 Northwest Ambassador Drive
P.O. Box 20404
Kansas City, MO 64195-0404

SECURITIES SALES WORKER (STOCKBROKER)

The job

When investors buy or sell stocks, bonds, or shares in mutual funds, they use the services of securities sales workers. These workers are also called *registered representatives*, *account executives*, or *customers' brokers*.

Securities sales workers relay the customer's buy or sell orders to the floor of the appropriate securities exchange or to the firm's trading department and notify the customer of the completed transaction and final price. They also provide related services such as financial counseling, the latest stock and bond quotations, and information on financial positions of corporations whose securities are being traded.

Securities sales workers can help a client accumulate a financial portfolio of securities, life insurance, and other investments geared either to long-term goals, such as capital growth or income, or to short-term goals. Some sales workers specialize in one type of customer, such as institutional investors, or in certain types of securities, such as mutual funds.

Beginners in this field spend much of their time searching for new customers. As they establish a clientele, they spend more time servicing their existing customers and less in seeking new ones.

Securities sales workers are employed by brokerage firms, investment banks, and mutual fund firms. Most work for a few large firms that have offices in cities throughout the country.

Places of employment and working conditions

Securities sales workers are employed in cities throughout the United States, mostly in the branch offices of a few large firms whose main offices usually are in New York.

Sales workers generally work in bustling, sometimes noisy offices. Beginners often put in long hours until they acquire a clientele, and sales workers occasionally meet with clients on evenings or weekends.

Each year, many sales workers leave the field because they are unable to establish a large enough clientele.

Qualifications, education, and training

Selling skills and ambition are necessary for success as a securities sales worker. A sales worker should also be mature, well groomed, and able to motivate people. Many employers prefer to hire applicants who have experience in sales or management positions.

A college education is preferred by the larger firms. A liberal arts background with training in economics, prelaw, business administration, or finance is particularly helpful.

Most employers provide training to new sales workers to help them meet registration requirements. In most firms, the training program lasts at least four months. Trainees working in larger firms often undergo a more extensive period of on-the-job training that lasts up to two years.

Almost all states require securities sales workers to be licensed. Licensing requirements usually include a written examination and the furnishing of a personal bond.

Sales workers must be registered as representatives of the firm for which they work. To qualify, they must have been an employee of a registered firm for at least four months and must pass the General Securities Registered Representative Examination. Most states require a second examination called the Uniform Securities Agents State Law Examination.

Potential and advancement

Nationwide, there are about 303,000 full-time securities sales workers and many others in other occupations who sell securities.

The demand for securities sales workers fluctuates with the economy, but currently the job outlook is good through 2008. There will be active competition for available jobs, though, because of the potential for high earnings. Job opportunities will be best for those with business and sales experience.

Income

Securities sales workers earn commissions on the transactions they broker for clients.

Earnings of full-time securities sales workers average between $31,400 and $103,040. Ten percent earn $124,800 or more.

Beginners earn a salary until they have completed their training. Experienced sales workers sometimes receive a base salary or "draw against commission."

Additional source of information

Securities Industry Association
120 Broadway
New York, NY 10271
www.sia.com

SINGER

The job

Professional singers are employed in every field of music. For every singing star of popular, classical, country and western, and musical comedy music, there are many more who work in choruses; who teach in churches, schools, and music conservatories; and who are employed by commercial advertising firms.

Employment opportunities exist in radio, movies, and television; on the concert stage, in opera, and in musical productions; in nightclubs; in elementary and secondary schools; and in colleges and universities. Many opportunities exist for part-time work in churches.

Anyone considering this field should be aware that few singers are able to secure full-time employment except in teaching. The time necessary for rehearsing and performing leaves little opportunity for other part-time work, and many singers are unable to support themselves with singing alone.

Professional singers usually belong to some branch of the Associated Actors and Artists of America.

Places of employment and working conditions

The most job opportunities for performers are in New York City, Los Angeles, Las Vegas, Miami, New Orleans, and Chicago. Nashville is one of the major centers of the recording industry and also offers many opportunities for musicians of all types.

Singers engaged in a performing career work evenings and weekends and must usually travel a great deal. The work is not steady, and many careers are short because of changes in public taste.

Qualifications, education, and training

In addition to a good voice, a singer needs poise, physical stamina, an attractive appearance and stage presence, perseverance, and determination.

Those persons who wish to pursue a singing career should acquire a broad background in music, including piano lessons (for music theory and composition) and dancing lessons, because singers are sometimes required to dance as well. Voice training should not begin until physical maturity is achieved, although young boys sometimes receive some training for church choirs before their voices change.

Singers who intend to perform classical music can take private voice lessons or enroll in a music conservatory or in the music department of a college or university. Those who attend a conservatory or college also receive training in such music-related subjects as foreign languages, dramatics, history, and literature. In four-year programs, the student receives a bachelor of arts or science (in music), a bachelor of music, or a bachelor of fine arts degree.

Singers who plan to teach music must also meet state teaching certification requirements, and those who expect to teach at the college level usually need a master's degree or a Ph.D.

In the field of popular music, voice training is an asset but is not always necessary. Many singers in this field start singing with groups or in amateur contests and go on to employment with better-known bands or groups as they gain experience and popularity.

Potential and advancement

This is a field in which there will always be many more qualified applicants than there are job openings. Except for a handful of top stars in opera and popular music, the only full-time steady employment for singers will continue to be in teaching positions.

Income

Singing teachers are paid on the same scale as other faculty members in the institutions in which they teach.

In an opera chorus, singers earn a base salary of more than $1,000 a week. Soloists who have earned a reputation for their talent earn much more, usually several thousand dollars per performance.

Additional sources of information

American Federation of Musicians of the United States and
  Canada
1501 Broadway, Suite 600
New York, NY 10036

American Guild of Musical Artists (concert stage and opera
  singers)
1727 Broadway
New York, NY 10019

Music Educators National Conference
1806 Robert Fulton Drive
Reston, VA 22091

National Association of Schools of Music
11250 Roger Bacon Drive, Suite 21
Reston, VA 22091
www.arts-accredit.org

SOCIAL WORKER

The job

Social workers strive to help individuals, families, groups, and communities solve their problems. They also work to increase and improve the community resources available to people.

Depending on the nature of the problem and the time and resources available for solving it, social workers may choose one of three approaches or a combination of them: casework, group work, or community organization.

In casework, social workers interview individuals or families to identify problems. They help people understand and solve their problems by securing appropriate social resources such as financial aid, education, job training, or medical assistance.

Social workers form therapeutic groups that help people understand one another. They plan and conduct activities for children, teenagers, adults, older persons, and other groups in community centers, hospitals, and nursing homes.

In community organizations, social workers coordinate the efforts of political, civic, religious, and business groups working to combat social problems. They help plan and develop health, housing, welfare, and recreation services.

Many social workers provide direct social services, working for public and voluntary agencies such as state and local departments of public assistance, and community welfare and religious organizations. Others work for schools, hospitals, and business and industry. Some social workers are in private practice and provide counseling services on a fee basis.

A related job is rehabilitation counselor.

Places of employment and working conditions

Social workers are employed throughout the United States, usually in urban areas.

Most social workers have a five-day, 35- to 40-hour workweek. Evening and weekend work may sometimes be necessary.

Qualifications, education, and training

A social worker must be sensitive, have concern for the needs of others, be objective and emotionally stable, and be willing to assume responsibility for projects.

A college preparatory course in high school should provide as broad a background as possible. Volunteer work and part-time or summer jobs in a community center, camp, or social welfare agency are good experience.

A bachelor's degree in social work (B.S.W.) or a major in sociology or psychology can prepare the student for some positions in this field, but the usual requirement is a master's degree in social work (M.S.W.). Those with only a bachelor's degree have limited promotion opportunities.

The M.S.W. degree is awarded after two years of specialized study and supervised field instruction. A graduate degree plus experience is necessary for supervisory and administrative positions.

A Ph.D. is usually required for teaching, research, and top administrative positions.

The National Association of Social Workers grants certifications and the title ACSW (Academy of Certified Social Workers) to members who qualify.

All states and the District of Columbia mandate certification, licensing, or registration of social workers. Requirements usually include specified experience plus an examination. Social workers employed by federal, state, and local government agencies are usually required to pass a civil service test before appointment to a position.

Potential and advancement

There are about 604,000 social workers in the country. Job opportunities should continue to be good, especially in rural areas and small towns. Rising crime rates, AIDS, and greater numbers of families in crisis will drive demand.

Advancement in this field depends on acquiring appropriate experience and education.

Income

Salaries for social workers vary by the type of agency and the geographic region. They are highest in large cities and in states with significant urban populations.

Annual earnings for full-time social workers are between $24,160 and $39,240, on average. Experienced social workers earn an average of $31,500 in hospitals and $45,300 in the federal government.

Additional sources of information

Council on Social Work Education
1600 Duke Street
Alexandria, VA 22314-3421
www.cswe.org

National Association of Social Workers
IC-Career Information
750 First Street NE, Suite 700
Washington, DC 20002-4241

SOCIOLOGIST

The job

Sociologists study human social behavior by examining the groups that human beings form: families, tribes, governments, and social, religious, and political organizations. Some sociologists study the characteristics of social groups and institutions; others study the way individuals are affected by the groups to which they belong.

Most sociologists are college and university teachers. Others are engaged in research and writing. Those doing research collect information, prepare case studies, and conduct surveys and laboratory experiments. Many research sociologists may apply statistical and computer techniques in their research.

The federal government employs sociologists in the Departments of Health and Human Services, Defense, Agriculture, and Interior.

Others work in private industry, social work, and public health.

Places of employment and working conditions

Sociologists work throughout the country but are heavily concentrated in areas with large colleges and universities.

Qualifications, education, and training

Study and research skills are necessary, as are communication skills.

In high school, a college preparatory course with a strong academic program is the best background.

A master's degree with a major in sociology is usually the minimum requirement in this field. A Ph.D. is required for professorship and tenure, for directors of major research projects, and for high-level administrative positions.

Those with only a bachelor's degree in sociology will be limited to jobs as interviewers, research or administrative assistants, or recreation workers. Some may be hired for social worker or counselor positions or teach in secondary schools.

Potential and advancement

Job competition will be stiff, as thousands of Ph.D.s with degrees in sociology are expected to vie for the limited number of job openings through 2008. Most job openings will occur to replace employees who retire or leave the profession.

Advancement in this field depends on experience and obtaining higher degrees.

Income

The annual salary of sociologists ranges from about $38,990 to $80,640.

Sociologists working for the federal government average annual earnings of $45,200.

Additional source of information

American Sociological Association
1722 N Street NW
Washington, DC 20036

SOIL CONSERVATIONIST

The job

Soil conservationists provide technical advice to farmers, ranchers, and others on soil and water conservation as well as land erosion.

Most soil conservationists are employed by the federal government in the Department of Agriculture's Soil Conservation Service or in the Department of Interior's Bureau of Land Management. Other soil conservationists work for state and local governments.

Related jobs are soil scientist, range manager, and forester.

Places of employment and working conditions

Soil conservationists work throughout the United States in nearly every county. Most of their work is done outdoors.

Qualifications, education, and training

A soil conservationist should have good communication skills, an analytical mind, and a liking for outdoor work.

High school courses should include chemistry and biology.

Few colleges and universities offer degrees in soil conservation. Soil conservationists usually have a bachelor's degree with a major in agronomy (interaction of plants and soils), agricultural education, general agriculture, or related fields of natural resource sciences such as wildlife biology or forestry. Courses in agricultural engineering and cartography (mapmaking) are also helpful.

An advanced degree is usually necessary for college teaching and research positions.

The Soil and Water Conservation Society offers the professional designation certified professional erosion and sediment control specialist. Candidates must meet education, experience, and testing guidelines.

Potential and advancement

Although the forecast is for growth of job opportunities in this field, the relatively small size of the field will mean competition for available openings.

Advancement is limited. Conservationists working at the county level can move up to state positions. They can also move on to similar occupations such as farm or ranch management adviser or land appraiser.

Income

Annual salaries for soil conservationists in the federal government average $53,600. Experienced soil conservationists working in the private sector earn an average of $42,340 a year.

Additional sources of information

American Society of Agronomy
677 South Segoe Road
Madison, WI 53711-1086

Soil Conservation Service
U.S. Department of Agriculture, Room 6155
P.O. Box 2890
Washington, DC 20013

SOIL SCIENTIST

The job

Soil scientists study the physical, chemical, biological, and behavioral characteristics of soils. Their work is important to farmers, builders, fertilizer manufacturers, real estate appraisers, and lending institutions.

A large part of soil science has to do with categorizing soils according to a national classification system. Once the soils in an area have been classified, the soil scientist prepares a map that shows soil types throughout the region.

A builder who wants to erect a factory or an apartment building will consult a soil-type map to locate a spot with a secure base. Farmers also consult soil-type maps. Some communities require a certified soil scientist to examine the soil and test the drainage capabilities of any building lot that will be used with a septic system.

Some soil scientists conduct research into the chemical and biological properties of soil to determine what crops grow best in which soils. They may test fertilizers and soils to determine ways to improve less productive soils. Soil scientists are also involved in pollution control programs and soil erosion prevention programs.

More than half of all soil scientists are employed by the Soil Conservation Service of the U.S. Department of Agriculture. Others are employed by the state agricultural experiment stations and agricultural colleges. Private institutions and industries that employ soil scientists include fertilizer companies, land appraisal firms, farm management agencies, and lending institutions such as banks and insurance companies.

Related jobs are soil conservationist, farmer, range manager, and forester.

Places of employment and working conditions

Soil scientists work in every state and in most counties of the United States.

They spend much of their time doing fieldwork in a particular area—usually a county. During bad weather, they work indoors preparing maps and writing reports. Soil scientists involved in research usually work in greenhouses or small farm fields.

Qualifications, education, and training

An interest in science and agriculture is necessary, as is a liking for outdoor work. Writing skills are also important.

High school courses should include chemistry and biology.

A bachelor's degree with a major in soil science or a closely related field such as agriculture or agronomy (interaction of plants and soils) is necessary. Courses in chemistry and cartography (mapmaking) are also important.

An advanced degree is necessary for many of the better-paying research positions.

Some states require certification of soil scientists who inspect soil conditions prior to building or highway construction. Certification usually entails a written examination plus specified combinations of education and experience.

Potential and advancement

Job openings in this rather small field usually occur to replace those who leave the field or retire, although some limited growth will probably occur. Competition for teaching jobs, however, will be intense.

Soil scientists who have training in environmental issues will have the best opportunities for advancement, especially if they have a high level of education.

Income

Soil scientists with a bachelor's degree start at about $27,600 a year.

Soil scientists working for the federal government have average annual earnings of $53,600.

Additional sources of information

American Society of Agronomy
677 South Segoe Road
Madison, WI 53711-1086

Soil Conservation Service
U.S. Department of Agriculture, Room 6155
P.O. Box 2890
Washington, DC 20013

SPEECH PATHOLOGIST AND AUDIOLOGIST

The job

Speech pathologists and audiologists evaluate speech and hearing disorders and provide treatment. *Speech pathologists* work with children and adults who have speech, language, and voice disorders because of hearing loss, brain injury, cleft palate, mental retardation, emotional problems, or foreign dialect. *Audiologists* assess and treat hearing problems. Speech and audiology are so interrelated that expertise in one field requires thorough knowledge of both.

Almost half of all speech pathologists and audiologists work in public schools; colleges and universities also employ large numbers in teaching and research. The remainder work in hospitals, clinics, government agencies, industry, and private practice.

Places of employment and working conditions

Speech pathologists and audiologists are employed throughout the country, with most located in urban areas.

Speech pathologists and audiologists usually work at a desk or table in an office setting. While the job is not physically strenuous, it does require concentration and attention to detail and can be mentally exhausting. Some speech pathologists and audiologists work at several different facilities and spend a lot of time traveling.

Qualifications, education, and training

Patience is an important personal characteristic for anyone who wants to work in this field because progress is usually slow. Therapists must also be able to encourage and motivate their clients, who are often frustrated by the inability to speak properly. Objectivity and the ability to take responsibility and work with detail are also necessary.

High school should include a strong science background.

A bachelor's degree with a major in speech and hearing or in a related field such as education or psychology is the usual first step in this career. Most jobs in this profession require a master's degree. Graduate course work includes supervised clinical training as well as advanced study. Many speech pathologists and audiologists have a Ph.D., and by 2012 a doctorate will be the required credential.

The American Speech-Language-Hearing Association confers a certificate of clinical competence (CCC) on those who have a master's degree and clinical experience, complete a nine-month internship, and pass a written examination. Certification is usually necessary to advance professionally.

In nearly all states, speech pathologists and audiologists must be licensed. A master's degree, clinical experience, a passing score on a national exam, and nine months of postgraduate experience are the usual requirements. In some states, those with a bachelor's degree and certification from the state educational agency can work in the public schools.

Potential and advancement

There are about 105,000 speech pathologists and audiologists in the United States. The field is expected to grow rapidly as a result of population growth among people age 55 and older, the trend toward earlier recognition and treatment of hearing and language problems in children, recent laws requiring services for people with disabilities, and the expanded coverage of Medicare and Medicaid programs. Any decreases in government-funded programs could change this employment picture.

If present trends continue, an increasing number of speech pathologists and audiologists will work in private practice.

Those with only a bachelor's degree will find limited job opportunities; advancement will be possible only for holders of graduate degrees.

Income

Average salaries for speech pathologists and audiologists are about $43,080 a year. Experienced speech pathologists and audiologists in hospitals earn about $44,800.

Most speech pathologists and audiologists working in schools are classified as teachers and are paid an average of $38,400.

Additional source of information

American Speech-Language-Hearing Association
10801 Rockville Pike
Rockville, MD 20852
www.asha.org

STATISTICIAN

The job

Statisticians gather and interpret numerical data and apply their knowledge of statistical methods to a particular subject such as economics, human behavior, natural science, or engineering. They may predict population growth, develop quality-control tests for manufactured products, or help business managers and government officials make decisions and evaluate programs.

Statisticians often obtain information about a group of people or objects by surveying a portion of the whole. They decide where to gather the data, determine the size and type of the sample group, and develop the survey questionnaire or reporting form. Statisticians who design experiments prepare mathematical models to test a particular theory. Those in analytical work interpret collected data and prepare tables, charts, and written reports on their findings. Mathematical statisticians use mathematical theory to design and improve statistical methods.

Most statisticians are employed in private industry: in manufacturing, finance, insurance companies, and business service firms. The federal government employs statisticians, primarily in the Departments of Commerce, Education, Health and Human Services, Labor, and Defense. The remaining statisticians are employed by state and local governments, colleges and universities, hospitals, and nonprofit organizations.

Related jobs are mathematician, economist, and actuary.

Qualifications, education, and training

Statisticians must have good reasoning ability, persistence, and the ability to apply principles to new types of problems.

High school courses in mathematics are important.

A bachelor's degree with a major in statistics or mathematics is the minimum requirement for this field. A bachelor's degree with a major in a related field such as economics or natural science and a minor in statistics is preferred for some jobs.

Teaching positions and many other jobs require graduate work in mathematics or statistics, and courses in computer use and techniques are becoming increasingly important. Economics and business administration courses are also helpful.

Potential and advancement

There are about 17,000 statisticians throughout the country, and the field is expected to grow slowly through 2008. Those who combine training in statistics with a background in engineering, health science, or computer science will have the best job opportunities. Competition for positions with the federal government will be especially intense.

Opportunities for promotion in this field are best for those with advanced degrees. Experienced statisticians may advance to positions of greater technical responsibility and to supervisory positions.

Income

Statisticians employed by the federal government have average annual salaries of $62,800. Those employed by colleges and universities receive salaries comparable to salaries of other faculty members and often earn extra income from outside consulting, research, and writing. The average salary for all types of statisticians is about $48,540.

Additional source of information

American Statistical Association
1429 Duke Street
Alexandria, VA 22314
www.amstat.org/index.html

SURVEYOR

The job

Surveyors measure construction sites, establish official land boundaries, assist in setting land valuations, and collect information for maps and charts.

Most surveyors serve as leaders of surveying teams; they are in charge of the field party and responsible for the accuracy of its work. They record the information disclosed by the survey, verify the accuracy of the survey data, and prepare the sketches, maps, and reports.

A typical field party consists of the *party chief* and three to six assistants and helpers. *Survey technicians* adjust and operate surveying instruments and electronic distance-measuring equipment to determine elevations, distances, and directions.

Surveyors are increasingly using the global positioning system (GPS) for larger projects. GPS technology uses radio signals transmitted by satellites to pinpoint precise locations on earth.

Photogrammetrists measure and interpret photographs to determine various characteristics of natural or artificial features of an area. They apply analytical processes and mathematical techniques to aerial, space, ground, and underwater photographs to prepare detailed maps of areas that are inaccessible or difficult to survey. These mapping scientists now use computerized databases of spatial data, data satellites, and improved aerial photography techniques.

Federal, state, and local government agencies employ about 25 percent of all surveyors. Those in state and local governments usually work for highway departments and urban planning and development agencies. Those in federal government work for the U.S. Geological Survey, Bureau of Land Management, Army Corps of Engineers, Forest Service, National Ocean Survey, and Defense Mapping Agency.

Many surveyors work for construction companies, engineering and architectural consulting firms, public utilities, and petroleum and natural gas companies. Others own or work for firms that conduct surveys for a fee.

Places of employment and working conditions

Surveyors work throughout the United States.

Surveying is outdoor work, with surveyors often walking long distances or climbing hills carrying equipment and instruments. They usually work an eight-hour, five-day week but may work much longer hours in summer months when conditions are more favorable for surveying.

Surveyors also spend a bulk of their time in offices, analyzing data, preparing reports, and creating maps. Most map drafting is now done on a computer.

Qualifications, education, and training

Surveyors should be in good physical condition. They need good eyesight, coordination, and hearing and must have the ability to visualize and understand objects, distances, sizes, and other abstract forms. They also need mathematical ability and strong computer skills.

High school courses should include algebra, geometry, trigonometry, drafting, and mechanical drawing.

Surveyors acquire their expertise through a combination of on-the-job training and courses in surveying. Technical institutes, vocational schools, and junior colleges offer one-, two-, and three-year programs in surveying. Universities offer four-year programs leading to a B.S. in surveying.

High school graduates without any training usually start as helpers. If they complete a surveying course and gain experience, they may advance to technician, senior survey technician, party chief, and finally, licensed surveyor.

Photogrammetrists usually need a bachelor's degree in engineering or the physical sciences.

All states require licensing or registration of land surveyors. Educational requirements for licensure are becoming more stringent because of technological advances in the field. Most states now require post–high school education, and more are requiring a bachelor's degree. Other requirements include work experience and passing state and national exams.

Potential and advancement

There are about 110,000 surveyors in the United States. Job opportunities are expected to increase at an average rate through 2008 due to replacement needs.

Advancement in this field depends on accumulating experience and mastering technological skills.

Income

The federal government pays surveyors an average of $52,400. Median earnings for all surveyors are $37,640.

Additional sources of information

American Congress on Surveying and Mapping
5410 Grosvenor Lane, Suite 100
Bethesda, MD 20814

American Society of Photogrammetry and Remote Sensing
5410 Grosvenor Lane, Suite 210
Bethesda, MD 20814

SYSTEMS ANALYST

The job

Systems analysts decide what new data need to be collected, the equipment needed to process the data, and the procedure to be followed in using the information within a given computer system. They use various techniques such as cost accounting, sampling, and mathematical model building to analyze a problem and devise a new system to solve it.

Once a system has been developed, the systems analyst prepares charts and diagrams that describe its operation in terms that the manager or customer who will use the system can understand. The analyst may also prepare a cost-benefit analysis of the newly developed system. If the system is accepted, the systems analyst then translates the logical requirements of the system into the capabilities of the particular computer hardware in use and prepares specifications for programmers to follow. The systems analyst will also work with the programmers to debug (eliminate errors from) a new system.

Because the work is complex and varied, systems analysts specialize in either business or scientific and engineering applications. Some analysts improve systems already in use or adapt existing systems to handle additional types of data. Those involved in research, called *advanced systems designers*, devise new methods of analysis.

Most systems analysts are employed by banks, insurance companies, large manufacturing firms, and data processing services. Others work for wholesale and retail businesses and government agencies.

In many industries, all systems analysts begin as computer programmers and are promoted to analyst positions only after gaining experience. In large data processing departments, they may start as junior systems analysts. Many persons enter this occupation after acquiring experience in accounting, economics, or business management (for business positions) or engineering (for scientific work).

Places of employment and working conditions

Opportunities for systems analysts exist throughout the country.

Systems analysts usually work a normal 40-hour week with occasional evening or weekend work.

Qualifications, education, and training

Systems analysts must be able to think logically, concentrate, and work with abstract ideas. They also must be able to communicate effectively with technical personnel such as programmers as well as with people who have no computer background.

High school should include as many mathematics courses as possible.

Because job requirements vary greatly, there is no universally accepted way of preparing for a career as a systems analyst. A background in accounting, business administration, or economics is preferred by employers in business. Courses in computer concepts, systems analysis, and data retrieval techniques are good preparation for any systems analyst.

Many employers require a college degree in computer science, information science, or data processing. Scientifically oriented organizations often require graduate work as well as some combination of computer science and a science or engineering specialty.

Because technological advances in the computer field come so rapidly, systems analysts must continue their technical education throughout their careers.

This training usually takes the form of one- and two-week courses offered by employers, computer manufacturers, and software vendors.

The Institute for Certification of Computing Professionals confers the designation of certified data processor (CDP) on systems analysts who have four years of experience, or two years of experience and a college degree. Applicants must also successfully complete a core examination and exams in two specialty areas.

Potential and advancement

There are about 1.5 million systems analysts in the country. This job field is expected to grow steadily because of the expanding use of computers. College graduates who have had courses in computer programming, systems analysis, and data processing will have the best opportunities, while those without a degree may face some competition for the available jobs that don't require a degree.

Systems analysts can advance to jobs as lead systems analysts or managers of systems analysis or data processing departments.

Income

Systems analysts who work full-time earn a median yearly salary of about $52,180. The middle 50 percent earn between $40,570 and $74,180. The bottom 10 percent earn less than $32,470, while the top 10 percent earn more than $87,810.

Additional sources of information

Association for Systems Management
24587 Bagley Road
Cleveland, OH 44138

Institute for the Certification of Computing Professionals
2200 East Devon Avenue, Suite 268
Des Plaines, IL 60018
www.iccp.org

T

TEACHER, COLLEGE AND UNIVERSITY

The job

The function of a teacher at the college or university level is to present in-depth analysis of or training in a particular subject.

Depending on the subject matter and grade level of the students, a teacher may conduct large lecture classes for basic courses, lead advanced seminars for only a few students, or work with students in laboratories. Many teachers at this level carry on research projects and act as consultants to business, industry, and government agencies. They are active in professional societies and write for publications in the field. Those who are *department heads* also have supervisory and administrative duties.

There are four academic ranks on college and university faculties: *instructor, assistant professor, associate professor,* and *full professor.* Beginners usually start as instructors. Education and experience govern advancement to higher rank. Many teachers are supported by part-time assistant instructors, teaching fellows, teaching assistants, and laboratory assistants. These posts are often filled by graduate students working toward advanced degrees.

Most teachers at this level teach in public colleges and universities. About 30 percent work part-time.

Places of employment and working conditions

One of the advantages college and university teachers have is their flexible schedule. They usually spend 12 to 16 hours a week in classes and set aside 3 to 6 office hours a week to assist students on an individual basis. They may also be required to attend faculty meetings. Otherwise, they are free to schedule study, class preparation, and research as they see fit. During the summer and school holidays, they may teach, do research, travel, write, and participate in other activities.

One of the current problems confronting college and university professors is that budget cutbacks are causing many institutions to replace full-time and permanent positions with part-time and temporary ones. Also, in order to advance, college and university teachers are under pressure to publish their research as books and articles, often leaving them less time to teach.

Qualifications, education, and training

A master's degree, which qualifies the teacher for instructor rank, is the minimum requirement for college and university teaching positions.

A master's degree or Ph.D. and a year or two of experience as an instructor are usually necessary for assistant professors. Associate professors frequently need a Ph.D. as well as three years or more of college teaching experience.

For a full professorship, a Ph.D. degree, extensive teaching experience at the college and university level, and published articles and books are usually required. Full professors may achieve tenure after a certain number of years, thus being assured of a teaching position for as long as they choose to remain at the school.

Potential and advancement

There are approximately 865,000 college and university teachers. Faster-than-average employment growth is expected in this field through 2008. Increased student enrollment and a high number of faculty retirements are expected to create job openings. However, many colleges and universities are relying on part-time faculty and leaving some positions vacant in response to financial difficulties. Job candidates should therefore expect competition for full-time positions.

Advancement usually depends on higher-level study and college teaching experience. Outstanding academic, administrative, or professional work as well as related research and publication can hasten advancement.

Income

Salaries for college and university professors vary by faculty rank, type of institution, and field. In general, faculty in four-year colleges earn more than those teaching in two-year schools.

For a 9- or 10-month academic year, salaries for full-time faculty average $56,300. The average for professors is $72,700; associate professors, $53,200; assistant professors, $43,800; and instructors, $33,400.

Many college and university professors supplement their income by consulting, writing, researching, teaching additional courses, or other employment.

Additional sources of information

Professional societies in the various subject fields will generally provide information on teaching requirements and employment opportunities. Another source of information is:

American Federation of Teachers
555 New Jersey Avenue NW
Washington, DC 20001

TEACHER, KINDERGARTEN AND ELEMENTARY SCHOOL

The job

Schoolteachers at the kindergarten and elementary levels introduce children to the basic concepts of mathematics, language, science, and social studies. They aid students in the development of good study and work habits and help them acquire the skills necessary for further education. They evaluate each child and work with parents to provide whatever help a child may need to develop his or her full potential.

Kindergarten and elementary teachers are also concerned with the social development and health of their students. They work to resolve behavioral or personality problems and are alert to health problems or illness. In these early school years, teachers try to give students as much individual attention as possible.

Most teachers at this level teach a single grade and cover all subjects, including music, art, and physical education. Recent trends, however, are for specialization in one or two subjects; the teacher then teaches these subjects to several classes or grades. Team teaching, with several teachers sharing responsibility for a group of students, is also popular in some areas.

Teachers have duties outside of the classroom as well. They attend faculty meetings, supervise after-school activities such as glee clubs, and monitor lunch and playground activities.

Most kindergarten and elementary teachers work in public school systems; the remainder work in private and parochial schools. During the summer, many teachers teach in summer-school programs or work as camp counselors. Others use the time to gain additional education.

Places of employment and working conditions

Elementary teachers work in every geographic area—in cities and towns of all sizes and in rural areas throughout the United States.

The workweek for elementary teachers is about 36½ hours, but time spent grading papers, preparing lessons, and attending meetings increases the total to about 46 hours a week.

At this level, teachers must be active physically. They are often walking, kneeling, or sitting on low stools or on the floor. In the lowest grades, they help children with boots and heavy clothing.

Most elementary teachers work a nine-month school year with a three-month summer vacation. Some school districts, however, function year-round; they have eight-week sessions, one week off, and a three-week midwinter break. This type of schedule makes extra employment difficult.

Many states provide for tenure after a certain number of years in a position; while tenure does not guarantee a job, it does provide some security.

Qualifications, education, and training

An enthusiasm for interacting with young children is a prime requisite for kindergarten and elementary teachers. Dependability, good judgment, creativity, and patience are also necessary.

In high school, a broad college preparatory course should be followed.

A bachelor's degree in an approved teacher education program is required. This includes a liberal arts program, education courses, and student-teaching experience.

Those with a bachelor's degree in another specialty may prepare to teach by taking the required education courses. One or two years of additional study is usually required. A provisional license allows teachers to work while completing their education.

All states require public school teachers to be licensed by the state board of education; some also require private and parochial teachers to be certified. State requirements vary and may include specific grade point averages, competency exams, and a master's degree or a fifth year of study.

Voluntary national licensure is available through the National Board for Professional Teaching Standards. It allows a teacher to teach in any state and may increase a teacher's salary.

Potential and advancement

There are about 1.9 million elementary school teachers in the country. Rising enrollments and retirement of experienced teachers will create average growth in this field. Job opportunities are expected to be best in inner cities and rural areas.

Income

Experienced elementary teachers average about $39,300 for a 9- or 10-month year. Teachers working in private schools usually earn less.

Additional sources of information

Information on certification requirements for local school systems is available from individual state departments of education. Other sources are:

American Federation of Teachers
555 New Jersey Avenue NW
Washington, DC 20001

National Education Association
1201 16th Street NW
Washington, DC 20036

TEACHER, SECONDARY SCHOOL

The job

Teachers at the high school level instruct students in specific subject areas such as English, science, or mathematics. They usually teach four or five classes each day and may teach different areas of their specialty to different grades. For example, a mathematics teacher might teach algebra to two 9th-grade classes, teach geometry to one 10th-grade class, and have two classes of seniors studying trigonometry.

The teacher must prepare lesson plans and examinations for each class and try to meet the needs of individual students. This could mean arranging tutoring for slower students or providing extra work for fast learners. Secondary school teachers also take students on field trips, attend faculty meetings and workshops, and supervise extracurricular activities such as sports, school plays, and student clubs.

Some teachers, called *vocational teachers*, train junior and senior high school students in specific job skills such as carpentry, auto mechanics, or distributive education (retail, production, and marketing training). They work with the actual tools of the particular trade.

Places of employment and working conditions

Teachers in secondary schools work in all parts of the country, with job concentrations in the most populated areas.

The average workweek is about 37 hours, but meetings, lesson preparation, and grading papers increase the total to about 48 hours per week. Most teachers work a nine-month school year with a three-month summer vacation. In school systems with a year-round schedule, teachers usually work eight weeks and have one week off, with a longer midwinter break.

Many states grant tenure after a certain number of years in a position; this provides teachers with some job security.

Qualifications, education, and training

Teachers at the high school level should enjoy working with adolescents, be interested in a specific subject area, and have the ability to motivate people.

A broad high school background with preparation for college is necessary. Courses in the student's specific area of interest should be included.

A bachelor's degree from an approved secondary teaching program, with course work in the specialty area, is the minimum requirement. Some states require a master's degree or a fifth year of education within a certain period after beginning employment.

Holders of a bachelor's degree in another specialty may prepare to teach by taking the required education courses. One or two years of additional study is usually required. A provisional license allows teachers to work while completing their education.

All states require certification, although specific requirements vary. A minimum grade point average and competency exams may be included in addition to education and student-teaching practice. Local school systems may have further requirements.

Teachers who intend to work as nonacademic specialists such as *guidance counselors, school psychologists,* and *reading specialists* need additional special education as well as separate certification in the specialty.

Voluntary national licensure is available through the National Board for Professional Teaching Standards. It allows a license holder to teach in any state and may lead to a higher salary.

Potential and advancement

There are more than 1.4 million secondary school teachers across the country. Rising enrollments and retirement of experienced teachers will create good opportunities in this field. Job opportunities are expected to be best in inner cities and rural areas.

Income

Experienced secondary school teachers average about $39,300 for a 9- or 10-month school year. Salaries tend to be higher in public than private schools.

Additional sources of information

Information on certification for local school systems is available from individual state departments of education. Other sources are:

American Federation of Teachers
555 New Jersey Avenue NW
Washington, DC 20001

National Education Association
1201 16th Street NW
Washington, DC 20036

TECHNICAL WRITER

The job

Writers who specialize in preparing scientific and technical material are much in demand. Technical writers may write for the professional members of a special field, detailing new developments and the work of others in the same field. On other assignments, the writer may write for a readership outside the field—the general public, equipment users, company officers, and stockholders.

Technical writers also compose operating manuals, catalogs, and instructional materials for manufacturers of scientific equipment. This material is used by company salespeople, technicians who install and maintain the equipment, and the people who operate the equipment. Writing manuals and training aids for military equipment and weapons is a highly specialized segment of this profession.

Research laboratories employ many technical writers who report on the results of research projects. Others draft proposals—requests for money or facilities to conduct research, to undertake a project, or to develop a prototype of a new product.

Technical writers also write technical books, articles for popular and trade magazines and newspapers, and advertising copy and press releases.

Technical writers are employed by firms in many industries, with the largest numbers working for electronics, aviation, aerospace, weapons, chemical, pharmaceutical, and computer-manufacturing industries. The energy, communications, and computer software fields are employing increasing numbers of technical writers.

The federal government employs many technical writers in the Departments of Interior, Agriculture, and Health and Human Services and in the National Aeronautics and Space Administration. The largest federal employer of technical writers is the Department of Defense.

Publishing houses employ substantial numbers of technical writers and *technical editors*. These companies publish business and trade publications and professional journals in engineering, medicine, physics, chemistry, and other sciences. Textbook publishers also employ technical writers and editors.

Many technical writers work as freelancers, sometimes in addition to holding a full-time technical writing job.

Most people do not enter this field directly from college. They usually spend several years or longer working as technicians, scientists, engineers, research assistants, or teachers before turning to technical writing or editing.

Places of employment and working conditions

Technical writers have mentally challenging work that requires creativity as well. They must be able to work well with other people, while freelance writers must also have the discipline to work alone and set schedules that will allow them to meet deadlines.

Technical writers usually work between 30 and 40 hours a week. They may be required to work extra hours at times to meet deadlines.

Qualifications, education, and training

In addition to having writing skills and scientific or technical knowledge, a technical writer should be logical and accurate, function effectively alone or as part of a team, and have disciplined work habits.

High school courses should develop writing skills and must include science and mathematics.

Technical writers come from a variety of educational backgrounds. Some employers prefer a degree in English, journalism, or technical communications plus course work or experience in a specific scientific or technical subject. Others prefer a degree in an appropriate science or in engineering with a minor in journalism or technical communications. A few colleges and universities offer bachelor's and graduate degrees in technical writing.

Many technical writing workshops and seminars, usually intensive one- and two-week courses, are also available at colleges and universities throughout the country.

Potential and advancement

This field is expanding. Job opportunities will be best for talented writers with education in a specific scientific or technical area. Those with the technical skills for working on the Internet will also have an advantage in the job market. Opportunities for federal employment have been declining and will probably continue to do so.

Technical writers can move up to technical editor or to supervisory and management positions. Some advance by opening their own firms, specializing in technical writing assignments as well as industrial publicity and technical advertising.

Income

Experienced technical writers average between $27,030 and $49,380 a year.

Additional source of information

Society for Technical Communication
901 North Stuart Street, Suite 904
Arlington, VA 22203
www.stc-va.org

TELEVISION AND RADIO SERVICE TECHNICIAN

The job

Skilled television and radio service technicians repair many electronic products in addition to radios and television sets. These include stereo components, tape recorders, intercom and public address systems, closed-circuit television systems, and some medical electronic equipment.

Most of the technicians in this field work in shops and stores that sell or service radios, television sets, and other electronic products. Some work for major manufacturers and service only the products of that manufacturer. About one in eight television and radio service technicians are self-employed.

Related jobs are appliance repairer, electrician, computer service technician, communications equipment mechanic, business machine service technician, and broadcast technician.

Places of employment and working conditions

Television and radio service technicians employed in local service shops or dealer service departments typically work between 40 and 44 hours a week.

Qualifications, education, and training

Work in this field requires mechanical ability; manual dexterity and good eye-hand coordination; normal hearing, good eyesight, and color vision; and the ability to work well with people.

High school courses should include mathematics and physics. Vocational or technical school courses in electronics or hobbies such as ham radio operation are also helpful.

About two years of technical training in electronics plus two to four years of on-the-job experience are usually necessary to become a fully qualified service technician. Training is available from a number of sources, including high schools, vocational-technical schools, junior and community colleges, and correspondence schools. The armed forces also offer training.

Many employers provide training through apprenticeship programs. The apprentice works under the supervision of a fully qualified technician, who is responsible for the apprentice's performance. Such programs usually include home-study courses or classroom instruction as well.

Many manufacturers, employers, and trade associations conduct training programs to keep service technicians up-to-date on new models or products. Manufacturers also provide service manuals and other technical material.

Some states require licensing of television and radio technicians, which usually entails a written examination. Voluntary certification is available through the International Society of Certified Electronics Technicians and the Electronics Technicians Association. Those who pass the exam and have four years of experience become certified electronics technicians.

Potential and advancement

There are about 138,000 service technicians in this field throughout the country. The size of the field is expected to increase through 2008. High turnover will create good job opportunities.

Income

Median hourly earnings in this career category are between $10.72 and $18.55.

Additional source of information

Electronics Technicians Association
604 North Jackson
Greencastle, IN 46135

TOOL-AND-DIE MAKER

The job

The production of the tools, dies, and special guiding and holding devices used by machining workers to mass-produce metal parts is the work of tool-and-die makers.

Toolmakers produce and repair jigs and fixtures (devices that hold metal while it's being stamped, shaved, or drilled). They also make gauges and other measuring devices for use on machinery-making precision metal parts.

Die makers construct and repair metal forms (called dies) for use on machinery that stamps out or forges metal parts. They also make metal molds for die casting and for molding plastics.

Tool-and-die makers usually receive training in the full range of skills needed to perform either job. They are required to have a broader knowledge of machining operations, mathematics, and blueprint reading than workers in related fields. They use a variety of hand and machining tools as well as precision measuring instruments.

Computer technology is changing the work of tool-and-die makers. Many companies use computer-aided design and drafting systems to electronically develop designs for tools and dies. These designs are then sent to computer numerically controlled (CNC) machines that produce the die. Tool-and-die makers still manually check and assemble the tool or die, but they may also spend time planning and writing programs for CNC machines.

Most tool-and-die makers work in plants that produce manufacturing, construction, and farm machinery. Others work in automobile, aircraft, and other transportation equipment industries; in small tool-and-die shops; and in the electrical machinery and fabricated metal industries.

A related job is machinist.

Places of employment and working conditions

Tool-and-die makers work throughout the United States, but job opportunities are best in large industrialized areas. Most work in the Midwest and Northeast, where many metalworking industries are centered.

Tool-and-die makers may come into direct contact with hazardous lubricants and cleaners in the course of their work and may be subject to injuries to hands and eyes caused by flying metal particles. They are usually required to wear special protective eyeglasses and to avoid loose clothing that could catch on machinery.

Qualifications, education, and training

Anyone interested in pursuing tool-and-die making should have mechanical ability, finger dexterity, and an aptitude for precision work.

High school or vocational school courses should include machine shop classes, mathematics, drafting, blueprint reading, and computer science, if possible.

Some tool-and-die makers learn their skills in vocational schools or through on-the-job training, but the best training is usually obtained in a formal apprenticeship program. Some companies have separate apprenticeship programs for toolmaking and die making.

An apprenticeship program lasts four or five years and combines practical shop training in all phases of tool-and-die making with classroom instruction in mathematics, shop theory, mechanical drawing, tool designing, and blueprint reading. After completion of an apprenticeship, several years of additional experience is usually necessary to qualify for the more difficult tool-and-die projects.

Some experienced machinists become tool-and-die makers without completing a formal tool-and-die apprenticeship. After years of experience and some additional classroom training, skilled machinists and machine tool operators can develop the skills necessary to qualify them as tool-and-die makers.

Potential and advancement

There are about 138,000 tool-and-die makers nationwide, and the size of the field is expected to decline through 2008. The use of electrical discharge machines and numerically controlled machines that require fewer special tools, jibs, and fixtures will reduce the need for tool-and-die makers in some industries. Job opportunities should remain good, however, because there is currently a shortage of qualified workers and many tool-and-die makers are expected to retire within the next decade.

Tool-and-die makers can advance to supervisory positions and, because of their broad knowledge, can change jobs within the machining occupations more easily than less-skilled workers. Some become tool designers; others open their own tool-and-die shops.

Income

Tool-and-die makers are among the highest-paid workers in the machining field. The median income for tool-and-die makers is $37,250 a year.

Additional source of information

National Tooling and Machining Association
9300 Livingston Road
Fort Washington, MD 20744
www.ntma.org

TRAFFIC MANAGER, INDUSTRIAL

The job

The efficient movement of materials into and finished products out of an industrial firm is the responsibility of an industrial traffic manager.

In the course of their work, traffic managers analyze various transportation possibilities—rail, air, truck, or water—and select the method most suited to the company's needs. They select the carrier and the route; prepare necessary shipping documents; process claims for lost or damaged shipments; consult company officials about purchasing, producing, and scheduling shipments; and sometimes appear before rate-making and government regulatory agencies to represent their companies.

Because many aspects of transportation are subject to federal, state, and local government regulations, industrial traffic managers must be well versed in all such regulations and any other legal matters that affect the shipping operations of the company. They must also be informed about advances in transportation technology and the current and future prices and availability of fuels necessary for the company's transportation requirements. Traffic managers often make decisions on or advise top management regarding purchasing versus contracting for railcars or trucking fleets.

Most traffic managers work for manufacturing firms. A substantial number are employed by wholesalers, large retail stores, and chain stores.

Places of employment and working conditions

Industrial traffic managers usually have standard working hours but may put in some extra time on paperwork, meetings, or travel to hearings before state and federal regulatory bodies.

Qualifications, education, and training

Traffic managers must be able to work independently, analyze technical and numerical data, and present facts and figures in a logical and convincing manner.

The high school curriculum should include mathematics courses.

Although some traffic managers arrive at their positions through experience only, college training is becoming more and more important. Traffic managers who argue cases before the Interstate Commerce Commission, for instance, must have at least two years of college education.

Some employers prefer to hire graduates of trade or technical schools or two-year college programs in traffic management. Other employers require a college degree with a major or course work in transportation, logistics, physical distribution, business administration, economics, statistics, marketing, computer science, or commercial law.

Potential and advancement

This relatively small field is expected to experience average growth through 2008. First consideration for job openings will go to college graduates with a major in traffic management or transportation.

Industrial traffic workers can advance to supervisory positions and to assistant traffic manager and traffic manager positions. Experienced industrial traffic managers often advance by moving to a larger company where job responsibilities are more complex.

Income

Beginners in traffic management earn about $31,790 a year.

Salaries of experienced industrial traffic managers average about $56,320 a year.

Additional sources of information

American Association of State Highway and Transportation
   Officials
444 North Capitol
Washington, DC 20001

Institute of Transportation Engineers
525 School Street SW
Washington, DC 20024

TRANSLATOR

The job

Translators render the written material of one language into written material in another language. Their work differs from that of interpreters, who provide oral translation.

Most translators work on a freelance basis. Those in full-time positions usually work for literary or technical publishers, banks, or large industrial firms with foreign subsidiaries and customers.

The largest single employer of translators is the U.S. government. Agencies such as the Joint Publications Research Service have in-house translation staffs, while other government agencies contract out their translating requirements to commercial agencies, which in turn employ freelancers.

A related job is interpreter.

Places of employment and working conditions

Many translators work for private companies and banks in large metropolitan areas such as Chicago and San Francisco. The largest concentrations, however, are in the New York City and Washington, D.C., areas, where government and publishing industry requirements provide the most career opportunities.

Working conditions vary from an office setting to the freelancer's own home. Occasionally, a rush assignment may mean long or irregular working hours, but in-house translators usually work a 37- to 40-hour week. Freelance translators can set their own schedules. Many work only part-time—some through choice, but many because they cannot obtain enough assignments to comprise a full workload.

Qualifications, education, and training

Translators need a working knowledge of one or more foreign languages. A translator's own foreign background, time spent living abroad, or intensive study of a language at the college or university level provides sufficient preparation for many translating jobs.

A college degree is usually necessary for this type of work. Course work should include foreign languages and writing. Studying abroad can also be a valuable experience for translators. Those who wish to work in literary translation should study the literature of foreign countries.

Potential and advancement

This is a small field. Exact numbers are difficult to calculate because those employed full-time, as well as those handling only an occasional assignment in conjunction with other work, are classified as translators. Job opportunities in this profession are limited because any full-time, in-house positions are usually filled from the existing pool of freelancers.

Advancement usually takes the form of better translating assignments through experience and reputation. Some translators form their own commercial translating agencies and solicit contract work for themselves and their in-house or freelance staff.

Income

The average income for translators is in excess of $26,000 a year. Freelance translators may charge by the word or by the hour. Some freelance translators charge more than $70 per thousand words.

Additional sources of information

American Association of Language Specialists
1000 Connecticut Avenue NW, Suite 9
Washington, DC 20036

American Translators Association
109 Croton Avenue
Ossining, NY 10562

TRAVEL AGENT

The job

Travel agents are specialists who make the best possible travel arrangements to fit the requirements and budgets of individuals or groups traveling anywhere in the world. A travel agent can provide a client with routine plane tickets and a hotel reservation or can plan a trip down to the last detail, including guided tours, rental car, passports and visas, and currency exchange rates.

Many services of a travel agency are provided free of charge to the customer, with a service fee imposed only for complicated travel and lodging arrangements.

Although personal travel experience is part of a successful agent's background, travel agents do not spend most of their time touring and vacationing. They are usually seated behind a desk, talking to a customer or completing necessary paperwork, or on the phone making airline, ship, or hotel reservations. Agents also address social and special-interest groups—often conducting slide or movie presentations of vacation tours—or meet with business executives to plan company-sponsored trips and business travel.

Some large companies whose employees do considerable traveling have experienced travel agents in-house to manage all of the company's travel arrangements.

Places of employment and working conditions

Travel agents work throughout the country, but most job opportunities are in urban areas.

During vacation seasons, travel agents may operate under intense pressure. They frequently have to work long hours.

Qualifications, education, and training

A travel agent is basically a sales representative and, as such, should have patience and a pleasant personality, like to interact with the public, and be willing to work with the hard-to-please customer as well as the timid or inexperienced traveler.

Travel experience is another important qualification. It is an asset to anyone who is applying for a job in this field, but it can also be acquired during years of training. Being able to speak from personal experience, an agent can provide more comprehensive advice to clients.

Part-time or summer jobs as a receptionist or reservation clerk in a travel agency or working as an airline ticket clerk can provide practical experience. Strong computer skills also are an asset.

Some travel agents receive on-the-job training, but more formal training is becoming important. Many vocational schools offer 3- to 12-week full-time programs as well as evening and Saturday programs. Courses for travel agents are sometimes offered in public adult-education classes and at community and four-year colleges. A few colleges offer bachelor's and master's degrees in travel and tourism. Home-study courses are also available from either the American Society of Travel Agents or the Institute of Certified Travel Agents.

Nine states—California, Florida, Hawaii, Illinois, Iowa, Ohio, Oregon, Rhode Island, and Washington—require licensing.

Potential and advancement

There are about 138,000 travel agents throughout America. The prospect for jobs in this field through 2008 is average.

Spending on travel is expected to increase significantly. Rising incomes and increased leisure time mean more people traveling more often than in the past. More efficient planes and the economics of group tour packages have brought even international travel within the budgets of more Americans than ever. In addition, increased business travel, much of it international, and a flood of foreign visitors to the United States will create demand for travel agents.

The travel industry, however, is sensitive to fluctuations in the economy. The price and availability of gasoline also have an effect on the travel industry because rapidly rising fuel costs could significantly raise the price of travel.

Technological advances, such as on-line computer systems that allow travelers to make their own reservations and electronic airline ticketing machines, may reduce demand for travel agents.

Travel agents in larger agencies can be promoted to supervisory or management positions. Some agents advance by opening their own agencies—many travel agents are self-employed.

Income

Salaries of travel agents average $23,010 a year. Agency managers earn more. Standard employee benefits such as pension plans, insurance, and paid vacations are usually available. Additional benefits in the form of substantially reduced travel rates and an occasional free holiday offered by a hotel or resort help to make this an attractive field.

Earnings of self-employed travel agents depend mainly on commissions from airlines and other carriers, tour operators, and hotels and resorts. Commissions for domestic travel arrangements, cruises, hotels, sight-seeing tours, and car rentals are about 7 to 10 percent; for international travel, commissions are about 11 percent.

Travel agents must have supplier or corporation approval before they can receive commissions. (Suppliers and corporations are organizations of ship lines, rail lines, or airlines—such as the International Air Transport Association.) To obtain corporation approval, the travel agency must demonstrate that it is in operation, that it is financially sound, and that it employs at least one experienced travel agent who can arrange foreign and domestic travel as well as hotel and resort accommodations. Obtaining corporation approval can take a year or more, which means that self-employed agents make little money during the first year except for hotel and tour-operation commissions. For this reason, starting capital of more than $50,000 is usually needed to carry a new agency through a profitless first year.

Additional sources of information

American Society of Travel Agents
1101 King Street
Alexandria, VA 22314

Institute of Certified Travel Agents
148 Linden Street
P.O. Box 812059
Wellesley, MA 02181-0012

TRUCK DRIVER

The job

The movement of goods throughout the country is the work of truck drivers. Many truck drivers are *owner-operators*, who own their trucks and operate independently. They may also lease their services to individual companies.

Local truck drivers move goods from warehouses and terminals to factories, offices, and homes within an area. Their skills include the ability to maneuver a truck through narrow streets and alleys, into tight parking spaces, and up to loading platforms. The work and schedule of a local truck driver depend on the product being transported. With some products, the driver starts out in the morning with a loaded truck, makes deliveries to a number of locations during the day, and returns at the end of the day. The driver who works for a lumber company, on the other hand, might return to the lumberyard after each large delivery, thus making several round trips each day.

Long-distance truck drivers, also called *over-the-road drivers*, move goods between cities and across the country. They are considered to be the top professional drivers and receive the highest wages of all drivers. These drivers work day and night; many prefer the night runs, when highways and turnpikes are less crowded.

The runs of long-distance truck drivers can include a short turnaround, in which the driver delivers a loaded trailer to a nearby city and then picks up another loaded trailer and returns it to home base, all within one day. Other runs take an entire day to complete, and the driver remains away overnight. On longer runs, the driver could be away for a week or longer.

On very long runs, many companies use two drivers. One sleeps in a berth behind the cab while the other drives. On these sleeper runs, the truck keeps moving day and night except for stops to eat or refuel. At the end of a trip, drivers file reports on the specifics of the assignment and on the condition of the truck; these are required by the U.S. Department of Transportation.

Depending on the product transported, a driver may or may not be responsible for unloading the truck. In deliveries to a warehouse or loading dock at a store or factory, the customer is usually responsible for unloading. On other deliveries, the driver, sometimes with a helper, does the unloading. Drivers hauling cargo that requires special handling always do their own unloading. A gasoline tank truck driver attaches the hoses and then pumps the gasoline into the gas station storage tanks; a truck driver transporting new cars drives the cars onto the racks and removes them at the final destination.

Most local truck drivers and a few long-distance truck drivers have regularly assigned runs. Drivers with smaller companies are more likely to be assigned regular runs early in their employment. In large companies, drivers usually start on an "extra board," where they bid for runs on the basis of seniority.

Most long-distance drivers and some local drivers are members of the International Brotherhood of Teamsters. Others who are union members usually belong to the unions that represent the plant employees of the companies for which they work.

Places of employment and working conditions

Every community needs local truck drivers, who usually work for businesses to deliver the company's products and goods. Most truckers, however, work in and around large communities and manufacturing centers.

Those who specialize in transporting agricultural products or minerals may live in rural areas.

Working conditions are somewhat different for local and long-distance truckers. Both must be excellent drivers, but the local operator faces a schedule that involves the strain of heavy city traffic, while the long-distance driver must contend with the fatigue of sustained highway driving. Time spent away from home for long-distance truck runs is another drawback.

Local truck drivers frequently work 48 hours or more a week; night or early-morning work is often necessary. The working hours and conditions of long-distance drivers are government regulated. They may not drive more than 60 hours in any seven-day period or drive more than 10 hours without at least 8 consecutive hours off.

Qualifications, education, and training

Reliability, sound judgment, and superior driving skills are necessary, as are good health and vision.

A high school diploma is not mandatory, but some trucking companies prefer it. Driver education courses and shop classes in automotive mechanics are helpful.

Truck drivers usually acquire their skills through experience. They may start as a helper or extra driver on smaller trucks, be given some company training on larger vehicles, and gradually work up to driving the largest trucks. Long-distance truck drivers usually do some local driving before handling long-distance assignments.

A few private and public technical and vocational schools offer truck-driving courses. Prospective students should check any courses out with local trucking companies before enrolling, since not all of them offer acceptable training.

All truck drivers must have a commercial driving license if they drive vehicles designed to transport at least 26,000 pounds. This is usually obtained by passing a written examination on driving regulations and a driving test.

The U.S. Department of Transportation establishes minimum qualifications for long-distance truck drivers who are engaged in interstate commerce. The driver must be at least 21 years old; pass a physical examination; and have good hearing, at least 20/40 vision with or without glasses, normal blood pressure, and normal use of arms and legs (unless a waiver is granted). Drivers must also pass a written examination on the motor carrier safety regulations of the Department of Transportation.

Some trucking companies may require a driver to be at least 25 years old, be able to lift heavy loads, and have three to five years of experience and a high school diploma. Many employers now also mandate periodic drug screening. Employers usually require a clean driving record as well.

Potential and advancement

There are about 3.3 million truck drivers in the United States. Because earnings are high and no formal training is required, truck drivers usually face competition for attractive job openings, even though the field is growing at an average rate. Opportunities for truck drivers will likely be favorable, as a growing population means increased movement of goods within every area.

Local truck drivers can advance to long-distance driving and occasionally to positions in scheduling or dispatching. Long-distance truck drivers have limited opportunities for advancement. Some move to positions as safety supervisors or driver supervisors, but the lower starting pay and lack of independence are often deterrents. Others become owner-operators, working independently or leasing their trucks and services to trucking companies.

Income

Average earnings for truck drivers are about $11.67 an hour. The range is from $8.80 to $15.57.

The earnings of long-distance truck drivers depend on miles driven, hours worked, and type of truck. Earnings generally range from a low of $20,000–$25,000 to a high of more than $40,000 a year.

Additional source of information

American Trucking Association
2200 Mill Road
Alexandria, VA 22314

UNDERWRITER

The job

Because insurance companies assume millions of dollars in risks by transferring the chance of loss from their policyholders to themselves, they employ underwriters to study and select the risks the company will insure. Underwriters analyze insurance applications, medical reports, actuarial studies, and other material. They must use personal judgment in making decisions that could cause the company to lose business to competitors (if they are too conservative) or to pay too many claims (if they are too liberal).

Most underwriters specialize in one of the three basic types of insurance: life, property-liability, or health. Property-liability underwriters also specialize by type of risk: fire, automobile, or workers' compensation, for example. Underwriters correspond with policyholders, insurance agents, and insurance office managers. They sometimes accompany salespeople as they call on customers and may attend meetings with union representatives or union members to explain the provisions of group policies.

Underwriters who specialize in commercial underwriting often evaluate a firm's entire operation before approving its application for insurance. The growing trend toward package underwriting of various types of risks under a single policy requires that the underwriter be familiar with several lines of insurance rather than specialize in just one line.

Beginners work under the close supervision of an experienced underwriter. They progress from evaluating routine applications to handling those that are more complex and have greater face value.

Related jobs are actuary, claim representative, and insurance agent and broker.

Places of employment and working conditions

Most underwriters are employed in the home offices of their companies, which are usually located in and around Boston, Chicago, Dallas, Hartford, New York City, Philadelphia, and San Francisco. Some are also employed in regional offices in other parts of the country.

Underwriting is basically a desk job. The average workweek is 37 hours, with occasional overtime required.

Qualifications, education, and training

A career as an underwriter can be satisfying to someone who likes to work with details and who enjoys relating and evaluating information. Underwriters must be able to make decisions and communicate well. They must often be both imaginative and aggressive when searching out information from outside sources. Underwriters must also be computer literate.

High school courses in mathematics are valuable.

Most insurance companies require a college degree, preferably in liberal arts, business administration, finance, or accounting.

As with all jobs in the insurance industry, strong emphasis is placed on the completion of independent-study programs throughout an employee's career. Salary increases and tuition costs are often provided by the company on completion of a course. The study programs are available through several insurance organizations and professional societies.

Potential and advancement

Countrywide, about 97,000 underwriters work for insurance companies at the present time. The field is expected to grow slowly as accelerating use of underwriting software systems shifts some of the workload to computers. The trend toward self-insurance, in which businesses set aside funds at their own rate in a reserve account, also will limit the need for underwriters.

Experienced underwriters can advance to senior or chief underwriter or to underwriting manager if they complete appropriate courses. Some are promoted to supervisory and senior management positions.

Income

Annual earnings for underwriters average $29,790 to $51,460, depending on the specialty and level of position.

Most insurance companies have liberal employee benefits, including life and health insurance and retirement pensions. Paid holidays are more numerous than in most other industries, and vacation policies are generous.

Additional sources of information

Insurance Information Institute
110 William Street
New York, NY 10038

Insurance Institute of America
720 Providence Road
Malvern, PA 19355-0716

URBAN PLANNER

The job

Urban planners develop plans and programs to provide for the growth of a community; revitalize run-down areas; and achieve more efficient uses of the land, social services, industry, and transportation.

Before preparing plans or programs, urban planners conduct detailed studies of local conditions and the current population. After preparing a plan, they develop cost estimates and other relevant materials and aid in the presentation of the program before community officials, planning boards, and citizens' groups.

Most urban planners (also called *city planners*, *community planners*, or *regional planners*) work for city, county, or regional planning agencies. State and federal agencies employ urban planners in the fields of housing, transportation, and environmental protection. Large land developers also employ urban planners, and some teach in colleges and universities.

Many urban planners do consulting work, either part-time in addition to a regular job or full-time for firms that provide planning services to private developers and government agencies.

Related jobs are architect, engineer, and landscape architect.

Places of employment and working conditions

Urban planners are employed throughout the United States in communities of all sizes.

A 40-hour workweek is usual, but evening and weekend hours are often necessary for meetings and community activities.

Qualifications, education, and training

The ability to analyze relationships and to visualize plans and designs is necessary for members of this vocation. Urban planners should be able to work well with people and cooperate with those who may have different viewpoints.

High school students interested in this career should take social science and mathematics courses. Part-time or summer jobs in community government offices can be helpful.

Almost all jobs in this field, even entry-level positions, require a master's degree in urban or regional planning. Most graduate programs take two years to complete. Part-time or summer work in a planning office is usually an established part of the advanced-degree program. Computer skills and an understanding of statistics are essential because urban planners increasingly rely on computer models and electronic geographic information systems.

Urban planners seeking employment with federal, state, or local governments usually must pass civil service examinations.

Voluntary certification, available from the American Institute of Certified Planners, may be helpful for promotion.

Potential and advancement

There are about 35,000 urban planners at work in the United States. The field is expected to grow through 2008. There will be many opportunities in smaller cities and in older areas, such as the Northeast, that are undergoing development and preservation.

Income

Average annual earnings for urban planners range from $32,920 to $56,150, depending on the type of employer and the worker's level of experience.

Additional sources of information

American Planning Association
Education Division
122 South Michigan Avenue, Suite 1600
Chicago, IL 60603

Association of Collegiate Schools of Planning
Department of Urban Planning
University of Wisconsin
P.O. Box 413
Milwaukee, WI 53201

VETERINARIAN

The job

Doctors of veterinary medicine diagnose, treat, and control diseases and injuries of animals. They treat animals in hospitals and clinics and on farms and ranches. They perform surgery and prescribe and administer drugs and vaccines.

While most familiar to the general public are those veterinarians who treat small animals and pets exclusively, some practitioners specialize in the health and breeding of cattle, horses, and other farm animals. Veterinarians are also employed by federal and state public health programs, where they function as meat and poultry inspectors. Others teach at veterinary colleges; conduct research on animal foods, diseases, and drugs; or take part in medical research for the treatment of human diseases. Veterinarians are also employed by zoos, large animal farms, horse-racing stables, and drug manufacturers.

In the army, the air force, and the U.S. Public Health Service, veterinarians are commissioned officers. Other federally employed veterinarians work for the Department of Agriculture.

Places of employment and working conditions

Veterinarians are located throughout the country—in rural areas, small towns, cities, and suburban areas.

Hours are often long and irregular, and those who primarily treat farm animals are outdoors in all kinds of weather. In the course of their work, all veterinarians are exposed to injury, disease, and infection.

Qualifications, education, and training

A veterinarian needs the ability to get along with animals and should have an interest in science. Physical stamina and a certain amount of strength are also necessary.

High school students interested in this field should emphasize science courses, especially biology. Summer jobs that involve the care of animals can provide valuable experience.

The veterinary-degree program (D.V.M. or V.M.D.) requires a minimum of 45 to 90 semester hours of college—at least two years of preveterinary study with emphasis on physical and biological sciences, followed by a four-year professional-degree program. Most successful applicants complete four years of college before entering veterinary school.

There are only 27 accredited colleges of veterinary medicine, many of them state-supported. Admission to all of these schools is highly competitive, with many more qualified applicants than the schools can accept. Successful applicants need preveterinary college grades of B or better, especially in science courses; part-time or summer job experience working with animals is a plus. State-supported colleges usually give preference to residents of the state or region.

The course of study in veterinary colleges is rigorous. It consists of classroom work and practical experience in diagnosing and treating animal diseases, surgery, laboratory work in anatomy and biochemistry, and other scientific and medical studies. Veterinarians who intend to teach or do research usually go on to earn a Ph.D.

In all states and the District of Columbia, veterinarians must be licensed. Licensing requires a doctor of veterinary medicine degree from an accredited college and passing a written state board of proficiency examination. Some states will issue licenses without examination to veterinarians licensed by another state.

Potential and advancement

There are about 57,000 active veterinarians, most of them in private practice. Employment opportunities for veterinarians are excellent primarily because of growth in the population of companion animals—horses, dogs, and other pets—and an increase in veterinary research. The growing emphasis on scientific methods of breeding and raising livestock and poultry as well as an increase in public health and disease-control programs will also contribute to demand. Demand for large-animal veterinarians will be significantly less than the demand in other areas, however.

Income

The incomes of veterinarians in private practice vary greatly and depend on type of practice, years of experience, and size and location of the community. They usually have higher incomes than veterinarians in salaried positions. The average starting salary for veterinarians is between $29,200 and $37,000, depending on the specialty. Large-animal vets earn the most. More experienced veterinarians earn between $39,580 and $78,670 on average in private practice and $61,600 on average with the federal government.

Additional source of information

American Veterinary Medical Association
1931 North Meacham Road, Suite 100
Schaumburg, IL 60173-4360

WAITER

The job

As a result of rising personal incomes and increased leisure time, eating out at restaurants has become a widely popular form of entertainment. Restaurants have also become a convenience for two-income families. Waiters play a primary role in the operation of the restaurant. Often, the type of service they provide determines whether the customer will return.

Waiters take orders, serve drinks and food, prepare checks, and accept payments. The manner in which they perform these tasks depends on the type of restaurant where they work. In restaurants that serve primarily sandwiches, often called coffee shops, waiters are expected to provide fast, friendly service. In more formal restaurants where gourmet food is served, waiters are expected to be able to make wine suggestions, explain how certain items on the menu are prepared, and prepare salads and other dishes at the table. Waiters at these restaurants work at a more leisurely pace.

Other duties often performed by waiters include showing customers to their seats, setting or clearing tables, and cashiering.

Places of employment and working conditions

Eating establishments are located throughout the country but are most plentiful in large cities and tourist areas. Most waiters work in restaurants, coffee shops, bars, and other retail eating and drinking places. Others work in hotels, bowling alleys, casinos, and country clubs.

Waiters spend most of their working time on their feet and have to carry heavy trays of food, dishes, and glassware. They are under pressure to work quickly and efficiently.

Some waiters work 40 or more hours a week, but most work part-time. They are often scheduled for duty on evenings, weekends, and holidays.

Qualifications, education, and training

Waiters must be friendly and should enjoy working with people. Other important qualities are a neat appearance, a good memory, and basic math skills.

There are no standard education requirements for waiters. Most employers prefer to hire high school graduates in more formal restaurants, but completing high school is usually not necessary for jobs in coffee shops.

Most waiters receive on-the-job training from more experienced workers.

Potential and advancement

There are more than 2 million waiters in the country, and opportunities should continue to be plentiful through 2008. This field has a high turnover rate, and most openings will occur as workers leave the occupation.

Opportunities for advancement are limited in small restaurants. Most waiters advance by getting jobs in larger restaurants where the potential for earning tips is greater. Some waiters move into management or supervisory positions.

Income

Waiters' earnings are usually made up of tips plus an hourly wage. Median hourly earnings for full-time waiters range from $5.58 to $6.32, not including tips.

Additional sources of information

Council on Hotel, Restaurant, and Institutional Education
1200 17th Street NW
Washington, DC 20036-3097

Educational Foundation of the National Restaurant Association
250 South Wacker Drive, Suite 1400
Chicago, IL 60606

WHOLESALER

The job

The wholesaler is a middle link in the distribution chain between the producer of goods and the retail store in which the goods are sold. Because no producer could possibly contact all the retail outlets or industries that use his or her products and no retail store manager has the time to contact all his or her suppliers individually, the wholesaler provides a valuable service to both segments of the marketplace.

The largest number of wholesalers are *merchant wholesalers*, who buy merchandise outright, warehouse the merchandise until needed, and then sell to retail outlets. They employ salespeople to call on retail customers, extend credit to customers, and lend money to suppliers in the form of prepaid orders.

The second largest group in wholesaling is *manufacturer's agents*. These are independent businesspeople who contract with a manufacturer to sell a specific product or group of products, usually in a specific geographic area. A manufacturer's agent usually represents several manufacturers and sells to retail stores, local distributors, industrial concerns, and institutions. If the business is large enough, the agent may employ additional sales personnel. An *industrial distributor* is a wholesaler who handles one or more products of only one manufacturer.

Merchandise brokers may represent either the buyer or seller in a wholesale transaction. The broker, however, does not buy or take direct responsibility for the goods being sold but acts as the agent of either the buyer or seller. Merchandise brokers work mainly in a few fields: food and grocery specialties, fresh fruits and vegetables, piece goods, cotton, grain, livestock, and petroleum products.

Commission merchants usually deal in agricultural products. They take possession of, but not title to, the merchandise. They may store it, transport it, and condition it for market (inspect, weigh, grade) before finding a buyer. They charge a commission for their services as a part of the final selling price.

Auction companies are wholesalers who sell a client's product at a public auction. Most sales of this nature are in tobacco, fresh fruits and vegetables, livestock, floor coverings, furs and skins, jewelry, and furniture.

Related jobs are retail buyer, retail store manager, manufacturer's sales representative, import/export worker, and sales manager.

Places of employment and working conditions

Some wholesalers, especially the largest and best known, are in major cities such as Chicago, Kansas City, Los Angeles, New York, and St. Louis. The others are located throughout the United States, many of them in small cities and towns.

Wholesalers, especially those dealing in perishable or seasonal goods, run the risk of sudden financial loss. They must have a secure financial base to carry them over lean periods.

Qualifications, education, and training

Good judgment, business and management skills, experience as a buyer or salesperson, and an ability to interact effectively with people are necessary.

There are no specific education requirements for this field. The largest wholesalers, however, usually require experience or training in business administration, sales and marketing, retailing, or a particular technical area such as electrical products or other industrial fields.

Potential and advancement

The best job opportunities for beginners are with smaller wholesalers, although persons with appropriate college education can often start in management-level positions with large wholesalers.

Income

Income varies greatly and depends in large part on the size of the business. Wholesalers earn from about $26,350 to $51,580 a year.

Additional source of information

Manufacturers' Agents National Association
P.O. Box 3467
Laguna Hills, CA 92654-3467
www.manaonline.org

WORD PROCESSOR

The job

Modern offices process volumes of information and data and keep numerous records. Word processors play a central role in maintaining this function.

Word processors use electronic equipment to make copies of reports, letters, and memorandums. They are also responsible for editing, storing, and revising these materials. In some large organizations, there is a word processing center where the typing for several departments is done, although this practice is becoming less common.

Word processors often have additional tasks such as answering telephones, filing, and operating copiers and other office machines.

Places of employment and working conditions

Word processors work throughout the country in firms that provide business services, educational institutions, health care facilities, law firms, and government offices.

Word processors work at desks and must sit for long hours.

Recent studies have shown that there can be physical and mental health hazards in this occupation, including musculoskeletal strain, eye problems, and stress. Women may risk pregnancy complications, miscarriages, and birth defects.

Word processors usually work 37 to 40 hours a week. There is a variety of work arrangements for word processors. Many hold temporary jobs or work part-time.

Qualifications, education, and training

Word processors need to have spelling, grammar, and punctuation skills. They should have familiarity with office procedures and different types of standard office equipment, including personal computers. Most employers prefer to hire high school graduates.

Word processing can be learned in high schools, community colleges, or business schools; through home-study courses; or by using self-teaching aids.

Potential and advancement

Employment of word processors is expected to decline through 2008 due to the productivity that has resulted from the increasing use of computers. In spite of this decline, there will still be thousands of job openings as workers leave the profession to retire or transfer to other occupations.

Word processing positions are often filled by workers who are beginning their first jobs. Often these positions serve as stepping-stones to better-paying jobs. Word processors often become secretaries, statistical clerks, or stenographers. They may also become the supervisor in a word processing department.

Income

Word processors earn average annual salaries of between $22,590 and $27,320. Salaries tend to be highest in transportation and public utilities and lowest in retail trade, finance, insurance, and real estate. The highest-paying region of the country is the West.

Additional sources of information

For information about job opportunities in word processing, contact the nearest office of the state employment service.